Making Sense of the Central African Republic

About the editors

Tatiana Carayannis is deputy director of the Social Science Research Council's Conflict Prevention and Peace Forum. She also directs the SSRC China-Africa Knowledge Project and is a research director of the LSE-based consortium, the Justice and Security Research Programme. A political scientist and seasoned field researcher, she is widely published on political mobilization and rebel governance, and UN peacekeeping and peacebuilding in Central Africa, particularly the DRC. She co-authored *UN Voices: The Struggle for Development and Social Justice* (2005) with Thomas G. Weiss, Louis Emmerij, and Richard Jolly, and is currently completing her next book, *Pioneers of Peacekeeping: ONUC, 1960–1964*.

Louisa Lombard is an assistant professor of anthropology at Yale University. She has worked in CAR as a field consultant to several international organizations, including Human Rights Watch, Small Arms Survey, Refugees International and the World Bank, in addition to her academic research. She is currently finishing two books about the country, one an ethnographic and historical account of the 'stateless' east, and the other an anthropological take on war and rebellion over the past decade.

Making Sense of the Central African Republic

Edited by
Tatiana Carayannis and Louisa Lombard

ZED

LONDON • NEW YORK • OXFORD • NEW DELHI • SYDNEY

Zed Books
Bloomsbury Publishing Plc
50 Bedford Square, London, WC1B 3DP, UK
1385 Broadway, New York, NY 10018, USA
29 Earlsfort Terrace, Dublin 2, Ireland

BLOOMSBURY and Zed Books are trademarks of Bloomsbury Publishing Plc

First published in Great Britain 2015
Reprinted 2021, 2022

Editorial copyright © Tatiana Carayannis and Louisa Lombard 2015
Copyright in this collection © Zed Books 2015

Tatiana Carayannis and Louisa Lombard have asserted their rights under the Copyright, Designs and Patents Act, 1988, to be identified as Editors of this work.

For legal purposes the Acknowledgments on pp. viii–x constitute an extension of this copyright page.

Cover designed by www.roguefour.co.uk

All rights reserved. No part of this publication may be reproduced or transmitted in any form or by any means, electronic or mechanical, including photocopying, recording, or any information storage or retrieval system, without prior permission in writing from the publishers.

Bloomsbury Publishing Plc does not have any control over, or responsibility for, any third-party websites referred to or in this book. All internet addresses given in this book were correct at the time of going to press. The author and publisher regret any inconvenience caused if addresses have changed or sites have ceased to exist, but can accept no responsibility for any such changes.

A catalogue record for this book is available from the British Library.

A catalog record for this book is available from the Library of Congress.

ISBN: PB: 978-1-7836-0379-4
ePDF: 978-1-7836-0381-7
eBook: 978-1-7836-0382-4

Typeset in Sabon by Saxon Graphics Ltd, Derby
Index by John Barker
Printed and bound in Great Britain

To find out more about our authors and books visit www.bloomsbury.com and sign up for our newsletters.

Contents

Acknowledgements	viii
List of maps	xi
List of abbreviations and acronyms	xii
Chronology	xix

1	Making Sense of CAR: An Introduction *Louisa Lombard and Tatiana Carayannis*	1
2	CAR's History: The Past of a Tense Present *Stephen W. Smith*	17
3	Being Rich, Being Poor: Wealth and Fear in the Central African Republic *Roland Marchal*	53
4	Local Dynamics in the Pk5 District of Bangui *Faouzi Kilembe*	76
5	The Elite's Road to Riches in a Poor Country *Stephen W. Smith*	102

6	A Multifaceted Business: Diamonds in the Central African Republic *Ned Dalby*	123
7	The Autonomous Zone Conundrum: Armed Conservation and Rebellion in North-Eastern CAR *Louisa Lombard*	142
8	CAR and the Regional (Dis)order *Roland Marchal*	166
9	Pathologies of Peacekeeping and Peacebuilding in CAR *Nathaniel Olin*	194
10	From Being Forgotten to Being Ignored: International Humanitarian Interventions in the Central African Republic *Enrica Picco*	219
11	CAR's Southern Identity: Congo, CAR, and International Justice *Tatiana Carayannis*	244
12	In Unclaimed Land: The Lord's Resistance Army in CAR *Ledio Cakaj*	267
13	A Central African Elite Perspective on the Struggles of the Central African Republic *Laurence D. Wohlers*	295
14	A Concluding Note on the Failure and Future of Peacebuilding in CAR *Tatiana Carayannis and Louisa Lombard*	319

About the contributors   342
Index   346

Our special thanks to all the scholars, practitioners, and others – from Central Africa and beyond – who have, over the years, tried to make sense of the Central African Republic for the betterment of all living in the region.

Acknowledgements

In late 2012, as the Central African Republic (CAR) seemed poised on the edge of another cycle of violence, and as the UN and regional partners prepared for yet another intervention, a few of us who work on (and in) this region began discussions about how to address the paucity of good, evidence-based, contemporary research on the country. The idea of this edited volume took shape while we were together in New York for an expert brainstorming on CAR for the United Nations Secretariat, a meeting convened by the Social Science Research Council's Conflict Prevention and Peace Forum (CPPF) to discuss national and regional dynamics affecting the country, and how the United Nations could best support a fragile peace between the Seleka rebellion and the national government. That brainstorming was held in light of the Security Council's request for a strategic review of UN engagement in CAR a few weeks before, and it followed an earlier CPPF expert brainstorming held in Bangui in June 2012 at the request of the late Dr. Margaret Vogt, then the UN Secretary-General's Special Representative to the Central African Republic. Both meetings brought together stakeholders across the UN, World Bank, and the international community with some of the contributors to this book to examine more deeply the social and religious cleavages emerging across the region. This book thus represents the culmination of an intensely interactive two-and-a-half-year process among a group of scholars and expert practitioners with a long history in this region. It is fair to say that much of this earlier work laid the foundation for this book.

First drafts of the chapters contained within were workshopped at a book contributors' meeting held in Paris in February 2014, generously hosted by Roland Marchal at Sciences-Po's CERI. Revised drafts were discussed at a second contributors' workshop held in June 2014 at the Social Science Research Council in New York. Our deepest debt of gratitude goes to our contributors who not only gave of their time to write chapters (some more than one), but who, by participating in these workshops and offering ideas, reactions, and comments to chapters along the way, also served as peer reviewers for the book. We are deeply grateful for their commitment to ensuring the quality of this work, which, as a result, is greater than the sum of its parts.

Making Sense of the Central African Republic was undertaken under the auspices of the CPPF founded in 2000 in response to the *Brahimi Report*, to connect UN decision-makers with scholars on and from conflict areas in which the UN is engaged and thus provide the UN with a deeper understanding of these places and their people; and the Justice and Security Research Programme (JSRP), a global research consortium based at the London School of Economics and Political Science. Our heartfelt thanks go to Bill O'Neill, Alex De Waal, Koen Vlassenroot, Tim Allen, and Mary Kaldor for their steadfast support of this project. Aaron Pangburn not only helped us organize the workshops, but compiled the chronology, helped with background research and fact-checking, proofread countless chapters, and hunted down stray footnotes. Mignonne Fowlis painstakingly sifted through the alphabet soup of missions, interventions, and armed groups to compile the list of acronyms, and helped with endless proofreading. We also wish to thank our editor at Zed Books, Ken Barlow, for enthusiastically agreeing to take on an edited volume on what was arguably then (and perhaps now) a 'B list' crisis; and to the rest of our team at Zed, our thanks to Dan Och for moving the manuscript along and keeping us on deadline, and to Rob Brown for his quick and thorough copyediting. Finally, we also wish to thank our respective partners, Maureen Burnley and Graeme Wood, for their patience with, and encouragement of, our lifelong obsession with this part of the world.

As one of the most prominent African women political scientists of her generation, Dr. Margaret Vogt's insistence on the UN's need for solid research and analysis for its work – particularly to strengthen its efforts on prevention – was spot on, though it may not have been sufficient to avert the current crisis in CAR. But the importance of good research and knowledge of history to good policy is an approach we share, and which we believe can only help strengthen our collective efforts to respond to this generation's social upheavals. We hope this book is a step in this direction.

Tatiana Carayannis and Louisa Lombard
New York and New Haven, CT, 8 May 2015

List of Maps

Map 1.1	United Nations map of the Central African Republic	10
	Permission acquired from the UN: http://www.un.org/Depts/Cartographic/map/profile/car.pdf	
Map 4.1	Local dynamics in Bangui's Pk5	83
	Permission acquired from the author, Faouzi Kilembe.	
Map 6.1	Diamonds and conflict: when natural resources feed rebellion	125
	Permission acquired from International Crisis Group.	
Map 12.1	LRA attacks against civilians: April 2012–March 2013	271
	Permission acquired from *The Resolve–LRA Crisis Initiative*. Created by Kenneth Transier.	

List of abbreviations and acronyms

ACCB	Association Centrafricaine des Commerçants en Bétail/Central African Association of Cattle Merchants
ACF	Action Contre la Faim/Action Against Hunger
ACOBECA	Association des Commerçants de Bétail de Centrafrique/Association of Cattle Merchants of Central Africa
AEF	Afrique Equatoriale Française/French Equatorial Africa
AFDL	Alliance des Forces Démocratiques pour la Libération du Congo-Zaïre/Alliance of Democratic Forces for the Liberation of Congo-Zaire
AFVP	Association Française des Volontaires du Progrès/The French Association of Volunteers for Progress
APFC	Association pour la Protection de la Faune Centrafricaine/Association for the Protection of Central African Wildlife

APRD	L'Armée Populaire pour la Restauration de la Démocratie/Army for the Restoration of the Republic and Democracy
ASSOMESCA	Association des Oeuvres Médicales pour la Santé en Centrafrique/Association of Medical Workers for Health in Central African Republic
AU	African Union
AUC	African Union Commission
AU-RCI	African Union Regional Cooperation Initiative
AU-RTF	African Union Regional Task Force
BFCE	French Foreign Trade Bank
BINUCA	Bureau Intégré de l'Organisation des Nations Unies en Centrafrique/The UN Integrated Peacebuilding Support Office in the Central African Republic
BONUCA	Bureau des Nations Unies pour la Consolidation de la Paix en République Centrafricaine/United Nations Peacebuilding Support Office in the Central African Republic
CAP	Consolidated Appeal Processes
CAR	Central African Republic
CDC	Centres for Disease Control and Prevention
CDS	Contribution au Développement Social/Corporate Social Responsibility Tax
CEEAC	Communauté Économique des États de l'Afrique Centrale/The Economic Community of Central African States
CEMAC	Communauté Économique et Monétaire des Etats de l'Afrique Centrale/Central African Economic and Monetary Union
CEMIDO	Cellule Mixte Impôt-Douane/Mixed Taxes and Customs Unit
CEMIFI	Cellule Mixte Impôt-Finance/Mixed Taxes and Finance Unit

CEN-SAD	Communauté des Etats Sahélo-Sahariens/Community of Sahel and Saharan States
CMRN	Comité Militaire de Redressement National/Military Committee for National Recovery
CNPC	China National Petroleum Corporation
COAC	Coalition pour les Actions Citoyennes/Coalition for Citizen Action
COCORA	Coalition Citoyenne d'Opposition aux Rebellions Armés/The Citizen's Coalition Opposing Armed Rebellion
COOPI	Cooperazione Internazionale/International Cooperation
CPJP	Convention des Patriotes pour la Justice et la Paix/Convention of Patriots for Justice and Peace
DDR	Disarmament, Demobilization and Reintegration
DGSE	Direction Générale de la Sécurité Extérieure/French secret service
DoD	Department of Defence
DRC	Democratic Republic of the Congo
ECHO	European Commission's Humanitarian Aid and Civil Protection Department
ECOFAC	Ecosystèmes Forestiers de l'Afrique Centrale/Conservation and Rational Use of Forest Ecosystems in Central Africa
ECOFAUNE	Ecosystèmes Fauniques du Nord-Est/Wildlife Ecosystems of the North East
EITI	Extractive Industry Transparency Initiative
EPI	Expanded Programme on Immunization
EU	European Union
EUFOR	European Union Force
EUFOR-RCA	European Union Force–Central African Republic
FAC	Forces Armées Congolaises/Congolese Armed Forces

FACA	Forces Armées Centrafricaines/Central African Armed Forces
FAO	Food and Agriculture Organization of the United Nations
FAZ	Forces Armées Zaïroises/Zairean Armed Forces
FDPC	Front Démocratique du Peuple Centrafricain/Democratic Front for the Central African People
FEA	French Equatorial Africa
FIDH	International Federation for Human Rights
FOMUC	Force Multinationale en Centrafrique/Multinational Forces in CAR
FORSDIR	Force Spéciale de Défense des Institutions Républicaines/Special Forces for the Defence of Republican Institutions
FROLINAT	Front de Libération Nationale du Tchad/National Liberation Front of Chad
FWA	French West Africa
GER	Gross Enrolment Ratio
GFATM	Global Fund to fight AIDS, Tuberculosis and Malaria
GTZ	German Cooperation Agency
HDI	Human Development Indicators
HDPT	Humanitarian and Development Partnership Team
HIV	Human Immunodeficiency Virus
ICC	International Criminal Court
ICRC	International Committee of the Red Cross
ICSID	International Centre for Settlement of Investment Disputes
IDPs	Internally Displaced Persons
IMF	International Monetary Fund
LRA	Lord's Resistance Army
MCLN	Mouvement Centrafricain pour la Libération Nationale/Central African Movement for National Liberation

MESAN	Movement for the Social Evolution of Black Africa
MICOPAX	Mission de Consolidation de la Paix en Centrafrique/Mission for the consolidation of peace in Central African Republic
MINURCA	Mission des Nations Unies en République Centrafricaine/United Nations Mission for the Central African Republic
MINUSCA	Mission Intégrée Multidimensionnelle de Stabilisation des Nations Unies en République Centrafricaine/United Nations Multidimensional Integrated Stabilization Mission in the Central African Republic
MISAB	Mission Interafricaine de Surveillance des Accords de Bangui/Inter-African Mission to Monitor the Bangui Accords
MISCA	Mission Internationale de Soutien à la Centrafrique sous Conduite Africaine/African-led International Support Mission to the Central African Republic
MLC	Mouvement pour la Libération du Congo/Movement for the Liberation of Congo
MLPC	Mouvement pour la Libération du Peuple Centrafricain/Movement for the Liberation of the Central African People
MONUC	Mission de l'Organisation de Nations Unies en Republique Democratique du Congo/United Nations Organization Mission in the Democratic Republic of the Congo
MONUSCO	Mission de l'Organisation des Nations Unies pour la Stabilisation en République Démocratique du Congo/United Nations Organization Stabilization Mission in the Democratic Republic of the Congo
MPLA	Movement for the Liberation of Angola

MSF	Médecins sans Frontières/Doctors Without Borders
NGO	Non-governmental organization
NOC	National Oil Corporation of Libya
OCHA	United Nations Office for the Coordination of Humanitarian Affairs
OLT	Operation Lightning Thunder
PAM	Programme Alimentaire Mondial/World Food Programme
PBC	United Nations Peacebuilding Commission
PCV	Per diem, Carburant, Voiture/Per diem, fuel, car
PDRN	Programme de Développement de la Région Nord/Northern Region Development Programme
RECAMP	Renforcement des Capacités Africaines de Maintien de la Paix/Reinforcement of African Peacekeeping Capabilities Programme
RSM	RSM Production Corporation
RTF	Regional Task Force
SAF	Sudanese Armed Forces
SAM	Société Anonyme Minière/Anonymous Mining Company
SODIF	Société de Détection des Importations Frauduleuses/Fraudulent Imports Detection Company
SPLA	Sudan People's Liberation Army
SPLM	Sudan People's Liberation Movement
SRSG	Special Representative of the Secretary-General
SSR	Security Sector Reform
TNC	Transitional National Council
UFDR	Union des Forces Démocratiques pour le Rassemblement/Union of Democratic Forces for Unity
UN	United Nations
UNDP	United Nations Development Programme

UNFPA	United Nations Population Fund
UNHCR	United Nations High Commissioner for Refugees
UNICEF	United Nations Children's Fund
UNOCA	United Nations Regional Office for Central Africa
UPDF	Uganda People's Defence Force
USAID	United States Agency for International Development
WES	Western Equatoria State
WFP	The World Food Programme
WHO	World Health Organization

Chronology

c. 1780: The Bandia-Nzakara founded the Kingdom of Bangassou around the Ubangi River basin.

c. 1820–1825: The Gbaya, Zande and Mandja peoples settled on Central African soil after escaping persecution from various regional slave traders.

c. 1830: The Dar al-Kuti, an Islamic Sultanate was established by a prince of the Banguir called Djougoultoum. Its zone of influence covered most of present north-eastern CAR and parts of modern-day Chad, and was active in slave raiding throughout its eighty-two year reign.

29 April 1887: France and Belgian King Leopold II established the north bank of the Ubangui River as the border between the French and Belgian zones of influence.

25 June 1889: The French post at Bangui was established.

July 1899: Paris subcontracted much of the French Congo – 667,000 of 1,233,000 sq km – to forty private companies that were granted a thirty-year monopoly on the exploitation of 'vacant and un-owned land'. Forced labour was common throughout this period.

29 December 1903: A French decree merged the region of Upper Ubangui and Upper Shari to create a new colony of French Congo, Ubangui–Shari, whose boundaries were close to what is modern-day CAR.

1910: Ubangui–Shari was absorbed into Afrique Equatoriale Francaise (AEF), a federal arrangement merging the French colonies of Chad, Gabon and Congo-Brazzaville.

1911: Dar al-Kuti's Sultan al-Sanusi assassinated by the French resident at Ndele.

1921–1929: Labour from the AEF was used to construct the Congo-Océan railway from Brazzaville to Pointe-Noir, but the project suffered from desertion, death, and massive illness and ultimately was embroiled in scandal after the horrific labour conditions were revealed.

1928–1931: In the western and south-western corners of the colony, the Kongo-Wara rebellion was a widespread anti-colonial workers revolt against the exploitative practices of concession industries in Oubangui-Chari. While the uprising was eventually squashed, once news of the abuses reached France, public pressure helped ensure that the concessions were not renewed.

1934–1946: Various administration reform efforts were attempted within AEF, to reduce costs, break up the structure into various territories and increase autonomy. The changes did little to satisfy growing local frustrations.

10 November 1946: Barthélemy Boganda became Oubangui-Chari's first national leader, and also its first native Catholic priest, as he was elected as the territory's Deputy to the French National Assembly in Paris.

28 September 1949: Boganda founded the Mouvement pour l'évolution sociale de l'Afrique noire (MESAN) to spread throughout the region, which provoked a hostile reaction from colonial administrations, and grew into the first political party of the Central African state.

17 June 1951: Boganda was re-elected as Deputy, despite strong opposition from many in the administration and colonial circles.

March–May 1957: MESAN won all of the seats in the Ubangui-Shari territorial assembly, and the constitution of the first Ubangui government was presided over by the newly appointed President and Vice-President of the Grand Council of the AEF, Boganda and Abel Goumba.

29 March–May 1959: Boganda died in a plane crash, Dr Goumba succeeded him, only to be excluded from the government by the National Assembly and replaced by David Dacko, the Minister of the Interior.

13–14 August 1960: The Central African Republic gained independence, with David Dacko named Provisional Chief of the Republic.

January–November 1962: The Central African Army was formed, opposition forces were put on trial, and MESAN was named the sole legal political party of the state.

15 November 1963–5 January 1964: CAR was changed from a constitutional to a presidential regime. Dacko was elected and named President of the Republic.

December 1964: Jean-Bédel Bokassa was appointed Chief of Staff of the Central African Army.

31 December 1965–1 January 1966: While the Commander of the Gendarmerie, Jean Izamo staged a coup attempt, Bokassa intervened, killed the commander, and took control of the capital after Dacko was arrested.

4 March 1972: Bokassa was proclaimed President for Life of the Central African Republic.

4 December 1976: A new constitution was adopted declaring CAR as a hereditary empire with a parliamentary-monarch system. Yet, the legislature was never convened and Jean Bédel Bokassa became Emperor in a lavish ceremony a year later on 4 December 1977.

January–June 1979: Student demonstrations over obligatory uniforms were met with mortar fire and the violent response killed hundreds of Central Africans. This response led France to sever ties with the Emperor and host the four largest opposition movements in Paris to come up with a common strategy to overthrow him.

20 September 1979: Operation Barracuda, composed of twenty-one paratroopers, facilitated the takeover of Bangui, while Bokassa was visiting Libya. David Dacko reluctantly returned to power and barely won his re-election over Ange-Félix Patassé in early 1981.

1–2 September 1981: President David Dacko was deposed in a military coup led by General André Kolingba. The Comité Militaire pour le Redressement National (CMRN), headed by General Kolingba, took control of the government and suspended the constitution.

October–November 1986: Bokassa returned to the country and was arrested on murder charges. A popular referendum on a new constitution was passed with 80 per cent approval, and Kolingba's Rassemblement Democratique Centrafricain (RDC) was established as the new single party of the nation, providing the president with another six-year term.

October 1991–October 1992: After growing calls for multipartyism culminated in an opposition meeting in Bangui of 10,000 people, and twenty opposition parties demanding an independent national conference, France intervened and conditioned any further aid on democratic progress. The results of a hastily convened vote were cancelled by the Supreme Court, and a French-observed presidential election was rescheduled for 1993.

19 September 1993: Ange-Félix Patassé of the Mouvement pour la Liberation du Peuple Centrafricain (MLPC) was elected President with 53 per cent of the vote in the second round of the presidential election and inaugurated as President on 22 October 1993.

April 1996–January 1997: A series of three army mutinies destabilized the capital, requiring a larger intervention by French forces. Regional leaders began to play a bigger role in diplomacy and peacekeeping, in part due to encouragement from France. The Bangui Accords were signed in January and led to the deployment of MISAB, CAR's first regional peacekeeping force.

28 May–October 2001: A coup was waged by a group of soldiers said to be loyal to former President Kolingba. Ten days of fighting ensued, with approximately 300 deaths and 50,000 displaced from the capital. The Yakoma, Kolinga's ethnic group, were targeted in a campaign of reprisal killings, and an increasingly paranoid President ordered the arrest of his Minister of Defence, and dismissed the army Chief of Staff, General François Bozizé, in October.

October 2002–March 2003: Under threat from Bozizé supporters, Patassé called upon Jean-Pierre Bemba, the leader of the Mouvement pour la Liberation du Congo (MLC), a rebel army from Equateur province in DRC, and Colonel Qaddafi of Libya to provide troops to reinforce the capital. Bemba's involvement in CAR eventually led to his indictment by the ICC in 2008.

16 March 2003: While President Patassé attended a regional conference in Niamey, General Bozizé took over the capital with Chadian and French support, dissolved the National Assembly, and became the self-proclaimed head of state.

13 March 2005–8 May 2005: Bozizé's party, the National Convergence 'Kwa Na Kwa' (NC-KNK) won 42 out of 105 seats in the National Assembly during the legislative vote. He was elected President with 65 per cent of the vote in the second round of the presidential election in May.

January 2005–October 2006: Three major rebellions emerged in the north of the country. Two of the groups – L'Armée Populaire pour la Restauration de la République et la Démocratie (APRD) and the Front Démocratique du People Centrafricaine (FDPC) – were remotely controlled by Patassé from his exile in Benin, while the Union des Forces Democratiques pour le Rassemblement (UFDR) was led by a convergence of local actors from the northeast of the country and former government officials.

June–December 2008: Representatives of the government and the three rebel groups (FDPC, UFDR, and APRD) signed a comprehensive peace agreement in Libreville, Gabon. This led to the passing of an amnesty law, preparations towards a demobilization, disarmament, and reintegration (DDR) programme and an inclusive political dialogue process that failed to live up to its name.

January–March 2011: Much-delayed legislative and presidential elections were held resulting in the re-election of President Bozizé (66 per cent of the vote) and the maintenance of a NC-KNK majority in the National Assembly. Opposition forces called fraud, and demanded the result be invalidated.

2 December 2012: The Seleka rebellion, a coalition of the various rebel groups from the north, issued its first press release, after taking the market town of Ndele, in which the coalition set out its demands. Chadian combatants, fighters from Darfur and heavily armed poachers soon swelled the rebellion's ranks, as they took over much of the north-east of the country.

11 January 2013: The Libreville Agreement was signed by President Bozizé and the Seleka rebellion to establish a union government and resolve the crisis in the Central African Republic. Nicolas Tiangaye was appointed Prime Minister a week later.

21–24 March 2013: The Seleka rebels crossed the red line set in Damara (an hour outside the capital), engaged the FACA and South African soldiers, and finally took Bangui on 24 March. Bozizé fled to the DRC and was then transferred to Cameroon.

18 August 2013: The transition period officially began, as Michel Djotodia was officially sworn in as Interim President, committing his government to national elections within eighteen months.

13 September 2013: President Djotodia formally dissolved the Seleka coalition, but this pronouncement did little to limit the series of abuses and counter-abuses between the former rebels and supporters of the Bozizé government.

5 December 2013: UN Security Council resolution 2127 authorized the deployment of an 'African-led International Support Mission to the Central African Republic', known by its French acronym MISCA, to stabilize CAR alongside a French mission, Operation Sangaris. In response, and to continue Seleka rule, a group of local self-defence militia, and former army officials attacked Bangui, under the name of Anti-Balaka. Additional offensives were launched around Christmas and on 5 January 2014.

10 January 2014: A regional Economic Community of Central African States (ECCAS) meeting of African leaders in N'Djamena strong-armed President Djotodia and his government into offering their resignation, after airlifting the Transitional National Council (TNC) to endorse the occasion. Upon its return to Bangui, the TNC chose from among eight candidates a new interim head of state, Catherine Samba-Panza, previously the mayor of Bangui, and only the third female head of state in Africa.

10 April 2014: The UN Security Council authorized a UN peacekeeping mission (MINUSCA) to be deployed in September 2014 and urged the holding of elections as soon as technically possible and no later than February 2015.

October 2014: Violence flared again in and around Bangui culminating in the arrival of international mediator Dennis Sassou Nguesso, the President of Congo-Brazzaville. After consultations and town hall meetings, a general agreement was achieved to hold a Bangui Forum in January 2015 and the National Electoral Authority chose to extend the electoral timeline, with the constitution referendum set for May 2015, and the two rounds of the presidential and legislative votes scheduled for July and August 2015.

26 January 2015: Secret negotiations between Anti-Balaka factions represented by Joachim Kokate and a Seleka faction by Nourredine Adam and Michel Djotodia in Nairobi led to the signing of a provisional agreement, with provisions on DDR, amnesty for all perpetrators of violence and the removal of current transitional authorities. The exclusion of CAR transitional authorities and international stakeholders caused resentment and the UN and AU refused to endorse the deal.

9–10 March 2015: The Security Council mission visited Bangui and Bria, underscoring the fragility of the environment across the country, and highlighting the importance of the Bangui Forum, which was delayed until 4 May 2015.

26 March 2015: MINUSCA received authorization from the Security Council for an additional 750 military personnel, 280 police personnel, and 20 corrections officers to support the original 10,000 that were approved in its initial 2014 mandate.

1 Making Sense of CAR
An Introduction

Louisa Lombard and Tatiana Carayannis

What has become increasingly clear with each successive crisis in the Central African Republic (CAR) is that, despite being such a low priority for the international community, it is, in fact, the crossroads of regional and international conflict and gamesmanship. Since its independence in 1960, CAR has had but one democratic transfer of power – in 1993, in an election organized by the United Nations. For its first thirty years, changes in executive office holders were spearheaded or otherwise facilitated by France, the country's former colonial power. Since then, army mutinies and serial rebellion that draws on collaboration with regional leaders and men-at-arms have resulted in two successful coups, one led by François Bozizé in 2003, and one in 2013, almost exactly ten years later, by a disparate rebel coalition called Seleka that ousted him. Moreover, over the last two decades, the country has become a kind of testing ground for peacebuilding initiatives. Just prior to the deployment of MINUSCA, in early September 2014, it was even proclaimed 'the world champion of peacekeeping missions' (AFP, 2014). The country has indeed hosted a two-decade-long succession of UN and regional (CEN-SAD, CEMAC, ECCAS,[1] European Union, African Union) peacekeeping missions, special political missions, peacebuilding missions, and bilateral (Chad, France) military interventions. Yet despite lying at the centre of a tumultuous region (its neighbours include Chad, Sudan, South Sudan, and the Democratic Republic of Congo – DRC), CAR and its turbulent history have often been overlooked by analysts. Indeed, no single volume has addressed the country's post-independence political economy, the role of conflict, and influence of regional and international actors. *Making Sense of the Central African Republic* begins to fill that gap – a gap whose breadth has become all the more glaringly apparent as people have scrambled to address the war that began in December 2012.

Again and again, interventions in CAR have failed, in part because those spearheading them have operated as if the crisis of the moment was the first of its kind. That is, they have failed to address the longer-running dynamics that have grown out of CAR's position in the world. The book argues that the CAR's history of turmoil and instability can only be understood in the context of its violent history of colonization, limited political institutionalization and centralization, and position (geographic as well as geopolitical) in the region. With this in mind, the book focuses less on explaining the post-Seleka crisis, and more on the dynamics that have animated the CAR political economy over the past two centuries, with a focus on the post-independence period. As much as the Seleka crisis reflects new tendencies and new actors, it also reflects these longer-running dynamics (*plus ça change*). Any attempt to help Central Africans emerge from this nadir will have to consider not just the symptoms but the underlying causes of their plight – a cliché that has been frequently uttered but rarely done when it comes to peacebuilding in CAR.

This book shows how the fault lines across the broader region (ethno-religious rivalries, north–south, transnational armed groups, etc.) are being replicated and re-energized in CAR, feeding off the absence of formal state institutions and creating increasingly complex transnational conflict dynamics. The peripheries of the Central African state – in particular the North, but really every border area – are now more connected to the peripheries of its neighbours than they are to the government in the capital, Bangui. But in contrast to the picture of a shapeless, amorphous political space that emerges in most accounts of this 'failed state', there is instead a hive of competing authorities across the region born of specific historical relationships and dynamics. CAR thus merits much more attention than it has received from researchers and international policymakers alike, and we continue to ignore it at our peril.

In this introduction, we offer a snapshot history of CAR and then provide a thematic overview of the book.

An 'unfortunate colony' becomes a 'failed state'

Central Africans, whose country was once known as the 'Cinderella' of the French Empire (or, less charitably, as *la colonie poubelle* – the trashcan colony [Brégeon, 1998]), have never had an easy time of it. When French colonists arrived at the end of the nineteenth century, they found sultans connected to trans-Saharan economic and social networks, as well as dynamic communities seeking both to participate in these new long-distance trades and avoid the wrath of the sultans' armies. The French saw their task as removing the 'foreign' sultans, arguing that they were a colonizing force with no right to rule over Central Africans (the irony of this stance was lost on the French). French colonization was alternately brutal and neglectful.[2] Rather than develop their colony themselves, the French leased most of the country's territory to concessionary companies to exploit (Coquéry-Vidrovitch, 1972). Penury, corruption, and the difficulty of retaining skilled officers plagued the colonial government. A century and a half of slave-raiding, forced labour (which did not officially end until 1954 and which continued unofficially even longer), and new diseases de-populated much of the country. Even today, after rapid post-independence population growth, only about four million people call this territory just larger than France (or the size of Texas) home.

At independence in 1960 the French admitted that of all their former holdings, this one was the least prepared to stand on its own (Brégeon, 1998). The country had only one hospital, and the few health dispensaries were perennially under-equipped. The country's first *lycée* had graduated its first class only four years prior. French 'technical advisers' effectively ran all the ministries. Central African politicians learned quickly that the powers that be of *françafrique* would support them decisively if they seemed able to prevent the spillover or repeat of their southern neighbour, the Republic of Congo's, political crisis (Kalck, 1971). Substantive democracy was among the victims of this policy, which continues into the present.

Despite these inauspicious conditions, a small middle class flourished. Coup leader-turned president ('for life', then emperor) Jean-Bédel Bokassa built and hired, and there remained a sense of opportunity for those educated during these decades, even though the economy had already begun its downward slope. The University of Bangui, created by Bokassa in 1969, attracted some of the region's top students. Given the dearth of qualified Central African civil servants at independence, all university graduates could count on a government job and pension. There had been no 'free and fair' elections (coups organized with French involvement had become the norm), but life mostly trundled along. The country even attracted many immigrants, among them a number of Muslim businesspeople from Chad and beyond.

Things began to change in the 1980s. Structural adjustment and a declining economy meant that government jobs dried up for all but the well-connected, and by the 1990s even the lucky few with jobs saw months upon months of salary arrears. As president, beginning in 1993, Ange-Félix Patassé abolished the head tax, and revenues from rural areas dwindled to almost nothing. At the same time, the French were eager to step back from the heavy-handed role they had played in CAR's independence politics, and by the time the century closed they had closed their military base at Bouar and withdrawn most of the soldiers based there and in Bangui.

Until the mid-1990s, civil conflict had been limited to relatively isolated incidents. The Central African Armed Forces had already established themselves as heavy-handed in dealing with possible unrest, but such incidents did not escalate into rebellion and war (Bigo, 1988).[3] Meanwhile, the region had already seen quite a bit of war, notably in Chad and Sudan. Militarization became further popularized through a range of factors, including demobilizations in Chad; an influx of weaponry (especially Kalashnikovs) after the Cold War; the demise of the Mobutu regime in the Democratic Republic of the Congo (then Zaire); and the broader social context of straightening economic circumstances and foundering governments. In 2002–2003, several of the region's leaders – chief among them Chad's Idriss Déby – decided to replace CAR's truculent Patassé with François Bozizé, a military man and former Patassé confidant. Bozizé took Bangui in March 2003 with a force that was seven-eighths Chadian (International Crisis Group – ICG, 2007), drawn from among that country's many mobile men-in-arms (Debos, 2008). These fighters, as well as the DR-Congolese rebels Patassé had called on for support, looted, raped, and murdered along the way.

In the following years, a number of rebellions emerged in rural areas, pointing to a recurring theme of the radicalization of those at the margins, while at least on the surface, life in the capital remained relatively calm. An ambitious mayor made a range of aesthetic improvements, like tending the city's parks and ensuring that the electrified BANGUI sign on the hillside beside town mostly glowed. A profusion of humanitarian and development organizations opened offices. The prospects for most Central Africans remained dismal, however. With time, the network of people benefiting from the Bozizé government became smaller, and more concentrated around his family and church. Many Central Africans lamented that they were moving steadily backward at a time when the rest of the world was, from their perspective, so obviously on a forward march.

Throughout the decade of *la Bozizie* the country went through a series of internationally-led peacebuilding and state-building initiatives. The government and rebel parties to these endeavours generally endorsed them in form rather than in spirit, and worked them to their own advantage. The international actors funding the processes were invested in presenting them as successful, and, moreover, reluctantly supported Bozizé because he seemed like the 'least bad option', defined as usual as the person most likely to be able to prevent the 'spillover' of the region's other conflicts into CAR. These calculations were a major part of why most diplomats only mutedly criticized the blatant rigging of the 2011 presidential elections. What all this meant was that grievances among the population and among the growing ranks of sidelined political elites grew in inverse proportion to the official channels (national dialogues, elections, etc.) to express them.

Even Déby, whose soldiers had helped Bozizé remain in power all this time, grew frustrated with the president. Bozizé was pursuing a new tutelary relationship with South Africa, and he appeared to have calculated that due to his new supporters (South African soldiers arrived in the country in 2007 and were reinforced in 2012–2013) he no longer needed Chad as he had before. Meanwhile, in mid-2012 a few Central African political–military entrepreneurs met in Niamey, Niger to begin planning a takeover of power. By the end of 2012, they had assembled a heterogeneous rebel coalition they called Seleka ('alliance' in Sango, CAR's main language) and obtained the go-ahead, if not direct funding, from Déby to begin their march on Bangui. Initially, many, if not most, of the Seleka fighters came from the Chad/Darfur borderland region, but when the likelihood of their success became apparent, north-eastern CAR's home-grown rebel groups joined as well.

Seleka leaders and the government were forced into a peace process in January 2013, but none of the parties seemed particularly interested in respecting its terms. On 24 March 2013, Seleka fighters claimed power in Bangui. Little united them other than the desire to take the capital and loot along the way. The new president, Michel Djotodia (a former CAR civil servant in the 1980s), had no real power over the various armed elements of his alliance, most of whom were politico-military entrepreneurs with much more battlefield experience than him. Seleka fighters spread throughout the country and ruled towns as their own fiefdoms, yet without the attachment to the terrain that the feudal model might suggest. Civilians suffered, and many were killed.

Whereas Bozizé had taken power through a kind of regional gentleman's agreement that included French support (ICG, 2007), Djotodia did not benefit from such regional cooperation. Some diplomats foresaw that a robust international peacekeeping mission would be necessary to restore some order, both in Bangui and in the countryside. But inertia and inaction mostly ruled the day among diplomatic actors. Crises elsewhere seemed more pressing.

In September 2013, Djotodia officially 'disbanded' Seleka. The move was an odd one for several reasons. On the one hand, Seleka was never really 'banded' in the first place, so why go to the trouble of *disbanding* it? For another, doing so removed any incentive the remaining Seleka elements had to work together or follow Djotodia's future orders. He ended up with even less bargaining power. In the wake of the disbanding, militias in the western part of the country and in Bangui began gaining strength. There is a long tradition of self-defence groups in most of CAR. These groups are less standing forces than networks that can be activated when the need arises. The new groups drew on these networks and traditions, but also far surpassed them. The various groups that mobilized in the wake of Seleka abuses called themselves the Anti-Balaka.[4]

As was the case with Seleka, the fact that the Anti-Balaka share a name masks that they consist of a number of different segments whose members do not share the same interests or objectives. (About half support a return for Bozizé and receive support from him; many of the others wanted Seleka pushed from power but do not support Bozizé.) This is one reason why a number of scholars of the region criticized the 'verge of genocide' or 'religious hatred' language that international actors and journalists used to draw attention to CAR when Anti-Balaka groups began their attacks. To the extent that people have asked them about their grievances, Anti-Balaka fighters have emphasized that theirs are political gripes, not religious ones. They describe their war in terms familiar to scholars of the region's autochthony movements; they see themselves only as standing up for the 'true' population of CAR, who, they argue, are being overrun – pillaged, raped – by foreigners. As Marchal describes in Chapters 3 and 8, this grievance is both understandable and not wholly fair.

Moreover, Anti-Balaka violence has exceeded its members' statements of purpose. All Muslims in the southern and western parts of the country have been persecuted, and only a few remain in the capital, where they are able to live only because they are continually guarded by peacekeepers.

Anti-Balaka groups launched a major offensive in Bangui on 5 December 2013, the day that French and African Union peacekeeping forces received mandates to deploy to CAR. Anti-Balaka battle success was yet another sign that Djotodia lacked any real control over violence in the country, and in early January 2014 Déby airlifted the entire Central African transitional government to Ndjamena where Déby met with Djotodia and convinced him to step down. Once back in Bangui, the transitional assembly chose a new president, Catherine Samba-Panza. In a different context, CAR's first, and Africa's third female president (a lawyer with both a business and advocacy background) might have augured well for the country. But given the ongoing war, she has been powerless to do much about the violence, despite accruing substantial power to benefit from the perks of her office, effectively consolidating power as surely as Bozizé and other CAR heads of state before her. In a telling incident that shows this paradox, in early February 2014, President Samba-Panza presided over a ceremony for new recruits to the Central African Armed Forces. As the event was wrapping up, soldiers identified someone they thought was a Seleka fighter in their midst and brutally killed him, a murder captured by the professional photographers there for the ceremony.

The peacekeepers have struggled to contain the violence and various contingents are seen as in collaboration with the different parties to the conflict: the French supporting Anti-Balaka; the Rwandans and Burundians protecting the few Muslims who remain in the capital; the Chadians actively fighting for Seleka (the Chadian contingent withdrew in late March 2014 following furore over an incident in which they killed more than twenty people at a market); and the French and AU peacekeepers actively hampering each other's objectives. In April 2014, the UN Security Council finally authorized the deployment of blue helmets to CAR. Given budget constraints and limited interest in CAR at UN headquarters and from troop-contributing countries, many of those peacekeepers were simply re-hatted from the AU mission. The UN took authority over its new force on 15 September 2014.

Today, outside of the capital, knowledge of what is going on is spotty. Large swathes of the country rarely make it into the news, but are experiencing rapid change and their own conflicts. In north-western Ouham-Pende prefecture, for instance, a new rebel group called the *Revolution Justice* has divvied up state jobs among its members. Travellers coming from Bangui must now transit past RJ customs officials. These rebels do not consider themselves separatists; they simply feel the government is not doing its job, so they must do it for themselves (which has the perk of drawing the salaries themselves as well). The safest part of the country is probably the far south-east, thanks to the presence of Ugandan and US troops there under the auspices of the long-running hunt for the Lord's Resistance Army (see Cakaj, Chapter 12). Hundreds of thousands of people are internally displaced or living as refugees. And there is no end in sight.

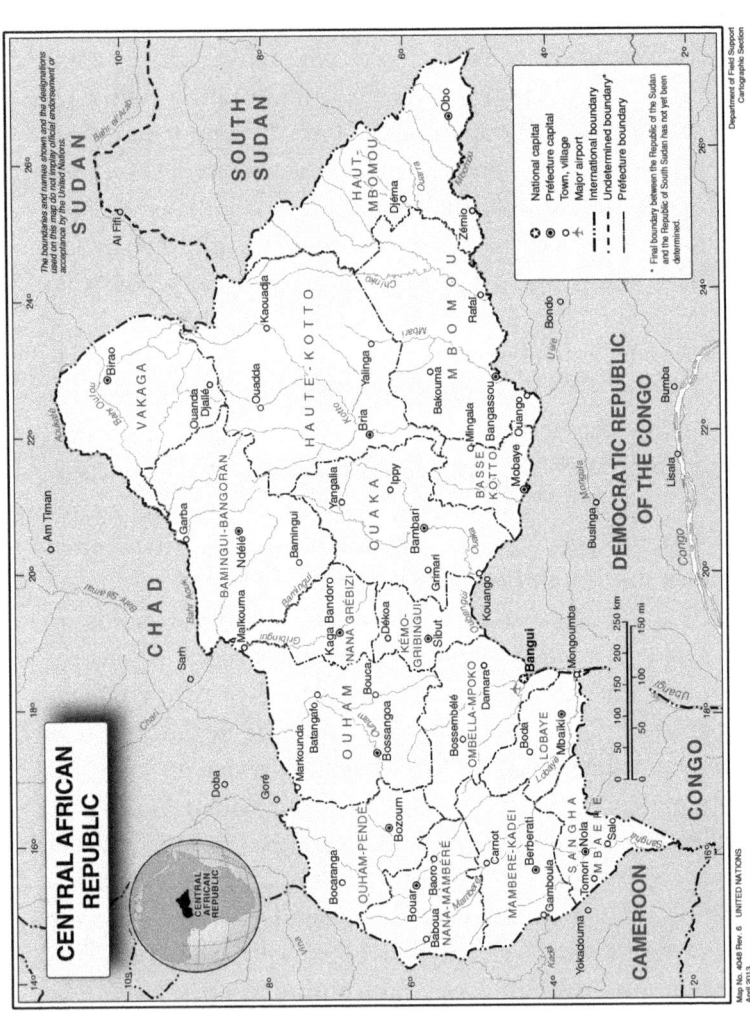

Map 1.1 United Nations map of the Central African Republic, April 2013.
Source: UN Department of Field Support, Cartographic Section.

Thematic overview of the book

A number of themes cut across the book's various chapters. These are, broadly speaking, the nature and importance of centre-periphery relationships in the regional system that CAR is a part of; modes of accumulation, often fraught, for government elites and the hoi polloi; the failures and misrecognitions of international interventions in CAR; and the growing insecurity in all aspects of life – that one might even call a 'spiritual insecurity' (Ashforth, 2005).

The chapters share in the understanding that states can only be understood as part of a broader system of states in the region and beyond (see Map 1.1). Therefore, we are sceptical of all those analyses that describe CAR's problems, including the ongoing war, as a function of its 'weakness' or even 'failure'. These descriptors tell us nothing about the nature of the *relationships* – within CAR's borders and beyond – that are the core dynamics of governance in the Central African Republic. So instead, we turn the usual centre-periphery model around. Where most such approaches focus on the centre and its determinative role, we probe the workings of political and economic life in the periphery with open minds as to the nature of its bonds with powerful actors outside its borders. CAR is, some might say, even a 'periphery of a periphery' (Cordell, 1985), but it has been an active player during the process of its *'mise en dépendence'* (the enactment of dependency) (Bayart, 2000), sometimes in surprising ways. This emphasis on relationships and their historical and geographical underpinnings runs through every chapter in the book.

Some of the chapters (Cakaj, Chapter 12; Lombard, Chapter 7) approach the question of the regional nature of the CAR state and people in the area by siting their analysis primarily in remote reaches of CAR territory. These chapters draw out the fact that the label 'peripheral' or 'marginal' connotes both a number of shared features and dynamics, but also hides important differences in the nature of the various regions' remotenesses and the connections and disjunctions it entails. Other chapters (Marchal, Chapter 8;

Carayannis, Chapter 11) make the region, and particular elements of it, their starting point for their questioning of the contours of peripheral statuses. The conclusion shared by all of these chapters is that even peripheral areas are centres of something.

A second set of themes has to do with the nature of the CAR state, and particularly the modes of accumulation associated with it. That is to say, in CAR, as Marchal draws out in his chapter ('Being Rich, Being Poor', Chapter 3), to be employed by the state has come to be seen as a way of amassing private wealth. Smith (Chapter 5) explains that the privatization of the CAR state is nothing new but rather began with the first years of French colonialism. Together, Marchal's and Smith's chapters (Chapters 3 and 5, respectively) explain how this logic of using state office for private gain has become popularized in the context of economic penury that ensued in earnest with the thinning of the civil servant ranks and devaluation of the CFA in the early 1990s. 'Thus', writes Smith, 'the Central African state is for most citizens a painful absence and a hurtful presence'.

At the same time as using public office for private gain has become a common practice that is lamented even as people justify it through a 'desperate times' mentality, other modes of wealth accumulation have come to be seen as increasingly suspicious. That is to say, if a person accumulates money through non-state based activities (commerce, etc.) people are likely to wonder whether dark arts (such as the mobilization of others' labour power while they ostensibly lie and sleep) are involved. The whole adds up to what Adam Ashforth has evocatively called 'spiritual insecurity' – the sense that not just one's physical body but one's whole metaphysical existence and understanding of the world is at risk. Dalby's chapter on diamond mining (Chapter 6) draws together these various threads related to state predation and the challenges of accumulation. Kilembe's (Chapter 4) does the same by instead looking at Bangui's most dynamic market neighbourhood through its historically cross-regional connections and recent upheaval. This upheaval has drawn out a tension long festering just below the surface of Central African social relations, namely the place of Muslims in Central African society. Kilembe writes,

> Today, the Muslim community of Central Africa is at a crossroads. Its future will depend on its approach to ending an internal crisis perpetuated by competition among different 'power-seeking' interests, but, above all, on its vision for establishing relations with other communities, particularly Christians, and its choice to pursue a nationalist or isolationist, group-centric approach on the national scene. (Chapter 4, this book)

A third theme relates to the reasons for CAR's long decline and the shortcomings of the efforts marshalled by the international community and other diplomatic actors to get the country on course. From the perspective of CAR's elites, the country's decline was in no way inevitable and rather relates to the personal failings of its leaders, particularly its presidents, as Wohlers' chapter draws out (Chapter 13). These elites might not be sufficiently accounting for the structural factors limiting their leaders' range of manoeuvring, but they add something important that outside observers often miss: the fact that the present is not the product of some inexorable process (i.e., the necessary decline of the CAR state), but rather reflects the concatenation of innumerable decisions, coincidences, and other factors, any number of which might have played out differently and led to a different CAR today.

Several chapters (Picco, Chapter 10; Olin, Chapter 9; Cakaj, Chapter 12; and Carayannis, Chapter 11) call attention to problems – at once structural and situational – related to the international humanitarian, peacebuilding, justice, and other diplomatic initiatives that have been deployed in CAR since the mid-1990s. One shortcoming of these efforts has been outsiders' tendency to view CAR's problems through the lens of the continent's other crises – (e.g., to see conflict in CAR as 'Darfur spillover') rather than seriously probe the nature of CAR's problems in and of themselves, as objects worthy of study and understanding rather than as corollaries of higher-profile crises.

This extends to the International Criminal Court (ICC). As with most international interventions in CAR, the first (and to date only) ICC case on CAR 'has been about something other than CAR' (Carayannis, Chapter 11). Another shortcoming has been the inability of this so-called international community, whose attention span for CAR is only as long as it takes for another more pressing crisis to emerge on the world scene, to focus on the necessary longer-term. As a result, 'a series of small patches' have been used to treat a large, open 'wound' (Picco, Chapter 10). The interests of these external actors always end up trumping the interests of Central Africans. At the same time, when diplomatic and donor agencies have tried to stay the course in CAR, they have been met with lip service from Central African leaders who are all too eager to accept donor funds but have little interest in translating them into action or reform. The inability of diplomatic actors to call the bluff of Central African heads of state has been among the reasons why the tens of millions of dollars spent on the country have done so little to improve the lot of people there.

Conclusion

Violence has long been an element of domination in Equatorial Africa, and in that sense the current war is no exception. Similarly, CAR sovereignty has always been relational, and Central African leaders have been adept at managing dependence with leaders from beyond the country's borders in order to bolster their own positions, in a classic example of what Jean-François Bayart (2000) called extraversion. These external actors – from France to the UN – have generally viewed CAR through the lens of the promotion of regional stability at the expense of standing firm for any kind of substantive democracy or inclusiveness in CAR politics. Of course, it may be beyond the capacity of an external intervention to do any such thing. What is clear is that any joint Central African/diplomatic endeavour must focus not so much on 'rebuilding' the state as on the *sources* of insecurity that act as brakes on economic and political development, as Marchal explains in his chapters in this volume (Chapters 3 and 8).

The dilemmas Central Africans now stand before reflect their country's turbulent history and marginalized place in the world. But at the same time, these challenges are not unique to the country. Throughout the region, a narrative of living together across religious lines has been sorely lacking. The schisms across the region as in CAR, however, have little to do with religion as such and much to do with struggles over power, wealth accumulation, and control over the invisible world. And these battles remain very much ongoing.

Notes

1 CEN-SAD: Community of Sahel–Saharan States; CEMAC: Economic and Monetary Community of Central Africa; ECCAS: Economic Community of Central African States.
2 Both of the country's two main independence-era figures, Barthélemy Boganda and Jean-Bédel Bokassa, had fathers who were killed by colonial militias. In Bokassa's case, his father had freed some people who had been jailed for failure to perform forced labour and was beaten to death in the town centre for this insubordination.
3 See Bigo (1988) for discussion of a rebellion in north-western CAR in the early 1980s.
4 The name Anti-Balaka has two commonly-cited etymologies: first, as a reference to the initiation ceremonies that members go through, which make them impervious to Kalashnikov bullets (*balles-AK*), and second as the term for machete in the Gbaya language, as spoken in the area around Bossangoa (Bozizé's home region).

Bibliography

Agence France-Presse – AFP (2014) 'La Centrafrique: Championne du monde des interventions internationales', Bangui: 2 September. Available from: http://www.lalibre.be/dernieres-depeches/afp/la-centrafrique-championne-du-monde-des-interventions-internationales-5405bef435708a6d4d52fe59

Ashforth, A. (2005) *Violence, Democracy, and Witchcraft in South Africa*, University of Chicago Press, Chicago, US.

Bayart, J. (2000) 'Africa in the World: A History of Extraversion', *African Affairs*, Volume 99, Issue 395.

Bigo, D. (1988) *Pouvoir et obéissance en Centrafrique*, Karthala, Paris.

Brégeon, J.J. (1998) *Un rêve d'Afrique. Administrateurs en Oubangui-Chari, la cendrillon de l'empire*, Denoël, Paris.

Cordell, D. (1985) *Dar al-Kuti and the Last Years of the Trans-Saharan Slave Trade*, University of Wisconsin Press, Madison, WI, US.

Coquéry-Vidrovitch, C. (1972) *Le Congo au temps des grandes compagnies concessionaires, 1890–1930*, Mouton, Paris.

Debos, M. (2008) 'Fluid loyalties in a regional crisis: Chadian "ex-liberators" in the Central African Republic', *African Affairs*, Volume 107, No. 427.

International Crisis Group – ICG (2007) *Anatomy of a Phantom State*, Africa Report No. 136, Nairobi–Brussels.

Kalck, P. (1971) *Central African Republic: A Failure in De-Colonisation*. Trans. by Barbara Thomson, Pall Mall Press, London.

2 CAR's History
The Past of a Tense Present

Stephen W. Smith

This chapter's ambition is both broad in scope and narrow in purpose: it aims at acquainting anyone interested in the Central African Republic (CAR) with the major events in, and protagonists of, the country's history since the nineteenth century. With a view to laying the groundwork for the subsequent chapters, it seeks to impart key dates, facts and figures – shoals of doubt or controversy will be duly signalled.

Inasmuch as any account of history is shaped by a perspective, and inasmuch as the past is instructed by our questions rather than 'teaching' us lessons, the narrative woven hereafter is a particular fabric. Two thematic threads – statehood and centre-periphery relations – constitute its warp and woof. Statehood is not explored here in functional or normative terms of 'success' or 'failure' but as a trajectory that has resulted, for the moment, in a 'phantom state' (International Crisis Group, 2007),[1] i.e. a state which – akin to a phantom limb – is experienced by most Central Africans as sorely lacking. Not only does the state fail to meet their expectations in providing public goods; it metes out extortionist and coercive abuse to a majority while purveying a 'sovereignty rent' to a minority in power. Thus, the Central African state is for most citizens a painful absence *and* a hurtful presence. How this has come to be, and which internal and external factors account for CAR's dark-matter statehood, will run as an open question through what follows. Centre-periphery dynamics are the second analytical leitmotiv. They are relevant for precolonial Central Africa within the wider, notably slave-trading world, for the relationship between the Oubangui-Chari colony and its French metropolis, for postcolonial Bangui and its hinterland as well as for the CAR vis-à-vis its defining regional context.

One caveat: to the extent to which this capsule account strives to be apposite for the crisis-stricken present, it fatally misconstrues CAR's history as a baneful, if not altogether tragic concatenation. To correct this distortion, one ought to bear in mind that, in the CAR like anywhere else, the past is not a genealogy of crime or a coherent sequence of 'causes'. It is merely the stage we revisit to make need-based sense of the unscripted interplay between necessity, contingency and human agency.

Precolonial Central Africa

From what we know about Central Africa in the nineteenth century, the territory destined to become Oubangui-Chari was not only demographically depleted but also politically and socio-economically organized in response to the devastating impact of sustained slave raiding (Rouget, 1906); (Davies, 1967); (Kalck, 1974). Early travel accounts describe the region as 'an archipelago of scattered ethnic groups' (Prioul, 1981, p. 71) more or less isolated from one another by unclaimed buffer zones. In addition to the 'river people' along the Oubangui, and the pygmies in the equatorial rain forest, the most important groups mentioned are the Gbaya in the west, the Mandja in the centre, and the Gbanda in the east.

A 'pervasive atmosphere of distrust' if not an 'endemic state of war' is said to have prevailed among the various peoples in the region (Prioul, 1981, p. 81). Notwithstanding, commerce was intense along the Oubangui River, and long-distance trade – in addition to slave trade – was also practiced. Caravans from Darfur linked the heart of Africa to the Nile valley, while in exchange for iron bars, bronze and rolls of cloth coming the other way, ivory, bush meat, honey and wax were ferried some 1,500 km down the Congo River. However, the value of these exchanges was surpassed by the slave trade toward Tripoli, Cairo and the Indian Ocean (Miege, 1981, p. 99).[2] Moreover, at the end of the nineteenth century, the human toll of the slave economy was compounded by the microbial shock of the 'colonial encounter'. Almost half of the Central African population perished between 1890 and 1940, when the number of inhabitants reached a historical low point of 750,000 (Saulnier, 1998, pp. 81–96). Since, population growth has been as spectacular here as in the rest of sub-Saharan Africa: CAR's population doubled by 1960, the year of the country's independence, and tripled over the next fifty years, reaching 4.5 million in 2010.

The slave-trading Wadai Sultanate in the north-east of today's Chad had launched razzias into the territories north of the Oubangui River since the mid-seventeenth century. But the pressure greatly increased after 1830 with the establishment of a vassal sultanate inside present CAR's north-east, the *Dar al-Kuti* (Kalck, 1974, p. 95). This Islamic frontier state extensively raided, and more tentatively proselytized (Cordell, 1977, pp. 119–191). For many Central Africans, Rabih Fadlallah, a Sudanese slave-trader who was killed in battle by the French in 1900, and his protégé as the 'emir' of *Dar al-Kuti* from 1890 until his death in 1911, Muhammad al-Sanusi, retain until today a spine-chilling ring to their names (Hallam, 1976).

France's cul-de-sac

Oubangui-Chari came into existence as an accident of colonial history. In 1896, a French military column left Gabon with the aim of linking France's territorial conquests in Africa along a west–east axis, from Senegal and the Atlantic Ocean all across to the newly proclaimed French Somaliland (today's Djibouti) and the Red Sea. The twin objective was to achieve territorial continuity and to ruin British attempts at a north–south colonization of Africa, 'from Cape to Cairo'. The clash of these rival ambitions has gone down in the annals of history as the 'Fashoda incident', which nearly sparked a war between France and Great Britain. Reaching the Upper Nile near to the small town of Fashoda after an adventurous three-year march, the French column – 12 Europeans, 150 African infantry and 13,500 porters – was summoned to turn on its heel by Horatio Kitchener, who had ferried up the Nile a much stronger detachment. Fashoda has since become in France a by-word for 'humiliation by Anglo-Saxons'.

The French column slogged back to Bangui, which had been founded ten years earlier, in 1889, by French explorers. 'The dream of a French Africa stretching from the Gulf of Guinea to the Indian Ocean evaporated and, instead of becoming the platform for this penetration, the Oubangui-Chari region became a cul-de-sac' (Brégeon, 1998, p. 24). A territory larger than metropolitan France was carved out and proclaimed a French colony in 1903. It joined the French Congo, the collective name given to France's possessions in Central Africa. Before long, Oubangui-Chari was dubbed the 'Cinderella of the Empire' for its lack of resources and advantages. Its capital, Bangui, where it rains from February/March until November/December, would never attract a strong European presence. Eighty expatriates lived there in 1900; 163 in 1915; 1,932 in 1921; and 4,696 in 1931, the year the colonial exhibition in the Park of Vincennes, near Paris, marked the apogee of popular interest in France's overseas ambitions (Colombani, 1991, p. 47).

The French state was not keen on investing heavily into its colonial dead-end street. What is more, the neighbouring Congo Free State – a misnomer as the vast territory was a colony privately owned by the Belgian king Leopold II – seemed to offer an expedient and profitable alternative. Inspired by its example, Paris subcontracted in 1899 much of the French Congo – 667,000 of 1,233,000 sq km – to forty private companies that were granted a thirty-year monopoly on the exploitation of putatively 'vacant and unowned land' (Cantournet, 1991, p. 7 and pp. 12–15). The state sold 'concessions' to operators who, in addition to the purchase price, were supposed to pay 15 per cent of their yearly net benefit as a flat fee. It was a wild bargain on both sides: the French state de facto outsourced its sovereign rights over recently conquered, not yet entirely pacified and barely administered overseas possessions (though, on paper, the delegation of state authority was explicitly ruled out); the private capital ventured into unknown territory bereft of basic infrastructure in hopes of a quick and massive return thanks to coffee, cocoa, cotton and, above all, ivory and the 'rubber boom'.[3]

Colonization 'on the cheap'

Fifteen of the forty concessionary companies – different only in name from the 'chartered companies' of earlier centuries – operated partly or totally in Oubangui-Chari. The most important one, the Compagnie des sultanats du Haut-Oubangui, administered 145,000 sq km. Taken together, the private companies covered about half of the colony where, in actuality though not legally, they 'made state'. However, they did not have the means to build roads, bridges, schools or hospitals. Unlike the companies in the Congo Free State, they were dramatically underfunded. Their investments represented barely 1 per cent of the overall capital invested in the French empire, and only 0.1 per cent of the total French foreign investment in 1905 (International Crisis Group, 2007).

It would be a mistake to assume that colonial administrators, private entrepreneurs, and Catholic missionaries in the French Congo were in league with one another. Oftentimes they were not, and their turf wars are abundantly documented. Yet, as the French colonized Oubangui-Chari 'on the cheap', the system was much more imbricated there than elsewhere. For instance, since 1895, the rules of engagement of the French army stipulated that 'if necessary, the head of a detachment takes local notables hostage' – a practice the concessionary companies liberally privatized

(Cantournet, 1991, p. 36), all the more easily as their security guards were often former members of the French army. On 19 March 1903, the fate of the state and of the concessionary companies was ultimately linked as colonial administrators were henceforth graded on the basis of how much head tax they levied on the 'indigenous people' – who mostly paid the tax in kind, i.e. in rubber the private companies collected (Jeaugeon, 1961, p. 396).

The upshot was that the French system in Central Africa, though less profitable,[4] resembled the exploitative, terror-based regime first introduced in the Congo Free State. While an international campaign against Leopold II's 'red rubber' – 'blood rubber' in modern parlance – was picking up steam, the French government was embarrassed by a concomitant series of scandals in its own Congo, and in particular in Oubangui-Chari. In one instance, in May 1904, fifty-eight women and ten children were taken hostage as a reprisal for their village's insufficient tax revenue and sent to Bangui, where they were detained in abhorrent conditions; forty-seven of the women and two of the children died. In another instance, on 14 July 1903, a colonial official in Fort-Crampel (today's Kaga-Bandoro) blew up a native prisoner sentenced to death by sticking a dynamite bar into his anus as a way of celebrating Bastille Day and deterring anti-colonial machinations.[5]

For the French authorities, such echoes from Central Africa were not only, and most likely not primarily, a humanitarian issue but a political one inasmuch as the public outcry about abuses in its Congo undermined France's efforts to position itself as 'heir presumptive' of Leopold II's private colony, if one day the Belgian king were to let go.[6] In 1905, a living legend, Pierre Savorgnan de Brazza, the explorer who had given his name to Brazzaville and who had administered the French Congo until 1898, was tasked with a mission of inquiry. His findings were damning but were only published in 2014 (Coquery-Vidrovitch, 2014, pp. 53–250).[7] As de Brazza had died on his voyage home from Central Africa, the French government replaced his commission of inquiry by a new and more complacent one and objected to the release of his report. Still, because of the reputational damage already incurred and the system's enduring inefficiency, the concessionary companies were restructured and finally disbanded after 1910, the year the French Congo was reorganized and renamed as French Equatorial Africa (FEA).

Independence in indigence

The hardship imposed by private profit-seeking endowed with state authority was added on to the 'ordinary' colonial practices such as forced labour and the impressment of unpaid porters. The colonial archives are replete with documents attesting to the difficulty of levying 3,000 bearers every month to transport loads from the Congo-Brazzaville river-front or Cameroon to Chad, where French troops depended on a steady provision of supplies. For lack of genuine volunteers, the authorities resorted to increasingly coercive methods. On 16 October 1901, a colonial circular ordered the construction of hostage camps, which were to be hidden in the forest lest travellers would see them (International Crisis Group, 2007, p. 3). A whole range of sanctions was inflicted on chiefs incapable of supplying the required number of porters: they were arrested or flogged with a strop made of hippopotamus rawhide, the *chicotte*: the women and children of their villages were taken prisoners and kept until the bearers returned. Finally, if this blackmail failed, punitive expeditions were organized against recalcitrant villages, which were burned down and their inhabitants killed as an example (Faes and Smith, 2000b, p. 284).

Armed resistance did occur, most notably in 1928, when the murder of a local chief sparked an uprising among the Gbaya in the north-west. The so-called 'war of the *kongo-wara*', which owes its name to the 'hoe handle' the rebel leaders brandished, was not definitively stamped out until 1930. Having taken on the character of an anti-colonial insurrection, it mobilized about 50,000 supporters against 1,000 infantry and regional guards, plus 3,000 auxiliaries, scouts and porters. In its final phase, when

10,000 implacable opponents were pursued into the caves to which they had retreated, the war resulted in thousands of deaths (Faes and Smith, 2000a, p. 65).

Oubangui-Chari was the weak link in FEA, which, as a whole, lagged enormously behind French West Africa (FWA). For example, FWA had about 500 teachers in 1930, 90 per cent of whom were Africans, while there were only 80 teachers, including some 60 Africans, in FEA. At the time, barely over 1 per cent of CAR's children attended school – it was still only 8 per cent in 1950 – and merely 3,500 Central Africans had converted to Christianity (Faes and Smith, 2000a, pp. 62–63). Barthélemy Boganda, Oubangui-Chari's first national leader, and also its first native Catholic priest, was thus doubly exceptional. Founder of the Movement for the Social Evolution of Black Africa (MESAN), he was elected as the territory's deputy at the French National Assembly in Paris in 1946. For over twenty years, he personified the awakening Central African nation. But on the eve of independence, on 29 March 1959, he died in a plane crash generally attributed by Central Africans – without irrefutable evidence – to an act of sabotage by French colonialists. His loss was one more setback for a country that had already accumulated a long list of handicaps.

Boganda's spiritual heir, Abel Goumba, a young teacher with socialist ideas, succeeded the deceased father of the nation as Oubangui-Chari's prime minister. As such, he benefited from the considerable advantage of incumbency when the territory became independent on 13 August 1960, two years after being granted internal autonomy. But the then minister of the interior, David Dacko, surrounded parliament with a group of pygmies armed with poison arrows. Adding inducement to open threat, Dacko promised the deputies an extension to their term in office without any obligation for them to face the uncertainties of re-election. He thus secured a majority in the national assembly and became CAR's first president.

Dacko's number one priority as head of state was to place Goumba under house arrest and ban his rival's party. An authoritarian regime was rapidly established. The rubber-stamp parliament adopted a series of repressive laws, dissolving political parties and trade unions; individuals presented as 'dangerous' were interned, and 'subversive writings' were censored. Both cynical about the postcolonial order and mindful of the 6,000 French nationals living in Bangui, Paris looked the other way and continued to support the government with generous development aid. Only in the face of runaway corruption in its former colony did France interfere by imposing a programme of economic recovery. To avoid cluttering up the prisons, it was pragmatically decided that only those responsible for misappropriations above twenty times the then average annual wage, would be given prison sentences. Nevertheless, between 1963 and 1965, twenty prefects and deputy prefects found themselves behind bars. As in other parts of sub-Saharan Africa, civil servants with exorbitant privileges formed a parasitic caste living from international aid funds and off the backs of a mostly peasant population.

At the end of 1963, Dacko requested the chamber of deputies to introduce universal suffrage for presidential elections. In January 1964, as candidate for the single party established two years before, he was elected president – officially by a unanimous vote! On 29 September, in search of new support, Dacko recognized the People's Republic of China and expressed his wish for a 'special partnership' with Beijing. Eyebrows were raised in Paris. Increasingly aware of his dwindling support at home and abroad, Dacko eventually slipped into depression, creating a power vacuum at the highest level of the state. He contemplated handing power to his trusted friend, the head of the gendarmerie, Colonel Jean Izamo. But Izamo was beaten to the punch by Colonel Jean-Bédel Bokassa, a former captain of the French army whom Dacko had appointed as the national army's chief of staff.[8]

Bokassa's empire

On the night of 31 December 1965, Colonel Bokassa took power. Though Dacko's life was spared, the coup was unnecessarily bloody. Bokassa killed his main rival, Colonel Izamo, with his own hands, lacerating him with a sword before leaving him to die a long and agonizing death. Several members of the presidential entourage were murdered at their homes. Despite the bloodshed, the New Year's Eve putsch was welcomed by many Central Africans with relief, if not with jubilation, as a redemption from corrupt and authoritarian rule. Until 1970, the new regime was able to retain its initial popularity. An ambitious economic recovery programme – 'Operation Bokassa' – reached some of its goals thanks to political will and despite its lack of method. In addition to a boom in CAR's cash-crop production, namely cotton and groundnuts, more streets were paved, traffic circles appeared and the first multistoried buildings were erected in 'Bangui-la-Coquette', a nickname that remained popular, despite the country's steady decline, until the mid-1990s.[9]

At first, de Gaulle wanted nothing to do with Bokassa. In 1966, the French president called him 'a bloody idiot' and refused to receive him. It took constant pleading by his long-serving chief of staff at the Élysée, Jacques Foccart, the mastermind of the postcolonial Franco-African network, for de Gaulle to reconsider. In 1969, when he finally agreed to meet with Bokassa, he called him a 'good bloke'. De Gaulle's successor, Georges Pompidou, similarly oscillated between utter exasperation and a certain sympathy for CAR's uncouth head of state. Foccart's policy of appeasement and behind-the-scenes manipulation again carried the day. 'If we combine a modicum of cleverness, flexibility and authority, Bokassa will never escape our friendship', Foccart summarized his view in 1970 (Faes and Smith, 2000a, p. 133). To his mind, Bokassa's 'Francophilia' – the CAR ruler held French nationality and took public pride in it – offset his 'eccentricities'. This was a lenient assessment regarding a man who made himself president for life in 1972, marshal two years later and, at one point, simultaneously head of ten ministries.

The indulgence displayed by Paris was further accentuated after 1974 with the election of Valéry Giscard d'Estaing who had a passion for big game trophy hunting. Already, as France's minister of finance, he had been a keen hunter in the CAR and, before long, he was Bokassa's 'dear cousin' in the aristocratic ways of France's *ancien régime*. However, CAR's strong man was growing more and more erratic. In 1976, he converted to Islam, becoming Salah Eddine Bokassa to please Colonel Qaddafi, who had a reputation for being munificent with his petrodollars. At home, Bokassa's acute paranoia led to increased repression as the years went by, with more and more victims of arbitrary rule.

On 4 December 1976, Bokassa heralded the creation of the Central African Empire. He also announced his coronation would take place in exactly one year, the same day his hero Napoleon had been crowned in 1804. The entire country was engulfed in a headlong rush to organize the imperial celebrations. Prime Minister Ange-Félix Patassé zealously spearheaded the operation and splurged the equivalent of CAR's annual budget on the great day, 4 December 1977. Diamond-studded crowns, ermine-trimmed flowing mantles, gilded carriages, 32 white-robed horses flown in from Normandy, 625 ceremonial swords, tons of fresh flowers, hectolitres of the finest French wines and the best champagne... – no effort was spared for the occasion. Five thousand guests attended. France was represented by its Minister of Cooperation. Public opinion ignored at the time that this 'tropical farce', which the international press ridiculed, was actually co-funded, and co-organized, by France, namely by the Élysée, the Ministries of Cooperation and Defence and also by the President's first cousin, François Giscard d'Estaing, the Director General of the French Foreign Trade Bank (BFCE).[10]

Resistance to the despotic ruler in Bangui, and to France, the power that sustained him, started to be more organized in January 1979, with the founding of a proper opposition party, the Movement for the Liberation of the Central African People (MLPC). Fallen from imperial grace, the former Prime Minister Patassé became its leader. Also in January 1979, school students demonstrating in CAR's capital were harshly repressed. Then, in

April, around 250 young people were picked up from the streets of Bangui and beaten up before being piled into cells at Ngaragba prison that were too small to contain them all. Dozens of them died, mostly from suffocation. In June 1987, when the criminal court of Bangui was called on to judge the ex-emperor who had returned from exile, it concluded that torture had resulted in the deaths although there had been no intention to kill. But in 1979, when Giscard d'Estaing gave his 'dear cousin' the thumbs down as he had become a liability for him, a commission of enquiry by African jurists concluded that the emperor had almost certainly personally put the imprisoned children to death.[11]

After the 'Ngaragba massacre', France severed all ties with Bokassa I. The Central African emperor sought out a saviour in Colonel Qaddafi. It was then that the French President gave orders to 'off-load' him (Faes and Smith, 2000b, p. 290). In retrospect, the same people who had kept quiet about the very real atrocities committed by a tropical dictator exaggerated his depravity to the extent that they falsely vilified him as a cannibal, after the discovery, completely fabricated, of human flesh in the imperial court's cold storage locker in Bérengo. The former master of CAR, forced into exile in Côte d'Ivoire, took revenge by revealing he had offered trays of diamonds – in fact small brilliants – to Giscard d'Estaing. The 'diamonds affair' was to play a role in the French President's failure to be re-elected in 1981.

The 'Barracuda syndrome'

On the night of 20 September 1979, Bokassa I was overthrown by a French military intervention – Operation Barracuda – while visiting Libya. David Dacko reluctantly returned to power in the hold of a French Transall aircraft packed with paratroopers. Paris argued that he remained the legitimate head of state, having been forcibly overthrown. This marked the beginning of the 'Barracuda syndrome', a term coined by Jean-Paul Ngoupandé[12] to describe the infantilization of a people that were so dispossessed of their own history that they were not even responsible for deposing their own tyrant. Reinstalled in the presidential seat by a seemingly perpetual tutelary power, Dacko himself doubted his capacity to reassert his leadership. Many of his compatriots, though they welcomed the end of the empire, shared his misgivings on account of his first spell in power. Demonstrations of discontent quickly followed. The French army was forced to stay to guarantee the security of the old regime it had restored to power. Except for a brief period at the turn of the century, French troops have since become a fixture in the CAR.

After the imperial dictatorship, which had finally exhausted its postcolonial patience, France retook full control of CAR. Independent in principle but in reality dependent on France for everything, Dacko's ex/new regime needed ever more foreign aid and troops to survive. Evacuated in 1965, the old French military base at Bouar, in the west, was reopened. In addition to the French advisers installed in all key administrative positions of the state, a safe pair of hands was eventually lodged at the very heart of power, the presidency: Lieutenant-Colonel Jean-Claude Mantion, a member of the French secret service (DGSE). He was quickly nicknamed 'the proconsul', because the proliferation of his duties made him the de facto ruler of CAR for thirteen years.

In 1981, Dacko campaigned for re-election in what resembled more a plebiscite a posteriori on his return to power. In the decisive second round, he defeated his challenger, Ange-Félix Patassé from the Movement for the Liberation of the Central African People (MPLC), with a margin so narrow – 50.2 per cent, i.e. a difference of 90,000 votes – that Dacko, reverting to type, preferred handing over power to the army's chief of staff, General André Kolingba, who formed a Military Committee for National Recovery (CMRN) to govern the country. Jean-Claude Mantion had a new boss but there was certainly no change in his mission. He soon had the opportunity to prove his usefulness. On 3 March 1982, he foiled an attempted coup instigated by Patassé and two prominent brigadiers who also originated from the north, François Bozizé and Alphonse Mbaïkoua.

To France's great embarrassment, Patassé had found refuge at its embassy in Bangui, disguised as a Muslim trader in a loose-fitting robe on a moped. In search of a solution, negotiations spread over two weeks with France's official representative – its ambassador – on one side of the table, and his countryman and DGSE agent, Colonel Mantion, representing CAR on the other. Their face-to-face captured the postcolonial moment: France was negotiating with France since, in the CAR of the 1980s, France was everywhere and on all sides. In this case, France reached an agreement with itself to provide safe conduct to Patassé, so that he could go into exile in Togo.

Shy and unassertive, General Kolingba gladly delegated swaths of his power to Colonel Mantion. However, while the watchful eye of Paris ensured the smooth operation of the state, the President was busy with what, in his eyes, was the main business: the affairs of his 'family' in the broadest sense of the word, starting with his kith and kin and extending to the Yakoma, his own ethnic group, which formed less than 5 per cent of the population and lived along the River Oubangui. So while Mantion carried out the tasks of a prime minister in the shadows, the President appointed his Yakoma relations to positions in the state apparatus and parastatal companies. In a country united by a true *lingua franca*, Sango, and which had previously given no heed to the manipulation of tribal solidarity for political ends, he promoted ethnicity. In 1993, after a 12-year reign, Kolingba left his successors an ethnically polarized country. For instance, 70 per cent of the national army was drawn from the small minority he belonged to (International Crisis Group, 2007, p. 8); (Marchés Tropicaux et Méditerranéens, 2002, p. 556).

Free elections, no democracy

The fall of the Berlin Wall, putting to rest the Cold War, and France's subsequent retreat from its role as the West's 'gendarme' of francophone Africa were tectonic forces that reshaped CAR's political landscape. In June 1990, at a Franco-African summit meeting, President François Mitterrand conditioned French aid on progress toward democratization in Africa. In this new context, the 'proconsul' in Bangui looked jarringly out of place, and General Kolingba could no longer resist the groundswell in favour of multiparty politics and free elections. Though he made attempts to derail the process by annulling a scheduled election at the end of 1992, and by pardoning the ex-emperor Bokassa in the hope of causing public disorder by releasing him from prison, in the end he had to give in. 'I comply because those who pay us asked me to', he bluntly admitted on national radio, in Sango ('Le président Kolingba concède le multipartisme', 1991). He knew that organizing a vote monitored by France amounted for him, politically, to assisted suicide.

In August and September 1993, Central Africans went to the polls for the first free and fair legislative and presidential elections in the country's history. Patassé triumphed over the Socialist Goumba in the second round with 52.5 per cent of the ballots cast. France stood by its word and saw the democratic process through. It recalled Colonel Mantion and cleared the road to power for a fiercely anti-French politician, former coup plotter and pillar of Bokassa's empire, whose campaign showed him to be an insuperable demagogue promising a money-printing press for every village.

For the first time, after three heads of state originating from the south, a 'son of the savannah' riding the tide of ethnic revanchism took the helm of the state. As Patassé was to repeat ad nauseam, he had been 'democratically elected' – a pleonasm which, in his eyes, gave him free rein to govern as he pleased. In due fairness, the new head of state inherited an onerous legacy on coming to power: his army and, even more so, his Presidential Guard was a tribal militia. He sought to improve his personal security by transferring the Yakoma in his guard into the ranks of the national army, the FACA (Forces armées centrafricaines). The move disgruntled those concerned, who had been given preferential treatment under the former president. Their discontent worsened, and spread inside the FACA, when it transpired that the new presidential security force was also a tribal militia, only this time almost exclusively comprised of Sara-Kaba, Patassé's larger ethnic group. Against the background of an unprecedented social crisis, the rivalry between this Praetorian Guard and the neglected national army went on to cause a series of mutinies-cum-looting-sprees that gutted CAR's economy and nipped democratization in the bud.

Three army mutinies in quick succession – on 18 April, 18 May and 15 November 1996 ('Le président Kolingba concède le multipartisme', 1991) – inaugurated a repetitive, escalatory pattern of national self-destruction. For France, at the risk of being called to account for its (post-)colonial failure, CAR's descent into chaos resulted in a growing challenge to prevent massive loss of life with limited effort, increasingly by burden-sharing with, or passing the buck to, regional African organizations and the United Nations as the institutionalized avatar of the 'international community'. For the CAR, the escalation of internecine violence amounted in the long run to ever more serious attempts at national suicide. The spasmodic outbursts seemed to express a desperate contestation of a world in which CAR always came out at the losing end, or an ultimate supplication to be taken care of, the latter with its share of collective irresponsibility and emotional blackmail.

The 1996 mutinies resembled a Russian nesting doll. Each matryoshka was swallowed by a bigger one. What started with 200 soldiers, with 7 dead and 40 wounded when the Presidential Guard stepped in, escalated into a more massive mutiny with 43 dead and 238 wounded, an all-out looting spree in Bangui, and a full-fledged French military intervention to protect foreign citizens and restore a semblance of peace and order. A government of national unity, with Ngoupandé as its prime minister, saw the day. But the third mutiny quickly pulled the plug on this attempt at cohabitation and political compromise. What is more, France's presence in CAR was called into question when two French soldiers on patrol were fatally shot in the back at one of the mutineers' roadblocks. In retaliation, the French army hunted down mutineers in Bangui's populous neighbourhoods. Scores of Central African civilians died in the crossfire.

Changing of the guard

Paris strived to extricate itself from the Central African quagmire with a two-step initiative, a troop surge followed by a phased withdrawal. First, the French military presence was increased from 1,400 to 2,300 soldiers to stabilize the country; then, at France's behest, six African countries – Burkina Faso, Gabon, Mali, Senegal, Chad and Togo – set up a regional peacekeeping force, the Inter-African Mission to Monitor the Bangui Accords (MISAB). In early 1997, 750 MISAB soldiers were deployed in CAR's capital. France covered the cost of this operation and provided the logistics on the ground. But, despite their best efforts, the African peacekeeping force could not prevent new clashes in Bangui in May and June 1997, which claimed 100 victims and forced 60,000 people to flee their homes ('Bangui, sens dessus dessous', 1997); nor could MISAB prevent President Patassé from creating a special force, outside the army, that was given responsibility to pacify the north of the country, which was in the throes of growing insecurity because of the *zaraguinas* (highwaymen) and the beginning of guerrilla warfare. This unit, soon accused of atrocities by human rights organizations, was placed under the command of Martin Koumtamadji, better known as Colonel Abdoulaye Miskine, a former rebel leader in the south of Chad. Patassé also financed a personal militia known as the *Karako*, which means 'groundnuts' in Sango. This allusion to the crop grown only in the north widened the gap with the 'people of the river', who felt targeted.

The professionalization and reform of the French army decided on by President Jacques Chirac served as a timely pretext for

Paris to justify the closure of its military bases in CAR. President Patassé felt 'dropped' by the French who maintained their contingents in other sub-Saharan countries, e.g. in neighbouring Chad. Irate, he requested the United States to take France's place as a protecting power, but his request fell on deaf ears in Washington. It was in these circumstances that Paris shut down its military base in Bouar, in December 1997, and in Bangui, in March 1998. Two hundred French soldiers remained at Bangui's airport to support MISAB and await the deployment of a UN peacekeeping force. On 27 March 1998, after intense French lobbying, the UN Security Council decided to deploy 1,350 blue helmets in CAR ('L'ONU a créé une force de maintien de la paix en République centrafricaine', 1998). In April, MISAB gave way to the 1,350 strong UN Mission for the Central African Republic (MINURCA). The French soldiers 'rehatted' and, under a blue helmet instead of their beret, stayed on until the UN force had superficially stabilized the country. Paris seized this window of opportunity to disengage completely. On 28 February 1999, the last French soldier left CAR.

In September 1999, Patassé officially won the presidential election in the first round with 51.63 per cent of the votes – a result disputed by the opposition. Nevertheless, the UN decided that their mission had been accomplished and withdrew MINURCA on 1 April 2000, leaving in its place the UN Peacebuilding Support Office in the Central African Republic (BONUCA) with some seventy civilians and no military backup. With the deterioration of the social situation in CAR and payment of civil servants' wages almost thirty months in arrears, the opposition parties supported a strike in the public administration that lasted almost five months. On 15 December 2000, they demanded that the head of state should step down 'in the superior interests of the nation'.

Five months later, violence returned to Bangui. On the night of 27–28 May 2001, a commando equipped with rocket-propelled grenades attacked the residence of President Patassé. The assault was repulsed in extremis, but clashes continued in Bangui for ten days. General Kolingba rather confusedly claimed responsibility for the coup on national radio.[13] In response, government supporters set to work hunting down any Yakoma they could find in Bangui, killing at least 300 and forcing 50,000 residents of the capital to flee their homes ('Discours et réalité: un fossé béant', 2002). Following the attempt to assassinate him, President Patassé turned increasingly paranoid. On 26 August 2001, he ordered the arrest of Jean-Jacques Démafouth, his Minister of Defence who had been tasked with restructuring the armed forces and who had reduced the Presidential Guard from 1,200 to 800 – while also reducing the FACA by a quarter, down to about 3,000 soldiers, and the percentage of Yakomas within the army from 70 to 40 per cent. Démafouth was cleared of any suspicion by the CAR judiciary on 7 October 2002. His acquittal came at a time when President Patassé had identified a new hidden hand behind the May 2001 coup: the FACA chief of staff, General François Bozizé.[14]

Regional dominion

Bozizé was dismissed on 26 October 2001, a week after the Evangelical church he founded – Le christianisme céleste Nouvelle Jérusalem – had been banned for 'illegal operation'. Attempts to arrest the cashiered army leader failed. Bozizé fled through CAR's north to Chad, and went into exile in France. From then on, insecurity reigned in northern CAR, which became a no-go area in the grip of rebels, highwaymen and Chad commando units in search of booty. From Paris, Bozizé claimed the birth of a guerrilla group under his orders. In desperate need of allies, President Patassé repeated a fatal error already committed by his political role model, ex-emperor Bokassa. He appealed to the regional organization formed by Colonel Qaddafi, the Community of Sahel and Saharan States (CEN-SAD). In December 2001, a CEN-SAD peacekeeping force of 300 men was deployed in Bangui.

On 26 October 2002, supporters of General Bozizé commemorated the first anniversary of their leader's dismissal by staging a lightning raid on Bangui. Although they counted little more than 150 soldiers, they entered the northern neighbourhoods of CAR's capital, from where they were only driven back by the intervention of Libyan forces and several hundred combatants of the Movement for the Liberation of Congo (MLC), reinforcements sent by the main Congo rebel leader, Jean-Pierre Bemba,[15] to help Patassé remain in power. Paris urged Colonel Qaddafi to repatriate his troops from Bangui. The Central African Economic and Monetary Union (CEMAC), anxious to reassert its regional pre-eminence, deployed 300 CEMAC soldiers in Bangui to replace the departing Libyan military and CEN-SAD forces.

The rebel raid on Bangui knocked the bottom out of relations between CAR and Chad. On 9 November 2002, Patassé accused the Chadian President Idriss Déby of fomenting an armed attempt to annex the north of the country and take control of its oil – the supposed extension of southern Chad's oilfields, near Doba. Forty-eight hours later, Chad's head of state denounced 'the massacre of many Chadian civilians, at least 120', ('Idriss Déby dénonce des massacres de Tchadiens en RCA', 2002) after loyalists and their Congolese allies retook control of the northern suburbs of Bangui.

The ensuing Franco-African division of labour that brought down Patassé was exemplary: without hindrance, General Bozizé evaded his police escort in France and made his way to Chad; in N'Djamena, President Déby placed personnel from his Presidential Guard at Bozizé's disposal; Congo-Kinshasa's head of state, Joseph Kabila, supplied the necessary armaments; his neighbour on the other bank of the River Congo, President Denis Sassou Nguesso, funded the operation to the tune of 3 billion CFA francs (over 6 million US dollars); and President Omar Bongo of Gabon, the most senior figure in the region who had long harboured doubts about Bozizé's capacity to govern CAR, finally gave his blessing (International Crisis Group, 2007, pp. 15–16).

Thereafter, events moved quickly. With only a handful of CAR officers and mostly Chadian troops General Bozizé took power in Bangui. On 15 March 2003, two rebel columns joined forces to seize the capital. They encountered no organized resistance. In the absence of President Patassé, who had left the country to attend a CEN-SAD summit meeting, the Central African army did not lift a finger. CEMAC forces had received instructions to not oppose Bozizé's entry into the city. France flatly dismissed President Patassé's formal request to apply the defence agreement between the two countries. However, Paris did send 300 soldiers, officially to protect the French community and foreign nationals in Bangui. In fact, Operation Boali helped stabilize the new regime. After only four years away, the French army was back in Bangui.

The Bozizé regime

François Bozizé took power 'on the cuff', as a general without troops who owed too much to many who expected to be paid back in spades. No sooner had his – mostly Chadian – forces invested him as CAR's new president than they helped themselves to a profitable return for their efforts: Bangui was plundered by its 'liberators'. More than 600 stolen vehicles, heavily laden with loot, left the capital for the north. In response, the popular outrage was such that, four days after taking office, Bozizé appealed to his brother-in-arms in N'Djamena, President Déby, to send him 500 soldiers to re-establish order in Bangui. This accomplished, about eighty of them took charge of President Bozizé's personal security while the remainder joined the CEMAC forces whose unchanged mandate – to secure Bangui and defend the state institutions – was renewed on 22 March 2003. At a summit meeting on 3 June, in an act redolent of self-congratulation, CEMAC's heads of state officially recognized the new regime in Bangui.

At first, acknowledging his political weakness, President Bozizé extended his hand to all CAR parties ready to support him. He appointed as his prime minister the Socialist Abel Goumba, and held the 'national dialogue' his predecessor had failed to organize.

But a mere six weeks after this attempt at consensus politics, he dismissed Goumba. By the end of the year, 'family politics'[16] were back in CAR, and the President's new political party – Kwa na Kwa, i.e. 'work, nothing but work' in Sango – garnered broad-based support in exchange for state patronage. Presidential and legislative elections in spring 2005 were won by General Bozizé; he defeated in the second round, with 64.6 per cent of the vote, Martin Ziguélé, a former prime minister under Patassé who accepted his loss and congratulated the winner.[17] Kwa na Kwa secured a plurality in parliament, with 42 out of 105 seats; alliance-building to find an overwhelming majority was made easier by the bandwagon effect of victory and deep divisions within the opposition.

Democracy was thus re-established as an electoral procedure, the ballots cast in his favour conferring the winner carte blanche to monopolize the levers of power and distribute plum positions among his kith and kin. As much as the Patassé regime before, the new power failed to render the judiciary independent and strengthen the rule of law (for example, no 'liberator' was brought to justice and punished), respect human rights and promote financial accountability. As a result, the country did not exit the vicious circle of its self-destructive politics. First incrementally, but then with the crushing speed of a juggernaut, misgovernment, corruption, nepotism, arbitrary rule, repression and armed rebellion compounded to fresh outbursts of escalatory violence.

Insurrections in the north

Only weeks after the spring 2005 presidential election, for which former President Patassé had not been allowed to stand, a new rebel group in CAR's north-west, the Army for the Restoration of the Republic and Democracy (APRD), claimed responsibility for attacks on FACA positions. In an attempt to restore order, President Bozizé sent in his Presidential Guard. But the loyalist forces conducted indiscriminate reprisals against civilians and such wide-ranging atrocities that it became difficult to know what was contributing most to the collapse of public order: the rebel activity or the army's scorched earth policy.[18] Over 100,000 people were displaced, according to the UN Office for the Coordination of Humanitarian Affairs (United Nations, 2007). Some of them would spend years bivouacking in huts made of twigs and leaves, well back from the main roads where they feared encountering armed men.

The APRD was remote-controlled by Patassé from his Togolese exile. On the ground in CAR, two local officers, Laurent Djimweï and Maradass Lakoué, commanded a fluctuating number of troops – never more than a few hundred – who joined forces with *zaraguinas* having rallied to their cause as much as the rebels partook in the latter's daily business of banditry. Another, smaller insurrectionist group, the Democratic Front for the Central African People (FDPC), was led by Colonel Miskine, the former head of a special unit tasked with 'pacifying' the north under Patassé. However, after an unsuccessful rebel attack on Paoua, in mid-January 2007, Miskine gave up.[19]

In spring 2006, a second insurrection, this time in the far northeast of the country, was launched by the Union of Democratic Forces for Unity (Union des Forces Démocratiques pour le Rassemblement, UFDR). The latter was a coalition of three armed groups led by a disgruntled 'liberator', Captain Abakar Sabone, a former member of Patassé's Presidential Guard, Major Hassan Justin, and Michel Djotodia.[20] Sabone and Djotodia acted, respectively, as spokesperson and President of the UFDR. Both lived in exile in Benin. In November 2006, after an arrest warrant against them had been issued in Bangui, they were taken into custody in Cotonou but continued to communicate from their prison cells. In their absence, the operational command of the UFDR rebels rested with 'General' Zakaria Damane, a former municipal councillor in a small town in CAR's north-eastern Vakaga province.

The extreme north-east of the CAR is singular in more than one regard. First, the national language, Sango, is hardly spoken in this far-flung corner of the land which, 1,000 km away from Bangui, is inaccessible by road for half the year, during the rainy season. Second, Muslims are in the majority in the Vakaga province while they represent only 15 per cent of CAR's overall population. Finally, the arid savannah of the north-east gravitates less toward Bangui and more toward Abéché, in Chad, and Nyala, in South Darfur, the spiritual centres and seats of power to which its local chiefs have traditionally pledged allegiance. As a result, the Vakaga prefecture is a borderland at least as susceptible to the fall-out of events in Chad and in Darfur, or in the wider Sudan, as to the backwash of events in the rest of the CAR.

The Darfur crisis, which took a slaughterous turn in 2003, and the conflict between Sudan and Chad, who mutually armed the other side's rebel factions between 2005 and 2010 to effect regime change, impacted CAR's north-east. The territory was used as a rear base, a safe haven or a transit corridor, the latter namely in 2006, when Chadian rebels launched a surprise attack on N'Djamena. However, the 'Darfurianization' of the Vakaga – a spectre raised in 2006/07[21] – was less a problem of 'spill-over effects' or 'regional conflict contamination' than a congruence of underlying structural factors such as demographic and environmental stress, attendant clashes between pastoralist and sedentary populations, war as a lifestyle for a lack of other alternatives and the dearth of public goods in the absence of a functional state.

On 30 October 2006, Birao, the most important town in the north-east with a population of 14,000, was attacked, and taken, by about fifty UFDR combatants. Transported and supervised by the French army, the FACA launched a successful counter-offensive on 27 November. Yet, over the weekend of 3–4 March 2007, UFDR rebels again attacked the town. Under the threat that eighteen French military advisers who had been left behind in Birao might be killed or taken hostage, France mounted – in the middle of a presidential election at home – an ambitious airborne operation (Merchet, 2007).[22] Birao was again secured, and some thirty rebels were killed during cleanup operations in the surrounding areas. Thereafter, 130 French paratroopers remained based in Birao. In light of this new situation, Zakaria Damane resolved to sign a peace agreement with the government on 13 April 2007. From their cells in Cotonou, Djotodia and Sabone disavowed the accord.

Feeling overly dependent on the French, President Bozizé strived to make new friends. In March 2007, he signed the first of two secret agreements with South Africa entrusting his new protector with the Presidential Guard and broader, unspecified 'military cooperation' (Marchal, 2013a, pp. 8–10). Though a degree of understanding was subsequently reached between Paris and Pretoria (Tshwane) to prevent being played off one against the other, CAR's president succeeded in diversifying his international support base. In the last hours before his downfall, in March 2013, Bozizé called upon Pretoria to halt the rebels' final assault on Bangui. South Africa engaged its military contingent in CAR in a senseless last stand and suffered its most crushing defeat since the end of apartheid.[23]

Bozizé's fall, Seleka's rise to power

A congeries of reasons and circumstances led to the end of the Bozizé regime. In autumn 2007, the UN stepped aside as a regional peacekeeper to make way for the European Union Force (EUFOR) Chad/CAR[24] which, in effect if not intent, was a mainly French operation to stabilize (Glaser and Smith, 2008, pp. 51–74).[25] In Bangui, 'family politics' became more and more pervasive, and the conduct of the Central African Nomenklatura increasingly predatory. Idriss Déby's exasperation vis-à-vis the liege-man he had helped to install and maintain in Bangui grew stronger as Bozizé strived to offset the Franco-Chadian military clout in CAR by a South African counterweight. Déby's lassitude was shared, in varying degrees, by other regional leaders and, in full measure, by Nicholas Sarkozy and then François Hollande in Paris. Last but not least, Bozizé and his party claimed to have won fraudulent presidential and legislative elections in January and March 2011, without being called to account for their arrogation of victory by the international community. The dashing of all hopes for an electoral turnover swung open the floodgates to armed rebellion.

Idriss Déby played a key role in the overthrow of François Bozizé (Marchal, 2013b). But the precise form, scope and rationale of the Chadian president's involvement are not entirely clear. Did the puppeteer simply cut the strings? Or did the Chadian president fund, staff and arm the insurgency that brought Bozizé down? Déby makes no bones about his ever more frequent dust-ups with the ousted Central African president.[26] But he denies any active role in the events that led to Bozizé's fall. According to him, the armed rebellion 'swept up the general discontent on its way from the north-east to Bangui'. The jetsam and flotsam of a pauperized country, in particular the unemployed urban youth, heeded the call to arms and joined the march on Bangui as self-styled liberators armed with machetes, bows and arrows, arriving on mopeds, bicycles and on foot.

In December 2012, the UFDR rebranded itself as a broad 'alliance' – *Seleka* in Sango. Chadian combatants, fighters from Darfur and heavily armed poachers swelled its ranks. Echoing the Arab Spring and its main slogan, *irhal* ('clear off!'), they were united only by a lowest common denominator: the uncompromising rejection of the Bozizé regime and the prospect of sharing among them the spoils of the country. The insurgency gathered momentum on its way from the north-east to Bangui. Its militants were all the more frustrated when, in December 2013, their sweeping advance was stopped within reach of the capital. Under international pressure to prevent yet another violent take-over, the Mission for the Consolidation of Peace in the Central African Republic (MICOPAX) peacekeepers – 2,300 soldiers and 380 policemen from five neighbouring countries, including Chad – stood in their way. A peace accord was negotiated in Libreville, Gabon. Bozizé remained president but he had to accept not only a prime minister from the legal opposition, Nicholas Tiangaye, but also Seleka's headman, Michel Djotodia, as the number two of the new government, in charge of Defence.

Neither side adhered to the agreement. President Bozizé tried to tip the balance in his favour by playing the South African card and distributing arms for a 'popular defence' of Bangui; Seleka tightened its grip on the rest of the country and, on 22 March 2013, closed in on the capital. Forty-eight hours later, with Bozizé having fled across the river into the Democratic Republic of Congo (DRC), the rebel alliance took power. Michel Djotodia pronounced himself the new head of state while, outside the presidential palace, pandemonium reigned in Bangui: unfettered by a chain of command or any other disciplinary restraint, the latest crop of 'liberators' was seeking revenge and cashing in on their victory. Armed men, who came from the very different world of CAR's north-east, abreacted a baneful mix of their old complex of inferiority and their new sense of entitlement. 'Our turn has come', they pretended. Soon, in their own eyes and in the eyes of their victims, their group identity came to be defined in religious terms.

The fallacy was predicated on the assumption that the 'Muslims' had seized power in CAR. To make things worse, non-Muslims tended to perceive Muslims as 'dubious Central Africans', i.e. aliens disguised as nationals to claim a seat at the table. In the end, faith became a shibboleth, a criterion to select who should live and who should die. For the first time in CAR's independent history, religion became a political field of leverage. But much like ethnicity in the 1980s, the politicization of religion did not come out of nowhere. The Muslim–Christian divide had deep historical roots in Central Africa, and powerfully resonated with the geopolitics of the present, all the more so as the 'Pentecostal Revolution' had brought Christianity back with a vengeance.

Over the next six months, until September 2013 when President Djotodia officially dissolved Seleka in reaction to the many crimes that had been committed in its name, the dramatic events in CAR did not attract much international attention. Only in the autumn of 2013 did France take its eyes off the Malian crisis, where it had intervened in January with 4,000 soldiers to quell a jihadist threat, and fully realized the bloody chaos in CAR. By then, more than 100,000 displaced non-Muslims had sought refuge around Bangui's international airport, and an estimated 1.5 million civilians – a third of the country's population – had been chased from their homes; the number of civilians killed was impossible to establish. What had been left of the state apparatus, and of state authority, had almost entirely vanished. In November, Paris began preparations for a limited military operation in its former colony which, named after a short-lived local butterfly, would become Operation Sangaris. 'We are seeing armed groups killing people under the guise of their religion', the UN's special adviser on the prevention of genocide, Adama Dieng, declared in New York. 'My feeling is that this will end with Christian communities, Muslim communities killing each other – which means that, if we don't act now and decisively, I will not exclude the possibility of a genocide occurring' (Nichols, 2013).

An international errand of mercy

On 5 December 2013, UN Security Council Resolution 2127 authorized the deployment of an 'African-led International Support Mission to the Central African Republic', known by its French acronym as MISCA. That very day, a French expeditionary force – first 600, then 1,200 and, as of December 2013, 2,000 soldiers – started to arrive in Bangui 'to re-establish public order and protect the civilian population' alongside the African peacekeepers who were already on the ground and whose number was to be raised to 6,000. After much diplomatic horse-trading, the European Union pledged in February 2014 to also contribute 600 – mostly French – soldiers to the international stop-gap operation in CAR. On 10 April 2014, the UN Security Council set 15 September 2014 as the date for the United Nations

Multidimensional Integrated Stabilization Mission in the Central African Republic (MINUSCA) to take over from MISCA.

As the French authorities readily admitted in hindsight, Paris had misjudged the situation in CAR.[27] What had been conceived as a short-term operation to halt exactions perpetrated under Seleka rule turned into a high-risk, protracted mission to prevent all-out killings in a religiously polarized nation as soon as the first French soldiers hit the ground. The very day Operation Sangaris was launched, on 5 December 2013, a motley force of grassroots self-defence groups and of remnants of the army, which had disintegrated into factions of diverse political allegiances, launched an attack on Bangui to oust Seleka. This rag-tag force became known as the 'Anti-Balaka', an umbrella term derived from the Sango word – *balaka* – for 'machete'.[28] But the 'anti-slaughterers' were as prone to kill civilians as their declared enemies. Worse, being in the majority in Bangui, they have since largely cleansed the capital of Muslims. For fear of being massacred, about 130,000 Muslims have fled to the north if not abroad. Some 55,000 have arrived in Chad alone, many of whom do not, or do no longer, possess any real links to their putative country of origin.

As a result of France's military intervention, the heightened media focus on CAR, and the onrush of the 'Anti-Balaka' forces, Seleka's misrule came to an end. On 10 January 2014, a summit meeting of African leaders in N'Djamena strong-armed President Djotodia and his government into offering their resignation.[29] To lend the regional diktat a sheen of constitutionality, the Central African parliament, the Transitional National Council (TNC), was airlifted for the occasion into the Chadian capital. Upon its return to Bangui, the TNC chose among eight candidates a new interim head of state, Catherine Samba-Panza, previously the mayor of Bangui.[30] Her administration was tasked with resuscitating CAR's state and organizing elections 'as soon as technically possible and no later than February 2015'.[31] However, with little to no institutional capacity and coercive power, entirely dependent on the international community and a farrago of foreign forces which were still not fully deployed in August 2014, the new government was hard-pressed to organize a free and fair vote in a country it neither controlled nor administered, and which faced a secessionist threat in the north. What is more, casting ballots would not perform the miracle of reviving a phantom state. For statehood to rise from the graves, Central Africans would need to accomplish as many steps toward national reconciliation, and the end of 'alimentary politics', as missteps had been made in the opposite direction since 1960; and the international community would need to stay positively engaged, possibly for as long as it took the postcolonial state in CAR to fall apart.

Notes

1 Cf. the first International Crisis Group (ICG) report on the Central African Republic, *Anatomy of a Phantom State,* which I authored in 2007.
2 In the mid-nineteenth century, according to Miege, up to 50,000 slaves arrived each year in the most important Mediterranean seaports, from Mogador (Morocco) to Berbera (Somalia). This figure does not account for the heavy losses of the trans-Saharan slave trade (estimated at 20 per cent), or for the slaves sold all over North Africa and who remained there. It also ignores Zanzibar, the primary outlet into the Indian Ocean.
3 In 1888 a Scottish veterinarian, John Boyd Dunlop, invented the inflatable rubber tire which very rapidly replaced the ironclad wooden wheels used until then. By the mid-1890s, the 'rubber boom' was in full swing; by 1925, it was over as rubber plantations and, increasingly, the synthetic variety derived from petroleum satisfied world demand.
4 During their heyday, between 1899 and 1905, all forty concessionary companies taken together exported 6,294 metric tons of natural rubber (Jeaugeon, 1961, p. 426) from the French Congo. By comparison, in 1901 alone, the Congo Free State produced 6,000 tons of rubber (Van Reybrouck, 2014, p. 87).

5 The official, Fernand-Léopold Gaud, explained: 'It is a bit stupid but it will dumbfound the natives. After this, they will probably keep quiet' (Faes and Smith, 2000a, p. 59).
6 At the Berlin Conference in 1884/5, to sway the French, Leopold II had granted them the right of pre-emption over the Congo Free State in the event he should prove incapable of administering the territory. He eventually sold his private colony to the Belgium State in November 1908 when the Congo Free State became the Belgian Congo.
7 In January 1906, a librarian with access to the material, Amédée Britsch, published a sympathetic though brief account (25 pages) of de Brazza's letters and notes written in the course of his inquiry to advocate for reforms in the French Congo.
8 Bokassa was both a victim and a beneficiary of the French presence. In 1927, when Bokassa was six, his father – a local chief perceived as a rabble-rouser – was killed by the French in front of the Lobaye prefecture in the south-west. Out of grief, his mother committed suicide – at the time an extremely rare event in local culture. Taken in by his paternal grandfather, Bokassa was admitted to one of the best missionary schools inside Oubangui-Chari, a clear sign that the Catholic clergy condemned the colonial crime which had made him an orphan. Having joined the French army and fought for the colonial power in Indochina, Bokassa was swiftly promoted through the ranks and groomed for a leadership position in the wake of CAR's independence.
9 'Bangui la Coquette' is the name of a poem published in 1961 by Marie-Jeanne Caron, the first principal of the secondary school for young girls in CAR's capital which still bears her name.
10 The full extent of France's implication was only revealed in Faes and Smith (2000a, pp. 15–50).
11 For a complete account, cf. Baccard (1987).
12 Ngoupandé, who died in May 2014, served as Minister of Education from 1985 to 1989, as Prime Minister of a government of national unity for eight months in 1996/97, and finally as Minister of Foreign Affairs in 2005/06. He is the author of – among other books – *Chronique de la crise centrafricaine 1976–1997: Le syndrome Barracuda*.
13 In August 2002, General Kolingba and twenty of his close associates were condemned to death in their absence. The former president had gone into exile in Uganda, from where he returned to Bangui in

October 2003 to attend the 'National Dialogue' sponsored by President Bozizé to promote reconciliation. He died in Paris on 7 February 2010.

14 A Gbaya, born in 1946 near Bossangoa, François Bozizé received his military training at Bouar, then in Fréjus, in the South of France. Bokassa's aide-de-camp, he owed his rapid rise in the army to the emperor. Co-instigator, with Patassé, of the 3 March 1982 coup against President Kolingba, he fled into exile in Benin from where he was extradited in 1989. Tortured and imprisoned in Bangui, he was released in 1991. In 1993, he stood as a candidate in the presidential elections won by Patassé, who appointed him in 1997 as head of the army.

15 On 14 February 2003, the International Federation for Human Rights (FIDH) lodged a complaint with the International Criminal Court (ICC) against President Patassé, Colonel Miskine and the Congolese rebel leader, Jean-Pierre Bemba. Only the latter has been prosecuted by the ICC for his 'command responsibility' in the massacre of about 200 residents of Bangui and the rape of 600 women by his rebel forces. For more see Chapter 11, 'CAR's Southern Identity: Congo, CAR, and International Justice' by Tatiana Carayannis.

16 For instance, Francis Bozizé, one of the president's sons, became director of his father's cabinet at the Ministry of Defence; a nephew of the head of state, Lieutenant-Colonel Sylvain Ndoutingaï, who – as a captain – had been the highest ranking Central-African officer in the former rebel movement, was appointed Minister of Mines and Minister of Energy (in July 2007, he became, in addition, CAR's treasurer); one of Ndoutingaï's cousins, Cyriaque Gonda, took over as the spokesperson for the presidency; a cousin of the President, Yvette Boissonnat, was given the Ministry of Tourism; another cousin of the head of state, Honorat Cocksis Willibona, became the party whip of Kwa na Kwa in parliament.

17 Martin Ziguélé was Patassé's prime minister between April 2001 and March 2003, before succeeding the former president as leader of the MPLC, the best structured party in CAR. Ziguélé was born in Paoua in 1956 and belongs to an ethnic minority of the north-west, the Karé. He has tried to overhaul the MPLC apparatus to diminish the preponderance within the party of Sara-Kaba, Patassé's ethnic group.

18 For further reading see: Amnesty International (30 November 2006) *Government tramples on the basic rights of detainees*, London; Diocesan Justice and Peace Commission (March 2007), *Rapport circonstancié sur les événements de Kaga-Bandoro, Période: août 2006-mars 2007*, Bangui; Human Rights Watch (September 2007) *State of Anarchy: Rebellion and Abuses Against Civilians*, Volume 19, No. 14(A).
19 Thanks to Colonel Qaddafi's intercession, Abdoulaye Miskine was appointed 'Special Adviser' at the presidency in Bangui on 13 July 2007. But, fearing for his life, he soon fled to Libya abandoning his fighters who, in his absence, were never integrated into the national army.
20 Michel Am-Nondokro Djotodia was born in the Vakaga province in 1949. He lived for almost ten years in the Soviet Union where he studied economic planning. After his return to CAR, he worked first at the Ministry of Planning and then in the Ministry of Foreign Affairs. He served for a time as consul in Nyala, the capital of Sudan's South Darfur province.
21 The immediate effect of this debate was a spike in humanitarian assistance: in 2006, CAR received more aid funds than throughout the three preceding years, from 2003 to 2005. The World Food Program (WFP) quintupled its budget within a year.
22 For operational detail, see the July 2007 issue of the monthly *Assaut*, published by the French army, pp. 10–13.
23 Thirteen South African soldiers were killed and twenty-seven wounded, and one soldier went missing, after their base on the outskirts of Bangui was attacked by up to 3,000 rebels. For a detailed though not entirely reliable account, cf. Helmoed Heitman (2013) *The Battle of Bangui. The Untold Inside Story*, Parktown Publishers, Johannesburg.
24 On 31 August 2006, UN Security Council Resolution 1706 provided for a multidimensional presence (political, humanitarian, military and civilian) in CAR, 'if necessary' to prevent the violence in Darfur spilling over the border. On 23 February 2007, Ban Ki-moon took a supplementary step by proposing to send 10,900 blue helmets to Chad and CAR. However, the UN shelved its plans when, in autumn 2007, the EU deployed in Chad and CAR 3,700 peacekeepers, 2,500 of whom were French.

25 Ironically, after a rebel raid on N'Djamena in June 2008, the Chadian President blamed EUFOR Chad/CAR for not doing enough to protect his regime; the European operation ended in March 2009.
26 Interview with Idriss Déby in N'Djamena, 22 November 2013.
27 Interview with Cédric Lewandowski, Chief of Staff of the French Minister of Defence, on 27 March 2014 in Paris.
28 Some sources contend that 'Anti-Balaka' alludes to the French for bullets from Kalashnikov assault rifles (*'balles AK'*). Either way, the generic term gained currency in 2008/9 as a designation for the self-defence units set up to protect communities from attacks by highway bandits or cattle raiders. A number of 'Anti-Balaka' groups joined Seleka in 2012/13 but most of them fell out with the 'alliance' in reaction to killings of non-Muslims.
29 Michel Djotodia left N'Djamena directly for Benin, where he was granted exile. Many of his close associates in power have retreated to CAR's far north-east, where some of them envision the proclamation of a secessionist state. For more detail see: *Jeune Afrique*, 10 April 2014, Interview with Abakar Sabone, formerly a 'Special Adviser' to President Djotodia who has founded the Organization of Muslim Resistance in CAR ('La guerre avec les anti-balaka commence').
30 Born in Chad, in 1954, to a Central-African mother and a Cameroonian father, Catherine Samba-Panza studied in Paris and worked as a corporate lawyer until she was appointed by the TNC, in June 2013, mayor of Bangui. Non-partisan, she was elected despite her lack of political and administrative experience in the hope she could build national and international consensus around her.
31 UN Security Council Resolution 2149, adopted on 10 April 2014.

Bibliography

Baccard, A. (1987) *Les martyrs de Bokassa*, Editions du Seuil, Paris.

'Bangui, sens dessus dessous' (1997) *L'Autre Afrique*, 25 June.

Brégeon, J-N. (1998), *Un rêve d'Afrique: Administrateurs en Oubangui-Chari, la Cendrillon de l'empire*, Denoël, Paris.

Britsch, A. (1906) 'Pour le Congo français. La dernière mission Brazza, d'après le registre de correspondance inédit de P. Savorgnan de

Brazza', Paris, Archives diplomatiques du Ministère français des Affaires étrangères 53 G 22 (2).
Cantournet, J. (1991) Des affaires et des hommes. Noirs et Blancs, commerçants et fonctionnaires dans l'Oubangui du début du siècle, *Recherches oubanguiennes* 10, Paris.
Colombani, O. (1991) *Mémoires coloniales : La fin de l'Empire français d'Afrique vue par les administrateurs coloniaux*, La Découverte, Paris.
Coquery-Vidrovitch, C. (ed.) (2014) *Le rapport Brazza, Mission d'enquête du Congo: Rapport et documents (1905–1907)*, Le Passager Clandestin, Paris.
Cordell, D. D. (1977) A History of the Slave Trade and State Formation on the Islamic Frontier in Northern Equatorial Africa in the nineteenth and twentieth century, Unpublished PhD thesis, Madison, University of Wisconsin, US.
Davies, O. (1967) *West Africa before the Europeans*, Methuen, London.
'Discours et réalité: un fossé béant' (2002) *Fédération internationale des ligues des droits de l'Homme (FIDH)*, Report 324, 9 February.
Faes, G. and S. Smith (2000a) *Bokassa 1er: Un empereur français*, Calmann-Lévy, Paris.
Faes, G. and S. Smith (2000b) 'République Centrafricaine: La solitude et le chaos', *Politique Internationale*, No, 88, Paris.
Français, J. (2004) *Le putsch de Bokassa: Histoire secrète*, l'Harmattan, Paris.
Glaser, A. and S. Smith (2008) *Sarko en Afrique*, Plon, Paris.
Hallam, W. K. R. (1976) *The Life and Times of Rabih Fadla Allah*, Arthur H. Stockwell, Ilfracombe, UK.
'Idriss Déby dénonce des massacres de Tchadiens en RCA' (2002), Reuters, 11 November.
International Crisis Group (2007) *Anatomy of a Phantom State*, Africa Report No.136, Nairobi–Brussels.
Jeaugeon, R. (1961) 'Les sociétés d'exploitation au Congo et l'opinion française de 1890 à 1906', *Revue française d'histoire d'outre-mer*, No. 172–173, Vol. 48, Paris, pp. 353–437.
Kalck, P. (1974) *Histoire de la République centrafricaine, des origines à nos jours*, Berger-Levrault, Paris.
'L'ONU a créé une force de maintien de la paix en République centrafricaine' (1998) *Le Monde*, 29–30 March.
'Le président Kolingba concède le multipartisme' (1991), Reuters, 23 April.

Marchal, R. (2009) 'Aux marges du monde, en Afrique centrale', *Les Études du CERI*, No. 153–154, March.

Marchal, R. (2013a) 'South Africa versus France: Rising versus Declining Powers in Africa?', unpublished work, CERI Sciences-Po, Paris.

Marchal, R. (2013b) 'Idriss Déby a officieusement aide les rebelles de la Seleka', *L'Humanité,* 13 November, Paris.

Marchés Tropicaux et Méditerranéens (2002) *Spécial Centrafrique*, No. 2940, 15 March.

Merchet, J-D. (2007) 'Les paras français ont sauté à la frontière du Darfour', *Liberation,* Paris.

Miege, J-L. (1981) 'Le commerce transsaharien au XIXe siècle', *Revue de l'Occident musulman et de la Méditerranée*, No. 32, pp. 93–119.

Ngoupandé, J-P. (1997) *Chronique de la crise centrafricaine 1976–1997: Le syndrome Barracuda*, L'Harmattan, Paris.

Nichols, M. (2013) 'U.N. officials see risk of genocide in Central African Republic', Reuters, 1 November, New York.

Prioul, C. (1981) 'Entre Oubangui et Chari vers 1890', *Recherches Oubanguiennes* 6, Paris.

Rouget, F. (1906) *L'expansion colonial au Congo français*, Larose, Paris.

Saulnier, P. (1998) *Le Centrafrique: Entre mythe et réalité*, l'Harmattan, Paris.

Tisserant, C. (1953) 'L'agriculture dans les savanes de l'Oubangui', *Bulletin de l'Institut des Études centrafricaines*, No. 6, Brazzaville, pp. 209–273.

United Nations Office for the Coordination of Humanitarian Affairs (February 2007) 'Central African Republic Fact Sheet.' New York.

Van Reybrouck, D. (2014) *Congo. The Epic History of a People*, HarperCollins, New York (Dutch original, 2010).

3 Being Rich, Being Poor
Wealth and Fear in the Central African Republic

Roland Marchal

This chapter discusses the historical and contemporary dynamics that have produced a profound insecurity in the moral and physical worlds inhabited by Central Africans. These insecurities manifest themselves frequently in the form of tensions over wealth, accumulation and social status, which could be described here as the 'economy from below'. Whereas using a state position for private gain is a source of wealth that people understand and expect, even as they decry when others do it, someone who becomes wealthy through business is frequently suspected of having used occult means to do so. This mistrust is part of the reason why nearly the entire commercial class is composed of 'foreigners'—people whose family ties lie elsewhere, though they may have been born in Bangui and legally be Central African citizens. If the economic arena is considered at a macroeconomic level, one can pinpoint a dynamic of devolution/extortion that is deeply connected with the history of state building in the Central African Republic (CAR) and the management of the economic arena between foreigners and autochthonous people, two categories that necessitate a bit of unpacking. This situation is the dynamic outcome of systemic tensions between an economic realm that is largely built through concessions managed by 'foreigners', a state affected by a deep ambivalence on the loss of sovereignty (this latter being given away to foreign companies to get its rulers richer) and the need to sustain itself at the risk of being overthrown, and a population that alternately seeks to escape and profit from state predation.

As a result, the state is primarily a vehicle for plundering, and business enterprises larger than the stalls operated by *wali gara* (market women) are often managed by foreigners. This feeds into a perception on the part of the population that their country is being pillaged by foreigners, and the end result is a growing arbitrary violence targeting the whole social arena. People try to grab whatever is left, while at the same time violence is used to chase away other contenders and bolster state authority, which comes neither from the law, nor from any widely accepted moral economy.

While understandable on one level, Central Africans' perception that they are being pillaged by foreigners does nothing about the *sources* of the absence of Central Africans from these types of work, particularly the profound insecurity people feel in all levels of social life. Rather than over-quick calls to rebuild the state, it is these dynamics of insecurity that should be the focus of attempts to improve the Central African economy.

The dynamics described below are not unique to CAR, though they reach a certain peak in the particular configuration they have taken in the country. A few examples illustrate how thoroughly insecurity wreaks havoc on social relations and how, as a consequence, the arbitrary exercise of power and symbolic or physical violence are overwhelmingly present in the daily life of most Central Africans.

Inheritance in CAR is a very complicated and divisive issue in most families, not only because the death of a father or a mother can cause relatives to suddenly discover that there are other offspring who were not known of (sexual nomadism is a prevalent pattern in CAR), but also because disagreements may result in stealing, looting or even destroying the properties of a close relative. Death in CAR is also a complicated issue because many possible causes of death may come to mind before age, sickness or bullet: a fatality is often seen as the consequence of a hidden conspiracy organized by close relatives or neighbours to take revenge or simply to appropriate their belongings. Social jealousy is extreme and people will often refer to obscure forces working in the shadows. Being rich can also bring about problems, because depending on the source of the wealth, people may assume you have woken up spirits to work for you (free of charge, one might add).

One should not laugh at or be surprised by the importance of witchcraft. While widespread in the region, it is at epidemic proportions in CAR, where it can result in death and years-long prison terms. Every single day someone is killed in CAR for having perpetrated witchcraft. These dynamics point to the problematic management of the border between the visible and invisible worlds among the population and provide some explanation of the predatory behaviour of those entitled to represent the state (the '*corps habillés*')[1] and the elites of the country (Debos and Glasman, 2013). It would be wrong to assume that the problematic management of the borders between the visible and invisible realms is simply connected with underdevelopment or the 'backwardness' of the population. Central Africans have in fact been highly adept at adopting many new practices brought in from the outside world in terms of family organization, farming, settlement patterns and political organizations. It would be better to refer to what Adam Ashforth called 'spiritual insecurity' (Ashforth, 2004).

According to Ashforth, spiritual insecurity is 'a sense of unease arising from the conditions of knowing that invisible forces are acting upon one's life but not knowing what they are and how to relate to them' (Ashforth, 2004, p. 127). In CAR, this exposure can take different forms: fetishes prepared by sorcerers (locally known as *likundu*), invisible stains that require constant purifications, spirits that are increasingly seen as evil due to the growing influence of Pentecostal Churches and the simultaneous weakening of others protecting the society, such as the witchcraft doctors and healers (locally known as *nganga*). Those invisible forces, what will be called here sorcery, merged the certainty of their existence with the uncertainty of their enforcers and the always-occult rationality of their effects. Sorcery, in this sense, is not strictly related to a specific ethnic environment and can be better understood as an attempt to make sense of injustice and insecurity in daily life.

This chapter focuses on popular political economy in CAR, and it argues that wealth accumulation in the country is often constrained by fears and practices that limit the spectrum of actors involved, focus on certain kinds of wealth and not others, and make the plunder of the state a safer activity than many others. Dialectically, it also points to a functioning of the state that entertains a kind of continuity with the concessionary mode of production as enforced from the early stage of the colonial period.

Sorcery and witchcraft are not new phenomena and hardly specific to CAR; their resilience correlates with other traumatic events and changes in the country such as democratization, mutinies and coups, as well as the collapse of the cash-crop economies and economic crisis more broadly. One may fear that the resolution of the Seleka/Anti-Balaka crisis will result in the growth of sorcery-related incidents.

If wealth accumulation eventually directs us to the state, state building in CAR is also largely connected to the structuring of a market inherited from the pre-colonial times but which emerged through an imperfect dialectic between two different actors: the state and the 'foreign' private sector. The state was only able to build and to sustain itself, and govern territories and people, through huge economic concessions allocated to foreign or non-native business people. Despite strategic discontinuities in the colonial policies and throughout the independence era, this paradigm is still shaping perceptions of the Central African political elites.[2]

While it would be easy to describe CAR's political history as a series of episodes led by highly corrupt and predatory cliques, this long-term analysis puts into consideration another aspect that is worth reflecting on: the tension between a state mostly concerned by extorting taxes for its own survival and a huge delegation of sovereignty to a foreign business class requested to produce wealth, pay for maintenance of the state apparatus and *de facto* rule the population. Violence and arbitrariness are again two systemic parameters of this dynamic.

Coercion and spiritual insecurity framing the social sphere

State building in CAR over the last two centuries is a history of oppression, coercion, mass killings and dispossession. Force and coercion more than social contracts were the drivers in building a Central African society: Machiavelli is more useful than Jean-Jacques Rousseau to understand these processes. This is illustrated by the slave trade that depopulated this part of the African continent, the violent tax liability and the boundless power of the *corps habillés* or other *gens en armes* 'men of arms' (such as the *zaraguina, coupeurs de route* or, currently, the Tongo-Tongo and Lord's Resistance Army fighters) after independence. Although those patterns fluctuated throughout time and space and did not mean a uniform harassment of the population (on the contrary, they created differences), they shaped a certain meaning of what mundane power is: violent, arbitrary and extortion-driven. The lay population has therefore been very ambivalent about state authority. Escapism has long been the best solution to cope with state encroachments and abuses. People would rather run away to the bush than submit to a 'civilization' that too often meant enslavement, starvation and forced labour.

This representation of power and authority (Bigo, 1988) has hardly been challenged despite some periods when the population received better care, for instance throughout the 'democratic' periods (1993–1996; 2003–2005) and some genuine—though fragile—achievements in terms of human rights after 1993. There were several openings when less-predatory state dynamics might have flourished: after the Second World War; in the mid-1960s when Bokassa was ambitious but not yet at the cost of the population he ruled; twenty years later when France claimed to control and guide Kolingba for the best of CAR's interests; and after Patassé won the first democratic elections.

But this did not happen, for reasons that were either linked to circumstances or to more structural legacies of the state. The collapse of cash-crop prices in the late 1980s meant that the state resource base diminished drastically, which left even a would-be benevolent state little to spare for the betterment of the population. The fear of a military take-over was more than paranoia in a country where the elites live off conspiracies and rumours, and it became the basis for action. Elites believe regional history most often repeats itself on the cheap in CAR, an efficient manner to deny any responsibility for the predicament of their society.

But, one should go beyond this unilateral vision. At the same time, the CAR society (or societies, since it is not a given that they are densely connected) showed a strong resilience and coping mechanisms that allowed them to adopt new crops, new cults, a new *lingua franca* (Sango), a monetized economy and many other aspects that make the colonial encounter and its aftermath a more complex moment than the enforcement of an oppression sometimes benign, sometimes totalitarian. What makes CAR distinctive is not a specific violent colonial moment. It is more the recurrence of certain arrangements and combinations that always emphasize the duality of a violent assertion of arbitrary authority and escapism into the wild world.

In July 2010, President Bozizé made a speech saying that the CAR police was 'full of bandits'[3] and that people should not trust them. How could a rational citizen make sense of this and not opt for other orders of rationality that privilege not constitutional rights but family or village or any other informal networks that might protect him better? The problem is that all alternatives exist at the same time and often overlap. Those informal networks are powerful and socially dense, but at the same time soldiers and police are asked to get involved in any dispute, not to be the law enforcers but to make decisions instead of a due legal process. In that dynamic, the population shares responsibility and pays a high price for it. The deinstitutionalization of the army is not only a product of state fragility in the long run but also of the existence of surrogate militias in the concessionary companies who were often at the forefront, solving local disputes, enforcing debatable decisions and living off the population. This militia paradigm was reasserted in using Chadian or Congolese people beside kinsmen in 1996–1997 and in 2003.[4] To a great extent, the Anti-Balaka forces in 2013 and 2014 demonstrate the same paradigm of militias set up for one purpose (initially securing farmed fields and village markets against livestock herders and *zaraguinas*) and acting for another (ruling populations, discriminating against them and plundering).

The contemporary period has also been characterized by the pervasive use of sorcery and witchcraft (Mbembe, 2000, p. 103) as a new attempt to domesticate—in the invisible world—forces that could not be contained in the visible one.

Occult forces are omnipresent in the daily life of most Central African people, including elites. A sad illustration of this is that in the 1970s more than 40 per cent of the cases brought to court were connected to sorcery and, in 2005, when an assessment of penal establishments was undertaken in CAR, it appeared that near to 80 per cent of the prisoners were there for sorcery and charlatanism crimes. Despite pressures by the international community and the Catholic Church, sorcery and charlatanism are still indicated as crimes in the Penal Code passed in 2010.

Of course, one should draw some differences within the population. Although sorcery beliefs are present almost everywhere in CAR, they differ slightly according to the region and the ethnic group, and do not affect life the same way or for the same duration (Ndjapou, 2008). These important nuances will not always be made here but they have to be kept in mind. Not all ethnic groups have the same consideration for the invisible forces: they are seen as powerful actors among the Ali, Gbaya and Banda but less so among the Yakoma. Another nuance has to be drawn between Muslims and others. On certain aspects (especially wealth and accumulation), the Islamic faith provides very clear indications from the Quran and the Sunnah that erase prohibitions that affect non-Muslim sectors of the population: wealth is seen very positively in Islam, and accumulation and sharing wealth or inheritance are also well codified by the Shari'a; aspects such as *zakat* or *sadaqa* are structural in defining a Muslim identity. This is part of the reason for the Muslims' ability to run the CAR commercial/trading sector.

Another mistake would be to interpret the prevalence of sorcery as a sign of under development and backwardness. As an anthropologist argues, 'African witchcraft may well be part of modernity but by no means needs to be about modernity' (Sanders, 2003). Each society relies on a specific perception of the invisible world. In Europe, the Counter Reform movement launched by the Catholic Church against Luther's supporters also served as an anti-sorcery movement and tried to eradicate pagan rituals that had coexisted within Christianity. The modern European, both the common people and political elites, may well believe in scientific progress but behind this belief lie many practices that hardly rely on hard sciences. A fortune-teller obtained her PhD from the prestigious Sorbonne University a few years ago and, the rumours say, mostly because she was consulted by leading politicians, including François Mitterrand.

A more pragmatic understanding would be to consider that some societies have been able to discipline the invisible world through adhesion to certain beliefs while others have not. Mainstream Christianity and Islam have been powerful tools for this, but they are not the only ones. It is crucial not to interpret those spiritual changes in normative ways but more in flows that are dialectically related to the challenges brought by the visible universe.

Alleged sorcerers are not outsiders: they live around their victims and are often relatives or neighbours. Increasingly, they are identified as old women and children, as in DRC (de Boeck, 2000). Yet, those accused of sorcery differ from their close environment in some way: an old woman might be living alone and unable to go to the fields, her children settled elsewhere in town; a boy might be shy, not well integrated within his age set; a physical handicap could singularize a person. Often, in the countryside children who show a difference can easily be labelled sorcerers; in an urban environment, reasons are more rooted in promiscuity and the lack of control of their daily universe. In all cases, this kind of targeting expresses a levelling down.

Youth and women are also the main targets of sorcery. The role played by them in the social division of labour is today undetermined. Clearly, customs defined their place within the household and the village. Today, this customary order is over; the new order defined by the state and the city is not constant enough to allow stability. In the colonial period, youth became adults when they could pay taxes. Today, even biological adults are unable to do so. Women and girls had babies under certain conditions—if not formal matrimonies, at least agreement between two families—today those conditions are rarely respected. Their targeting underlines the fact that their behaviour illustrates the deficiency of the new order, the inability of the social bonds to produce a clear situation that makes sense of the position of everyone. The economic depression from the late 1980s onward strengthened this dynamic and its depth may explain why sorcery allegations are often related to wealth accumulation (even in poorer neighbourhoods). By accusing young people and women of sorcery, people intend to protect what they believe should still be the normalcy of their lives, the redistribution of wealth and economic opportunities.

Sorcery cannot be understood, and should not be considered, without reference to other occult forces: pagan (and brought in by the *nganga*) or monotheist beliefs brought in by churches (and mosques). Often the *nganga* explain their weakening as a function of the lack of means and knowledge that should allow them to fight back the occult negative forces. Their discourse is also framed as an opposition between now and the past, us and our forefathers. Without over-interpreting, their rhetoric is about how social changes and access to modernity reshaped the invisible world and altered their own ability to domesticate it.

In urban areas, their influence was also drastically reduced by the growth of the new Awakening Churches, which defined themselves first and foremost as anti-sorcery institutions. Making the sorcerer evil is more paradoxical than first imagined because this latter becomes a paramount figure in the social realm. At the same time, the churches are successful because they offer local solutions, not metaphysical solutions (by the reconfiguration of the invisible world, for instance). During collective prayers, children are incited to confess publicly their 'true' nature as sorcerers and tell about their sins. The identification of the sorcerer means an end to the insecurity, if only for a while.

The Awakening Churches are also important because they are part of the global processes promoting individuation: the sorcerer and the victims are indeed individuals, not elements of a group that could have its own rationales. There is no collective responsibility even if sorcerers are perceived as numerous in the same neighbourhood. The solution is within and from the church: to protect yourself or confess yourself, you have to attend a religious service and tell first the priest then everyone of your sins and misfortunes. It is better to do so while gifts are given to the church.

The important point is that this healing process is based on a gift (*don*) and a counter gift (*contre-don*), as underlined by the anthropologists: getting rid of the effects of sorcery is accomplished by actively participating in the church and promoting it as a successful anti-sorcery institution. If sorcery has to be seen as a metaphor of the visible word (which is a partial and somewhat debatable understanding), then it emphasizes the crisis of reciprocity relations and the new dominance of monetized relations, to follow Peter Geschiere's analysis (Geschiere, 1992).

Two last remarks are needed. The new churches have many other social roles that are reminiscent of the colonial state: these include inciting people to work, economic accumulation (at least for the clerics), and harsh criticism of idleness since the devil finds work for idle hands. They also powerfully advocate against Islam, which they portray in spatial–political terms, familiar from the period of slave raiding, as a hostile region opposed to Bantu people. Nonetheless, they have problems retaining followers for very long because they recurrently—and unsurprisingly—fail to eradicate sorcery. So, their followers move to other churches.

Also, people point to the need to 'protect yourself before going to church to get protection'. The churches are only present in the urban centres and do not offer protection beyond them, while, whether for survival or for family reasons, the people move frequently between town and rural areas. In rural areas, the witch doctors remain the only ones who can address the spiritual needs of the population, though, as explained earlier, they are not as influential as in pre-independence times.

Sorcery also plays an important role in defining what counts as legitimate wealth. In the countryside, a successful farmer is likely to become suspect if he makes more than his neighbours and stays overtime in the fields while others are already resting in the village. Sooner or later he will be accused of sorcery, such as capturing people's labour power while they sleep, and his success will become illegitimate—or even criminal. Relatives who have been successful in cities will not return to their villages to celebrate their wealth. For one thing, they would have to pay their village relatives' expenses. But, more importantly, their wealth may be considered suspect. In contrast to countries such as Côte d'Ivoire, the 'return to the village' is not common among high ranking civil servants or (Christian) traders. It is only in the last five years that a number of regional associations have sprung up, with the aim of lobbying to bring state or NGO resources to their home areas.

The most legitimate wealth is therefore seen as an outcome of interacting with the state or having a successful career outside the country in the *Moundjou* world (the world of white people). A politician can be rich but a private entrepreneur has to be careful and make sure that his family legitimates his wealth, which can come at a high cost. This sheds some light on why the traditional business sector is largely in the hands of non-natives and why Muslims are more represented than Christians.

It also shows that wealth or accumulation attained through direct work is often a cause for suspicion. In the same way, if a person cannot understand why she has become a target of sorcery, violence may be used in the most extreme way to make someone accused of being a sorcerer acknowledge the accusation. Arbitrary authority and violence are connected to the process of legitimizing (or delegitimizing) wealth.

Between concession economy and a tax obsessed state

The turbulent but very active invisible universe also echoes an entrenched economic realm characterized by the profusion of informal activities and deeply-rooted doubts about property and wealth. This situation is the dynamic outcome of systemic tensions between, on the one hand, an economic realm that is built according to the concessionary model and largely controlled by a non-native social strata and a state affected by a deep ambivalence about the loss of sovereignty (this latter having been given away to foreign companies to the profit of CAR's rulers) and the need to sustain itself at the risk of being overthrown on the other (civil servants have to be paid because if they are not the aid system would basically lose its main aim, which is to allow the CAR state to survive).

In 1899, nearly 70 per cent of what would become French Equatorial Africa was attributed to about forty concessionary companies: 700,000 square kilometres of the 900,000 square kilometres that today represent Chad, Gabon and Congo-Brazzaville (Coquery-Vidrovitch, 2001). The firms had to pay a fixed amount of money and 15 per cent of their profits every year to the French state. In exchange, they had a monopoly on all agricultural products, ivory and rubber. They could, this way, dispossess all people settled on the territory they controlled. Paris expected that the concessionary companies would fund the required infrastructures to increase their benefits. Colonization, they believed, should not cost a single centime to metropolitan France. This first wave of concessions failed dramatically because those companies were more interested in quick profits than in a longer and more rational exploitation of the territories they had authority over. From 1910 onwards, the French state tried to respond to the failures and recuperated a large part of the territories that had previously been allocated. The new deal was the same everywhere in Equatorial Africa: the companies gave back a part of 'their' territory and had to limit their monopoly of exploitation on one product (timber or rubber). In exchange, the remaining land became their full property. Yet, these changes were not significant for the Central African people themselves. Dispossession continued but was more mediated by the colonial administration.

This paradigm has persisted until today, even though at certain periods parastatal companies have taken over some sectors (water and electricity supply and distribution being the two most important today). There are good reasons for that permanence. The concessionary model is a very flexible and adaptable model that builds relations of patronage, ownership and power, and allows them to be renegotiated at any time by new discretionary arrangements at different levels.

Another key reason is the weak potential of the state apparatus to monitor specialized economic activities. This expertise, in the case of CAR, has always been weak. Little was done after independence to bolster the anaemic colonial accounting competence. There are few means of verifying contract implementation. The only interest of the state has always been the fiscal implications of concessions, particularly elites' cuts. The concession model does indeed frame the main sectors of CAR economy, as Smith draws out in his chapter (Chapter 5). Of course, those are not the only sectors but there is a key commonality the former share with the others, namely the over-representation of foreign entrepreneurs. As an official said to the author, 'The Central African people never learnt trading and just let others do so on their behalf'. In the same way, most of the people involved in business are running for quick profits and do not give much recognition to long-term investment and accumulation: it is therefore very different from Côte d'Ivoire or Kenya. The various regimes never managed to promote a local autochthonous entrepreneurial bourgeoisie, although Kolingba tried by exempting autochthonous traders from paying import taxes. Soon all goods were imported through these traders, but the absence of a strong identity of autochthony at the time eventually rendered this effort null, and Kolingba gave up. In CAR, the majority of the middle class belongs either to the civil service or to the political class.

The category of 'foreigner' is frequently used in CAR, but it is a very slippery one. Passports can be bought easily, which creates even more doubts about national identities. Legally, people born from one Central African parent are Central African citizens. But most people will not acknowledge this because laws in CAR may be passed but are barely known of by the *corps habillés* and are therefore enforced in a capricious manner (Lombard, 2013, pp. 157–173). For several reasons, most Muslims are basically considered foreigners. First, they do not have a Christian name, and most people believe that CAR is a secular yet Christian state. Second, they may be of foreign descent. Whatever the nationality code states, they are not 'from the land'. Third, many do not speak Sango, the national language, instead using a pidgin Arabic that is a reminder of how close the country is to Chad and Sudan (even though the people in question may be from Mauritania or Senegal).

There are also different categories of foreigners. If West Africans are met with little hostility, Nigerian and Cameroonian small traders are viewed less favourably, in part because of their status as petty traders who Central Africans must frequently negotiate with. Congolese people are present in all petty works (they are the most populous category among foreigners) and except at moments of great tensions (2001–2003) are accepted. Chadians (and Sudanese) are labelled the 'absolute' foreigners, those whose offspring cannot become CAR citizens, according to most CAR people. Syro-Lebanese, Portuguese, Greek and French people belong to another world and are 'far away' (and therefore not dangerous in the same way as, say, Chadians) foreigners. Therefore, in CAR one should be cautious about terms such as foreigners or autochthonous. Citizenship laws are powerless in the face of autochthony movements as seen tragically in 2013–2014, and the status of 'alien' is not homogeneous.

Greek, Portuguese and French were at first the most prominent business people. The two former often came from Congo-Kinshasa while the French were linked to the colonial era. In the independence period, there was also a surge of African migrants who became involved especially in petty trade and diamond exploitation (notably Senegalese, Mauritanian and Malian people), while Chadian and Cameroonian traders have a longer tradition of settlement. While the former are mostly in the distribution sector, the latter today have a good share of transportation and building material imports.

The Lebanese are therefore latecomers, although some families were already settled in Bangui when President/Emperor Bokassa offered them important start-up facilities in 1973. There are numerous allegations explaining this decision. Some argue that the CAR president, soured on the French, made the decision while visiting Lebanon. Others argue that he made this invitation after visiting Abidjan, where he was amazed by the urban development, and the role of Lebanese businessmen in that growth. Today, the Lebanese business community appears uniquely important in popular perceptions of the key private economic actors in CAR. They are present in the trade and service sectors and also have interests in transportation and diamond mining. They benefited from the departure of many other non-native entrepreneurs who decided that they could no longer cope with predatory practices or/and found new and more profitable places to settle (as it seems today Angola has become for African-Portuguese business families). For instance, after the mutinies in 1996 and 1997, there were still a number of French companies that had survived the general looting of the formal sector in Bangui. But they could no longer endure the new fiscal policies enacted by a whimsical and greedy president. Others also left because they did not have the same political protections as their Lebanese competitors. The main point is that, although there are many skilled and educated Central Africans, very few hold prominent positions in the business sector on their own.

In parallel with (and shaped by) the concession paradigm, no CAR president ever had a vision of his future beyond enforcing fiscal policies and embezzling money: political programmes and ambitions were indeed very narrow. At the time of David Dacko (1960–1965), the old colonial order was not contested. The concessionary companies dictated their policies and the old system went on. Cotton, coffee and cash crops were grown for their interests and there was little else. Once salaries were paid to the workers, these latter had to pay the poll tax, the phytosanitary tax, the contribution to the Société indigène de prévoyance (Native Provident Societies) and to the ruling party (Goulbert 2002). The parastatal sector was taking shape but again the real beneficiaries were restricted to a small stratum of the urban society, including high rank civil servants, leading politicians and non-native economic operators.

Under President/Emperor Bokassa, things changed. His erratic management of the state did not mean that he was willing to reduce it. Primary education became compulsory in 1966 but achievements are debatable despite an increase in the number of children sent to school. In the 1970s, most of the budgets were passed with a positive balance but all led to important deficits. More than two-thirds of the budget was then spent on salaries: the ranks of the civil service increased from 14,714 in January

1973 to 25,542 in September 1979. As seems always to be the case with coups, the commitment to fight corruption and bring to justice those (numerous) officials who had embezzled money evaporated after a few months.

Bokassa was also an innovator in the way he systematically bled the wealth of the country: he expelled companies to create *ex nihilo* his own ones and jailed businessmen to convince them to comply with his requests. This example has been followed by his successors. Ange-Félix Patassé was the most impressive and the least secretive about this achievement. Catadiam, Centrafondor, Omac, Camco, Colombe-Forêt, and Colombe-Mine are all companies that he set up to grab whatever was possible. This behaviour did not end with the take-over by François Bozizé, though it never reached the same level. While this straddling is not uncommon, it has reached a level in CAR that is beyond comparison, with the possible exception of Equatorial Guinea. Yet this happens under constraints. From time to time the international community may show its discontent.

The government's inability to pay civil servants on time has been a recurrent problem over at least the last thirty years. It was both a factor and an outcome of a specific working of the state apparatus. Beyond easy explanations (embezzlement), two features deserve attention. The first is rulers' refusal to get rid of parastatal companies that are often in structural deficit or could generate more profits for the state budget if managed by a private company. The second is the ability of the state to capture foreign companies with attractive contracts and then make their stay so rough that they eventually prefer to close their offices and lose their investment to the profit of a small clique at the presidency.

As a legacy of the first post-colonial years, many parastatal companies still exist but only two are important for the state budget: electricity and water supply. Many others are small and so inefficient that they would disappear without trouble. Past presidents were adamant about keeping them and subsidized them for two main reasons. One was patronage. Being a civil servant may provide a very low salary, but it also provides access to further revenues and employment is thus a useful thing to be able to dole out. The second was the expectation that the international community would get involved and spend a fair amount of money on them. History has so far proved those presidents right on both counts.

Everyone acknowledges the limited capabilities of the state[5] and invokes political appointments and corruption as the main explanations. Foreign observers have cynically called ministries 'PCVs',[6] a reference to their distracting interest in per diems and other perquisites (Mehler and da Cruz, 2001). At the same time, the ministries are still producing decrees, draft laws and regulations, which further complicate the lack of transparency and cultivated confusion in relations between the state and the private sector. While no one criticizes the impetus to reform old laws, the previous ones are never abolished, and the decrees that clarify the implications of a new law are never published. This creates legal chaos. As a businessman said, 'Here in CAR, there is no legality. There might be many legalities, plural enough to make you always near to a delinquent or ready to bribe someone'.[7]

Over the last decade, a number of fears have grown in Bangui which are mentioned by many people, regardless of the position they have in the society. Two are relevant for this discussion. Long before the Seleka reached Bangui, there was the fear of being invaded, that the country would be taken over by hordes of foreigners. This feeling coalesces with the second fear: foreigners are in CAR to loot, to take away the little the Central African people have and destroy their country.

The fear of being invaded by foreigners is both implausible and understandable. History has not been generous with this country, as this and other chapters draw out. Besides insurgencies and their own army and police, the lay population has still to survive the *zaraguinas*, the poachers and the pastoralist groups that are heavily armed and uncompromising. The Seleka made that nightmare a reality for most of the Christian population.

CAR elites and lay people alike argue that foreigners are in CAR to loot. Those foreigners no longer have a specific nationality: they can be French (a love–hate relationship rooted in the colonial encounter, as French Operation Sangaris soldiers have had to deal with) but also Lebanese, Chadian, or from somewhere else. People sarcastically refer to international conspiracies to keep CAR a poor country. Such discourses are common (for instance, in Sudan today), but the striking element in CAR is that they are often pronounced by very well-educated people who happen to have a French passport and belong to the middle class. This is also strange because in rural areas, the situation may be quite diverse and working with foreigners the best way to survive.[8]

The state's behaviour towards foreign businesspeople also reflects the broader social ambivalence about foreigners. When a foreign company shows interest in investing in CAR, it is warmly welcomed and often given facilities and other perks. Yet, it does not take long before whatever was agreed upon has to be renegotiated. Due to the recurrent lack of expertise of the state apparatus, one may understand this will to change a few articles but the striking aspect is that there is no arbitration. Often a director general or a minister will come with several police officers or soldiers to ask for the immediate payment of some taxes, as if money was kept in the office of the company manager. The discourse is always the same and accuses the (foreign) businesspeople of looting CAR and capturing all the country's wealth. This is not a personal problem, the result of a few bad apples, but rather a structural one that in its recurrence evidences a deeper logic and behaviour. Also, very interestingly, the nationality of the businessperson alone is taken as grounds of an infraction, above and beyond any possible disrespect of a regulation.

This economic insecurity also affects daily life for Central African people themselves. For instance, judges decide cases based on a calculation as to who among the parties will be able to pay the highest fine: that person will be declared guilty. Or the reverse: the wealthier person can pay off the judge ahead of time and thus obtain a decision in his favour. There are also many African businessmen who are expelled once their bank account is fat enough that the police officer and judge who execute and sign the expulsion order will be able to eat well.

A person will buy a house or a plot of land, build on it, inhabit it and then, for whatever reason, leave for some period of time—perhaps a month, perhaps a year. Upon seeing a house or plot thus abandoned the *chef de quartier* (neighbourhood chief) will often seize the opportunity to put the lot up for sale. Or, even more surreal, the following: a court in Ndele found a certain man guilty of 'failure to maintain his property'. He had been away working on a cotton plantation and did not return to sweep his yard and otherwise keep up appearances. The judge sentenced him to prison time and/or a hefty fine.[9]

Conclusion

This chapter is a reminder that the Seleka crisis is only the most flamboyant or bloody aspect of ongoing dynamics that forestall the building of better institutions in CAR. None of the dynamics described in this chapter are unique to CAR. Neither can any of them alone make sense of the societal fragility. The argument here is to point out to a specific configuration of strategic societal patterns that produce a profound insecurity in the moral and physical worlds of the population. The analysis shows that the physical insecurity is based on a tumultuous history of migrations to escape slave raids, brutal colonialism and predatory regimes. While so doing, people learn to adapt but also to show an ambivalent attitude towards authority and cultivate an escapism that is today reflected in the stance towards the various insurgencies in the countryside and urban informal activities.

The invisible Central African world is not serene but very strong and turbulent. It has to make sense of the profound changes in people's daily universes, provide a rationale for questioning the social and sexual division of labour, and give moral strength to address modernity represented by money, market, city and a still-hostile universe marked by wildness.

This spiritual insecurity is exacerbated by an economic uncertainty that is provoked by the capturing of the market by non-native and foreign operators and a state that tries to survive and provide adequate means for its greedy leaders. More than nationalism and the will to build a community of citizens in the abstract, the complex reactions of the population reflect the short-term logic of survival rather than a desire to accumulate and develop.

Any policy that tries to transform this situation should be undertaken within a timeframe that goes much beyond the Seleka crisis and addresses the deeply entrenched realities of the Central African social setting. The production of a national narrative by Central Africans themselves on their own history would be the best starting place. But there is no indication that they are ready to produce one.

Notes

1 *'Corps habillés'* is an often used expression in Francophone Africa to name those who are in charge of enforcing state order, such as the police, gendarmes, military, customs officers and park rangers.
2 See Chapter 5 by Stephen Smith, 'The Elite's Road to Riches in a Poor Country'.
3 This speech was made when the police went on strike to get higher stipends. Roadblocks were erected in the capital city and people were fined for whatever reasons. Eventually, the French Ambassador convinced the CAR army to intervene and clear the roadblocks. For once, not only Central Africans but also French people were suffering from the misbehaviour of the police.
4 See Chapter 2 by Stephen Smith, 'CAR's History: The Past of a Tense Present'.
5 Fourteen Central Africans graduated from the prestigious Ecole Nationale d'Administration (that trained most of the high ranking

French civil servants). Only six are employed according to their expertise. The other eight are kept idle, often for political reasons. (Interview with a French expert in Bangui, September 2010.)
6 Based on a French joke: a PCV is a call for which the receiver has to pay. In the CAR context, PCV means *per diem, voiture, carburant* (per diem, car and petrol) all eventually paid by the donors.
7 Interview, Bangui, March 2010.
8 In timber concessions, the workers have been able to negotiate further commitments from the foreign companies that today pay for funerals and transportation for those kinds of ceremonies. To a large extent, to date, companies there are a substitute for the state and a better one. Interview, Bangui, July and September 2010. See also Alain Karsenty, 2006.
9 Examples taken from the author's fieldwork, Mehler and da Cruz, 2001, and Louisa Lombard's blog (http://foolesnomansland.blogspot.com/).

Bibliography

Ashforth, A. (2004) *Witchcraft, Violence and Democracy in South Africa*, Chicago University Press, Chicago, US.

Bigo, D. (1988) *Pouvoir et Obéissance en Centrafrique*, Karthala, Paris.

de Boeck, F. (2000) 'République démocratique du Congo', *Politique Africaine*, No. 80.

Coquery-Vidrovitch, C. (2001) *Le Congo au temps des grandes compagnies concessionnaires 1898–1930*, Editions de l'Ecole des Hautes Etudes en Sciences Sociales, Paris.

Debos, M. and J. Glasman (2013) 'Politique des métiers de l'ordre', *Politique Africaine*, No. 128, February.

Geschiere, P. (1992) 'Kinship, witchcraft and the market' in Roy Dilley (ed.) *Contested Markets*, University of Edinburgh Press, Edinburgh, UK.

Goulbert, Y. (2002) 'Le Centrafrique au seuil du troisième millénaire', *Géographie*, No. 1506, September.

Karsenty, Alain, *Les concessions forestières en Afrique centrale*, CIRAD/GEPAC/Union Européenne.

Lombard, L. (2013) 'Navigational tools for Central African Roadblocks', *POLAR: The Political and Legal Anthropology Review*, Vol. 36, Issue 1, pp. 157–173.

Mbembe, A. (2000) *De la postcolonie: Essai sur l'imagination politique dans l'Afrique contemporaine*, Karthala, Paris.

Mehler, A. and V. da Cruz (2001) 'République centrafricaine. La démocratie n'est pas un vaccin', *L'Afrique politique 2000*, Karthala, Paris.

Ndjapou, E. (2008) 'Au nom de la sorcellerie, je te tue', in *Colloque Sorcellerie et justice en République centrafricaine*, Bangui, August, available at: http://recaa.mmsh.univ-aix.fr/site_Bangui/numero2.html

Sanders, T. (2003) 'Reconsidering Witchcraft: postcolonial and analytic (un)certainties', *American Anthropologist*, Vol. 105, No. 2.

4 Local Dynamics in the Pk5 District of Bangui

Faouzi Kilembe

Pk5 or Km5, also known as '*Cinq kilos*' to many residents of Bangui, are the names given to a zone, or the group of districts, located 5 km to the west of the city centre (Pk0). This zone is well known for its vibrant atmosphere, which it owes to its celebrated market, as well as to the diversity and dynamism of its population. It is a densely-populated zone characterized by improvised housing and extreme overcrowding. This density also has an impact on commercial activities in the area.

Built around the Mamadou Mbaïki market created in 1914, Pk5 is the zone par excellence of the savvy and resourceful, where things are said, seen, experienced, encountered, exchanged and confronted in a situation of conflicted harmony, marked by contentious relationships rooted in history. For approximately two decades, this zone, where resident communities once maintained amicable relations, has been at the centre of a number of events that have had, and continue to have, serious consequences for intercommunity relations and the future of the country.

This chapter presents the experiences of the author, as I grew up in the Pk5 zone, and also attempts to objectively report the events that have shaped Pk5 over time, and the various internal and external influences that have disturbed the local dynamics. This chapter aims to provide information that will lead to a fuller understanding of the evolution and transformation of this small, indigenous colonial-era district that has developed over time into a fully-fledged economic hub driven chiefly by an immigrant community. It also probes the causes of an intercommunity crisis that stands to endanger the district's robust economic activity.

It should be noted that this piece was written under duress, after I was forced into exile in Cameroon in late December 2013. Upon my return to Bangui I was unable to enter the Pk5 zone. Being unable to go there to collect certain information, I was obliged to bring informants to me in the city centre, bearing in mind the risks this would involve for them. Some of them simply refused to leave the district out of fear for their lives. This piece therefore contains the author's experiences in addition to reports from some of the current and former inhabitants of Pk5.

The chapter is composed of three main parts that provide insight into the evolution of the local dynamics of Pk5 in time and space. The first part describes the historical circumstances surrounding the creation of Pk5 during the colonial period. The second part covers Pk5 from 1960 to December 2012, providing an overview of the various events at the national and regional levels and their impact on the national political climate. Finally, the last part analyses the dynamics resulting from the crisis connected with the Seleka coalition's rise to power.

Pk5 of the colonial period

The history of the creation and settlement of this district dates back to the colonial period. The city of Bangui was founded on the right bank of the Ubangi River on 26 June 1889 by the explorers Uzac and Albert Dolisie. Later, with the arrival of the colonists and the development of trading posts, African villages, according to a discriminatory scheme, were grouped at considerable distances around an administrative and commercial district (city centre). Against that backdrop, the city continued to grow gradually toward the west, south-west and north in the marshy plain (Boute-Mbamba, 2010). Pk5 was one of the first indigenous districts of the city of Bangui from the colonial period. A Pk5 elder tells us:

> Historically, the origin of Pk5 was closely linked to the destiny of the Hausa village of Bangui, one of the native villages that were located at the current site of the national police department, around what would become the city of Bangui. In the context of colonial expansion and urbanization efforts, the first Muslims reportedly agreed to follow colonists' orders to transfer first to the Lakouanga district then to the current location of Pk5, originally called Kolongo. It was an inhospitable place that required enormous sacrifice to become the lucrative zone it is today, the heart of commercial activity in the city of Bangui, and a prime source of tax revenues.[1]

Pk5 is a densely-populated zone with populations of various origins. This melting pot originally consisted of populations that had come from the backcountry via rural exodus, in addition to immigrant populations. The names of certain districts (e.g., the Gbaya, Ali, Issongo and Sara districts) derive from names of certain ethnic groups in the country or African ex-patriates (from Cameroon, Senegal, etc.) who reside there. Although some districts of Bangui, such as Miskine, Boy-Rabe, Combattant and Pk12, harbour a strong Muslim community, the composition of Pk5 is somewhat atypical in its heterogeneity. Although most of the Muslim community of Pk5 came from immigration, the Miskine and Combattant communities consist of Rounga and Goula, ethnic groups originating in the north-east of Central Africa, particularly the prefectures of Vakaga and Bamingui-Bangoran.

The populations from elsewhere engaged in several types of activity. Some became *commis* (clerks)[2] and domestic employees of the colonists who worked in the city centre, while others were farmers with fields located inside the city, as well as in the western and south-western outskirts of Bangui. Still others were merchants, the majority of whom were Muslims.

The following analysis focuses on this last population. This segment of Pk5's population is mostly Muslim and primarily came to Bangui through immigration from much further afield –

from Chad, Cameroon, Nigeria, Benin, Togo, Senegal, Mali, Niger, Lebanon, Yemen, etc.

Muslims began arriving gradually. Precise information on the arrival of the first Muslims in Bangui is difficult to obtain, but some reports note a Muslim presence in Pk5 (in the Hausa district) even during the early colonial period. These reports refer to Muslims who had come from Chad in search of wealth, as well as pilgrims from West Africa en route to Mecca. At the time, for those with insufficient means, the cross-country pilgrimage to Mecca was done on foot or on the back of a donkey or horse, often taking several months or years.

In addition, forced population displacements were frequently carried out by the colonial administration in the zone of French Equatorial Africa (AEF):

- Deportation of the Gbaya populations from the north to the forested south for rubber tree cultivation;
- Settlements, established by the French, of Mbororos, wealthy Fula livestock breeders in the western pastures (savannahs of Bouar) after the revolt of 1928–1931 (Gourdin, 2013);
- Deportation of the populations of Chad and Ubangi-Chari toward Congo-Brazza for the construction of the Congo-Ocean railroad;
- Deportation of (Muslim) merchants from Salamat in the south of Chad toward the southernmost agricultural zones of Ubangi-Chari.

Some fled their native villages to escape the policy of forced labour instituted in 1898 and subsequently, the imposition of taxes in 1903 (Gourdin, 2013), as well as social sanctions levelled against crimes, sorcery and adultery.

Some of the migrations from (primarily southern) Chad were economically motivated. Ubangi-Chari, which had become the Central African Republic (CAR) in 1958, was and still is considered a place where a quick fortune can be made, particularly in the commercial sector. Most Central Africans work in agricultural and/or artisanal production, or else work as civil servants. Few are engaged in commerce. Migrants have stepped in to fill the strong demand for commercial products and services and have gained considerable wealth in the process. In addition, the mining sector, particularly diamonds and gold, drew many Chadians, Cameroonians, Sudanese[3] and West Africans (Senegalese, Malians, Mauritanians, Guineans, etc.) to the region. The only Ubangi merchants at the time belonged to the Yakoma and Sango ethnic groups, small populations along the Ubangi River whose constituents had been recruited as intermediaries or managers of stores run by the colonists.

The movement of the Fula from North Cameroon was primarily driven by conflicts in Adamaoua between the Gbaya populations and the *lamibe* of Usman Dan Fodio around 1830, on the one hand, and by the search for green pastures in the south, on the other. The migrants who arrived at Bangui often settled in Pk5 owing to the presence of Muslims in the district, as well as its prosperous market. Some stayed for several months or years in the cities or villages outside the capital before coming to settle in Bangui.

Some reports indicate that the first Muslim families arriving in Bangui around the 1900s were Bouhari (Hausa), Kabara (Hausa), Mamadou M'baïki (Hausa), and Sambo (Fula). Some important places in Pk5 are named after these families, e.g., the market and dispensary of Mamadou M'baïki and Sambo market. The Sambo market is the area where people used to, and still currently, sell foodstuffs imported from Chad, Cameroon and Nigeria (for example, peanuts, cereals, onions, garlic, dates and dried fish).

The intermingling of communities that characterizes Pk5 is also related to religious dynamics. Two monotheistic religions, Christianity and Islam, closely intertwined with African traditions (animist practices), have been historically dominant in Pk5. Though most of the district's population was initially made up of Christians and animists, beginning in the 1970s and 1980s, the Muslim population increased with the massive influx of Chadians and West Africans, and with the increase in new converts to Islam, evidenced by the construction of new mosques, sometimes in districts far removed from the traditional Muslim neighbourhoods. The first Muslim settlers who conducted trade in Pk5 and other Central African cities were highly respected by their Christian neighbours owing to their reputation as honest and respectful.

The presence and the proximity of churches (Fatima, Boulata and St. Mathias) and mosques (the central mosque and the mosque in the Hausa district) – some of which were erected on the same street – is remarkable today as evidence of a long-standing mutual respect and harmonious cohabitation. Constructed in 1947 on land graciously granted by a certain Hassan Kabara, the mosque in the Hausa district was the first to be built by the Muslim community. The central mosque was built in 1967 by the Central African government, and was rehabilitated a few years later with support from Libya, during a period of amicable relations between Emperor Bokassa and Qaddafi. This friendship led to the conversion of Bokassa and several members of the Central African political community at the time to Islam.

The cohabitation among those communities also resulted in marital unions. Several generations of Central Africans are the product of relationships (either within or outside the context of marriage) between Muslim immigrant men (Chadian, Cameroonian, and West African) and Christian women of Central Africa. The migrants, who were either unmarried or had families back home, quickly formed relationships with local women, despite the sometimes-expressed reservations expressed by natives about unions with foreigners of another religion.

There are reports of close friendly relations between the Ubangi elite of the time (Boganda, Goumba, Dacko, Bokassa, etc.) and some Muslim dignitaries from Pk5. There are even reports that Prime Minister Boganda, himself an ordained priest for a time, occasionally hid at the homes of his Muslim friends in Pk5 when being pursued by the colonial authorities.

1960 to December 2012

Pk5, an important commercial centre

Let us take a trip back in time, prior to the crisis that set in in earnest at the end of 2012. Until then, Pk5 was primarily characterized by its large market (see Map 4.1). It was the largest market of several that developed around a core, Mamadou M'baïki, created in 1914 under the colonial administration. It grew considerably with the urban expansion and growth of the Bangui population, and extended along the avenues Koudoukou and Boganda, where various stores and kiosks thrive. As of 2012, this market covered several hectares and extended across the entire zone. Around the Mamadou M'baïki sector, the following sectors developed, each with its own distinctive features: Béa Rex, Kokoro, Fodé, Magalé, ABC, Ngawi, Sudanese, Sambo, Etoile-Koudoukou, Guédéma-Senegalese.

The Mamadou M'baïki sector comprised several zones where various activities were conducted. It was home to several groceries and various other stores. At the centre of Mamadou M'baïki was an establishment with butcher's shops managed by Christian women and Hausa butchers. Various speculative enterprises were also found there. Muslim and Christian merchants operated side by side, sometimes offering the same products. Hardware and second-hand clothing were featured as well. Impromptu displays featuring vegetables and trinkets were often set up directly on the ground on the sides of streets, where young pick-pockets also circulated.

The Kokoro sector offered fresh farm produce (cassava, vegetables, tubers, plantains, etc.) and produce from gatherers (mushrooms, caterpillars, sheets of Koko/*Gnetum africanum*, etc.). Though some were men, Kokoro merchants were typically female.

The zone of Magalé, located in the Fatima district in southern Pk5, was the section for wood (boards, beams and slats), which has given rise to other types of business related to construction.

The zones of Rex and Béa Rex were the sectors where building materials and equipment was sold. This area was mostly managed by Muslim merchants, with occasional exceptions (chiefly Central

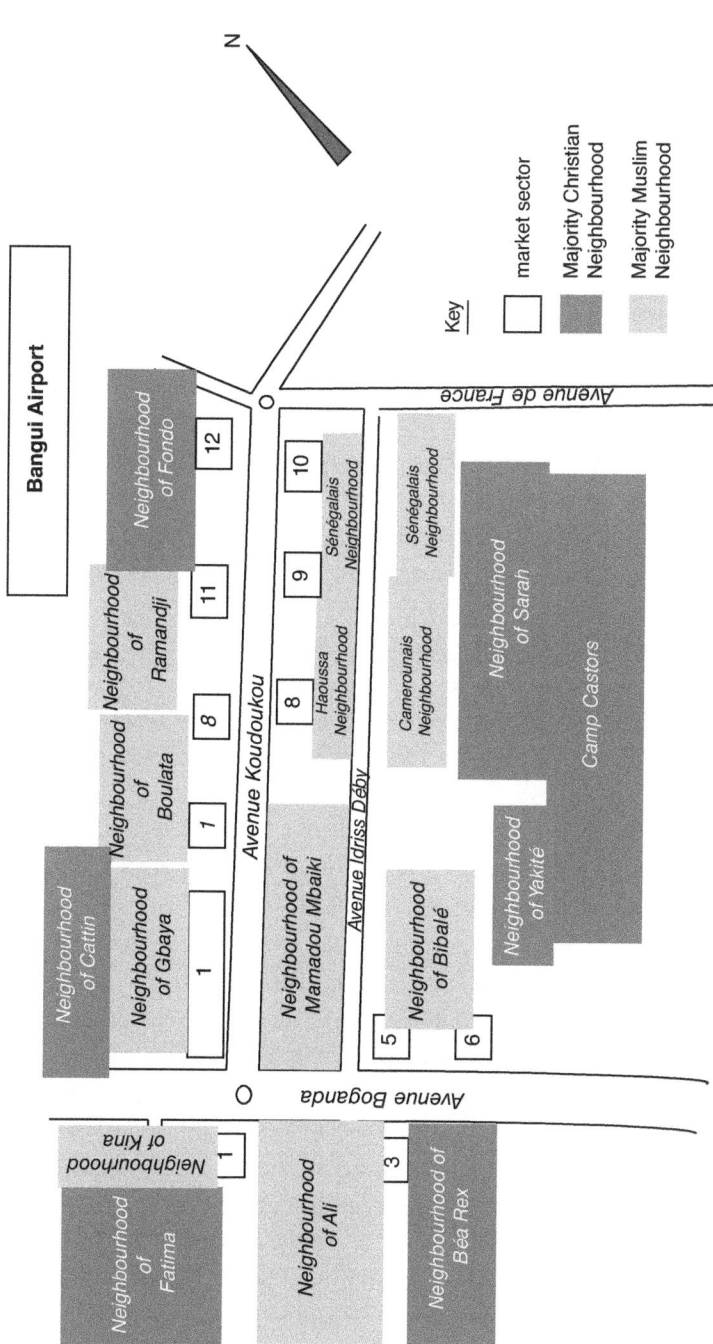

Map 4.1 Local dynamics in Bangui's Pk5: A map of the Pk5 district of Bangui (author's own map).

Africans, Cameroonians and Nigerians). It should be underscored that the building materials business prospered from 2003 to 2012, with buildings cropping up like mushrooms in the cities and their outskirts, despite the perennial shortage of cement, which must be shipped in from abroad.

Fodé was the very prosperous sector of used clothes and shoes (second-hand clothing shops), where most merchants were of Chadian origin. However, more and more young Christians became involved in commerce there, sometimes acting as retailers.

The ABC sector (named for a former bar where a national orchestra used to play) was previously home to butcher's shops and grills, but was overtaken in subsequent years by stores run by new Chadian and Senegalese immigrants (a term used to refer to all West African natives) and vegetable sellers. It was also home to mattress sellers and restaurants featuring Chadian and Sudanese specialties.

The Ngawi market was the sector where products specific to Muslim culture were sold – boubous, sandals, robes, veils, carpets, religious books, etc. It was also the sheep market. Activity in the zone often picked up as the Muslim year-end holidays of Ramadan and Tabaski approached.

The Sambo sector, which was several decades old, was the area for condiments and other foods imported from Chad, Cameroon and Nigeria: onions, garlic, peanuts, beans, ginger and spices. For about the past ten years, trade in counterfeit medications has grown, largely conducted by Kanembous from Kanem (Chad).

Next door was the Sudanese market run by Muslim women (Chadian and Sudanese) who sold various imported products (clothes, dates, kitchen utensils, glassware, decorative objects, etc.) from Chad, Sudan or Dubai. It was initially a seasonal market run by merchants who arrived, in the dry season, with various products offered at very low prices. Since war broke out in Darfur, however, and owing to ongoing obstacles faced by Sudanese merchants, these merchants stopped coming and the market was taken over by newcomers.

Etoile and Koudoukou were the areas where 'new' or 'used' spare parts, for vehicles and motor bikes, often imported from Europe, were sold. The shops were run by Nigerian nationals (Biafran) alongside some Fulas and young Central Africans.

Finally, in the Senegalese district, alongside the shops that skirt Koudoukou Avenue, was the extensive Ramandji market known for its moderately-priced butcher's shops (it was previously a market that sold beef from clandestine slaughterhouses) and vegetables produced around Bangui airport.

The Pk5 market underwent a dramatic expansion as a result of the increase in domestic and foreign merchants in the 2000s. The sides of the streets and lanes were overtaken daily with kiosks and displays selling various staple goods in direct proximity to consumers. Upon arriving in Pk5, one was immediately struck by the presence of a strong Muslim community operating within the business sector, mines (gold and diamond) and the transportation sector. Although some districts of Bangui, such as Miskine, Boy-Rabé, Combattant, Pétévo, Ouango, etc., had the potential to develop large markets, Pk5 remained a central hub and chief

---

Box 4.1: Bilal's story, Part 1

I was born around 1960 in Boali [95 km from Bangui]. I arrived in Bangui around 1975. My uncle, who worked as a merchant there, asked me to come to help him sell the diverse products (onions, garlic, peanuts, beans, etc.) he sold, which came both from rural CAR as well as Chad and Nigeria. After five years, my uncle gave me some capital to start my own shop. I started by selling the same things as him, just by his side. After two years, I started selling cloth. I did well and after three years had opened a shop. I bought wares from the wholesalers in Bangui as well as in Cameroon. Customers came from Bangui and also from elsewhere in the country. The biggest orders came from Zongo, the city across the Oubangui in Congo. The market was full of both Christian and Muslim merchants, women and men, all working together.

supplier to surrounding markets. The inhabitants of Pk5 described their zone as a capital within a capital. With the variety of activities carried out in the formal and informal sectors, one could find everything there.

Pk5 has been dubbed 'the district of atmosphere', where one could eat, drink, dance and party from morning till night. From the 1960s to the end of the 1990s, Pk5 was the epicentre of Bangui night life, owing to the presence of attractions like bar-dance halls and movie theatres, the most famous of which were Ciel d'Afrique (which later became ABC), Morisson (which became 5/5), Le Punch Coco, Jamaïque, Piano Bar, Etoile cinéma-bar, cinéma le Rex, etc. By 2012, all of these famous places had disappeared to make way for stores or bakeries, and even places of worship (e.g., Evangelical churches). The presence of the Evangelical churches, which frequently distributed speeches and written material (leaflets) exposing attempts by Muslims to convert Christians through marriage and land acquisitions, has given rise to a new vision of intercommunity relations. Anti-Islamist pamphlets have been published with mounting frequency. The terrorist acts of Islamists and other radical groups throughout the world have only reinforced these positions, though it would be misleading to extrapolate a direct causal relation between the two phenomena.

Beyond being a commercial centre, Pk5 offered a prime example of community intermingling, as most of the Muslims in this zone were the product of relationships that developed between the first Muslim immigrants from Central Africa or West Africa and non-Muslims. Many young Muslims in Pk5 become romantically involved with young Christian women. Unions between Muslim men and Christian women are very frequent and have increased over the years. Until the arrival of Seleka and subsequent fall-out, it was not uncommon to see young Muslim women with Christian men. In fact, many young Christian men dreamed of having a Muslim girlfriend, and more and more Muslim men favoured Christian women over those of their own religion. Over time, this situation has consolidated family ties and friendships between families.

Owing to simple circumstance, then, many people end up members of a family (in the broad sense of the term) that have been moulded by interdenominational relationships, many of which increasingly occur outside of marriage. However, the political and military events of recent years, especially the government takeover by the Seleka coalition in March 2013 and the retaliation of the Anti-Balaka, resulted in the weakening of that cohesion and the undermining of several years of social construction efforts.

Pk5, a state within a state

The diversity of the socio-economic activities conducted in Pk5 has contributed to the high level of dynamism in the district. Running parallel to this bustling economy, however, is an undercurrent of informal and frequently illegal activities, which include the production of counterfeit documents (diplomas, transcripts of grades, civil registry documents, identification papers, passports, etc.), counterfeit bank notes and swindling. Any government document can be forged in Pk5.

Some intermediaries in Pk5 even work in collaboration with government officials to procure genuine government documents, a common practice that enables uninformed Central African Muslims, and especially foreigners, to obtain official papers (birth certificates, certificates of nationality, passports, and national identity documents) for large sums of money. This situation is compounded by widespread corruption within the government and by the fact that a Muslim, even a Central African one, often faces difficulties obtaining documents from the national government. In addition, vehicle theft and other suspicious trafficking activities are commonplace in Pk5.

As early as the 1980s, a sector of the Pk5 market was dubbed Sambo University, owing to its reputation for issuing counterfeit university degrees. Over time, this practice has spread to the city of Bangui. In addition to government documents, drugs (Indian marijuana, amphetamines, etc.) and weapons are also sold. Indian marijuana comes from the backcountry, especially from the north of the Democratic Republic of Congo (DRC), while amphetamines are brought in from Cameroon and Nigeria.

The network of actors involved in weapons trafficking is rather broad (encompassing the DRC, Chad and Sudan) and dates back several years. Already at the time of President Kolingba, some dignitaries of the regime were supplying large merchants, particularly those in the diamond sector, with weapons for self-defence. The practice increased under the successive regimes, reaching its peak under Bozizé and Djotodia. The network is primarily composed of persons in power or their close relations, though it is difficult to speak of a connection among the various types of trafficking (weapons, drugs and diamonds). In recent years, Central Africa has become a trafficking hub, where explorers and swindlers from around the world come to ply their trade with the complicity of the men in power or executives of the administration in a climate of corruption and underhanded dealing.

Pk5 and the impact of outside events

This period was marked by a series of events at the national and sub-regional levels that have had a direct and indirect impact on sociopolitical life in CAR. Indeed, beyond the internal causes of political instability in Central Africa, the sub-regional crises, particularly in Chad, Sudan and the DRC, have had a major impact on, or are partly to blame for, the security upheavals in Central Africa. As explained in Chapter 2, CAR has had more than its share of domestic upheaval related to coups and attempted coups. This upheaval centred on the capital area especially during the periods 1996–2003 and 2012–2014. Peacekeepers dispatched in response to violence have frequently been of Chadian origin and have gravitated toward areas with a large Muslim presence like Pk5. Throughout this period, these Chadian soldiers have developed a reputation for turning quickly to violence and enjoying total impunity for their abuses, which has contributed to rising anti-Chadian and anti-Muslim sentiment among non-Muslim Central Africans. In addition to the officially-present Chadian soldiers, in the run-up to Bozizé's successful coup in March 2003, both he and his adversary, Patassé, recruited Chadian mercenaries (as well as people of Chadian origin living in CAR), and all targeted civilians for physical violence and looting. The recurring crises in Central Africa have had a deep impact on the education system, resulting in years of wasted potential beginning in the late 1980s. Young Central Africans, especially Bangui residents, typically either quit school to pursue agriculture and small business (the less common route), or to do nothing (as was the case for a number of young people who have now reached adulthood, including many of the actors at the centre of events in Central Africa today).

Influence of the sub-region

The various crises in Chad since 1979 and Sudan, (the rebellions of John Garang in South Sudan and Darfur) have caused populations to seek refuge in CAR, among them former rebels or opponents of the regime of Déby (e.g., Ladé Baba or Adoum Yacoub) as well as rebels from Darfur. Some refugees settled along the borders, while others came to Bangui, most of them settling in Pk5, attracted by the strong presence of communities from their country or region of origin. Many of them are involved in various types of trade, trafficking and commercial activities. The recurring crises in Central Africa have led to the intervention of sub-regional and international troops on numerous occasions.[4]

The Chadians (soldiers from international forces, former rebels or others) who arrive in Bangui typically head for Pk5, where there is a strong Chadian and, more importantly, Muslim community. Most of the time ethnic or family connections play a role in this decision. Even though the cohabitation between Christian and Muslim communities has tended to be relatively peaceful, conflicts have been triggered by some minor events that have centred on the Muslim community:

- The aggressive intervention of MISAB's Chadian contingent in 1997 led to feelings of rejection toward the Chadian community, and often toward the entire Muslim community by association;
- The use of knives in brawls between Muslims (especially of Chadian origin) and 'natives', which resulted in the loss of human life, has spurred violent demonstrations against the entire Muslim community. An act of violence committed by a Muslim is often blamed upon the entire Muslim community, while responsibility for an act perpetrated by a non-Muslim is treated as purely individual;
- Blame for car-jackings in the backcountry has often been attributed, wrongly or rightly, to Muslims;
- The recurring conflicts between livestock breeders and farmers (and particularly Chadian livestock breeders, often heavily armed, who travel each year toward the south in search of green pastures) have multiplied over the years. Some of those livestock breeders have settled in Central Africa, particularly Bangui (Pk5, Pk12 and Pk13), and display aggression toward their urban neighbours;
- Disputes between Muslims and Christians over land ownership in the districts of Bangui have been a source of conflict.[5]

In addition, migratory trends in Central Africa have brought in different types of migrants. While during the colonial period, and shortly after independence, Muslims who settled in Central Africa had very cordial relations with the Christian or animist 'natives'; as of the 1990s, populations of livestock breeders arrived from Chad, displaying weapons and violence toward the local populations. They settled in Pk5 and laid claim to the cattle business and small-scale trade, especially in items such as second-hand clothes, hardware and building materials/equipment. Frequent conflicts and clashes have arisen from interactions between this new, more arrogant and aggressive generation of Muslim merchants and the Christian merchants at the market of Pk5.

Dissensions have even arisen between the new arrivals and other Muslim livestock breeders (Fulas and other ethnic groups of Chadian origin) at the cattle market of Pk13 on Boali Road, causing a rift within the Central African Association of Cattle Merchants (ACCB). The dissidents withdrew to form the ACOBECA (Association of Cattle Merchants of Central Africa).

Complexity of the situation of Muslims in Central Africa

Since independence, Central African Muslims have faced exclusion perpetuated by public authorities, particularly at an administrative level. Although tensions among communities are not often apparent, debates over the Central African 'status' of Muslims in Central Africa, chiefly emerging from clashes surrounding routine procedures, have increased, particularly after Bozizé took power in 2003.

In CAR, Muslims are automatically considered foreigners. Having an 'Arab' name (e.g., Mahamat, Issa or Oumar) can lead to harassment, swindling, exclusion, and degrading treatment in Central Africa, in situations where anyone else, even a foreigner who happened to be named Pierre, Jean, or Paul would be left alone. One could cite thousands of incidents to illustrate this point. A 'Christian' Sara from Chad would circulate even more freely than a Muslim native to northern CAR (Ndele or Birao).

During raids and checks by the police or gendarmerie, even Muslims who hold a Central African national identity card must present a birth certificate and certificate of nationality, and are then required to pay a large sum of money, while their Christian compatriots, even those without government documents, are not hassled.

> **Box 4.2: Bilal's story, Part 2**
>
> Beginning in the 1980s, Muslims like me started to have trouble with the abusive checks by the police and gendarmes. The situation got worse when Patassé took power [1993]. At that point the searches of Muslims at Pk5 became more frequent. Even if your papers were in order, you would be accused of having false papers, and in addition to a national identity card, they would demand your birth certificate and a certificate of nationality, neither of which are required for Christians. Over the course of the years, Central African Muslims were increasingly viewed as foreigners. When Seleka arrived, our situation became impossible.

Before the Seleka coalition entered Bangui, Pk5 was always the focal point for checks by the police and gendarmerie. Although Pk5 is located within the jurisdiction of the third district police precinct, it was not uncommon to see police officers and gendarmes from other districts operating there, hoping to fill their pockets at the town 'hotspot'. Their targets were often Muslims, particularly from Chad, or Fula Mbororo, who are easy to intimidate, because their nomadism renders them perpetual outsiders. Though known to the political authorities, the situation has never concerned anyone except the victims, who react by revolting or defending themselves with knives, eliciting even more violent reactions from the police and occasionally the non-Muslim civilian public.

Once Bozizé seized power with the 'liberators', many of them inhabitants of Pk5, the impromptu raids and checks in that zone declined as many former victims and their relatives became soldiers in the army. Several clashes, some of them very violent, broke out between Muslim citizens or liberators and the defence and security forces (police and gendarmerie) during checks of identification papers.

For a Muslim, obtaining a national identification certificate can be a genuine ordeal, as significantly more documents are required of an 'Abakar' than a 'Jean'. In addition to the legally required documents, presumed Muslims are asked to present identity or civil registry documents, as well as certificates of nationality from their parents in order to prove their 'Central African status'. Most of the time, a large sum of money is also required, in addition to the legal expenses. When a dispute arises between two Central Africans, one of whom is Muslim, comments to the effect of 'A Central African was involved in a dispute with so-and-so' can be heard from private individuals and political authorities alike, as if the Muslim was not also Central African.

On top of this, the 'sale' of genuine government documents (birth certificates, national identity cards, certificates of nationality and even passports) by corrupt, greedy government officials to foreigners who arrive in Central Africa is prevalent. It is common for foreigners, freshly arrived in Central Africa, to obtain those documents from (sometimes quite high-level) local authorities in exchange for a sum of money, bearing in mind that issuers of illegally-obtained official documents (most of whom are concentrated in Pk5) are ubiquitous in Bangui. As a result, it is often difficult to tell the difference between a true Central African Muslim and a foreigner with a genuine or counterfeit certificate of Central African nationality.

These practices have created a situation of disorder and mistrust toward the already-marginalized Central African Muslims. The opaque and inconsistently-applied rules governing the treatment of certain citizens of this country have led to serious frustrations within the Muslim community of Central Africa as well as sustained tensions that have contributed to the most recent episodes of the country's crisis.

Strategies of survival and integration

It should be noted that the Muslim community is characterized by a very low level of schooling, since Muslims have, since the colonial period, considered school to be a 'sinful' device deployed by colonists to undermine the Islamic religion. Muslim parents have always prioritized Koranic study over traditional education. It is also fairly common for Muslim parents to encourage their sons to give up their studies in favour of going into business. Even more obstacles exist for young girls, as they frequently marry young, and few employment opportunities exist for those with more extensive education.

With many of their parents already involved in the trade sector, young Muslims traditionally go into commerce. Those who manage to finish their school and university programmes often face considerable difficulties attempting to enter the civil service or state-owned and semi-state-owned companies. Against that backdrop of exclusion, Muslims have developed various strategies to facilitate their integration into society. Graduates often go into trade or mining (diamonds and gold) or create their own micro-businesses. Their parents' involvement in that sector is an asset, and the community network affords them easy access to seed capital.

Those who do not have that opportunity often take Christian first and last names in an attempt to change their civil status, but their features frequently betray them. There are stereotypical differences in appearance between Bantu and Sahelian features. Many young Muslims become unemployed at a rate comparable to that of their Christian counterparts, sometimes adopting marginal lifestyles as drug users[6] or criminals (theft, car-jackings and rebellion). Lastly, some work on development projects for international agencies and some emigrate abroad, though few young people have this opportunity.

> ### Box 4.3: Dido's story
>
> I was born into a mixed family. My father is a Muslim who was born in CAR but his father came from southern Chad, and my Christian mother comes from a town near Bangui. Already during my first year of school I faced discrimination. My mother came to the school to pay the 250 Francs tuition, but the school director said that since I had a Muslim name I must be a foreigner and hence should pay

> 1,000 Francs. My mother was both panicked and furious, and she went to see her brother, who was a court clerk. He changed both my and my younger brother's names to Christian ones. But even with a Christian name, I would be hassled at checkpoints because I looked like I had a 'Muslim face'. People would say, 'Why do you have a Christian name if you look like a Muslim?' I kept this name until I was thirty, at which point I decided to go back to my original names. I left school at 26 with a Master's in social sciences but I have not managed to get a job in the civil service. To get by, I do small business activities as well as teaching in private secondary schools.

Pk5 at the centre of the recent crisis

Pk5, formerly a hotspot for commerce, social bricolage, music, dance and parties has been at the centre of several conflicts in recent years. The eventual destination of most Muslim migrants, Pk5 is a zone of vibrant social interaction characterized by occasionally-turbulent but generally peaceful getting along among communities, which began a precipitous decline in the mid-1990s. Pk5 has a strong Muslim community, most of whom are property owners. This significant population, which dominates the sectors of commerce and transportation, is the locus of considerable conflict.

Although rejection or reluctance vis-à-vis Islam has always been manifested in Central Africa (Islam is still considered an unfamiliar and mystical religion, and Muslims are often automatically stereotyped as unpredictable and wealthy foreigners), relations have always been cordial between the communities. Although the first Muslims in Pk5 and Central Africa more generally earned the respect and friendship of their non-Muslim neighbours, the new generation has been cast as violent, knife-carrying swindlers, killers, etc. As their behaviour is judged to betray the purer values of their parents and grandparents, it is common to hear people say that the Muslims of today are not true Muslims.

Conflict between these communities began to emerge around 1996, with the aggressive intervention of the Chadian troops of MISAB and MINURCA at the time of the mutinies by the national army under the Patassé regime. But when Bozizé seized power with the support of the liberators, most of whom were recruited from among the young Muslim merchants of Pk5, these relations began to deteriorate in earnest. The vindictive brutality of those 'liberators' toward the Christian civilians and the plundering that followed Bozizé's coup were at the origin of an increasingly apparent enmity toward all Muslims. Some Muslim civilians were glad to finally see their own in power in Central Africa, and some of them supported the abuses and settling of scores against non-Muslim civilians.

Beginning in December 2012, with the rise of the (largely Muslim) Seleka[7] rebel coalition, several public speeches were delivered which expressed hatred toward the Muslim community. President Bozizé and his cohorts, rightly or wrongly, accused Muslims of supporting Seleka. Raids and arrests were carried out in Pk5, sometimes leading to lethal confrontations. Several movements, such as the Coalition Citoyenne d'Opposition aux Rebellions Armés (COCORA), the Coalition pour les Actions Citoyennes (COAC), and others, were set up with the goal of 'keeping Bangui's Muslim population under better control'. Barriers were erected in the city, and ID checks and vehicle raids by young drug addicts armed with machetes increased throughout the city, for which several Muslims paid the price (arrests, physical violence and murder).

Seleka's coup on 24 March 2013, and the accompanying abuses perpetrated against the non-Muslim populations, were the final straw. Many in Bangui were surprised to see young Pk5 merchants become Seleka officers. Score settlings between Seleka and Christian merchants were carried out, which exacerbated the damage that had been done to social cohesion in Pk5. All Muslim civilians began to be accused of being in collusion with Seleka, especially since some of their (previously docile and humble) constituents had begun to exert authority in the zone with arrogance that elicited contempt from their neighbours.

On 5 December 2013, an especially brutal attack was waged by the Anti-Balaka (a militia supported by a part of the elements of the Central African armed forces, FACA) against Christian and Muslim civilians. As the conflict evolved, Pk5 became the only enclave harbouring Muslims from the city of Bangui and the backcountry, particularly Njoh, Bossembélé and Bossangoa, where the Anti-Balaka movement originated.

The need for self-preservation led to new dynamics within the Muslim community in Central Africa: community bonds were strengthened as members witnessed even new converts being massacred. Some members banded together to help others escape the country, generally to Chad and Cameroon, and in solidarity against the Anti-Balaka's repeated attacks on Pk5. Even though some Muslims criticized the actions of the Seleka constituents and continue to do so, Seleka became the de facto protectors of that community.

The position of some Muslims vis-à-vis the behaviour of Seleka and the Djotodia regime created dissension within the Muslim community of Pk5. On the one hand, there are those who supported the Seleka coup as an opportunity for Muslims to claim power and exact retribution for the wrongs suffered by Central African and foreign-born Muslims. Others criticized the coup and foresaw the backlash it would bring upon the entire Muslim community, but their voices were generally too weak to be heard, and the relentlessness of the Seleka constituents only served to stifle it further.

At the height of the crisis, there were disagreements among the imams of Bangui, some of whom reproached supporters of Seleka for their actions, which they considered a violation of the mission of an imam. Notwithstanding, the Seleka constituents remained the only group able to defend the Muslims from attacks by the Anti-Balaka. The president of the Islamic community of Central Africa, Imam Kobine Layama, is among those who criticized

Seleka fighters' actions at the time and predicted their consequences. Efforts to resolve the crisis carried out by Layama and Christian leaders were criticized harshly and sometimes violently by certain Muslims in Pk5. Some called for Layama's dismissal, claiming he had betrayed his community by denouncing Seleka, while others sought to delegitimize him by pointing out that he was not Muslim by birth. (In the mid-2000s, conflict arose over the stronghold maintained by children of immigrants over the Muslim community's leadership. Iman Kobine Layama was elected with the support of new converts, garnered through the association of Muslim leaders of Central Africa.)

Conclusion

In CAR, a poor country in the heart of Africa, intercommunity crises are a persistent problem. They stem from, among other things, bad governance and the exclusion of much of the population from the management of public affairs. The most recent developments in that crisis have brought to light an issue that had always been swept under the table – the place of Muslims in the Central African community. This minority community, estimated at between 5 and 15 per cent of the general population, has always been marginalized and treated as foreign. The community nevertheless remains a driving force of the nation's economy, owing to its stronghold over the commercial and mining sectors in a country dominated by agriculture. The community has expanded to include an increasing number of immigrants from Chad, Cameroon and several West African countries.

Muslim involvement in the conflicts leading up to General Bozizé's coup in 2003 and the Seleka coup in 2013, and their participation in the ensuing violence, brought about the deterioration of intercommunity relations, eliciting open hatred against the Muslim community as a whole. The intercommunity or interdenominational massacres and the mass exodus of Muslims from the country over the course of 2014 raise the issue of how the Central African public and decision-makers view Islam in Central Africa.

The Seleka coup was a source of some optimism for the Muslim community of Central Africa, which had often been the object of social exclusion. That optimism was nonetheless short-lived owing to poor management, abuses and inability on the part of Bangui's new strongmen to gain control of the national territory, which was in the hands of (Chadian and Sudanese) foreign mercenaries as well as other uncontrolled elements.

Today, Muslims in Bangui, who have become a minority in Pk5, are fighting for their survival, an effort that has been complicated by conflicts among Muslims themselves. At the height of the tension, dissent emerged among Muslims between proponents of peaceful reconciliation and radical supporters of war against the Christians.

In addition, entitlement to leadership positions has become the subject of contention between those claiming to be Muslim by birth and converts. Today, the Muslim community of Central Africa is at a crossroads. Its future will depend on its approach to ending an internal crisis perpetuated by competition among different 'power-seeking' interests, but, above all, on its vision for establishing relations with other communities, particularly Christians, and its choice to pursue a nationalist or isolationist, group-centric or atomized approach on the national scene.

The massacre of Central African Muslims and unclear aims of international intervention have furthermore triggered reactions by radical currents of Islam (Boko Haram and Al-Qaeda). The displacement of Muslim populations toward the north and adjoining countries (Chad and Cameroon) has prompted some to fear the partitioning of the country, as well as the infiltration of pro-Muslim terrorist groups seeking revenge against the Christians and international troops accused of supporting the killings of Muslims.

In this chapter I have created a portrait of Pk5, once the dynamic heart of urban CAR. I have done so in order to contrast the long history of peaceful relations even in this at-times chaotic market space with the current predicament, and particularly the tensions between and among Christians and Muslims. And yet at the same time I show how bit by bit the tensions began to rise, owing not to any one factor but rather to a concatenation of several, all of which exacerbated the others: the fact that Muslims are never considered 'true' Central Africans, the dominance of commerce by 'foreign' Muslims, the rise of Pentecostal churches, the regionalization of Central African political instability and particularly the increasing involvement of mercenaries in changes in power in Bangui. Time will tell if Pk5 will ever again be the geographic and symbolic centre of cultural and commercial dynamism in CAR.

Notes

1   Interview with Mr Moussa (70 years of age), on 15 April 2014.
2   Name given to the indigenous people working in the colonial administration.
3   It is difficult to determine the period of the first migrations of Sudanese into the Central African Republic. The proximity of that country has always fostered movements and exchanges between the two countries. In Pk5, there is still a Sudanese 'club' that was created in the 1970s as a space for meetings and events among Sudanese residents in Bangui.
4   See Chapter 9, 'Pathologies of Peacekeeping and Peacebuilding' by Nathaniel Olin.
5   The sale of land in the Central African Republic is not governed by clear legislation. 'Customary' law and law texts are superimposed. Most often, land is sold without the knowledge of the proper authorities. Thus, facing financial difficulties, several families in Pk5 have been forced to sell their houses to their Muslim neighbours without informing the authorities beforehand.
6   Tramadol, a pain medication imported from Cameroon and Nigeria in large quantities, has had devastating effects on young people in the Central African Republic. For more information regarding the spread and abuse of the drug in Africa see, 'Analysis of the world

situation – Africa' (2012) *Report of the International Narcotics Control Board.* Available from: http://incb.org/documents/Publications/AnnualReports/AR2012/AR_2012_E_Chapter_III.pdf

7 This rebel movement was formed from the coalition of several groups, of which the most important came from the Muslim communities of Goula and Rounga in the northern and north-eastern Central African Republic. They enlisted the aid of Chadian and Sudanese mercenaries, some of whom lived in Pk5.

Bibliography

Boukanga, A. (2014) Note à la très haute attention de son Excellence Monsieur le Secrétaire général des nations Unies. Available from: <http://www.centrafriquelibre.info/?p=10962>.

Boute-Mbamba, C. (2010) 'Bangui est-il notre avenir? 26 juin 1889–26 juin 2010: Cent vingt et un ans', *Sango Net*, June. Available from: <http://www.sangonet.com/afriqg/PAFF/Dic/HistoireRCA/bangui-121ans.pdf>.

Gourdin, P. (2013) 'République centrafricaine, géopolitique: d'un pays oublié' *Diploweb.* Available from: <http://www.diploweb.com/Republique-centrafricaine.html>.

Niewiadowski, D. (2014) 'La République centrafricaine: le naufrage d'un Etat, l'agonie d'une Nation'. Available from: <http://rue89.nouvelobs.com/sites/news/files/assets/document/2014/01/la___republique_centrafricaine.pdf>.

5 The Elite's Road to Riches in a Poor Country

Stephen W. Smith

This chapter addresses the 'paradox of scarcity' in the Central African Republic (CAR) by way of analysing the country's political economy and the role the ruling elite plays in it. It aims at explaining the *a priori* surprising fact that the Nomenklatura in control of CAR's state apparatus is capable of turning the lack of institutional capacity into a lucrative resource for private appropriation. It argues that a pattern of outsourced governance rooted in colonial practices – 'concessionary politics'[1] – has become engrained.[2] The system benefits the few in power to the detriment of the overall population and the public weal. Hereafter, concessionary politics are understood as: a) legal arrangements by which national sources of income are temporarily demarcated for specific uses by outside, i.e. non-national, interests in exchange for compensation; and b) asset-based practices of patronage which undergird a political economy.

After a brief introduction to concessionary politics as an analytical tool, the core of this chapter provides a case study of CAR's economy in early 2012, i.e. at a moment when there was still a centrally administered, state-tethered economy to speak of.[3] Since the diamond sector as a resource base for rebellion is assessed in the next chapter of this book, four other examples of outsourced assets are examined here: timber, petroleum, uranium and the national customs service.[4] However, the timeframe of this chapter does not imply that concessionary politics have run their course after Seleka's rise to power in March 2013 or, in January 2014, the take-over by an interim government. On the contrary, as the conclusion will argue, the more exceptionally underperforming CAR's state becomes, the more frequent, and widespread, becomes the ruling elite's recourse to concessionary politics. The reason thereof is simple: at heart, concessionary politics are a 'sovereignty rent'. Hence, the more sovereignty is outsourced, the higher the yield.

Concessionary politics

Within the context of the so-called 'resource curse', Terry L. Karl has pointed to the 'paradox of plenty' (Karl, 1997), i.e. the production of mass poverty through the massive exploitation of oil inasmuch as the proceeds derived from the mineral resource innervate a neo-patrimonial petro-state. An even more intriguing conundrum verging on political alchemy is the 'paradox of scarcity', i.e. the ability of a ruling elite to draw substantial benefits from its own incompetence and the broader lack of institutional capacity in a poor country. Here, neither the presence nor the absence of natural resources is *per se* material. What matters is that assets of any sort and importance, natural resources as well as other state sources of revenue, become all the more lucrative for those in power as they are 'outsourced' to external, non-national actors. This nexus feeds a vicious cycle inasmuch as local deficiencies are aggravated by the abdication of governance, and the forfeiture of managerial skills, in return for pecuniary compensation or specific services.

In CAR, this pattern is rooted in history. Between 1899 and 1910, the former colony was largely 'subcontracted' by Paris to concessionary companies, which exploited the territory's assets in lieu of the French state. A regal prerogative under France's *ancien régime*, concessions date back to the eighteenth century and, as Rebecca Hardin highlights:

reinforced sovereign power and extended that power through various actors and across varied geographical and social contexts. It conferred rights as specific as the planting or cutting of particular trees by clergy or the placement of vendor stalls in the gardens of the *Palais Royal* in Paris and as extensive as the right to explore and trade products from within entire river basins or within entire colonies as empires expanded. (Hardin, 2011)

In practical terms, concessionary politics are performed through the cyclical repetition of three phases: prospection, delimitation and negotiation. Cycles recur not only as new assets are constantly being discovered (from animal skins and ivory to diamonds or uranium) but, also, as already 'conceded' assets continuously come up for renegotiation because of, and contributing to, political instability.

Most concessionary arrangements fall somewhere between warlords ruling in a failed state and a centralized state exercising effective control over resources and revenues. Several factors combine to determine where on this continuum a state (or a sub-region) is located at any time. These include the nature and wealth of the resource base, privatization or decentralization of resources, and the political and cultural legacy of the *longue durée*. (Hardin, 2011)

Timber, CAR's MVP

Timber is by far CAR's most valuable natural resource. In 2012, the logging industry accounted for 10 per cent of the country's GDP, for two-thirds of its export earnings and one-third of state revenue.[5] The sector directly employed about 4,000 people, and indirectly provided work for approximately 100,000 more. Historically, since the colonial conquest at the end of the nineteenth century, timber has continuously been at the heart of concessionary politics. In CAR's 'forest production zone' of 3.6 million hectares in the south-west of the country the forest companies currently holding permits[6] have largely substituted themselves to the failing Central African state. They construct roads, bridges, schools and small clinics; they employ teachers and health workers in addition to transporting local police and customs officials; they even pay the daily allowances (per diem) of the state controllers from the *brigades d'agents fiscaux* who are dispatched from Bangui to assess their tax obligations. The aggregate tax rate for the logging industry in CAR has risen to 27 per cent, by far the highest in the Congo River basin. By comparison, the overall tax rate in neighbouring Cameroon, where subsidized fuel is sold for 520 CFA francs a litre, caps at 17 per cent. Moreover, operators in CAR, where fuel costs 830 CFA francs, export the same tropical species as their regional competitors but need to factor into their price the cost for transporting their logs overland to the Cameroonian seaport of Douala, 1,500 kilometres away from their production zone. Finally, the aggregate tax rate in CAR actually reaches in-between 30 and 35 per cent, when the social expenditure for minimal welfare in the logging concessions is included. Indeed, the state imposes a levy of 10 per cent as *Contribution au développement social* (CDS). Absurdly, the CDS tithe is also clamped on, for example, school furniture or basic drugs such as antimalarials purchased by a forest company for the benefit of the population living inside its concession.

The extortionist logic of the Central African rentier state is an important way in which concessionary politics affect the logging industry. Fluctuating in its arbitrariness, the extraction of revenue replicates the cyclical exhaustion of successive regimes. Toward the end of Patassé's rule, special logging permits (*droits spéciaux de coupe*), and the unprincipled admission of up to seventeen forest companies, had all but ruined the ecology of the sector. The incoming Bozizé regime convened a quasi-revolutionary Estates-General of all stakeholders (*états généraux du secteur forestier*) to reshuffle the cards. Upon the insistence of donor countries, notably France, the new deal laid strong emphasis on the long-term sustainability of CAR's timber resources. As a result, prior to the current turmoil, CAR had become a regional leader in the global management of its forests. But over the same period, in sync with the progressive exhaustion of the Bozizé regime, and exacerbated by a worldwide recession since 2008, the fiscal vice almost squeezed the logging industry into bankruptcy. 'I don't even pay the interest of my debt any longer, let alone the principal', admitted in March 2012, under cover of anonymity, the CEO of one of the three leading operators. 'Like my competitors, I'm technically bankrupt. If we weren't "too big to fail", our suppliers would already be all over us, and it would be plain for everybody to see'. President Bozizé strongly disagreed. 'They always lament and pass over the huge profits they raked in before the crisis. I have much more reason to complain: since 2008, the state revenue from the logging industry has been divided by ten.'[7]

Petroleum in the north

Against the backdrop of a continental oil rush since the late 1990s, Central African hopes for windfall earnings are pegged to three sedimentary basins straggling CAR's border with Chad. The first, the basin of the Logone River, has been exploited since 2003 around Doba, in Chad, by a consortium led by ExxonMobil, and is linked by a pipeline to the Cameroonian seaport of Kribi. Its oil layer is said to extend on the Central African side to the area between Markounda and Batangafo. However, the petroleum south of the border has not yet been tapped, and many sources in Bangui believe a 'Chadian veto' to be the chief impediment. During his time in office, President Patassé had refused to negotiate a joint venture with his Chadian counterpart's special adviser for oil affairs, Loïc Le Floch-Prigent, a former CEO of the French state oil company Elf.[8] Instead, he had tried to close a deal with China's National Petroleum Corporation (CNPC) in association with the Malaysian state-company Petronas and the Libyan National Oil Company (NOC).[9] Once toppled with the help of Chadian troops, Patassé claimed on several occasions that he had been overthrown by the Chadian

President 'because of the oil'.[10] His successor in power reputedly did not dare to challenge Idriss Déby's exclusive grip on the Logone basin – a claim François Bozizé however denied in March 2012, a year prior to his fall.[11] The fact is that the Logone basin's extension into CAR has not yet been attributed for exploitation.

In addition to the Salamat basin, which reaches into CAR around Ndele, the Doséo basin straddles not only Chad and CAR, but also Sudan. It is here in CAR's far north-east that prospection started as early as 1976, and that the chances of finding oil were perceived by President Bozizé to be 'by far the most promising' (Soudan, 9 February 2012). On 17 December 1999, under Patassé, an exploration contract had been signed with RSM Production Corporation (RSM), a company headquartered in Denver (Colorado) and headed by Jack J. Grynberg.[12] The area of license application covered 55,504 square kilometres along the common border with Chad, roughly from Birao to north of Bossongoa. Yet after Bozizé's seizure of power, RSM invoked *force majeure* to suspend its operations and, as a result, became entangled in a protracted legal dispute with the new regime which accused the US operator of non-execution of its contractual obligations. While a US court ruled in favour of RSM, and a Bangui court in favour of CAR, the International Centre for Settlement of Investment Disputes (ICSID) – the adjudicating branch of the World Bank based in Paris – rejected on 7 December 2010 the claims for compensation made by the Central African authorities and ruled that, rather, RSM was entitled to 'reparations'. However, the ICSID also affirmed that RSM's exploration rights had expired on 23 November 2004. This opened the way for the attribution of new concessions on RSM's former perimeter. On 22 July 2011, a Chinese company, PTIAL, signed a contract for the exploration (during four years, plus two possible four-year extensions) and exploitation (during thirty years) of petroleum in CAR's north-east.[13] On the Central African side, the contract was signed by the new junior minister in charge of Mines placed under the direct authority of the President, Obed Namsio, and the new Minister of Finance and the Budget, Colonel Ndoutingaï – in breach of legal requirements stipulating that only CAR's Minister of Economy and Planning was entitled to sign loan conventions with foreign states or companies. For concessionary politics to prevail, short shrift was made of the law.

Uranium at Bakouma

In 1959–61, while the French colony was emerging as an independent country, a uranium survey revealed phosphatic sediments around Bakouma, a sub-prefecture in the south-eastern part of the country. The phosphates were said to contain the highest grade of uranium in sub-Saharan Africa, 0.27 per cent on average, i.e. 20 times more than, for example, the resources in Trekkopje, Namibia. However, for a host of reasons, primarily doubts about the commercial viability of the project, industrial exploitation never took off. Eventually, in May 2006, a Canadian company, UraMin, entered a joint venture with CAR's government (10 per cent), represented by its then Minister of Mines, Colonel Sylvain Ndoutingaï. Yet before production could start, and despite the discovery in August 2006 that the uranium was located significantly deeper than previous studies had indicated, the French parastatal Areva[14] acquired UraMin in 2007 for 1.8 billion Euro. In hindsight, the transaction has been labelled 'the worst deal ever in Areva's history' (Pauron, 2012), and has prompted an internal as well as a parliamentary inquiry into potential fraud. Whether or not the soil around Bakouma should be expected to hold some 60,000 tons of uranium has become a hotly disputed issue pitching the former head of Areva, Anne Lauvergeon, against her successor in June 2011, Luc Oursel. In point of fact, Areva in December 2011 wrote off in its bookkeeping 1.46 billion Euro against the value of UraMin at its acquisition; that is 81 per cent of the price Areva had paid ('UraMin: Lauvergeon dément qu'Areva ait dissimulé des éléments à l'Etat', 2012).

The Central African side of the Bakouma story illustrates concessionary politics in a postcolonial moment of both connivance and acrimony. As production was planned to start in January 2010, hopeful expectation led Central African mothers to baptize their newborn girls 'Areva', as a promise of a better future (Soudan, 2012). Yet, after stalling for time until December 2011, Areva eventually made public that the extraction of uranium at Bakouma would be 'postponed' for two more years. Officially, the nuclear accident in Fukushima in March 2011 and its disastrous impact on the uranium market were cited as reasons. But President Bozizé contested what he called 'the rewriting of history' and, in March 2012, stated that the Bakouma concession was again up for grabs:

> Our lawyers are currently busy negotiating the future of Bokouma. For the moment, the project is 'suspended'. Areva claims that they don't have the necessary funds to invest in Bakouma. But they also say that they are ready to give up their exclusive rights and will accept a third party. I hope that in two or three months, China will be our new partner in the project – and that we will finally go ahead.[15]

The President's intention to impose China as his 'new partner' threw into sharp relief the postcolonial roller coaster between Bangui and Paris since 2007. Back then, François Bozizé had viewed the purchase of UraMin as a signal that France would eventually 'stop considering CAR's uranium as a convenient reserve for her to tap into if, one day, it would please her to do so'.[16] But subsequent episodes, most notably France's urging that he should sack his Minister of Mines, Colonel Ndoutingaï, who was at loggerheads with Areva (and other French operators in CAR, such as Total), as well as an acrimonious tête-à-tête with President Sarkozy at the Elysée on 19 September 2007, had persuaded François Bozizé of, 'at least malign neglect in Paris if not a plan of destabilization'.[17] In angry hindsight, CAR's President had erased from his memory more cordial and less official episodes, such as Areva's undisclosed 'entry ticket' into

CAR, and an amendment to the initial contract, which had been negotiated in the summer of 2008 for an additional $40 million to be paid by Areva over a period of five years.[18] The ratchet-wheel of concessionary politics – negotiation, amendment, real or imputed default, renegotiation – was meant to turn in China's favour. But in the end, no deal was reached with Beijing before Bozizé's fall in March 2013.

Customs as a concession

How lack of institutional capacity and the donor community's inability to constructively engage the Central African state feed into concessionary politics was best exemplified in 2012 by CAR's customs service. The latter had undergone constant reform since Bozizé's seizure of power: in 2005, the World Bank had inspired the creation of a task force of twenty-one officials from both the customs service and the tax administration, CEMIDO, (Cellule mixte impôt-douane) who were meant to spearhead a complete overhaul of all levies and their modes of collection; the result was such a disaster that, on 22 August 2006, President Bozizé dissolved the country's customs, bringing international trade to a total standstill for two weeks with long lines of trucks blocked at CAR's land borders and tons of goods piled up in hangars at Bangui airport while almost 500 customs officials, accused of 'dubious morality', remained sidelined. Forty-eight 'virtuous elements' were then reinstated, and soon were joined by Ivorian colleagues brought in to teach new recruits an ethical lesson. The mission ended in utter failure, bad practices in lieu of best practices being shared. In 2007, the World Bank tried again what had already failed, this time instituting a task force of twenty-six officials, CEMIFI, (Cellule mixte impôt-finance) from the customs service and the Treasury. But as the same causes produced the same effects, President Bozizé requested in early 2008 a foreign private businessman in Bangui, and an old friend of his, to take over CEMIFI and run it more efficiently. Armand

Ianarelli[19] declined the presidential offer but submitted a counter-proposal. In essence, he asked for a 'concession' within the customs service, which he subsequently ran as a private–public joint venture in close association with the head of state.

On 28 April 2008, a MOU concluded between CAR's government and Ianaralli's SODIF (Société de détection des importations frauduleuses) granted the latter legal rights to effectively operate as a fraud squad within the national customs service. With the help of two customs officials and a gendarme, who were put on 'special temporary assignment', Ianarelli started chasing illegal importations all over the country, at the borders (namely with Cameroon) as well as in Bangui and in the interior of the country. He high-handedly impounded suspicious goods and, when deemed necessary, drove seized trucks right into the courtyard of the presidency where they remained blocked pending arbitration by the head of state. Stockpiled in warehouses, Ianarelli's other impoundments were secured by three padlocks: one from SODIF, one from the regular customs service, and one from the owner – a display of tripartite distrust. The penalties imposed were subject to negotiation. Once agreement was reached, the amount due was shared between the state (two-thirds) and SODIF (one-third). Starting in 2009, month after month, SODIF invariably earned the state more penalty money than some 400 regular customs officials were able to recover, or willing to remit to the state coffers. In 2011, Ianarelli and his aides, aka 'Zorro and his three deputies', accounted for 12 per cent of CAR's entire customs revenue.

In March 2012, a brief visit to the customs headquarters in Bangui bespoke the baneful downward spiral of concessionary politics. Crammed in a single office, Ianarelli and his aides were both insulated from, and besieged by, the bulk of ordinary customs officials. Their room was an extraterritorial enclave as much as a tempting island of unrivalled drive and prosperity. For the customs' rank and file, mounting an operation with SODIF constituted self-repudiation but, also, a gainful alternative to the corrupt pecking order of which they were the underdogs. For each 'lead' given to him that prompted an impoundment, Ianarelli paid his informer a substantial 'commission' – and there was no lack of informers, or snitches, all over the country. 'We're swamped with files to investigate', Armand Ianarelli rejoiced at his good fortune. Alain Fred Pépin Bonezoui, the Director General of the Customs and Excise Services, was less gleeful. 'Our relationship with Mr. Ianarelli and his collaborators is very good but, inevitably, it is ambivalent', he stated, promising to 'further develop [his] thoughts' in an interview which he successfully shunned.[20]

Evidently, the Director General's position was delicate. Both outperformed by Ianarelli, and undercut at the presidency, his best agents ran over to where the money and the power were. To top it off, he had to be grateful to his rival for refurbishing his headquarters, i.e. for a fresh coat of paint and urgently needed new lavatories. 'Let me see whether I can also get the access road tarred again', Ianarelli incidentally dropped during our conversation with the Director General. The message was as clear as a bell: in the end, concessionary politics benefited not only the President, Ianarelli and the venal telltales but, also, the dysfunctional customs service reduced to a foil. All pride swallowed, it was a perfect 'win–win'.

A default mode of governance

Concessionary politics are by no means exclusive to CAR or to Africa. However, in most countries, including states in sub-Saharan Africa, concessions are more of an exception, and the rule is self-reliance, at least in the minimal sense of some degree of national involvement in gainful local endeavours. Obvious examples are the mineral-extractive industries, sometimes cash crops and, since the wave of privatizations in the 1990s, the generation and distribution of water and electricity.[21] Yet, in CAR, the prospection, delimitation, negotiation, and often renegotiation, of concessions have become the default mode of governance. By 2012, even the defence of the country's territorial integrity had been largely 'conceded' to outsiders while the internal security apparatus was stacked with members of the presidential 'family'.[22] In addition to some eighty Chadian bodyguards, President Bozizé employed South African military advisers and pilots to sign off on his personal protection. The Chadian army had a free rein in the northern part of the country, and so had the Ugandan army in the south-east where they had been joined in late 2011 by American military; in March 2012, they were reinforced by, or 're-hatted' as members of a 5,000 men contingent mandated by the African Union to arrest and bring to justice the Ugandan warlord Joseph Kony.[23] In addition, the Economic Community of Central African States had deployed in CAR 440 soldiers and 150 policemen as a 'peace-fostering force' (MICOPAX, Mission de consolidation de la paix en République centrafricaine). In support of MICOPAX, France had redeployed 200 military in Bangui after having shut down its permanent bases in CAR since independence, in Bangui and Bouar, in 1999. In sum, CAR was already then a motley of military constituencies under foreign command. Today it is even more of a patchwork and, in fact, a multinational protectorate.

At the end of the Bozizé regime, the Humanitarian and Development Partnership Team (HDPT) in CAR presented the country's economic trajectory on its website as follows:

> Since independence in 1960, the Central African Republic's (CAR) economy has hardly developed. Today, two out of three Central Africans live on less than one dollar a day and in rural areas it is three out of four. Time has also not brought much improvement to CAR: people are not any better off today than they were more than two decades ago. (...) GDP in sub-Saharan African countries has risen an average of eighty percent since 1985, but in CAR, growth was ten percent and was entirely erratic. (...) Of 5,400 km of roads, only 700 km are actually in serviceable conditions. (Website no longer exists.)

The UN Office for the Coordination of Humanitarian Affairs (OCHA) estimated in March 2012 that nearly half of the Central

African population was in need of relief. 'Two-thirds of the people in CAR do not have access to clean drinking water or health facilities, with one health worker for 7,000 people. About a third of the children do not have access to primary school education: many are crowded into classrooms with 95 pupils per teacher' (OCHA, 2012).

In a report released in November 2011, Médecins sans Frontières (MSF) highlighted that the under-five mortality rate in Carnot, a town between Bouar and Berbérati, was three times as high as the under-five mortality rate in Kenya's Dadaab camp, a receptacle for Somalis and, then, the biggest refugee camp in the world. Pointing out that life expectancy in CAR – 48 years – was the second lowest in the world. MSF concluded that one of the reasons for high mortality, in addition to holoendemic malaria, preventable diseases and armed conflict, was:

> a phantom healthcare system which has failed to make even minimum-quality care available and accessible to the population. (...) Humanitarian assistance can help lower deaths from endemic and epidemic diseases and from the health effects of crisis, conflict and displacement. But if the country is to have a functioning health system, the government of CAR, in collaboration with its international partners, will need to start taking responsibility for its own citizens' health. (MSF, 2011, pp. 6 and 14)

That objective today is farther removed than ever before.

Conclusion

In 2011, CAR's state budget equalled that of the public hospital in Aix-en-Provence, a Mediterranean French town of 140,000 inhabitants. Faced with a scale conundrum, the outside world's reaction to comparisons of this sort has been a seemingly self-evident conclusion: CAR is urgently in need of assistance. Yet, the budget of the hospital in Aix-en-Provence, modest as it may be in a wealthy country like France, is a fabulous treasure island in CAR's endless sea of need. In the eyes of those in Bangui who are in a position to lay their hands on state funds, or for that matter on any other monies flowing into the country, this treasure is not only worth stealing but, actually, *ought to be stolen* because its equitable use for the benefit of all would hardly alleviate pandemic poverty, at least not in the short and medium term – and the Keynesian insight that 'in the long run we are all dead' is a low-hanging horizon in a place where life expectancy is a Procrustean death bed of small size. What is more, the lack of institutional capacity is only a different name for the absence of long-term perspectives inasmuch as institutions are the breeding ground for norms, values and procedures capable of (re-) producing predictable outcomes. Where they do not exist, for whatever reason, instability is systemic. And in an intrinsically unstable environment, ethical considerations left aside, it would amount to an irrational choice to predicate one's conduct on any long-term outcome which is structurally improbable.

Against this background, concessionary politics can be understood as a privileged mode of turning lack of institutional capacity into a productive resource. The more governance is outsourced the more can be charged by a rentier-cum-gatekeeper state which monetizes its own deficiencies. Put differently: the greater the local needs the more numerous the opportunities to carve out 'concessions' and to allot them to outsiders in return for pecuniary compensation or particular services. And the more concessions are handed over to foreigners the less nationals will be capable of doing what others are busy doing for them. In this regard, the myriad donor-funded projects 'to build local capacity' are quixotic attempts to tilt at the windmills that the self-same donors power to grind the grist for the happy few in power in Bangui. In the final analysis, they are only fig leaves to hide the outside world's respect of, and compliance with, the local nomenclature's raw sovereignty.

If there is truth in Carl Schmitt's assertion that 'sovereign is who decides upon the exception' (Schmitt, 2005), then CAR is one of the world's most sovereign states. Its President is *de facto* unfettered by constitutional rules and performs almost daily political miracles, i.e. ruptures with routine expectations thanks to his original, apparently underivative and godlike power to make exceptions. Just how far these exceptions went at the end of the Bozizé regime was documented by an International Monetary Fund (IMF) *aide mémoire* summarizing the findings of a mission dispatched to Bangui by the guardian of international financial orthodoxy between 30 June and 13 July 2011. The document stated that 'the official, computerized recording of state expenditures – GESCO – had been systematically circumvented in 2010, in advance of presidential and legislative elections in January 2011, to the extent that 49 billion CFA francs had been spent outside of normal procedure while only 46.2 billion had been properly accounted for'.[24] In short, half of the state funds had been illegally disbursed by the Comité de trésorerie, an ad-hoc executive body of the Treasury created in 2007 which had the last word on all expenditures and was chaired by the President in person. In January 2011, without prior consultation of his government or the parliament, François Bozizé had dissolved the boards of all state or state-tethered companies. From then on, he chaired the Conseil spécial de surveillance et de redressement, which directly administered the state-controlled sector of the economy. In the eyes of Nicolas Tiangaye, then a leading opposition figure in Bangui, 'Bozizé's efforts to rake in money by all means resemble[d] the last spasms of a moribund'.[25]

Since then, Nicolas Tiangaye has worked as Prime Minister, first with President Bozizé, and then with the latter's successor, Michel Djotodia, after Seleka's seizure of power in March 2013. In December 2013, France embarked on a large-scale military intervention to save a country 'on the brink of genocide',[26] and CAR's neighbours – with the notable exception of Chad, which withdrew its contingent in April 2014 – have sent thousands of additional peacekeepers. An interim administration has been put in place in Bangui under the authority of Catherine Samba-Panza to organize general elections 'at the latest in February 2015'.²⁷ In other words: CAR's ruling elite has transacted the country's sovereignty wholesale and no longer piecemeal, and is now asking to be generously funded to take it back. It has been an all-out triumph of concessionary politics. A country which has descended into chaos by dint of outsourcing its state attributes in the first place is digging itself deeper into a hole with the altruistic help of the outside world.

Notes

1 Rebecca D. Hardin, who currently teaches as Associate Professor in the School of Natural Resources and Environment at the University of Michigan, coined the concept of 'concessionary politics' in her PhD dissertation (2000). This chapter leans, in particular, on her article 'Concessionary Politics: Property, Patronage, and Political Rivalry in Central African Forest' (Hardin, 2011).
2 It is not premised here that concessionary politics in CAR are in some way the 'return of the repressed' in the collective psyche, i.e. the re-enactment of a traumatic experience under colonial rule. Such an assumption would require careful scrutiny, and regional comparison, beyond the aim and scope of this chapter. For our purpose, the colonial practice is simply regarded as a precedent which, after independence, has been gainfully replicated by the postcolonial elite and has become a 'habitus' in the Bourdieusian sense of a generative principle of regulated improvisations representing pregnant dispositions to 're-act' acquired over time.
3 The field work for this study was completed in March 2012, and an earlier version of this analysis was circulated within the United Nations in April 2012.
4 Foreign aid is arguably the most pervasive form of outsourced sovereignty. However, strictly speaking, it does not fall within the remit of 'concessionary politics' as no national asset is forfeited and turned into a source of income. Moreover, foreign assistance to CAR has wildly varied over time. For example, it reached 44 billion CFA francs in 1994 but plummeted to minus 10 billion in 2004 (the negative balance is due to debt repayments conditioning access to

further public aid disbursements). Between 1985 and 2004, the average yearly amount of foreign aid received by CAR was 26 billion CFA francs, i.e. approximately four times the cumulative proceeds the Central African state took in from the timber and diamond sectors of the national economy (Bonda, 2009, pp. 50–51).

5   Interview in Bangui with CAR's Minister of Water, Forestry, Fisheries and Hunting, Emmanuel Bizot, on 26 March 2012. In 2011, the logging industry stood for 67.3 per cent of CAR's export earnings, another 32.3 per cent coming from the diamond sector, the country's second natural resource.

6   In 2012, eight companies held eleven permits, out of a total of fourteen that were potentially open for attribution. The 'big three' were the French IFP (Industries forestières de Batalimo), the Lebanese-owned SEFCA (Société d'Exploitation Forestière Centrafricaine) and the Chinese company Wickwood. All three had been operating in CAR for at least fifteen years and each exploited roughly 600,000 hectares.

7   Interview with François Bozizé on 28 March 2012. According to the ex-President, the monthly state revenue generated by the logging industry had dropped from 450 million CFA francs before the crisis to 'somewhere between 25 and 50 million'.

8   In the wake of a scandal exposing Elf Aquitaine as a conduit of institutionalized corruption between France and several African countries, the company was absorbed, in 1999, by its privately-owned rival Total.

9   This deal had been facilitated by Tidjani Thiam, another of Déby's petroleum advisers who, subsequently, fell out with the Chadian President and took the helm of a rebel movement operating out of Darfur with the support of the Khartoum government.

10 Patassé voiced his suspicion in my own presence and, independently, in a conversation with Martin Ziguélé, who shared his testimony with me in an email message dated 24 March 2012.

11 In our interview on 28 March 2012, François Bozizé stated: 'There is no Chadian overlord who has a final say on CAR's oil production! Chad extracts a lot of oil, not only in Doba but also around Abéché and in the West, close to its borders with Nigeria and Niger. President Déby is very proud of his achievements. He wouldn't bother about us exploiting our own oil'.

12 The contract, 'signed at 9:50pm' according to Grynberg's handwriting above his signature, was to run over an initial period of five years, which could be twice extended, first by three and then by two years. The royalty rate 'for anything but natural gas', which would have yielded 5 per cent, was fixed at 12.5 per cent.
13 In addition to a signature bonus of $10 million, the contract foresaw a loan of $15 million per year for a three-year period. If oil had been discovered, CAR should have been granted a 15 per cent share of PTIAL's capital.
14 The French state holds 87 per cent of Areva's capital.
15 Interview with President Bozizé in Bangui, 28 March 2012.
16 Ibid.
17 Ibid. President Bozizé was received by the French head of state for seventeen minutes, just enough time for Nicolas Sarkozy to reiterate his request for Colonel Ndoutingaï to be sacked. Not only did CAR's President not oblige upon his return to Bangui but, in April 2011, he appointed his nephew Minister of Finance and the Budget, the No. 2 position in the government. The same reshuffle stripped the Ministry of Mines of its autonomy and placed it under the direct authority of the President. Given that Ndoutingaï's former chief of staff in the Ministry of Mines, Obed Namsio, remained in charge of the sector under Bozizé's control, CAR's mineral riches continued to be *de facto* co-administered by the head of state and his nephew.
18 For Areva's 'joining fee', newspapers in Bangui advanced unverifiable claims as high as $200 million. The conclusion of the amendment signed in August 2008 was 'facilitated' by George Forrest, a mining operator in the neighbouring DRC, as well as by Patrick Balkany, a long-standing personal friend of President Sarkozy, and Balkany's adviser for Africa, Renaud Guillot-Corail. On the Central African side, in addition to Colonel Ndoutingaï, President Bozizé's 'Special Adviser for Economic Affairs', Fabien Singaye, a Rwandan national, was part of the negotiating team.
19 Prior to settling down in CAR in 2004, at the age of seventy, Armand Ianaralli, a French national of Italian descent, had been a life-long mercenary, successively in the former Belgian Congo, in Angola and in South Sudan. In 2003, the French brewer Castel had acquired CAR's national sugar factory in Ngakobo. In exchange for saving 1,200 jobs in the anaemic formal sector of the country's economy, Castel urged

the President to pull the plug on allegedly mostly Lebanese traders illegally importing sugar to undercut local production. The head of state explained that he didn't have the means to curb the contraband. So Castel brought in Ianarelli, who had befriended Bozizé in Paris during the latter's impecunious years in exile. Castel underwrote Ianarelli's remuneration and operational expenses, i.e. his local residence and office, yearly air fares to France and a four-wheel drive vehicle. CAR's President bestowed 'special executive power' upon Ianarelli, who subsequently all but halted illegal sugar importations. In 2012, the Ngakobo factory ran at a moderate loss (800 million CFA francs in 2011). On account of a MOU (memorandum of understanding) signed with the government, Castel benefited from a legally guaranteed quasi-monopoly (90 per cent) on sugar importations. As a result, the French brewer did exceedingly well in a poor state.

20 My conversation at the customs headquarters in Bangui with Armand Ianarelli and Alain Fred Pépin Bonezoui, 26 March 2012.

21 Surprisingly, electricity and water supply are a state monopoly in CAR. In March 2012, the then Minister of Energy and Hydraulic Power, Léopold Mboli Fatran, explained that 'administrative inertia' accounted for 'a certain delay in outsourcing both sectors'. Indeed, the law privatizing the electricity and water supply had been passed by the Central African parliament in January 2005 but, seven years later, the implementing legal instruments (*'décrets d'application'*), which would have rendered the law effective, had not yet been adopted. In 2012, 3 per cent of the population had access to electricity – a very irregular access, even in the capital where load shedding and outages were an integral part of the daily life as the demand (24 MW) by far outstripped the installed capacity (18.75 MW). Since, things have gone from bad to worse.

22 At the end of the Bozizé regime, the state security apparatus was fragmented into fiefdoms which were parcelled out to foreigners or to 'the family', the generic term for relatives of President Bozizé, for his fellow tribesmen from the Bossangoa region or, simply, for close and trusted friends. One of the President's sons, Colonel Jean-Francis Bozizé, acted under his father's tutelage as Junior Minister in Charge of Defence while several of his (half-)brothers held commanding positions in the army. Yet another presidential son, Aimé Vincent Bozizé, aka 'Papy', led a special unit of the gendarmerie

(Section de recherche et d'investigation) which, in tandem with a biddable Public Prosecutor, went after 'white collar criminals', most often arresting them first and investigating thereafter.
23 See Chapter 12, 'In Unclaimed Land: The Lord's Resistance Army in CAR' by Ledio Cakaj.
24 For additional information, see the IMF press release 'Statement at the Conclusion of an IMF Mission to the Central African Republic' published on 13 July 2011. Available from: http://www.imf.org/external/np/sec/pr/2011/pr11278.htm
25 Interview with Nicolas Tiangaye in Bangui on 25 March 2012.
26 Interview with Laurent Fabius on state television, France 2, on 21 November 2013. When President Hollande announced the French military intervention, on 5 December 2013, he insisted that 'France [had] no other objective than to save human lives'.
27 The transitional roadmap, agreed by regional leaders and supported by the UN Security Council and African Union, stipulates that elections must occur within eighteen months of the establishment of the transitional authority, which officially began on 18 August 2013. Given this framework, elections must be held 'no later than February 2015'.

Bibliography

Bonda, A. (2009) 'Problématique du crédit au secteur privé face aux défis de la croissance économique en Centrafrique', unpublished manuscript (BA in Economics), University of Bangui, CAR.

Hardin, R. (2000) *Translating the Forest: Tourism, Trophy Hunting, and the Transformation of Resource Use in the Central African Republic (CAR)*, PhD Dissertation, Yale University, New Haven, CT, US.

Hardin, R. (2011) 'Concessionary Politics: Property, Patronage, and Political Rivalry in Central African Forest', *Current Anthropology*, Vol. 52, April, pp. 113–125.

Karl, T. L. (1997) *The Paradox of Plenty: Oil Booms and Petro-States*, University of California Press, Berkeley, US.

Médecins sans Frontières – MSF (2011) 'Central African Republic: State of Silent Crisis', MSF, Amsterdam. Available from: http://www.doctorswithoutborders.org/sites/usa/files/A%20State%20of%20Silent%20Crisis%20EN.pdf

Office for the Coordination of Humanitarian Affairs – OCHA (2012) 'Central African Republic Situation Report No. 8', Bangui, CAR.

Pauron, M. (2012) 'Mines – Uranium: Pékin, chevalier blanc du minerai jaune', *Jeune Afrique*. Available from: <http://www.jeuneafrique.com/Articles/Dossier/JA2664p124.xml0/niger-namibie-chine-minesmines-uranium-pekin-chevalier-blanc-du-minerai-jaune.html

Schmitt, C. (2005) *Political Theology: Four Chapters on the Concept of Sovereignty*, trans. George Schwab, The University of Chicago Press, Chicago, US and London.

Soudan, F. (2012) 'Tchad – Idriss Déby Itno: J'ai trop longtemps prêché dans le désert', *Jeune Afrique*. Available from: <http://www.jeuneafrique.com/Article/JA2688p003–004-bis.xml0/>.

Soudan, F. (9 February 2012) 'François Bozizé: "Il suffirait d'un rien pour que la Centrafrique renaisse"', *Jeune Afrique*. Available from: http://www.jeuneafrique.com/Article/JA2664p038–043.xml0/

'UraMin: Lauvergeon dément qu'Areva ait dissimulé des éléments à l'Etat' (2012), *Agence France-Presse*. 25 January. Available from <http://www.lepoint.fr/societe/uramin-lauvergeon-dement-qu-areva-ait-dissimule-des-elements-a-l-etat-25–01–2012-1423727_23.php.>

6 A Multifaceted Business
Diamonds in the Central African Republic

Ned Dalby

This chapter examines diamond mining and trading in the Central African Republic (CAR) from the points of view of rural mining communities, the presidential palace, and entrepreneurial rebel leaders. It argues that the diamond business illustrates several engrained characteristics of the country's political economy that help explain its current situation.

For thousands of miners, digging for diamonds is a gruelling way of life that shapes their economic, social, cultural and political outlook, including their attitude to the state. When faced on a daily basis with the venality of state officials on the one hand and the lucrative black market on the other, most miners opt to steer clear of officialdom and operate entirely outside state regulations. This is symptomatic of how the state, by abusing its power, has become an obstacle that Central Africans are at pains to avoid, if not escape altogether. The illicit diamond smuggling networks that have flourished as a result stretch into Cameroon, the Democratic Republic of the Congo (DRC), Chad, and Sudan. This pattern is indicative of the regional and transnational commercial linkages that characterize CAR's economy.

A backwards glance at how successive presidents have governed the diamond business reveals how the powerful few have exploited the sector for their own personal gain at the expense of the many. From self-proclaimed Emperor Bokassa to

François Bozizé, the 'big men' have sought to maximize their profits mainly by heavily taxing the mining operations of outsiders. This reflects the wider tendency of those in power in CAR, dating back to colonial times, to subcontract the management of national goods to non-nationals in return for hefty compensation. Such concessionary politics makes it all the more difficult for local business and expertise to grow.

Finally, diamonds stand out as one of the few resources – a source of money and influence – for political entrepreneurs in the hinterland seeking to gain a foothold in the political marketplace. They throw into sharp relief the concentration of power in the capital, Bangui, and at the same time the web of commercial and political connections that spans the region. It was in part these cross-border contacts that enabled Seleka's leaders to mount a rebellion worthy of the name.

In CAR, diamonds have become intertwined with economic survival, social and political status, citizenship and organized violence. Consequently a closer look at these 'dangerous little stones' (International Crisis Group, 2010) offers valuable insights into the country's political economy.

A way of living and a worldview

Diamond mining and trading organizes the lives of thousands of Central Africans in the two large diamond zones in the south-west and east of the country (see Map 6.1).[1] It has a greater impact on the psychological, economic, and political life of CAR than the country's other natural resources (timber, gold or uranium) because it affects a much larger slice of the population, and because it alone nurtures dreams of quick riches that are attractive to dispossessed rural residents. The worldviews of miners and their families are shaped by localized dynamics that are related to, among other things, family, spiritual beliefs, and politics. Though the specific configurations of these dynamics vary greatly from place to place, there are nevertheless some aspects that are broadly shared in all mining communities, including those which relate to the process of mining itself.

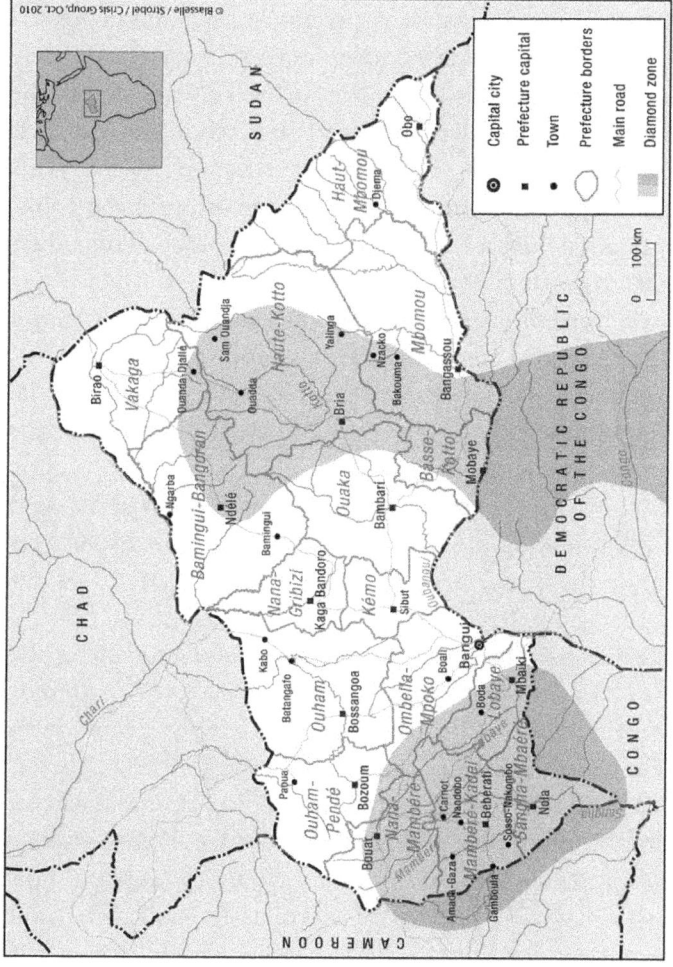

Map 6.1 Diamonds and conflict: When natural resources feed rebellion, 16 December 2010.

Source: 'Map of CAR diamond fields' from *Dangerous Little Stones: Diamonds in the Central African Republic*, International Crisis Group, Africa Report No. 167, Nairobi–Brussels.

Diamonds affect the lives of so many because of their shallow depth and wide spread, the weak enforcement of mining regulations, and the lure of quick riches. All the diamonds so far unearthed in CAR are alluvial. This term describes those diamonds that shifting land masses and river systems have picked up from their Kimberlite[2] source rock, transported and deposited elsewhere, typically spread thinly over a large area. In CAR, they are found about ten metres below the surface. At this depth, the process of extraction is relatively simple but labour-intensive. It involves excavating gravel and sieving it in shallow water. This artisanal mining requires only a little know-how, basic tools, muscle, and good luck. Numerous, mostly foreign companies have tried to mine diamonds on an industrial scale using heavy machinery such as bulldozers and drag-line excavators. But major obstacles have ended their operations one after the other. Importing machinery to landlocked CAR is costly; finding alluvial diamonds in sufficiently high concentrations to justify the equipment outlays is difficult; and chronically poor infrastructure makes accessing and operating in remote areas unviable. As a result, diamond mining in CAR has remained almost exclusively artisanal and, therefore, a potential source of income for the rural poor.

The large number of miners is also a result of the financing and production chain, through which money is invested in mining and diamonds are channelled from mine to export. Five months after the country gained independence in August 1960 a new law granted Central Africans the right to mine gold and diamonds for the first time. Many had previously worked for French mining companies, and in so doing had learned where to look and how to extract the stones. Thousands picked up their tools. Over time a production chain developed, which has since been written into law. A head miner (*exploitant artisan*) employs a team of diggers (*ouvriers miniers*) to find diamonds, which the former is entitled to sell. Middlemen with expertise in valuing diamonds, known as collectors (*collecteurs*), buy from miners and sell to exporting companies, called buying offices (*bureaux d'achat*). Buying office agents in mining towns send their purchases to Bangui from where the diamonds are flown to international trading hubs.

The system only works because the buying offices inject the capital needed to pay for licence fees, equipment and diggers' salaries. They finance a handful of collectors, who in turn finance miners in many different pits. Since neither buying offices, collectors nor miners can ever be sure whether a mine will be rich or barren, buying offices need to invest in multiple pits to minimize the risk of loss. This means that a small number of buying offices and collectors need to keep busy a large number of miners spread over many mine sites. In 2010, six buying offices were up and running (Initiative pour la Transparence des Industries Extractives – ITIE, 2012, 20) while the number of licensed collectors has oscillated in the last decade around the 300 mark (Initiative pour la Transparence des Industries Extractives–République Centrafricaine – ITIE–CAR, 2009, 32). The number of miners is difficult to pin down but by 2010 there were an estimated 80,000 to 100,000 people working in the pits. Taking into account miners' families, diamonds could be a direct source of subsistence living for some 600,000 people (Matthysen and Clarkson, 2013, 13). This does not include those running the small businesses that spring up in mining areas.

CAR's other natural resources do not touch the lives of so many. Gold, found in the west in particular, can be mined with basic tools, but since it is not so widespread and the potential rewards are smaller it attracts fewer people.[3] Timber has consistently accounted for a greater share of the state's revenues,[4] but logging on a profitable scale requires specialized equipment and lorries unobtainable for most Central Africans. Similarly, the machinery, expertise, and capital needed to exploit CAR's uranium or oil make such enterprises the preserve of specialists.

For the thousands who dig diamonds in CAR, whether in the south-west or east, some aspects of the experience of mining are the same. An essential characteristic is the simultaneity of gruelling, dangerous conditions and the ever-present hope of immediate, massive rewards. Diamond mining is a gamble. Buying offices and collectors gamble with their money, but it is the miners who take the greatest risks. They put their health and, in some cases, their lives on the line. By shifting heaps of earth, miners are prone to hernias and exhaustion. Prostitution in the temporary mining-site settlements has also boosted HIV rates there. Injuries are common. Collapsing pit walls on occasion crush diggers to death and some who dive in rivers to bring up gravel from the bed never resurface. But against these dangers, miners weigh the imagined serendipitous moment of finding a large rough diamond, the proceeds from which could dramatically change their social position.

In response to the risk and uncertainty that runs through their work, miners have developed a range of practices based in spiritual beliefs about managing occult forces. These practices express differently in different places. In some places, including Boda in the south-west, at the start of the day miners sacrifice an animal in the pit, often a white chicken, to keep the spirits on their side. In others, diamonds are known as the devil's stones, as if they themselves had the power to lure a man to his death or raise him up out of poverty. The way in which diamonds have accrued supernatural associations and have become part of miners' wider spiritual understanding of the world strengthens the hold they have on the imagination and aspirations of mining communities.

In mining areas, much of the population's economic prospects and social capital depends on their place in the production chain and the strength of their relationships with others who are more influential. For instance, diggers cultivate relationships with head miners, and they in turn nurture relationships with collectors and buying office agents. These relationships are hierarchical in that those further up the production chain have vastly more capital, expertise in valuing diamonds, and knowledge of their worth on the international market. Collectors can amass savings but miners, largely ignorant of diamonds' worth and dependent on pre-financing from collectors, have very little bargaining power and mostly fail to garner the vast sums that drive them to the mines. Those who leave off farming in order to dig must purchase their food at the market. When global diamond prices dropped in 2009, it caused widespread malnutrition in the south-western mining regions because people could no longer afford to buy their daily essentials. Many diggers, though they dream of the transformation a big find could bring, are balanced on the sharp edge between poverty and destitution.

Whereas the diggers are frequently (but not always) from the areas where they dig, the collectors and buying office agents are frequently outsiders. For many years buying office agents and collectors have mostly been immigrants from Chad, West African countries such as Mali, Senegal, Mauritania, and Guinea, and also Lebanon. They are predominantly Muslim and speak Arabic. This shared religion and language eases communication, builds trust, and forges strong business relationships. Miners, on the other hand, are mostly Christian Central Africans who speak their tribal language, Sango, and possibly French and have difficulty breaking into this higher business echelon. In part, in order to join these social networks, some Central Africans in eastern mining areas were, in the late 2000s at least, converting to Islam.[5] At the same time, the power dynamics between local diggers and richer, often foreign, collectors and buyers feeds discontent and fears of exploitation on the part of the diggers and other locals.

For those Central Africans who depend wholly, or in part, on the diamond business, the government's interventions in diamond affairs have coloured their attitudes to the state, the nature of its authority, and the notion of the law. Throughout the fifty-four years of CAR's existence state parasitism on the mining sector has been a constant. In the provinces, individuals experience this venality first-hand through dealings with self-serving mining authorities – mining ministry officials in Bangui have admitted entrenched corruption in the mining brigade – and attempts by other authorities including the police and security forces to make money from diamonds by illicit means. Because they perceive the state as rotten, miners have few qualms about neglecting to purchase the expensive prospecting and mining licences the law stipulates.[6] Only an estimated 5 per cent go to the trouble of paying the various fees. Many object to buying a licence to dig on land that they consider their own by virtue of customary land agreements. Furthermore, when state authorities are clearly less powerful than, and in some cases dependent on, collectors and buying office agents (in mining areas the former often borrow vehicles from the latter) the government ceases to be a credible bearer of authority.

These attitudes to the state and the authority of the law, the weakness of law enforcement agencies, economic incentives, and the ease with which diamonds can be hidden explain the long-standing prevalence of illicit mining, black market diamond trading, and international smuggling – an escape from the state, as Marchal puts it elsewhere in this volume (see Chapter 3).[7] It starts at the mine where illegal traders known as *débrouillards* (resourceful ones) offer higher prices to miners than licensed collectors. From mining zones some illicit diamonds are taken to Bangui and leave the country through the airport in the hands of Central Africans or foreigners, some of whom come to CAR specifically to buy. Others are taken across CAR's long, largely uncontrolled land borders to Cameroon, DRC, Sudan, and Chad.

The illegal trading network and the legal production chain overlap as miners and collectors who operate above board also trade illegally to buoy their profits. The network spans the socio-economic spectrum from small-time traders in rural areas to businessmen in Bangui. Since its clandestine nature puts a premium on trust, it extends organically through family and cultural communities throughout the country and across into neighbouring countries. It is a borderless, transnational network of relationships that operates irrespective of the centralized and border-bound state. Indeed, the two are in competition. The state has tried to curtail these transactions so more diamonds pass through official channels and generate more tax revenue. But for those mining and trading in the hinterland, doing business outside the ken of state officials and bypassing state channels in Bangui is often more lucrative and carries little risk of penalty.

One diamond smuggler in Bangui joked that trading diamonds illegally is CAR's national sport. High-level officials and diggers alike play it. In a sense, the one activity that unites everyone in CAR is finding ways around state control. The joke also captures the idea that just as illegal diamond trading has been going on for a long time; it is also likely to continue far into the future.[8]

The organization of diamond mining also fosters the mistrust that has come to characterize CAR social relations more broadly (see chapters by Smith on CAR's history [Chapter 2] and Marchal on wealth and fear [Chapter 3] in this volume for more on the origins and nature of this mistrust). Many artisanal miners are reluctant to share the proceeds of their own good fortune or carry other people's risk. Cooperatives rarely take off. What is more, clandestine mining and trading, corruption, and the mining brigade's use of spies feed high levels of suspicion in diamond areas, in the face of which those involved in the business tend to limit their transactions when possible to those with whom they share family, ethnic, linguistic or religious identity.

The perks and performance of power

While diamond mining and trading play a central role in the lives of many in the diamond zones of the hinterland, the business also looms large in the halls of power in the capital, Bangui. Since independence, CAR's presidents have exploited the diamond sector for their own benefit and that of their close circle, leaving the mining authorities to function as a façade. At times they have run their own diamond businesses, but mostly they have outsourced the extraction and export of diamonds to outsiders – industrial mining companies and buying offices – in return for hefty compensation. This practice exemplifies the long-standing tradition of concessionary politics elaborated in Chapter 5, which dates back to colonial days. This repeated and largely overt exploitation of the diamond business by successive presidents, notably François Bozizé, has entrenched a common understanding among the political class in CAR that diamond profits are a perquisite of high office.

Diamonds, by virtue of their opulence, have also played a particular role as an accoutrement, part of the costume, in the performance of power. To take the presidency by force or to be elected into the role is one thing, but to be seen as president by the political class and the population at large has required that Central African politicians inhabit a particular kind of 'big man' persona (Bigo, 1988). In CAR one of those characteristics that has crystallized over time is a strong hold on the diamond business and, if the right opportunity arises, boldly showing off the fruits of it. Bokassa was infamous in this regard, but he was not alone. After initially putting in place a diamond consortium that helped increase production to the highest on record (636,000 carats exported in 1968), Bokassa disbanded it and created a company in which he was the major shareholder, which he exempted from taxation (Titley, 1997).

Of the presidents who followed, Ange-Félix Patassé, former prime minister under Bokassa, stands out for his lack of scruple in profiteering from diamonds. He owned his own mining company, Colombe Mines, which operated near Ngore in the south-west and, like a buying office, financed collectors to buy for him. Other mining companies to which he granted concessions were allowed to circumvent the 1961 mining code in return for a cut. These concessions covered almost three-quarters of the diamond zones (International Crisis Group, 2010, 3).

François Bozizé took measures to establish his own, personal control over mining. He cancelled his predecessor's concessions and in February 2004 brought in a new mining code, the first since 1961. Despite this and some collaboration with international agencies keen to reform the sector, Bozizé's governance of the business was still marked by the policies of his predecessors, including the concentration of power in his own family circle. Colonel Sylvain Ndoutingaï, the president's nephew who helped him take power in 2003, was Minister of Mines, Energy and Water before his promotion to the Finance Ministry. In the mining code the government gave priority to industrial mining above artisanal because mining companies hand over significantly more in tax, from which the Bangui elite benefit (ITIE, 2012). Meanwhile, in the provinces, mining brigade officials extorted money and diamonds with near-total impunity.

The government's self-serving approach took a bullish turn in late 2008. After eight out of eleven buying offices refused to pay fines for infringement of the mining code, claiming the penalties were illegal, the government, on 5 October, executed Operation Closing Gate. Ministry officials, mining brigade officers and soldiers from Bangui descended on the buying offices' branches in mining towns as well as some collectors and seized diamonds, cash, and other belongings. The confiscated diamonds, normally sold to the highest bidder in Bangui, were never seen again.

The biggest change to the diamond sector during the Bozizé era, then, was the co-existence of the old patterns through which heads of state and their associates profited from the industry, and the country's new participation in internationally-led reform efforts such as the Kimberley Process and the Extractive Industry Transparency Initiative (EITI), without the latter seeming to seriously challenge the former. Both the Kimberley Process and the EITI were in effect rubber stamps on a thoroughly dysfunctional system controlled by the powerful few in Bangui for their own benefit. The decision of the EITI, a coalition of governments, companies and civil society working to increase openness and accountability of natural resource management, to declare CAR 'EITI Compliant' on 1 March 2011 misleadingly gave the impression that the mining sector enjoyed a healthy degree of good governance. Likewise, CAR's membership in the Kimberley Process was a façade of respectability and changes in the bureaucratic systems such as the use of Kimberly Process certificates were surface-level. They had done nothing to alter the reality rooted in CAR's political history of political entrepreneurs in Bangui intent on making the most of their short time in office. Like peacebuilding and other internationally-led initiatives to 'improve' Central African politics, reform of the diamond sector has floundered given the disconnect between what politicians and diplomats say (their espousal of support for reform and accountability) and what they do (neglecting reform or otherwise looking the other way rather than enforcing standards).

Bozizé's tenure further reinforced the perception held within CAR and further afield, summed up by one former politician, that 'Central African heads of state are first and foremost diamond merchants' (Ngoupandé, 1997, 179). By this measure, Seleka leader Michel Djotodia had some claim to presidential expertise because he had previously worked as a diamond trader in the north-east. For his inauguration as president in August 2013 he commissioned a gold chain that entwined one 5-carat diamond and twenty-two smaller ones (Agger, 2014, 9). Diamonds remain a core part of the performance of power in CAR.

The business of rebellion

Though they are far from sufficient to explain the rise of rebellion in CAR, diamonds have still been an important part of the process of rebellion in the north-east over the past decade. The geo-political location of the north-eastern diamond fields, far from the reach of state power centralized in Bangui, has made them a valuable resource available to political entrepreneurs seeking to launch a rebellion. In addition, those very individuals accrued the wherewithal (transnational business contacts, technical expertise) to initiate their plans in part through mining and trading diamonds. As one Seleka leader explained, 'When we started this movement about the exclusion of the north, we brought local communities together, and they gave us some support, but it was not enough.

Then slowly we started to trade diamonds, and it became like a business for us'(Senior Seleka leader, Agger, 2014, 9).

Conducive geo-politics

The presence of diamonds has not led inevitably to rebellion (none have sprung from the diamond-rich south-west) nor have rebellions depended on the presence of diamonds (several rebel groups have formed in the north-west and centre-north where there are no diamonds to be found). However, alluvial diamonds in the north-east constituted a resource to which budding rebel groups operating in the country's impoverished hinterland were able to gain and maintain access. As noted, it requires only manpower and basic tools. This characteristic of diamonds – that they are a resource accessible in the hinterland – makes them the exception that illustrates the general rule, namely that power and resources are concentrated in Bangui.

Since independence the political elite have sought to benefit from their privileged position and have therefore concentrated power and resources in Bangui while largely neglecting and excluding those in the hinterland. But to reduce the risk of being supplanted, when necessary, they have used the tools at their disposal – money, jobs, licence to loot – to buy the loyalty of potential rivals. Recent rebellions have formed in marginalized areas of the hinterland and been led by politicians sidelined by the Bozizé regime. They have used violence as a means either to attempt to replace the government entirely or, more often, to demonstrate that the government must offer a higher price to buy their loyalty. To launch a rebellion in CAR is to claim a place at the negotiating table. The government may challenge that claim and retort with force or recognize it, make an offer and begin negotiations to reach a settlement. That ceasefires and peace agreements have repeatedly broken down shows that in CAR any settlement is open to renegotiation.[9]

The case of the Union of Democratic Forces for Unity (Union des Forces Démocratiques pour le Rassemblement, UFDR) illustrates the point. In 2006, the UFDR formed in the north-east under the operational command of Zakaria Damane. That month the group took control of Sam Ouandja, a small town in Haute-Kotto prefecture around which diamond mining has proved lucrative since colonial times. The first part of the town's name, which distinguishes it from nearby Ouandja, is even derived from the name of the French mining company that used to operate there, Société Anonyme Minière (SAM). On arrival the rebels demanded $2,000 from each of the local collectors and continued to extort from them $40 each month for 'security'. In addition, individual UFDR members acting autonomously took control of productive mines and used the threat of force inherent in their membership in the group and the weapon slung across their shoulders, to steal diamonds or buy them at rates far below the going rate. Rebels sold diamonds both to licensed collectors and buying office employees who would send them to Bangui for export onto the international market and to black market traders who would smuggle them out of the country, especially overland into nearby Sudan.[10]

This concentration of diamond wealth in Sam Ouandja, a place far removed from the centre of power in Bangui and lesser provincial capitals, offered the UFDR a valuable boost at the very start of its rebellion. It helped the group pose enough of a threat to the government as to warrant negotiations. Diamonds, therefore, by virtue of their accessibility in a remote and difficult-to-govern area, undermined Bozizé's efforts to keep the north-easterners weak by excluding them from centralized power.

The UFDR then advanced south and west towards Bangui. But in March 2007 a combined French and Central African force stopped them at Mouka, eighty kilometres north of Bria. Following negotiations, and in return for refraining from another offensive, Bozizé gave Damane the salary of a presidential adviser and licence to remain in control of Sam Ouandja and its diamonds until a disarmament, demobilization and reintegration (DDR) programme should start. The government even sent them ammunition. Thus to keep Damane compliant Bozizé offered access to diamonds and the opportunity to tax the production chain. This arrangement suited Bozizé well as it kept the rebel force anchored far from his seat of power in Bangui.

Right men for the job

It is striking that several of the main personalities in the north-eastern rebel groups had past experience in the diamond sector. Damane was a head miner in the east, including at Damalango near Bria, before he gained military training as a park ranger. In late 2012, the UFDR commander took a prominent role in the newly formed Seleka. In addition, Oumar Younnous, originally from southern Darfur in Sudan, was a diamond trader at Nzacko, Bria, and Sam Ouandja where he became an agent for a buying office. In 2006 he collaborated with the UFDR to extort money from collectors and in late 2009 he joined the group and gave himself the rank of general. He continued to finance diamond mining in the area and trade illegally in CAR and Sudan and has remained close to the Seleka leadership.

Abdoulaye Hissene was onetime president of the Convention of Patriots for Justice and Peace (Convention des patriotes pour la justice et la paix, CPJP), a rebel group originally formed by miners of Runga ethnicitity whom Gula members of the UFDR and army soldiers pushed out of the mines near Bria in 2007–2008. Previously he was a successful collector at Nzacko, Sam Ouandja and Ndele, but he ran into debt. One buying office tried to take him to court in 2000. He went to Chad to avoid these troubles, but returned when rebellion offered an opportunity for a comeback. Hissene has since been sidelined and played no role in Seleka. Abdoulaye Youssouf was a collector in Sam Ouandja for many years. There he held the post of second deputy mayor until 2003. He joined the UFDR but later, when the group became dominated by one ethnic group, the Gula, and turned against his own group, the Runga, he joined the CPJP.

These trajectories illustrate how the legal and illegal diamond sector in the north-east is enmeshed with the business of armed rebellion. The transnational criminal network of diamond smuggling is indistinguishable from the transnational network from which CAR's recent rebellions have emerged. Business and family ties weave them together (e.g. Oumar Younnous is the brother-in-law of Abakar Sabone, onetime leader of the UFDR). They are both aspects of the same political and economic marketplace in which canny operators seek to gain influence. But smuggling and rebellion involve different levels of risk. For those who take up arms, the penalties for losing are more severe. They include forced exile, imprisonment or death. Charles Massi, a former minister, joined the UFDR and then the CPJP but in early 2010 died in custody, after allegations of torture.

Conclusion

Diamond mining and trading has been a strand of CAR's political economy since the early twentieth century and illustrates elements of the country's chronic political instability and economic malaise. The abuse of state power by the government in Bangui and officials in the provinces explains why miners have no incentive to abide by the regulations of institutions that have been hijacked for private gain. Instead they seek to escape the state when possible and survive by means of parallel, transnational commercial networks. With neither state employees nor citizens committed to the improvement of state institutions, the latter cannot provide the predictability and stability the country so badly needs, or the reform international actors (the Kimberley Process, the EITI) have attempted to foster.

These entrenched elements of CAR's political economy – a population that tries to escape the state; self-seeking office holders in Bangui; and the ability of political entrepreneurs in the periphery to mount violent challenges on the centre – explain in part the great difficulty faced by international actors trying to inject some degree of political stability in the country. The obstacles to collective action frustrate outsiders' efforts to build a functioning system of governance and impose international norms. These norms cover up, but do not fundamentally alter, the real political dynamics that keep the diamond industry from substantially bettering Central Africans' lives or otherwise bolstering the failed economy.

Notes

1 The western zone centres on the geological formation known as the Carnot sandstones that lies underneath the towns of Carnot, Berberati and Nola but which also extends into Cameroon and Congo-Brazzaville. The eastern diamond zone includes the Mouka-Ouadda sandstones and extends from north-eastern Vakaga prefecture along the River Kotto basin to the south and continues into the Democratic Republic of the Congo (DRC).
2 Kimberlite is a dark coloured volcanic rock that is best known for its potential to contain diamonds. It was named after the town of Kimberley in South Africa, where the discovery of a massive diamond in 1871 set off a major diamond rush.
3 In 2010 artisanal miners officially produced only 60 kilos of gold. 'Central African Republic's mining revenue doubles' (2013) *Extractive Industries Transparency Initiative*. Available from: <http://eiti.org/news/central-african-republic-mining-revenue-doubles>.
4 According to the African Economic Outlook, in 2007 mining contributed 2.8 per cent of CAR's GDP while agriculture, forestry, hunting and fishing contributed 54.3 per cent. In 2011, they contributed 2 per cent and 54.1 per cent respectively. Available from: <www.africaneconomicoutlook.org/en/countries/central-africa/central-african-republic/>.
5 By converting for political and economic reasons, these miners follow in the footsteps of Emperor Bokassa himself. In search of external support after France had turned her back, in 1976 he converted to Islam in an attempt to endear himself to Libya's Muammar Qaddafi (International Crisis Group, 2007, 5).
6 The 2009 mining code says an artisanal miner at the head of a team of diggers should pay the state 258,850 CFA francs (about $518) for the first year of mining and 158,850 CFA francs (about $318) for the second.

7 The level of smuggling has fluctuated according to various factors including how hard the government tries to squeeze exporting companies. When Patassé introduced an export quota that buying offices had to meet, some buying offices left the country, those remaining upped their prices and traders smuggled more so that by 2000 a quarter of CAR's diamonds were being smuggled out (Kimberley Process, 2003, 3). When the government closed eight buying offices, official exports dropped dramatically and illegal exports are estimated to have risen from 20 to 30 per cent.
8 Recent research estimates that CAR's subsoil still holds 39,000,000 carats of alluvial diamonds; about twice the total amount of diamonds reportedly exported since 1931 (Chirico, Barthélémy and Ngbokoto, 2010, 1).
9 De Waal's analysis of the political marketplace in patrimonial states illuminates well the underlying political games that have been played in CAR in the last fifteen years (De Waal, 2009).
10 In 2014 the United Nations Panel of Experts on CAR reported that diamonds were being smuggled from eastern CAR into Sudan and DRC and from western mining zones into Cameroon. It also told how in May 2014 Belgian authorities picked up a package of diamonds in Antwerp containing some stones from western mining zones and some from the east. They were most likely smuggled to Kinshasa, DRC from where they were sent with Kimberley Process certificates to Dubai before being sent to Belgium (United Nations, 2014, a and b).

Bibliography

Chirico, P., Barthélémy, F. and Ngbokoto, F. (2010). *Alluvial Diamond Resource Potential and Production Capacity Assessment of the Central African Republic*, US Geological Survey Scientific Investigations. Available from: <http://pubs.usgs.gov/sir/2010/5043/>.

Agger, K. (2014) *Behind the Headlines: Drivers of Violence in the Central African Republic*, Enough Project, Washington, DC, US.

Bigo, D. (1988) *Pouvoir et obéissance en Centrafrique*, Karthala, Paris.

De Waal, A. (2009) 'Mission without end? Peacekeeping in the African political marketplace', *International Affairs*, 85: 1.

Initiative pour la Transparence des Industries Extractives–République Centrafricaine – ITIE–CAR (2009), 'Premier rapport de l'ITIE-RCA, collecte et réconciliation des données statistiques du secteur minier, Année 2006', Bangui.

Initiative pour la Transparence des Industries Extractives – ITIE (2012) 'Rapport de l'administrateur indépendant de l'ITIE pour les revenus de l'année 2010', *ITIE*, Paris-London.

International Crisis Group (2007) *Central African Republic: Anatomy of a Phantom State*, Africa Report No. 136, Nairobi–Brussels.

International Crisis Group (2010) *Dangerous Little Stones: Diamonds in the Central African Republic*, Africa Report No. 167, Nairobi-Brussels.

International Crisis Group (2013) *Central African Republic: Priorities of the Transition*, Africa Report No. 203, Nairobi–Brussels.

Kalck, P. (1959) *Realités Oubanguiennes*, Berger-Levrault, Paris.

Kimberley Process (2003) *Report of the Review Mission of the Kimberley Process to the Central African Republic*, Johannesburg, South Africa.

Lombard, L. (2011) 'Central African Republic: Peacebuilding without Peace', German Institute for International and Security Affairs, Berlin.

Matthysen, K. and Clarkson, I. (2013) *Gold and Diamonds in the Central African Republic. The Country's Mining Sector, and Related Social, Economic and Environmental Issues,* International Peace Information Service, Antwerp, Belgium.

Ngoupandé, J. (1997) *Chronique de la crise Centrafricaine 1996–1997: Le syndrome Barracuda*, Karthala, Paris.

Titley, B. (1997) *Dark Age: The Political Odyssey of Emperor Bokassa*, McGill-Queens University Press, Montreal, Canada.

United Nations (2014a) *Report of the Panel of Experts on the Central African Republic established pursuant to Security Council resolution 2127 (2013), S/2014/452*, New York, US.

United Nations (2014b) *Report of the Panel of Experts on the Central African Republic established pursuant to Security Council resolution 2127 (2013), S/2014/762*, New York, US.

7 The Autonomous Zone Conundrum

Armed Conservation and Rebellion in North-Eastern CAR

Louisa Lombard

Since the emergence of the Seleka rebel alliance in the Central African Republic at the end of 2012, the 'foreignness' of the Seleka has been among the main grievances of the fighters opposing them. Its president, Michel Djotodia had lived for years in Benin and (as Central African consul) in Nyala, South Darfur where he met several of the military entrepreneurs who later helped him take power. Seleka was constituted not in CAR, but in Niamey, Niger, in mid-2012. It began its assault on Bangui from CAR's north-east, and only after it seized Ndele in December 2012 did large numbers of Central Africans join the movement. Because the activity of political–military entrepreneurs like Djotodia has international origins, it is easy to overlook the micro-dynamics of governance in the marginalized, peripheral areas of CAR where rebellion found its strongest support. Seleka's military chief (appointed in May 2014), Joseph Zindeko, had already had a long career policing CAR's parklands before he became a rebel. That this former anti-poaching guard (*pisteur*) has risen to prominence shows that recent decades' conflicts in north-eastern CAR have been important battlegrounds in rebels' military educations. These conflicts frequently pit 'poachers' and herders against Central African wildlife guards in intense battles that the international humanitarian–diplomatic media audience rarely notices.

This chapter focuses on two centuries of the political economy of violence and visibility in north-eastern CAR. In their study of rural power in CAR, Bierschenk and Olivier de Sardan observed that 'the absence of the state... is so striking that the position in certain respects has almost reached the level of caricature' (1997, 441). The experience of state absence has created a contested, pluralized local political arena. This chapter asks: what is the relationship between people in north-eastern CAR and their central government, and through what dynamics do they attempt to establish a livelihood?

Through a study of the North East's major economic activity – conservation and hunting regulation – I demonstrate the tendencies through which people in the area[1] simultaneously decry the lack of an all-powerful state and take advantage of state absence, which offers them space to pursue a range of livelihood-generating projects – to 'escape', as Marchal puts it elsewhere in this volume. The armed conservation initiatives carried out by a variety of parastatal and private actors over the past thirty years, which sought to erect boundaries and police them where previously none had existed, intensified these dynamics and in the process caused new conflicts and rebellion to arise.

People in north-eastern CAR seek order and predictability, and they lament the absence of a state capable of building roads, operating schools and clinics, and employing people. At the same time, their only way of getting 'the state' to pay attention to them is by threatening rebellion and armed disorder. One rebel from the region's Union des Forces Democratiques pour le Rassemblement (UFDR)[2] in Tiringoulou summed up this conundrum when he asked me, 'What if we took up arms again and became road robbers to prove to the state that we have been neglected – what would you think of that?'[3] This bind is a feature of local political life, and it is one that has entangled all with interests in the area, from dispossessed youth to diplomats and donors who pay attention to conflict, but not to other forms of agitation.

The north-eastern expanses of CAR are a particular kind of space that I call an 'autonomous zone'. Autonomous zones are marked by a minimal government presence. To whatever extent any government *could* control the territory and its people (likely not very much), no one has ever shown much interest in doing so. Governments have instead treated the area's residents as foreigners and ignored them. And yet people in the area are Central African, and their home is part of CAR. In short, they are stuck between their *lived reality* of abandonment by any government and their *formal reality* of being bound to CAR. They respond to this bind by simultaneously making pleas for inclusion and also operating in ways that subvert any unitary model of governance or control.

Autonomous zones are difficult for states to govern partly because of geography.[4] For much of the year, the region is a half-flooded swamp. At the end of the colonial era, secret French military assessments described the 'ungovernability' of the autonomous zone as a natural phenomenon:

> Oubangui, country of wooded savannah, with its population concentrated along the roads and its vast open spaces, seems the perfect terrain for the guerrilla: ambushes are easy to launch against the main roads, destruction of bridges and ferries can have big effects since all movement depends on them, and it is possible to disappear in the bush and to there be less vulnerable due to the difficulties of penetrating and the quasi-impossibility for aerial surveillance of individuals or small detachments… large spaces escape all control. Interventions can only be undertaken on foot, with all the slowness and fatigue that this kind of movement entails. They would require a formidable number of men because the Oubanguian bush with its lack of a horizon and absence of clear routes is an 'eater of men' (Oubangui-Chari, ND).

But of course autonomous zones are not simply the product of the natural environment. They are products of governance. In this respect, hunting and conservation – the main sources of revenues, both licit and illicit, since the early twentieth century – have shaped this area as an autonomous zone. These dynamics have fed rebellion as the most dramatic, visible expression of the bind mentioned above. They have become violent as the region has militarized over the past decades, a process that manifested in the autonomous zone first as conservation battles and then as rebellion.

Birth of an autonomous zone

Where southern CAR is a lush, wet, green expanse with many tall trees when viewed from the air, the North East becomes drier the further north-east one travels. That green blanket becomes thinner, interspersed with varied hues of tan, as well as, in the far north-east of the region, the grey tones of thorn trees. In these forested savannahs, most people are Muslim, many adhering to the Tijaniyya sect, a Sufi brotherhood prominent in West Africa. Chadian and Sudanese Arabic dialects are most widely spoken, but Sango is prominent and has gained speakers over the past thirty years due to its official status and importance in business, especially to the south in Bangui.

During the eighteenth and nineteenth centuries, the area saw many migrants seeking refuge from the militarized polities in the surrounding areas (especially to the north and west). They fled slave-raiders and hunters who came to seize other goods (ivory, foodstuffs, etc.) and innovated in hunting tactics to do so. People settling here tended to live in small, fluidly-defined groups. As trade intensified, a few individuals became especially powerful and were known as sultans. These sultans developed trade networks. Itinerant merchants (*jellaba*) set up storehouses and thorn-fenced forts (*zara'ib*) to facilitate their own work and the passage of Hajj pilgrims. The political economy was a 'zaribas system', organized through militarized trading posts that sometimes became cities but never lost their militarized-mercantile nature (Santandrea, 1964).

The most powerful sultan was the Sultan Sanusi (about 1840–1911), who founded and built the town of Ndele to reach its greatest-ever wealth and largest population. At the turn of the twentieth century, Ndele counted some twenty to twenty-five thousand inhabitants, three times more than its current population. Sanusi's army was perhaps six thousand strong – larger than the Central African armed forces today.[5] Partly due to relationships with his powerful northern neighbours (principally *Rabah*, in Wadai) and the French, he amassed a formidable arsenal (Cordell, 1985). The terror his raiders wreaked would today be classified as a humanitarian catastrophe – tens of thousands displaced, tens of thousands taken captive, untold numbers of houses looted and burned (Cordell, 2002).[6] But he also brought access to new modes of knowledge, goods, and social organization. A French captain dispatched to the sultan's territory in 1909 wrote that for Sanusi, 'slavery is a process of governance and raids are the only truly productive commercial operations' (Modat, 1909). The French assassinated Sanusi, in 1911, citing (without apparent irony) the illegitimacy of his rule as a 'foreigner' colonizing these lands for his own profit (Prioul, 1982). The French also wanted to impose a 'legitimate' economy and government. They did not get what they wanted. With Sanusi gone, people dispersed. Ndele became a ghost town. By the 1930s, official French documents recognized that the area's prosperity had declined since their take-over.

The French never invested the vast sums that would have been necessary to install the physical infrastructure and human resources of a coherent administration in north-eastern Oubangui-Chari (as the territory was then known). Their few government outposts in the zone were each staffed with a single administrator/officer and a few regional guards. Given how long it took for anything – people, information – to reach these remote locations, the government declared the area an 'autonomous district'. This meant that, though part of the colony, it was not expected to keep up with government directives and was mostly ignored and neglected. To a certain extent, this liminal status characterized French Equatorial Africa (AEF) as a whole. In the late 1920s, journalist Albert Londres described AEF as a 'skeleton' of a house, with no walls, no windows, no furnishings (2006 [1929]). In the autonomous zone, it was barely a skeleton. The colonial officer sent to Ndele in the mid-1930s begged his superiors in Bangui to send him scrap metal that he could fashion into chains for securing prisoners. He found himself targeted on all sides – by the prisoners he could not contain, by the bugs and snakes that filled his house, and by the guards who would not follow his orders (Lignier, 1936). Administration was to be funded by tax-paying natives, but the already small population continued to dwindle due to the problem of *transfuges* (deserters) as many people left Oubangui-Chari for Sudan or the Belgian Congo, which had better services (for instance, sleeping sickness pills) and jobs.

The French colonial view of north-easterners as exploitative, slave-raiding foreigners remained in place after independence. Though educated elites from the North East have ascended to ministerial positions, Central African nationalism (to the extent it exists) is strongly coded Christian, and non-north-eastern. The North East is associated with Islam and foreignness – regardless of how many generations a Muslim family has lived in the country. When north-easterners travelled to Bangui, they faced roadblocks by government officials and/or freelancers who, upon hearing a Muslim name, demanded extra fees and denied that the person could be a Central African. Those who could not speak Sango had extra trouble. In Bangui, during a World Bank-sponsored research workshop in late 2010 whose goal was to enumerate the causes of CAR's 'fragility', a sociology professor at the University of Bangui told her audience of the indignity of having to pay her electric bill to a man with a Central African identity card but no ability to speak Sango, the national language. When another participant sought to sanitize the professor's comments ('Of course, it is *possible* to be Central African but not speak Sango…'), most in the room disagreed.

On rare occasions, government officials and the representatives of international diplomatic and humanitarian agencies visit the

North East. They make promises understood by most to be empty, to a local population that lacks means to bring them to account. Even the eager-to-help humanitarians are frequently constrained by cost–benefit calculations showing that the per-person cost of work in the North East are exponentially higher than in more densely populated and safer areas in the south, and so their statements of a desire to help frequently amount to less than people expect.

The run-up to the 2011 presidential elections brought an occasional representative from the president's party, Kwa na Kwa ('work, nothing but work', KNK), out to campaign. On one such visit in Tiringoulou in late 2009, the KNK rep arrived in a small plane. He rested for a while on the sofas of the fanciest house in town, built to serve as a show piece by the leader of the town's rebel group. That rebel group, the UFDR, had signed a peace agreement with the government and were waiting for the benefits of the state's Disarmament, Demobilization and Reintegration (DDR) programme. By this point they had waited well over a year. After his rest, the party representative received supplicants. His golfing attire (khaki shorts, loafers, and a striped polo shirt stretched like a hammock for his growing belly) was revealing of the disconnect between him and the town's residents, whose clothes bore the marks of agricultural work. One by one, men sought work as wildlife guards, schoolteachers sought chalk, and gendarmes asked for motorcycles to do their jobs. His advice: 'Write a letter to the president. I myself will place it on his desk. I will make sure he reads it.' A youth member of the rebel group expressed scepticism. The party representative responded as if personally offended: 'You think the president won't reply? You think that when I present him with this letter, he will not answer?' Later that afternoon, he made a speech drawing on familiar themes: this is a rich region, full of resources, and our party is committed to transforming it so it realizes its potential. He added that before his party left power, they would drill for oil here. This last promise drew the loudest cheers.

The next morning, people handed the representative their requests, penned in careful cursive. His laptop bag full of letters, the KNK representative flew away. He never returned, and the letter-writers never received any response. As one rebel explained in French, 'We don't have the kinds of mouths that can speak to the government'. The man had joined the rebels because he felt his gun could speak when his mouth could not. But at the same time as people lament their abandonment, they have taken advantage of the state's absence and developed a range of livelihood- and authority-generating projects. Many of these projects exploit the gap between the unitary, ideal-type state imagined in laws and regulations, and the plural authorities in north-eastern CAR. In this gap, different actors negotiate with each other (or else try to hide from each other) for access to the resources in the area's vast open spaces, chief among them its wildlife.

Official policy from the colonial era into the present has focused on wildlife. It was first quarry for European professional hunters and then became 'protected' for the sake of safari hunters. Oubangui-Chari became known as a place where lax oversight made it possible to hunt and trade ivory. Tusks from Bahr-el-Ghazal would be transported to Oubangui-Chari because they could there be traded for firearms or exported northward (Sikainga, 1990). Much of the ivory hunted in the Belgian Congo also found its way to Oubangui-Chari for sale and export, because AEF lacked Belgian export quotas (Roulet, 2004, 112). The autonomous zone hosted a number of adventurers, both 'Arab' and European, who came to hunt for a living. Some colonial administrators decried this state of affairs. In 1934, the administrator at Birao lamented that though the region had once known great prosperity thanks to ivory and hunting, overhunting by 'Arabs' had caused a precipitous economic decline. Other administrators hunted with gusto (Brégeon, 1998, 253).

By 1929, officials in Brazzaville decided better regulation of hunting was needed. They drafted a range of provisions taxing white hunters and limiting hunting by Africans. The governor of

Oubangui-Chari critiqued the proposed law as beyond their ability to enforce, particularly in the North East, which had the best hunting. He argued that the law was a 'façade' that was impossible to enforce ('no effective control is possible.... The hunters are at home [*chez eux*] and there is little risk they will be disturbed') and that it incentivized tax evasion ('we can be sure that pretty much all the trophies from this zone will elude us') (Antonetti, 1929).

In the 1940s and 1950s, safari hunting developed in the area. Oubangui-Chari was, as the title of a 1956 guidebook put it, a 'paradise' for trophy hunting (Gauze, 1958). Both for conservation and for the maintenance of safari hunting, the French declared a number of areas as hunting and faunal reserves in north-eastern CAR and legally categorized the eastern lands as 'zones of hunting interest'. The human population of the area was already low, so the park creation did not entail massive displacement, but about 20,000 people were forcibly moved to the roadsides near towns. Today, 51,060 square kilometres of north-eastern CAR (an area two and a half times the size of Wales) are consecrated as parkland (Blom *et al.*, 2004), with additional land dedicated to no-go safari hunting catchment zones.[7] All of eastern CAR has been designated a Zone of Hunting Interest (*zone d'intérêt cynégetique*). CAR has the highest proportion of its territory (31 per cent) dedicated to safari hunting of any country in Africa (Binot *et al.*, 2006). Many laws regulate this industry. For instance, only male animals are to be shot; females and young animals should be left to reproduce. In practice, though, these rules are frequently and secretly broken (Van der Elsken, 1958). Because hunting takes place in areas that are difficult to keep under surveillance, hunting ethics are defined more by personal honour or professionalism than by law (Roulet, 2004). But at the same time as ivory hunting was flourishing, in its niche way, the number of illicit ivory hunters and herders taking advantage of the area's green pastures was on the rise as well.[8] These dynamics justified a more bellicose approach to parkland interlopers.

Renewed militarization and armed conservation

From the late 1970s onward, even remote parts of the region were affected by war. The autonomous zone was too remote, unpopulated, and difficult to traverse for it to represent a valuable military objective, though it may have served infrequently as a rear base (Lombard, 2007). It was, however, a site where the region's political–military entrepreneurs could pursue a range of other militarized economic activities (ivory hunting, cattle-herding, road-robbing). At the same time, desertification was driving herders southward.[9] Beginning in the late 1970s, the autonomous zone became important for large-scale hunting (particularly of elephants) and herding by well-armed people with connections to military, rebel and commercial leaders in Chad and Sudan. The autonomous zone became an attractive site for cattle-rustling and road-robbing (Marchal, 2009), leading to a vicious cycle of militarization and the entrenchment of arms-carrying (toward whatever end) as one of the region's primary money-generating occupations (Thomas, 2010, 97).

The combination of desertification, 'industrialized' elephant hunting and cattle-herding justified the armed patrols of the area's parklands that began in earnest in the mid-1980s. Since then, conservation patrols have been carried out by parastatal militiamen, private associations, French soldiers, and safari hunting concession operators and their guards. Armed conservation's proponents frequently see it as a stop-gap and a first step toward 'the state' taking enforceable control of the area and its resources and ending the situation of pluralized authorities that has characterized the area for more than 150 years. However, 'the state' has remained absent. Instead, armed conservation has intensified localized dynamics whereby people maintain access to competing livelihood strategies through shows/threats of force and hiding.

Much of what now goes on in this zone can be hidden, and people have learned to hedge their bets by seeking rents wherever they can, and playing opposing interests off each other. In a militarized context, this can become a driver of violence.[10] The parties to these interactions share rhetoric about the importance of 'the state', but they also operate in atomized ways, and villages sometimes find themselves pitted against each other in attempts to regulate access to the area and its resources. In the case of armed conservation, people living in the autonomous zone hold on to the state as utopian ideal, but in so doing are distracted from thinking through practical ways in which their lives might be improved. And they are not the only ones who fetishize the state: diplomats and donors who seek to intervene there, such as the European Union (the main source of conservation funding in the autonomous zone from the mid-1980s into the present) also see the state as the ideal form to respond to the area's challenges, without any realistic expectation that it will have any significant role in the conflict.

Beginning in 1987, the EU financed conservation, including anti-poaching militias, in north-eastern CAR. The first of these, the Programme de Développement de la Région Nord (PDRN), lasted from 1987–2000. The PDRN was the largest governing undertaking the autonomous zone had seen since Sanusi. Heavy equipment was brought into the area to build roads and bases in the parklands (which is now disused and broken down). The PDRN became known simply as 'the Project' – the lack of a further qualifier owing to its uniqueness in living memory. It was followed by the Ecosystèmes Forestiers de l'Afrique Centrale (ECOFAC) in 2000–2004 and 2007–2010. In the 2004–2007 funding gap, a private outfit, the Association pour la Protection de la Faune Centrafricaine (APFC), took over, with anti-poaching headed by mercenaries with weapons-procurement connections in Russia. Their units became known for terror tactics, such as ambushes and desecrating bodies. The Ecosystèmes Fauniques du Nord-Est (ECOFAUNE), another EU endeavour, was slated to continue the conservation agenda in 2011, but was repeatedly delayed due to bureaucratic wrangling and then war.

New tensions among the area's plural authorities

New modes of surveillance stemming from armed conservation intensified collaboration and conflict among the autonomous zone's disparate neighbours. Armed conservation helped the struggling safari hunting industry. And yet in the early years of the PDRN, safari hunting operators were among some of the Project's anti-poaching guards' main opponents – in at least a stealthy way. The most notorious in this regard was Manovo A/S, a concession managed by the Laboureur family, principally *pere* Jean and *fils* Matthieu. In the 1960s, they took on a concession in the autonomous zone that was officially the size of Swaziland (unofficially, they made use of additional parkland space as well). After leaving for part of the Bokassa era, they returned in the early 1980s. In his memoir *Sans défense* (1988), Matthieu Laboureur describes ambushing and killing a handful of people he described as illegal poachers, as well as their donkeys and other pack animals. Laboureur justified his shoot-first policy because, he wrote, he could as easily be killed by his adversaries. The Laboureurs, according to Project leaders, acted as sovereigns, and they resented getting pushed out of the areas they alone knew, and that they alone had protected, by newcomers without that knowledge and long-term commitment. The Project leaders, meanwhile, saw themselves as bringing rationality and science to domains that the hunting guides knew personally. The shooting dead of a PDRN employee – he was clearing trails that would facilitate LAB (*lutte anti-braconnage* – the anti-poaching struggle) surveillance – by one of the Laboureurs became the symbol of a widening rift between the two groups. Jean Laboureur said the man was a poacher and a foreigner, since he was not speaking Sango. As a result of the killing (which most people in the area were sure had actually been done by his son) he had to leave the country but was not otherwise punished.

Why did apparent allies in the conservation struggle take such a hostile stance to each other? The personalities of the people involved played a role, but the animosity also stemmed from their potential to disrupt each other as they engaged in simultaneous 'rival resource use regimes' (Hardin, 2000) – that is, sometimes sidestepping the conservation laws they at other times enforced. The EU conservation archives are replete with incidents in which *pisteurs* and game-lodge operators were found hunting animals or mining in protected areas. A theme in all of these accounts is the difficulty of enforcement. Unless the sanction is applied non-judicially – in which case it is usually death, justified on the grounds of 'legitimate self-defence' in an encounter between poacher and guard – everyone agrees that the punisher should be 'the state'. But the state never responds. For instance, in 1994 a group of *pisteurs* surprised Matthieu Laboureur and a client hunting in the Sangba Ecosystem Protection Zone, an area where human activity is prohibited. Laboureur and his client had killed two baboons illegally and were hanging leopard bait when the guards discovered them. The guards' leader wrote,

> This transgression is very serious, principally because it was done by a concessionaire and a hunting guide, in an area with the status of national park. We transmitted our report to the Minister, but no sanction has been applied. In contrast, he has received his permit to be a hunting guide! (PDRN, 1995; emphasis in original).[11]

The autonomous zone is not stateless; though the guides were not punished, they did take the time to secure permits. Rather, because of the ways people *experience* the state as absent, laws and other state dictates become flexible forms from which a wide range of actors draw some livelihoods and authority, yet without ever seeing themselves as the (proper) authorities.

Idongo, the Project's 'model village', is another example of how people develop rival resource-use practices. In 2003, Idongo was the subject of several glowing journalistic accounts, including a profile on the French–German television channel *Arte*, which described how the safari hunting revenues the village received in exchange for agreeing to refrain from hunting had transformed village life. Now, in Idongo, 'the elderly have a right to a small pension' ('A Idongo, les anciens ont droit meme a une petite pension', 2003)![12] But later that year, the anti-poaching guards caught several people from the village hunting in a protected area and seized six guns. The following night the *pisteurs* caught the son of the president of the Idongo conservation committee hunting. Jean-Baptiste Mamang-Kanga, then head of the anti-poaching base near Idongo, called Sangba, who was washing up for church the morning after the arrests when he heard shots from an AK-47. An angry crowd confronted him outside. He estimated that there were three or four hundred people destroying a radio post and attempting to confiscate the *pisteurs*' weapons. Members of the crowd were shooting (mostly in the air) and threatening the *pisteurs*. One *pisteur* had his clothes ripped from his back. The captured Idongans were released, with détente between the Idongans and the *pisteurs*.

The destruction of the radio post showed local anger over being monitored and a desire to cut off the *pisteurs*' privileged access to people and resources in the capital and beyond. Another incident that year also demonstrates the importance of radio posts. An Italian biologist had outfitted three Lord Derby elands (the largest of all antelopes, found only in CAR and Benin, and safari hunters' most-sought-after prize) with radio collars so that he could monitor their movements and health. Over the course of six months, two collared elands were killed. Local people understood the animals' importance to the struggling safari industry; they killed them because they believed the collars were for keeping their own activities under surveillance (Pampaloni, 2003). Idongans worked for conservation – but not to the extent that it would crowd out other livelihood strategies. They welcomed the rationality of conservation management, while also pursuing other projects.

Cattleherders (some of whom also hunt on a wide scale) frequently get caught in villagers' livelihood-generating projects.[13] Many of the disputes that result centre on the flexible, imprecise and atomized terms of the *taxe de pacage* (grazing tax). In many places, herders pay a *taxe de pacage* to local chiefs. (There are official *taxes de pacage* levied by the mayors' offices, but these seem less frequently harvested than unofficial ones.) For instance, when they started arriving in 2001, Mbororo herders displaced into south-eastern CAR from the Democratic Republic of the Congo and what is now South Sudan paid a fee of 1,000 CFA francs per cow to the Sultan Pombolo (in Mboki) to use the land near the Chinko River. This arrangement became annual. Though it brings revenues to the sultanate, farmers in the area see these herders as having caused other problems, especially a rise in insecurity due to the *coupeurs de route* who often follow the herders, known to these robbers as *banquiers ambulants* – walking ATMs – thanks to their cows (Bonal et al., 2008).

Other chiefs or officials who do not receive *taxes de pacage*, often call on anti-poaching militiamen or local defence forces to chase the same herders out. In 2009, four members of an anti-poaching militia unit at Gordil, including the foreign 'technical assistant' leading them, were transporting a guard – injured during a battle with hunters – to the closest airstrip, at Tiringoulou, to be evacuated to Bangui. As they traversed the park, they found a large cattle herd. Though the guards wanted to shoot at the cows, the technical assistant convinced them not to, since they were too few to defend themselves – or, for that matter, the nearby villages – should the herders retaliate. At the first village they passed, Mele, the chief waved down their vehicle. He implored them to shoot the cattle. When they refused, the chief produced twenty armed villagers to accompany them. After making sure that the chief understood that the anti-poaching unit could not stay to protect the village, the technical assistant doled out ammunition to the assembled local forces. During the resulting firefight, one herder was killed. The next day, '*janjaweed*'[14] (some observers said forty, others eighty) surrounded Mele and held the village hostage. They demanded a blood payment of ten million CFA francs (about US$20,000). Contributions from throughout the area eventually freed the village. Given the high level of armament among the local (farming) population, it is unlikely that herders would have been allowed so close without paying some kind of tax, but in the absence of either an overarching authority or a process of mediation, these arrangements' terms are always up for dispute, especially when one leader does not agree with a neighbour's decision. About a month later, the Gordil anti-poaching base found itself surrounded by hundreds of armed herders/*janjaweed*. The anti-poaching unit retreated, deeming it impossible to do effective work there. The tensions and outright conflict around armed conservation – including among people who are ostensibly allies – draw out the ways in which many people in the area simultaneously avow interest in the existence of a more-effective unitary authority and actively pursue ways of maintaining autonomy and possibilities for escape from oversight. Rebellion, to which I will next turn, is the latest instantiation of this two-faced tendency.

The arrival of rebellion

Though the idea with armed conservation was that it would contribute to establishing unitary control over north-eastern CAR, in fact it strengthened and entrenched the pluralized authorities who, whether they drew benefit from conservation or not, also sought to maintain access to competing sources of revenues. The Caliph Yaya Ramadan was a good example of how armed conservation strengthened pluralized authorities, and the fallout from his engagement in armed conservation contributed to the creation of the UFDR. Ramadan, a prominent figure in the region, lived in an area that stood to profit from safari hunting revenues. He rallied men into a militia that would patrol the area and for these efforts received gasoline and ammunition from the conservation project. In May 2002, two days after Ramadan had himself killed two 'poachers' (one carried a *taxe de pacage* receipt from a chief in Mossabio, near the border with Chad) and nine donkeys and confiscated 1,500 kg of meat, herders killed Ramadan. The Caliph's supporters rallied for vengeance, and raids by them and their opponents, which lasted until 2005, killed hundreds. Moreover, while initially the Caliph's supporters had been ethnically diverse, suspicions arose over the course of the battles and mistrust and hostility between Gula (like Ramadan) and Runga grew.

In 2006, a mysterious plane landed near Tiringoulou, the Caliph's home, and offloaded military equipment and armed men – Chadian rebels who disappeared into the bush to the north. When locals managed to get word to the authorities in Bangui, Presidential Guard soldiers sent to the area accused the locals of complicity and attacked them. Angry, the Ramadan-avenging militia regrouped, this time drawing others from the region into their ranks. Another factor also pushed them to rebel: when the government promoted anti-poaching guards and made them employees of the Ministry of Water and Forests, not a single *pisteur* from north-eastern most Vakaga prefecture was chosen, despite the fact that the Vakagans comprised the majority of anti-poaching guards (though parastatal projects paid more money in the short term, they offered far less job security than a state post). Vakagans felt their only way of being taken seriously was to threaten violence.

At some point, their leader, Zakaria Damane, made an alliance with Abakar Sabone, a former 'liberator'[15] from Vakaga who split with Bozizé, and Michel Djotodia, then a Central African diplomat to Nyala.[16] The newly-christened UFDR launched a surprise attack on Birao on 30 October 2006. They then took one town after another until they were eventually turned back by French and Central African soldiers at the end of that year. Damane subsequently signed a peace agreement with the government, but Djotodia refused and quietly sought a new opportunity to take power. When I met UFDR fighters in 2009 to 2010, they were waiting for a promised DDR programme.

At the end of 2012, they somewhat reluctantly joined Djotodia's Seleka in its assault on Bangui. In the ensuing war, former anti-poaching guards have taken important rebel positions. Zindeko is only the most prominent. They have turned the military tactics they learned for the anti-poaching struggle to new ends, using them to train fellow fighters. When I asked UFDR members (in 2009 and 2010) about their decision to take up arms, they were unanimous in ascribing it to their 'abandonment' by the government and treatment as foreigners whenever they travelled out of the autonomous zone and toward the capital. They also cited the Presidential Guard attacks on their towns and villages in 2006. Their desire for inclusion and for a state to care for them was sincere. And yet, embedded, as they were, in a region simultaneously atomized and militarized, and not subject to exclusive surveillance, they also worked to maintain access to livelihoods that required 'escaping' from any attempts at enforcement of state laws.

Most international attention (donors, diplomats) to CAR has focused on either the lack of access people have to state services or to the ways that they appreciate escaping it, but rarely are these two tendencies considered together, as equally valid stances toward state power. This failure to recognize the usefulness of an exit option – for both elites and rural folk – has compromised efforts to establish more accountable, coherent governance relationships.

Conclusion

The current war in CAR is symptomatic of the two general trends, both for and against the consolidation of state power. The area's history of violent raiding and the legal/social bind that it has produced are directly responsible for this state of affairs.

These two trends are inherent in the political dynamics of an autonomous zone. Whether the zone is naturally an 'eater of men' (Oubangui-Chari ND) or was made dangerous and remote by political–economic processes over the last 150 years, its isolation has only increased in the wake of Anti-Balaka/Seleka violence. The desire to secede is the latest expression of the fetishized position that 'the state' occupies here. Rebellion – whose fighters see it as a way of 'shocking' (a word many used in my interviews with them) the state into providing for them – has taken over from armed conservation (and in part grew out of it) as the main mode through which the armed aspects of this ambivalent position play out. The militarization of conservation efforts and the militarization of their foes have resulted in a rise in human–human conflict over the past twenty-five years. If, during years of stepped-up anti-poaching presence, its proponents can cite a reduction in the number of large animals killed, that reduction has quickly been erased during breaks in project funding cycles. Experiences with armed conservation in the Central African autonomous zone suggest that belligerent tactics do little to protect animals while heightening tensions and conflicts between human users of the space.

It has become ever more difficult to do something about this state of affairs; even the Uganda People's Defence Force (UPDF) – certainly among the best-equipped and best-trained armies in the region – has been soundly bested by hunters. On 26 May 2010, a contingent of Ugandan soldiers based in eastern CAR, with the objective of fighting the Lord's Resistance Army (LRA) went out on patrol. About twenty[17] returned to Uganda dead. Many questions arose surrounding the killing of these soldiers. The LRA, just a few hundred fighters living in a dispersed fashion, could not have launched such an attack. Military officials later claimed the culprits were poachers, but no definitive answers have emerged. In short, the most threatening elements in the area may be the least-known, and armed actors can slip away into the bush, as the writer of the colonial intelligence report (Oubangui-Chari, ND) cited in the introduction foresaw.

North-eastern CAR is not the world's only autonomous zone. Many other remote spots experience the bind of legal inclusion/effective exclusion. With militarization, such a position becomes not just one of refuge, like those sought by the state-avoiding Zomians Scott describes (2009), but one of violence, structural and otherwise. Changing these dynamics will require more than initiatives designed to bolster 'the state'. It will require fundamental re-thinking of the relationships of governance and modes of inclusion and exclusion that crisscross the autonomous zone and tie it into the broader region, which create a tangled web of nationality-transcending interests. Such a re-thinking would require minute attention to micro-dynamics that simultaneously recognizes the ways they are embedded in further-flung relationships of governance and sociability. The state – whether considered as an ideal type or as an assortment of actors and projects – is poorly positioned to respond to such a challenge. Rebellion has not been able to do so, either, and people in the autonomous zone feel more abandoned than ever.

Notes

1 The prefectures in question are primarily Vakaga, Haut Kotto, and Bamingui-Bangoran.
2 Zindeko was also a member of the UFDR.
3 Interview, Tiringoulou, CAR, October 2009.
4 They resemble, in many cases, those zones of South East Asia that James C. Scott (2009) referred to as Zomia, a refuge inaccessible to centralized rule.
5 The Central African Armed Forces employ some five thousand people, less than a third of them operational (Spittaels and Hilgert, 2009).
6 Marchal (2009) states that of six million people in the region at the outset of late-eighteenth and nineteenth century slave trades, only one million remained by the beginning of the twentieth.
7 ECOFAC (Ecosystèmes Forestiers de l'Afrique Centrale) covered 85,000 square kilometres, or about the area of Austria.
8 As early as 1959, the administrator at Birao exhorted his higher-ups to take action against pastoralism and hunting, which he portrayed as grave, related problems threatening regional security and economic viability. In fact, herding and hunting were productive industries. But because they evaded taxation, they were vilified. 'Other than at the border, in all the places where the pastoralists cannot be monitored, it is certain that arms in great quantities pass as they do every year, by the poachers.' In addition to causing the 'total disappearance' of the rhinoceros, 'Everywhere the pastoralists

pass, desert sets in'. He lobbied for the dispatch of two airplanes to Birao for better surveillance, as well as the interdiction of all horses from entering CAR. (Hunters and herders used horses for transport.) Neither measure ever came into being, though the colonial military did carry out patrols during which they killed cows found in parklands, a practice that their parastatal anti-poaching successors have continued (see below).

9   By the turn of the twenty-first century, Lake Chad – the source of many of the area's rivers – was 10 per cent of its 1960s size (Tomety, 2009).

10 These themes are elaborated on in Louisa Lombard, 2012; Lombard, 2015 (in preparation); and Lombard (in preparation).

11 By the mid-1990s it had become clear to most game lodge operators and Project staffers that they would have to collaborate, at least somewhat, and safari hunters began to contribute to the salaries of LAB 'technical assistants' (AT, freelance military trainers). By ECOFAC IV, which ran from 2007 to 2010, the LAB ATs, though they had EU contracts, were funded by the safari hunters' association. At the same time, given the escalation in armed conflict between the *pisteurs* and their opponents, it had become necessary to shift the criteria in AT hiring. No longer was ecological expertise a prerequisite for the job. Now, the emphasis was on finding someone who would know how to keep himself from getting killed, such as former Parachutists (the French Special Forces).

12 Because it lay beside profitable safari hunting outfits, as of 2002 Idongo alone accounted for more than 60 per cent of the total revenues of the nine ZCVs (*zones cynégétiques villageoises*, Lloveras, 2002) and so if any ZCV was to succeed, it would have been Idongo.

13 Cattleherders in the autonomous zone are highly diverse. They can be divided into two broad categories. First, there are herders in family groups with small numbers of cattle. They tend not to be well-armed or belligerent. Then there are young men guiding herds of cattle on their own, who are well-armed and who hunt and smoke meat on a massive scale. They are financed by bosses in places like Nyala, in South Darfur, and are by reputation much more hostile.

14 This is the term of choice in the region for mobile guns-for-hire from the Chad/Darfur borderlands.

15 This is the term used to denote those who helped Bozizé seize power in 2003. Most liberators were from Chad, Sabone included.
16 Interview, Tiringoulou, CAR, March 2010.
17 This according to military sources; other estimates vary from ten to fifty-eight.

Bibliography

'A Idongo, les anciens ont droit meme a une petite pension' (2003) *Agence France-Presse – AFP*, 10 May.

Antonetti (1929) Letter (Untitled), Archives Nationales de l'outre-mer (ANOM).

Bierschenk, T. and J.P. Olivier de Sardan (1997) 'Local Powers and a Distant State in Rural Central African Republic', *The Journal of Modern African Studies*, Volume 35, Number 3.

Binot, A., V. Castel and A. Caron (2006) 'L'interface faune-bétail en Afrique Subsaharienne', *Science et changements planétaires/Sécheresse*, Volume 17, Issue 1.

Blom, A., J. Yamindou and H.H.T. Prins (2004) 'Status of the Protected Areas of the Central African Republic', *Biological Conservation*, Volume 118, pp. 479–487.

Bonal, E., I. Templaar and P. De Munck (2008) 'Etude sur les Dynamiques et les Perspectives de Gestion de la Transhumance transfrontalière et interne dans les préfectures de la Vakaga et la Bamingui-Bangoran en RCA', Intermediate Report, *Agrifor Consult*, Isnes, Belgium.

Brégeon, J. (1998) *Un Rêve d'Afrique: Administrateurs en Oubangui-Chari, la Cendrillon de l'Empire*, Denoël, Paris.

Cordell, D. (1985) *Dar al-Kuti and the Last Years of the Trans-Saharan Slave Trade*, University of Wisconsin Press, Madison, WI, US.

Cordell, D. (2002) 'Des 'réfugiés' dans l'Afrique précoloniale?', *Politique Africaine*, no. 85, pp. 16–28.

'Entre Oubangui et Chari vers 1890.' (Recherches oubangiennes, 6), *Service de Publication du Laboratoire d'Ethnologie et de Sociologie Comparative*, Université de Paris X, Nanterre, France.

Gauze, R. (1958) *Oubangui-Chari: Paradis du Tourisme Cynégétique*, Ozanne, Caen, France.

Hardin, R. (2000) 'Translating the Forest: Tourism, Trophy Hunting, and the Transformation of Forest Use in the Southwestern Central

African Republic,' Unpublished PhD thesis, Yale University, New Haven, CT, US.

Laboureur, M. (1988) *Sans défense*, Lafon, Paris.

Lejoly, M. (ed.) (1959) on 'everywhere the herders pass', extract of a report edited 16 April 1959, Administrateur en Chef de la France d'Outre-Mer, Chef du District Autonome de BIRAO et addressé à M. Le Ministre de l'agriculture, de l'elevage, des eaux, forêts et chasses de la République Centrafricaine. Service Historique de la Défense, Vincennes, France, Carton 6H 47.

Lignier (1936), 'Rapport du 3eme trimestre par le chef de subdivision', *Archives nationales de l'Outre-Mer (ANOM)*, 30 September.

Lloveras, J. (2002) 'Reflexions sur le programme ECOFAC en RCA, Composante ZCV', *European Commission*, Bangui, 15 March.

Lombard, L. (2007) 'A Widening War around Sudan', *Small Arms Survey*, Geneva.

Lombard, L. (2012) 'Raiding Sovereignty in Central African Borderlands', Unpublished PhD thesis, Duke University, Durham, NC, US. Available from: <http://dukespace.lib.duke.edu/dspace/bitstream/handle/10161/5861/Lombard_duke_0066D_11603.pdf?sequence=1>.

Lombard, L. (2015, in preparation) 'Camouflage and Violence in Armed Conservation and Rebellion in the Central African Republic'.

Lombard, L. (in preparation) *Hunting Game: Politics in an African Frontier* (provisional title).

Londres, A. (2006 [1929]) *Terre d'Ebène: La Traite des Noirs*, Group Privat/Le Rocher, Paris.

Marchal, R. (2009) 'Aux marges du monde en Afrique Centrale', *Les Etudes du CERI*, Paris.

Modat (1909) Letter 48, dated 30 November 1909, *Archives nationales de l'Outre-Mer (ANOM)*, Carton 6H 124.

Oubangui-Chari (ND) Présentation sommaire du territoire de l'Oubangui-Chari, marked 'très secret', *Service Historique de l'Armée de la Terre*, 6H 127.

Pampaloni, C. (2003) Note du Dossier—ECOFAC ZCV, *European Commission*, Bangui, (September 12).

PDRN (Programme de Developpement de la Region Nord) (1995), 'Rapport d'activites pour l'année de programme 1994–1995', *NORCADEV*, Bangui.

Prioul, C. (1982) 'Entre Oubangui et Charí vers 1890', *Service de Publication du Laboratoire d'Ethnologie et de Sociologie Comparative*, Recherches Oubangiennes, 6, Université de Paris X, Nanterre.

Prins, Pierre (1907) on Sanusi as a foreigner, 'L'Islam et les musulmans étrangers dans les sultanats du Haut Oubangui', *Renseignements Coloniaux: Bulletin du Comité de l'Afrique Française*, 17(6): pp. 136–142 and 17(7): pp. 163–173.

Roulet, P.A. (2004) 'Chasseur blanc, Coeur noir? La Chasse sportive en Afrique Centrale: Une analyse de son rôle dans la conservation de la faune sauvage et le développement rural au travers des programmes de gestion de la chasse communautaire,' Unpublished PhD thesis, University of Orleans, LA, US.

Santandrea, S. (1964) *A Tribal History of the Western Bahr El Ghazal*, Editrice Negrizia, Bologna, Italy.

Scott, J.C. (2009) *The Art of Not Being Governed*, Yale University Press, New Haven, CT, US.

Sikainga, A.A. (1990) *The Western Bahr al-Ghazal Under British Rule, 1898–1956*, Ohio University Press, Athens, OH, US.

Spittaels, S. and F. Hilgert (2009) 'Mapping Conflict Motives: Central African Republic', *International Peace Information Service*, Antwerp, Belgium, 17 February.

Thomas, E. (2010) *The Kafia-Kingi Enclave: People, Politics, and History in the North-South Boundary Zone of Western Sudan*, Rift Valley Institute, London/Nairobi.

Tomety, S.N. (2009) 'Analyse de la dimension transfrontalière des conflits ruraux dans l'Est de la République Centrafricaine', *European Commission*, Bangui.

Van der Elsken, E. (1958) *Bagara*, De Bezige Bij, Cape Town.

8 CAR and the Regional (Dis)order

Roland Marchal

The crisis in the Central African Republic (CAR) did not start on 5 December 2013, when French forces intervened a few hours after Resolution 2127 was passed at the United Nations Security Council. It took months for the international community at large to reluctantly recognize that a creeping civil war was unfolding in a small country only known to be the backyard of France. The arguments used to mobilize international attention were based on a recurrent assumption: this was the terrible outcome of a dysfunctional state, unable to deliver minimal services to its population for years, if not decades. This is flawed analysis, and it has led to flawed 'solutions'.

The 'dysfunctional state' argument is indeed flawed on at least two accounts. First, a quick glance at the ability of CAR's neighbours like Cameroon, Chad, Congo-Brazzaville, Sudan, and South Sudan to deliver services and public goods to their respective populations on the border with CAR, shows that these communities are already peripheries in their own countries, as this capacity is reduced at best. If such a challenge to the social fabric were to take place in CAR, it should therefore also happen in those neighbouring areas. This has not been the case despite the flow of refugees and military clashes at the borders. This analytical discrepancy is rooted in a normative understanding of what the state is supposed to be and to do that ignores other important parameters. This argument ignores, for instance, that although neighbours, national situations are rather distinctive and the state does not always or everywhere have a central role in defining how livelihoods on the ground are shaped. To a large extent, this criticism could be extended to the very state-centric approach of international paradigms such as fragility or state collapse. The state, arguably, collapsed in many of CAR's regions years ago but this did not produce the violence witnessed in 2013 and 2014.

A second flaw is that the 'dysfunctional state' argument does not pay much attention to another systemic dimension – the fact that CAR is part of a regional system of states as historical sociology has taught us.[1] As is explained elsewhere, one could argue that the CAR state actually works the way it does because of the ways it fits into a regional process of state building. State building processes in the region have been extremely violent and characterized by internal wars and high levels of coercion. It is easy to recall the Sudan wars, the Chadian episodes of prolonged conflict, and also the way Zaire/DRC has been ruled since independence. This 'regressive crystallization of state building' also had a dramatic impact on the CAR polity (Shaw, 2001).

This raises an important question, namely how the region has dramatically impacted the growth of the CAR polity, well beyond the last decade. CAR has to be seen as a 'periphery of peripheries' (Cordell, 1985) and logically inherits some of its weaknesses from that situation. The endless crisis in Darfur, the growing discontent in southern Chad, the spillover of Boko Haram in northern Cameroon and the ongoing instability in DRC, not to mention the collapse of the new political order in South Sudan all impact in a way that explains some of the current predicament faced by the CAR population and the challenges to the CAR state.

Very few structural improvements are likely in CAR if the regional environment remains the same as it has been over the last two decades. Improvements are not impossible – at one time the independent CAR state performed much better than it does today – but one must identify the causes restricting the state's capacity to deliver. The 2013–2014 crisis and the difficulty of restoring some kind of normalcy, despite the presence of thousands of African and French peacekeepers, raises several questions about the regional management of what by June 2013 was a predictable crisis and also points to longer-term issues, including relations with Chad, forced migration, the shape of regional elites, and the culture of illegality that may have a profound influence on the way the CAR state is able to function and respond in the future to grievances raised by its population.

One further confusion should be avoided. A reading of this past history may give the impression that CAR's fate has been more in the hands of foreigners than under the control of its own elites. This narrative was re-enforced at the moment of the French/AU/UN military intervention, when Central African elites relied on foreign money but also on external conditionalities. Such a narrative is very popular among the Central African lay population, but leaves out a crucial interrogation on the nature of its elites and the multiple connections built over time with their regional counterparts (often through the former colonial power).[2] While reactions from the rulers of CAR may often sound parochial and short-sighted, they are the outcome of an extraversion that goes beyond a dialogue involving relatives, friends, or decision makers in Paris. This extraversion may be one of the many problems faced by elites who have long forgotten their own populations for the sake of getting co-opted elsewhere.

Coping with the region (1800–1959)

At a time when the issues of Islam and autochthony are the cornerstones of the Central African political debate, it is useful to remind readers how this country has been shaped by traumatic events in the last two centuries, including the slave trade, colonialism, and their direct or unintended consequences, such as forced migration.

The consequences of the nineteenth-century slave trade on the region cannot be over-stated. Dramatic demographic changes illustrate the magnitude of this disruption (Cordell, 2002). Many CAR intellectuals would say that, by the end of the eighteenth century, the territory of what is nowadays CAR would have had a larger population than today. The very low population density seen today in eastern CAR is not a consequence of the environment, but of the catastrophe induced by the slave raids more than a century ago.

In a matter of less than a century, ethnic groups such as the Banda and the Gbaya, which today make up the majority of the Central African population, moved into CAR to escape slave raids and find fragile sanctuaries. The Banda came from Darfur in the middle of the nineteenth century to run away from the Waddai and Darfur Sultanates. In about the 1820s, the Gbaya escaped from the Fulbe Adamawa Kingdom in northern Cameroon, which they confronted again later in the nineteenth century. Autochthony is therefore rooted in a very contemporary (and traumatic) moment.

Slave raids also provoked major societal changes. The best way to escape them was to run away and get deeper in the savannah at the risk of dying in a hostile environment. Another strategy was to give up life in small hamlets and gather in bigger villages easier to defend – the Gbaya, Bada, Manza, Banda, and Sara ethnic groups used this method with some success. But, these concentrations of population also created conditions for the break out of smallpox epidemics that decimated local communities.

To put it mildly, French colonization was not exactly executed in order to provide peace, security, and development either. France had little interest in the Central African territory itself. Its conquest was intended to pre-empt further Belgian, German, and British colonial ambitions. The borders of what currently defines CAR were slowly agreed by negotiating different treaties with other colonial powers. Throughout the first decades of French rule, the simple idea that the territory deserved attention and care was much beyond the thinking of the colonial state apparatus.

Even when Paris decided in the 1920s to end the concessionary way of governing CAR and enforced a more orthodox way to rule, it mostly failed to improve the fate of the local population. The poll tax, porterage, and the construction of the Congo-Ocean railway were as lethal before as they were after the colonial reform of the mid-1920s. Funding was not available and most colonial policies in CAR were created to gain high profits, regardless of the human costs. The colonial administration even after the Second World War was not specifically enlightened as the political struggle and suspicious 1959 plane crash of Central African national leader Barthélemy Boganda tragically illustrates (Kalck, 1974; Kinata, 2008).

This period, nevertheless, brought important changes. The first one, not obvious given the lack of infrastructure and interest, was a certain sense of regional belonging for the meagre elites. This was tangible in the political agenda set up by Barthélemy Boganda – the United States of Latin Africa was made up of the countries that belonged to French Equatorial Africa (AEF) but also included Cameroon and Belgian Congo. Beyond the federalist argument that was discussed (and given up) by most African nationalists long before the Second World War, there was also a sense that CAR was not ready for independence and needed more cadres, who could be found elsewhere in AEF.

The capital of AEF was Brazzaville and people used the Oubangui River to travel there. Chad also became an important place, not only because of the extension of cotton growth that eventually became a major agricultural output in CAR as well, but also because it provided most of the trading class in Bangui, Bambari, and other big cities at a time when native traders were few.

The inability of the colonial regime to organize in a decent manner the transition to independence was reflected in the very limited number of educated natives and the strong dependence on outsiders, either from the region or France, to provide the administrative staff for the independent state (Kalck, 1974). A major consequence of this situation was the centrality France had for years after independence for the elites. In the 1980s and 1990s French people were still perceived as superior and that whatever came from France was higher in quality and value.[3]

Regional connections were also built through religious networks that played an important role in the colonization (especially the Catholic Church) and in propagating the Sango language in large parts of the territory (the New Testament was translated into Sango by 1937 and the Old Testament a few years after by Protestant clerics who created more than 200 parishes before 1939).

Schooling also played a part because Central African students could travel to neighbouring countries to get educated either as a priest or a clerk. These connections eventually became crucial when Masonic and Rosicrucian societies grew at the dawn of independence and in the following decades. Those secret societies at first recruited mostly individuals who were politically or culturally acquainted with colonial administrators, but soon grew on their own terms. They became a way to select elites, to get protected (the rule being that Freemasons should protect each other and not revert to violence when competition occurs), and to also build new networks beyond ethnicity or political means. Since the independence decades Freemasonry has become an important regional forum and network in Central Africa thanks to the role of Congo-Brazzaville President Denis Sassou Nguesso and the late President Omar Bongo of Gabon, who recurrently funded its activities. It is an important aspect, though not an overwhelming one, that should be considered in many situations. Rosicrucians in Central as in West Africa, did not enjoy the same success, though they had some significance when André Kolingba was the president of CAR (1981–1993). Student associations were also a fantastic regional melting pot and became a necessary conduit for having access to or becoming *'les grands monsieurs'* (Gagliardi-Baysse, 2008).

The French neo-colonial order and the Chadian civil war (1960–1990)

For over two decades after independence in August 1960, the French sway over CAR was overwhelming and regional players had little to say. The reasons were rooted in Paris's interest in keeping a strong influence in its former colonies to consolidate its international status, and not offer a divergent alternative to more important countries of the region such as Congo-Brazzaville or Gabon, where oil was already exploited by French companies. The east/west competition also obliged Paris to enforce a western order on its former colonies. Furthermore, the activism of Muammar Qaddafi who took over Tripoli in September 1969, added a regional dimension that shaped events up to his death in 2011. Had he been alive in 2012 and 2013, the Seleka crisis would have unfolded in a quite different (if not better) way.

A first warning shot for France was the visit to Tripoli made by Jean-Bédel Bokassa in 1976 and his conversion to Islam, a religious move followed nearly instantly by several members of his cabinet, including Ange-Félix Patassé. While few in Paris or Bangui were concerned by Bokassa embracing Islam, many more were by the impact an alliance between Tripoli and Bangui could have on the civil war in Chad, since Qaddafi had made it clear from the early 1970s that France should leave, and Chadian and Libyan influence on that country should be uncontested. However, Bokassa wanted to become emperor and in the typical schizophrenia of Françafrique, decision makers in Paris mocked the coronation and yet funded the ceremony as a proof of reconciliation.

This alert would become a main concern in the following years due to new developments in Ndjamena. In 1978, Hissène Habré and the then Chad President, Félix Malloum, struck a deal in Khartoum that allowed Hissène Habré to become Prime Minister in Ndjamena. A few months later, in February 1979, violent incidents changed into riots, and fighting broke out in Ndjamena. This period was the very moment when Chadian politics, which had previously centred on 'southerners' from independence onward, shifted in favour of 'northerners'. As a consequence of the killings in the capital city, many southerners escaped Ndjamena and went to their ethnic homeland (Buijtenhuijs, 1987; Lemarchand, 1986). Discussions then took off to declare a Logone Republic, independent from northern Chad and possibly annexing a part of CAR that had many ethnic commonalities with the other side of the border. Those debates became more vivid in 1982 when Hissène Habré, who had been expelled from Ndjamena in 1980 and was a refugee in Darfur, fought his way back to Ndjamena thanks to US, French, and Sudanese support. For the following two years, he and his associates (including Idriss Déby Itno) waged war in southern Chad to enforce the authority of the new regime at the cost of huge displacements of population and violent coercion.

This episode of the Chadian civil war had many consequences for CAR. First of all, many Chadians looked for refuge in CAR and they were not only southern Chadians, but Arabs from the Salamat region whose allegiance went to a faction opposed to Habré. Some stayed near the border, but many fighters actually settled in cities with their kinsmen and became small traders or shopkeepers (Marchal, 2009).

A similar episode was reproduced after December 1990 when Idriss Déby, after an unsuccessful coup attempt in March 1989, was able to come back to Ndjamena victorious, this time supported by strange bedfellows – Sudanese Islamists, France, and Libya. Again, the escape of Hissène Habré's supporters (including many Gorane based in Sahr) from Chad brought about the expansion of a small arms regional market and a growing insecurity in CAR (the early 1990s saw a new episode of highway bandits in north-western CAR).

Meanwhile, Libya had also tried to build an armed opposition in CAR by training activists close to the Mouvement Centrafricain pour la Libération Nationale (MCLN) led by Dr Rudolph Idi Lala, an opponent to Jean-Bédel Bokassa and his successor David Dacko. Libya's efforts were inspired by the perception that those two presidents were France's puppets, or supported attempted coups such as the one orchestrated in March 1982 by a close colleague of André Kolingba (who took over from Dacko in 1981), General Mbaikoua, in Bangui. The overwhelming argument was the increasing availability of weapons and the population shifts of those who had acquired genuine military skills (Marchal, 2009, 32–39).

Despite those events, the relationship between Hissène Habré and André Kolingba was excellent, as they knew they needed each other while France was their best common friend. Indeed, France, once uncontested in Chad, had to face a Libyan interventionism that justified itself by an anti-imperialist rhetoric and was able to mobilize local supporters and mercenaries from all over the region to oppose France and its local clients. French military facilities in CAR (notably in Bangui and Bouar) were extended to provide sanctuary to combat aircraft and, up until 1990, CAR was considered a significant military base for France.

This decade of the 1980s was also a crucial moment for connecting oppositions in both countries. In the 1960s and 1970s, there had been hardly any contact between those who opposed regimes in Ndjamena and Bangui because they were too different in terms of location, ethnicity, and religion. However, new opportunities came up due to the political instability in the two countries. In the early 1980s, opponents were closer both in pure geographical terms, but also culturally and ethnically. This period was the first moment when Chadians and CAR insurgents were involved in the same military adventures. A point of convergence that today has become of renewed importance, is the idea to set up a Logone Republic that would include southern Chad and a variable part of CAR (this has varied a bit depending on the time of, and people involved in, the discussion). While that claim was never really popular on either side of the border, it offered a narrative to protest the behaviour of the respective state and call for a more decentralized, or federal rule of the country.

A dangerous neighbourhood (1990–2003)

The 1990s were more tumultuous and bloody. The regulations of the previous period evaporated. France had lost its stamina to micromanage CAR politics. This was expressed by the dismissal of Colonel Mantion, a French Secret Service operative, who was called the Pro-Consul in Bangui (and closest adviser to President Kolingba) for more than a decade. While they did keep their respective consuls in Gabon and Chad, France also wished to normalize its Africa policy at a time the European Union was becoming a more tangible reality. The Cold War was also over and it could no longer justify military adventures based on the fear that the Soviet Union and its African allies could benefit from a hesitant France. French troops were still present in CAR but their numbers decreased and, after 1996, Paris wanted to close all its military facilities in CAR. This was achieved in 1999, even though a small contingent of the French military stayed behind within a regional or international force.[4]

This new era was well described in the new assessment made in Paris on Chad. Idriss Déby Itno benefited from a paradoxical alliance (France and Libya). In Paris, this meant that the Chadian civil war was over since the sole real patron of any armed opposition to Ndjamena for two decades had been Muammar Qaddafi. However, events were going to prove that not everyone was convinced by this geopolitical argument.

Idriss Déby, despite his commitment to bring democracy and freedom, repeated the mistakes made by his predecessor and quickly had to face several armed groups, either based in the Lake Chad region, in southern Chad, or in Waddai. Initially, those groups had little or no connections with CAR rulers or opposition forces. But events in CAR provided new opportunities to build social and military connections. The newly elected President, Ange-Félix Patassé, did not trust his army and therefore tried to keep it in its barracks rather than deploy it to unsafe areas in the countryside. The state budget was also in dire condition and did not allow ambitious policies to restore law and order in zones that were increasingly considered peripheries.[5] Remnants of armed movements that had fought in Chad or in Darfur (1987–1989) found asylum in CAR, without any difficulties.

A first major consequence was the over-militarization of the herdsmen who moved livestock from Chad to CAR throughout the dry season. While they were always armed, after 1990, their military capability increased dramatically in terms of weapons and skills. This became even truer in the 2000s. Often, Chadian military officers used their own troops or hired former ones to take care of their large livestock. Because of the conflicts in Chad and Darfur, weapons were distributed without much control or were looted from military arsenals by defecting soldiers.

A second consequence that became paramount in the 2000s was that the Chadian community (a loose term as it was never really structured) became an actor *per se* in CAR politics, beyond the usual patronage networks entertained by business people. Ange-Félix Patassé offered hospitality to well-known figures of the armed Chadian opposition such as Adoum Yakoub Kougou, which provoked the outrage of Idriss Déby. The reasons were linked to his wish to increase his leverage in negotiating with Paris but also to a sense of ethnic solidarity. He was a Kaba and was well connected with the Sara, a major ethnic group in South Chad, who accused Idriss Déby of having killed many of their kinsmen between 1982 and 1984 but also in the 1990s, when armed groups tried to control potential oil producing areas.

In 1996 and 1997, mutinies broke out in Bangui mostly over issues related to salaries and corporatist issues concerning the army.[6] To protect himself, as he doubted the good faith of the French contingent, Ange-Félix Patassé armed Chadian residents who often had significant military experience having been active in various Front de Libération Nationale du Tchad (FROLINAT)[7] factions or in Hissène Habré's army. Years before François Bozizé took over Bangui, the population had to come to terms with the fact that its president was actually protected by a Pretorian Guard made up of foreigners, mostly Muslim Chadians.

Libya was somewhat involved in those events. Patassé was an old friend of the Libyan ruler and, as a very talented demagogue, had little to do to convince his interlocutor that he distrusted the French and wanted them to leave (which they eventually did in 1999 despite his request not to do so at the last moment). In 1996 and 1997, Tripoli provided weapons and ammunitions. In 2001, when a more serious coup attempt took place in Bangui, Libya sent troops that were as unimpressive as they had been in Ndjamena twenty years before.

CAR was not made fragile only through its northern border. The wars in Sudan also affected the security situation in the eastern part of the country. As the Anyanya movement in the 1960s, the Sudan People Liberation Movement (SPLM) led by John Garang used to collect gold, diamonds, and ivory to be sold in Uganda or Kenya. The Sudan Armed Forces also sent soldiers illegally into CAR to control the movements of the South Sudanese insurgents and became equally involved in the same economic predation. This consolidated the marginal and unsafe status of CAR's most eastern zone, long before the Lord's Resistance Army showed up.[8] Because that area was unpopulated and economically polarized by Sudan, politicians in Bangui did not pay much attention.

A first major outbreak of fighting in Darfur was concluded by a peace agreement in June 1989, but significant skirmishes broke out again in 1994 and 1998 before becoming recurrent in 2002 and a full-fledged civil war in 2003. Those events provoked forced migrations of different groups, sometimes only civilians, sometimes militias, in the three border areas at the junction of Chad, Sudan and CAR. This area became a zone with multiple sovereignties enforced at different moments by armed authorities, sometimes states, and sometimes powerful armed groups from any nationality. This also sheds light on the blurred citizenship notions in that zone that help explain the sociological ambiguities of many armed groups in the 2000s (Marchal, 2006; Debos, 2008).

The 1990s also brought a chaotic and eventually failed transition to democracy in Zaire and the Great Lakes region. In the previous period, Mobutu Sésé Séko (whose ethnic group was related to the Yakoma of André Kolingba) was instrumental in keeping a secure border with CAR, since the neighbouring Congolese province of Equateur was his homeland. The Congo wars in 1996 and 1998 produced a constellation of local conflicts often manipulated by external players, including Uganda and Rwanda (Belaid, 2008).[9] As Carayannis explains elsewhere in this volume, Jean-Pierre Bemba, leader of the Mouvement de Libération du Congo (MLC) and initially supported by Uganda, struck a deal with Ange-Félix Patassé, which in essence was not that different from what the Chadians did with Bozizé later – he put his own troops at the disposal of the president of CAR and used CAR as a hub for economic and military activities (see Carayannis, Chapter 11).

MLC fighters were known locally as 'Banyamulenge'. This does not refer to the regional or ethnic origin of the combatants, but rather to the fact that they – like the actual Banyamulenge in South Kivu – were opposed to the Kinshasa government. Their interventions, at the request of Patassé to support him against coup attempts in Bangui in 2002 and 2003 were more violent than any previous event in CAR. When François Bozizé successfully took over in March 2003, many Congolese were killed and their belongings taken away as revenge for the MLC intervention in 2002 and 2003 – a consequence that went largely unnoticed during the confusion of that period. Before 2003, Congolese people represented 51 per cent of the foreigners living in CAR,[10] but many escaped back home after those killings.

Even Congo-Brazzaville went through a chaotic cycle of crises in its 'return to democracy'. Although the fighting in 1997 opposed national figures, many people in the region argue that Denis Sassou Nguesso eventually succeeded thanks to the support he got from mercenaries sent by Chad and CAR. In comparison to Bozizé several years later, Sassou Nguesso took strong steps to reward the mercenaries and render them toothless after his victory.[11] Although not as central as in CAR, the short Congo-Brazzaville war (1997–1999) proved that exporting mercenaries was not so unusual for states in the region, and that France could eventually close its eyes if the outcome met its requirements.

The 1990s were a decade short of economic achievements in CAR. Cash crops like cotton, coffee, and tobacco had played an important role in its agriculture for decades. Their success was not permanent but nevertheless organized the daily life and mode of production for a huge majority of the population in rural areas. In the mid-1980s, the international price of cotton collapsed and put at risk the whole farming organization in the richest agricultural regions of the country. It did not recover and this shortage of resource for both the farmers and the state became one of the leading factors of fiscal tension and unrest.

Ange-Félix Patassé's governance style helped grow the informal economy – mostly because people attempted to escape the fiscal obsession of the state (or the plundering of its agents). The mutinies in 1996 and 1997 destroyed more than 70 per cent of the formal economy, and those companies were never able to restart. A 'mechanical consequence' was an extension of regional networks of smuggling, poaching, and illegal accumulation rooted either in Zaire, Sudan, Chad, or even Cameroon. The difference with the 2000s is that the key operatives in those networks saw pushing for regime change in Bangui as too bold and unlikely a move that could elicit a strong reaction from some regional states and international players. This decency did not exist anymore in the 2000s.

Patronizing Bangui (2003–2013)

The end of Ange-Félix Patassé was a clear illustration that the region (and Paris) could work jointly to decide who should preside over the destiny of CAR. Ange-Félix Patassé, especially after 1997, got lost in adventurous calculations and dangerous alliances. Libya was hardly seen as a friendly state in a region dominated by pro-western regimes led by political dinosaurs such as Cameroon's President Paul Biya and Gabon's Omar Bongo. Idriss Déby could not accept the hospitality provided to some of his most dangerous opponents. Denis Sassou Nguesso had long before lost his patience with Patassé and wanted to please Déby and Chirac for the support he got against his contenders, Pascal Lissouba and Bernard Kolelas, in 1997.

However, it is important to emphasize that the decision to overthrow Ange-Félix Patassé was not as easy as it would seem retrospectively – even Idriss Déby in February 2003 had a moment of hesitation, certainly because he understood that he was crossing a red line and that kind of move could set a precedent elsewhere in the region. Moreover, regional actors expressed significant nuances on the reasons to get rid of the incumbent, given the previous record of the new contender, François Bozizé. Omar Bongo was not a fan of this latter and this lack of enthusiasm strengthened with time and was very visible in the multiple meetings he chaired in 2007 and 2008 to find a settlement between the CAR regime and its armed opposition: the Gabonese president often said that Bozizé missed the point of rewarding his supporters and allocating money to his real friends.[12] Déby saw him as a military officer, but had some doubt about his intellectual smartness. Sassou Nguesso had a new recruit in his Freemasonry, but knew that it might not be a good enough guarantee. Nevertheless, François Bozizé appeared then as the best possible solution of the day, or maybe the least problematic.

Chad, Congo-Brazzaville, and Gabon also thought that they had leverage enough on CAR political elites to guide François Bozizé and make him behave smartly within the regional team. Despite a few small hitches, in their view, things went the right way until the Darfur conflict broke out as a regional crisis. Even François Bozizé's election in 2005 – despite his commitment to not being a presidential candidate – did not upset either his regional colleagues or France.

Retrospectively, few paid enough attention to the way Bozizé was protected up until 2012. Two military units were supposed to protect the President. The Presidential Guard was made up of *ex-libérateurs* and military recruited from the same ethnic group (Gbaya) as the President, especially after 2011 (Debos, 2008).[13] This was not uncommon in CAR's history,[14] but the behaviour of those soldiers increasingly created tensions in Bangui and, wherever they intervened, they misbehaved. By 2012, the hatred against them had reached a peak. But that was little compared to Bozizé's second layer of protection.

After March 2003, Idriss Déby intervened to restore some law and order against the *ex-libérateurs* who could not stop plundering Bangui. He agreed to provide half a company (about seventy) of elite Chadian soldiers (under the Chadian flag and in Chadian uniform) to be the personal guards of François Bozizé. Those Chadian soldiers were often closely connected to kinsmen who were big traders or dubious traffickers at the main Bangui market at Pk5, protecting them against the police and helping them settle their scores with competitors. By 2011, they were seen as the sole (and foreign) guarantee for Bozizé to stay in power (a debatable yet widely shared perception, including by Déby himself). When François Bozizé, upset by the pressures exercised by Idriss Déby in 2012, decided to get rid of them, all CAR actors knew that the *roi était nu* ('the king was naked').

The Darfur conflict changed the regional equation in many ways that were not always perceived immediately by regional actors. First, it involved many states that had ambivalent agendas such as Libya (the main arms supplier for the Darfur insurgency), Chad (that benefited from the transit of this equipment but got intimately connected to the conflict because of the role Zaghawa played in the power structure in Ndjamena and in the Darfur insurgency), and Sudan (that felt that its old friend Idriss Déby was betraying them for the sake of pleasing his western allies) (Marchal, 2008; Tubiana, 2011).

France and the US did everything to save their ally Déby at the cost of governance reforms in Chad, and ultimately the emergence of armed groups in CAR. The various armed groups that emerged in CAR in 2005–2006 were somewhat a consequence of the Chadian and Sudanese insurgencies (Lombard and Berman, 2007). Even L'Armée Populaire pour la Restauration de la Démocratie (APRD), led by Jean-Jacques Démafouth, benefited from Chadian know-how. For instance, one of the main APRD military leaders was Maradas Lakoué who in 1997 was a key military commander in Mahmouth Nahor's short-lived insurgent group. Baba Laddé, once a gendarme in Am Timan and an opponent to Déby, was called in 2008 to provide military training to APRD by Démafouth before becoming the commander of a Fulbe/Peul ethno-nationalist armed group located in the centre of CAR that was dismantled in February 2012 (Marchal, 2011).[15] The Union des Forces Démocratiques pour le Rassemblement (UFDR) and its splinter group the Convention des Patriotes pour la Justice et la Paix (CPJP) benefited from campaigns of recruitment in the three-border area and those recruits who could be also called Sudanese or Chadian very often were people with a history of involvement in the Chadian armed groups after 1991 (Debos, 2008; Lombard, 2012).

After the Chadian armed opposition's defeat in February 2008 in Ndjamena, the logic of events was unsurprising. Many of these rebels tried in 2009 to get back home and some were reintegrated in the army (to be later sent to CAR as part of a Chadian MICOPAX contingent). Others stayed in Darfur, mostly idle, and became enthusiastic recruits for the Seleka in 2012. Huge amounts of money were promised (up to fifteen million CFA francs per fighter), and looting was not forbidden.[16] Of course, as always, some moved to Bangui, Bambari, Berberati, and other cities where the Chadian community was already well represented.

When in April 2006 Chadian rebels reached Ndjamena to the despair of the French government, Chadians in Pk5 demonstrated their joy – Idriss Déby was not popular there and then. This offered a glance into the ethnic make-up of this diaspora – Gorane, Arabs from Salamat, and ethnic groups from Waddai (Kibet, Dajo, for instance) were well represented in Pk5, which explains why years later the Seleka foreign recruits were welcomed in Bangui because they often belonged to the same ethnic constituencies. Idriss Déby was smart enough not to let the armed opposition find open supporters in the trading community in Bangui. From summer 2006 up to the Seleka crisis, he spent money to regain support among Chadians settled in CAR and not allow this armed opposition to move unnoticed. Those social dynamics were not carefully considered by Paris either under Chirac or Sarkozy, especially under the latter, because the French President's friends were in lucrative businesses with the CAR regime (including UraMin, which was bought back at a very high price by the French company Areva, a case that is under judicial investigation in France in 2014).

If those aspects shed light on the behaviour of the Seleka fighters and their social connections in CAR, they do not explain why relations deteriorated between Bozizé and CEMAC (Communauté Économique et Monétaire des Etats de l'Afrique Centrale) colleagues. Actually, there were many reasons, but none taken alone was significant enough to explain what happened in December 2012.

Idriss Déby considered himself the kingmaker in CAR and indeed he was. A number of issues came up in the last years of Bozizé's rule that pushed him to reverse the support to the president he had installed to power in Bangui. First, he found that on many occasions Bozizé was not reliable. In December 2006, when the tensions between Khartoum and Ndjamena reached a peak, he had to threaten to take his troops back to stop François Bozizé from travelling to Khartoum at the invitation of Omar al-Bashir. In 2009, when Nicolas Sarkozy decided to revamp the Defence Agreement between France and CAR and erase the trigger of a French military intervention in case of internal rebellion, François Bozizé sent his right-hand man Sylvain Ndoutingaï (then Minister of Energy and Mining) to negotiate an alternative support package with the South African President, Jacob Zuma, and did not even discuss the problem with Idriss

Déby. The killing of a former minister and leader of the CPJP, Charles Massi, who had been called to Ndjamena to be handed over to Bozizé's men, was a further humiliation in December 2009 – the goal for Déby was some kind of reconciliation, not an assassination. Bozizé also refused to use the same channel as Chad to negotiate with Chinese companies and, allegedly, Idriss Déby thought that Bozizé was trying to launch exploration and exploitation of oil fields that likely straddle the border between the two countries.[17] In 2011 and early 2012, alarmed by the growing decay in CAR politics, Idriss Déby called for a national dialogue, if not some kind of power sharing. Bozizé accepted, only to renege on his commitment soon after. In 2012, aware of his growing unpopularity, François Bozizé made a further strategic mistake – he tried to direct the discontents towards the Chadian community in Bangui and later in the year, in October 2012, sent back home the few dozens of Chadian soldiers who were his personal guards to prove that whoever was to be blamed, they were Chadian. He had crossed the red line for Déby.

Denis Sassou Nguesso, like most heads of state in the region, felt that François Bozizé never tried to convert from predatory military leader to head of state, albeit one with the ability to steal money from state coffers, while also sharing the wealth with his followers. The Congolese leader could not accept the killing of Charles Massi, as that went counter to a major tenet of Freemasonry in which he had invested so much – killing Massi even though he did not pose a real threat to Bozizé. Regional politics – or to say it more concretely – the distribution of positions within the CEMAC and La Communauté Économique des États de l'Afrique Centrale (CEEAC) were also contentious as François Bozizé did not want to accommodate his neighbours despite the fact that they had been generous with him at certain times (for example, five billion CFA francs were disbursed by the region for a DDR programme in CAR in 2008, and not even two billion CFA francs were actually used for it). Ali Bongo, for instance, long before the Seleka emerged, had given up hope on

Bozizé. He was seen as dead wood whose end was expected sooner or later.

There was also the very complicated game of seduction with Paris. The night in May 2012 when François Hollande was elected in France was not the best one for Idriss Déby. Naively, the latter thought that Hollande would reflect the Socialist Party criticisms of his regime and that the disappearance of Ibni Oumar Mahamat Saleh on 3 February 2008[18] would become a major argument for stopping the support he had enjoyed from Paris, thanks to Nicolas Sarkozy and a military and diplomatic lobby. As we know, Idriss Déby was wrong on all counts – Hollande paid lip service to the fate of his former colleague at the International Socialist Organization, and the presence of Chadian soldiers in Mali muted all possible critics in the French government. Yet, Déby and some of his colleagues in the region were adamant to please Paris to avoid a diplomatic confrontation. François Bozizé was a small price to pay to prove to Paris that the region wanted to do better. This could have taken place without Paris mentioning anything.

The history of the Seleka is not yet fully known and different narratives try to explain how a coalition of dissident factions of unimpressive armed groups were able, in December 2012, to reach the outskirts of Bangui and several months later, overthrow François Bozizé with no international reaction. There should be no doubt that the Seleka growth visible in December 2012 hugely benefited from the green light given in Ndjamena. People such as the former Minister Bashir Ahmed played a major role in convincing Idriss Déby that he could trust the Seleka to rid CAR of a useless and selfish leader and install instead, for the first time in history, a Muslim as president of the country.

Yet, Idriss Déby had to take into account the views of his colleagues in the region. In December 2012, though earlier in the month he wanted to launch a *blitzkrieg* in Bangui, he had to cool down and convince his colleagues in the region that the Seleka was not a gang of Islamist Janjaweed.[19] He was also increasingly concerned by the huge contingent of former Chadian rebels among the Seleka rank and file. Before the Libreville meeting in January 2013 he requested Nur ed-Din Adam, the Seleka military mastermind, to remove those people and also get rid of those who still had a Chadian agenda (which was partially done even before March 2013) ('Déby's enemies crowd in', 2013).[20]

The Libreville meeting that took place in January 2013 under Seleka pressure on Bangui was again a show of strategic misunderstanding by François Bozizé. He could not accept that he had lost the confrontation with the Seleka and was still in power only because the CEMAC leaders had decided it so. A good tactician would have shown flexibility and would have been patient to regain leverage. Instead, he naively played a South African card that irritated the whole region that did not want 'external' (including continental) actors to get involved.[21] Whether he had respected the Libreville Agreement or not is today an academic discussion. The Seleka (supported by Chadian soldiers not in uniform) launched a new offensive on 1 March 2013 and took over Bangui on 24 March 2013.

History never repeats itself. The Seleka victory was not celebrated in all capitals of the region. Despite poor relations with him mainly due to strong disagreements on allocating positions at the CEMAC, President Paul Biya of Cameroon was extremely concerned by the Seleka Islamic dimension and provided hospitality for months to François Bozizé and his followers as an expression of his bitterness towards Idriss Déby who had gone too far, and too fast. Only the common threat represented by Boko Haram today may reconcile the two heads of state.

Denis Sassou Nguesso's behaviour (in response to the lack of follow up by Idriss Déby himself) illustrated well the weakness of the regional management. While Congolese President Sassou Nguesso worked hard to have people attached to him in charge, he did not do much to ensure a smooth transition or exit to the crisis. Sassou Nguesso was only an intermittent mediator with no ambition other than to have his men in charge and please Paris and the international community by proving his effectiveness in solving the CAR quagmire at a time he wanted to have a new presidential mandate for 2016.

The other heads of state quickly lost interest in the CAR file. They needed to settle scores but were hardly interested in more than that. Angola's late involvement in the CAR crisis does not seem to have been so natural. Many of CAR's political elites believe that Luanda got involved at the request of Paris to find a middle ground between Sassou Nguesso and Idriss Déby who were divided on the newly appointed CAR President Samba-Panza's qualities, and also to provide some funds to the CAR government at a time negotiations with the IMF were stalled because of the misbehaviour of some of her entourage.

Conclusion: external actors and the re-foundation of a Central African polity

What emerged from the latest CAR crisis is a more divided region that has had to reluctantly accept the involvement of other actors, the African Union and the United Nations. France, itself, despite its lip service to celebrate the region's commitment to CAR would not trust the region the same way it did in December 2012–March 2013. The mistakes made at that time were core reasons for the intervention in December 2013, an intervention that is going to last a long time and not be as successful as once expected in Paris.[22] The question of whether those new players can do more and better than the region is left open. The Brazzaville agreement signed in July 2014 is not really proof that more can be achieved, because the same mistakes were made by regional and international players or, to say it better, divisions on external agendas were as important.

Chad for the first time is identified as having played a Muslim card without measuring the consequences on the region. Despite being an elected member at the UN Security Council and hosting the HQs of the French Barkhane Operation that encompasses all of Western Sahel, Chad today feels cornered. In April 2014, Idriss Déby had to pull out his troops from the African Union's Mission internationale de soutien à la Centrafrique sous conduite africaine (MISCA) under strong allegations that they shot down civilians, helped rearm the Seleka, and might have committed war crimes. Relations with Samba-Panza have gone from bad to worse and Chad's policy towards CAR in recent months has left the impression that Chad is playing the deterioration more than stabilization card.

Ndjamena can gain some recognition from several Islamic states since the narrative in Khartoum, the Gulf, and international Islamic fora is that France led a quasi-genocide of Muslims in CAR. This may bring additional financial and diplomatic capital to Chad, but also make the inconsistencies of its policies more visible. Idriss Déby, after quitting the MISCA, is also in a difficult situation at home. He has had to spend time and money to reassure Chadian returnees that France, not Chad, was responsible for the mess in Bangui.

The Seleka discourse on secession also puts Idriss Déby in a very difficult position. The secession card is the best leverage the Seleka has on Bangui, even though it may look very unlikely from a legal perspective or even politically (as the huge majority of the population in the region claimed by the Seleka is Christian and not represented within the Seleka). At the same time, the reminder of secession has strong resonance in Southern Chad, a zone that produces most of Chad's oil, but gets little reward for it from the central state.

Denis Sassou Nguesso is not in a better position. The diplomatic community managing the CAR portfolio has been blaming the poor quality of his personal representative in the mediation, Noel Léonard Essongo, and the ups and downs of the Congolese regional diplomacy. Congolese troops have not been impressive, regardless of whether they belonged to MICOPAX or MISCA. Sassou Nguesso also illustrates well a persistent pattern of the regional diplomacy – an inability to keep a file open until problems have been solved. Congo-Brazzaville, despite significant financial investment to support the CAR government and political initiatives, such as the July 2014 Brazzaville meeting, has not yet spent enough political capital to make a striking difference with what the African Union or the United Nations claim to achieve.

Yaoundé is bitter because it never wanted things to go that far, and although it had hardly paid attention to CAR for decades, it is nowadays subjected to a humanitarian stress up north, insecurity on the border, and the still unlikely convergence between disenfranchised Peulh and Boko Haram. While its troops in MISCA do not do much, its reaction in northern Cameroon is expressed purely by security reinforcements that may have counterproductive effects if not accompanied by a more civilian reassertion of the state. Relations with Chad and Nigeria are going to be tested for quite some time.

The earthquake represented by the Anti-Balaka and the spread of hostility against Islam and Muslims cannot be dismissed. It has somewhat echoed everywhere in the region. In Angola, Congo-Brazzaville, Democratic Republic of the Congo, over the last two years there have been movements of hostility against Muslims, who are in the minority, that never took such a violent turn, but shared the common assumption that Muslims are foreigners, even outsiders, and have to go. One can argue whether this is a strategy designed by some or the reshaping of social tensions fed by regimes that are hardly concerned by their own populations.

Months after the international intervention took off in CAR, no regional narrative has been defined to provide a sense of living together despite differing on religion. It is so because this issue relies not on religious differences as such, but on positions of power and wealth accumulation, on the control of the invisible world, which is a crucial issue in all societies of the region, and on rivalries between regional players. It is far from certain that the Anti-Balaka could spread beyond CAR's borders as they express a predicament of social bonds hardly visible elsewhere in the region, and roots in Gbaya culture and rural order. However, the

Anti-Balaka's emergence keeps open the question of who benefits from an unjust political order. This question is also shared by many people coping with authoritarian regimes across the region.

Notes

1 See, for a good reminder, the two books authored by Anthony Giddens on the Nation-State and Violence.
2 For more see Chapter 13, 'A Central African Elite Perspective on the Struggles of the Central African Republic' by Laurence Wohlers.
3 Interviews, Bangui, 2007–2010. The French Sangaris Operation assumed that it would enjoy the same respect as their colleagues who had intervened in 1996 to stop mutineers.
4 See Chapter 9, 'Pathologies of Peacekeeping and Peacebuilding' by Nathaniel Olin. MISAB was actually seen as the new paradigm for the French military cooperation with African States (Marchal, 1998).
5 See Chapter 2, 'CAR's History: The Past of a Tense Present' by Stephen Smith.
6 Ibid.
7 The FROLINAT or Front de Libération Nationale du Tchad, was an insurgent group and active player in the Chadian civil war (1965–1979).
8 See Chapter 12, 'In Unclaimed Land: The Lord's Resistance Army in CAR' by Ledio Cakaj.
9 For more detail see Chapter 11, 'CAR's Southern Identity: Congo, CAR, and International Justice' by Tatiana Carayannis.
10 See National Census 2003. It is also interesting to note that Chadian and Sudanese people represented more or less the same proportion: 16.7 per cent and 17.6 per cent, respectively.
11 Some of them were parts of the MICOPAX contingent present in CAR until the re-hatting as MISCA. For more detail see Chapter 9, 'Pathologies of Peacekeeping and Peacebuilding' by Nathaniel Olin.
12 Interview with UN diplomat, 2008. The exact quote is *'Il ne comprend pas qu'il faut savoir préparer de temps en temps la soupe juste pour la distribuer pas pour la manger seul'*.
13 Interviews with French Defence attachés (2007, 2011, 2013).
14 Bokassa did it and Kolingba made it a key rule in re-organizing the army.

15 Interviews in Ndjamena and Bangui, 2011 and 2013.
16 Many thought that if a friendly regime was installed in Bangui maybe northern CAR could become a sanctuary to launch new attacks against Déby. Plundering was also a motivation. Many ex-Seleka fighters opened shops in Sahr and Moundou after March 2013. No one in Chad tried to bother them.
17 A story that started with Ange-Félix Patassé and Jack Grynberg, allegedly a financier of the Seleka in 2012. Interviews in Ndjamena, January 2013.
18 Ibni Oumar Mahamat Salah, Chadian opposition leader and spokesperson for the Coordination des Partis Politiques pour la Défense de la Constitution (CPDC), was arrested by around twenty Chadian Presidential Guard soldiers at his house on 3 February 2008, and was never seen again. The 'February 2008 incidents' were the source of much criticism of Déby and France for keeping troops in Chad that effectively supported him.
19 Interviews with Seleka leaders and dissidents in Bangui, December 2013 and May 2014.
20 Interviews with Chadian and EU officials and Seleka dissidents, Bangui and Brussels, May 2013.
21 Interviews in Paris and Bangui with French officials and CAR politicians, January and March 2013. On details about South African involvement in CAR in 2012–2013, see Marchal, 2014.
22 For more detail see Chapter 9, 'Pathologies of Peacekeeping and Peacebuilding' by Nathaniel Olin.

Bibliography

Belaid, M. (2008) *Le Mouvement de libération du Congo en RDC. De la guérilla au parti politique*, L'Harmattan, Paris.

Buijtenhuijs, R. (1987) *Le Frolinat et les guerres civiles du Tchad, 1977–1984: La révolution introuvable*, Afrika-Studiecentrum, Leiden, Netherlands and Karthala, Paris.

Cordell, D. (1985) *Dar al-Kuti and the Last Years of the Trans-Saharan Slave Trade*, University of Wisconsin Press, Madison, WI, US.

Cordell, D. (2002) 'Des 'réfugiés' dans l'Afrique précoloniale? Le cas de la Centrafrique (1850–1910)', *Politique Africaine*, no. 85, March. Available from: <http://www.politique-africaine.com/numeros/pdf/085016.pdf >.

Debos, M. (2008) 'Fluid loyalties in a regional crisis: Chadian "ex-liberators" in the Central African Republic', *African Affairs*, vol. 107, no. 427.

'Déby's enemies crowd in' (2013) *Africa Confidential*, vol. 54, no. 11, 24 May.

Faes, G. and S. Smith (2000) *Bokassa: Un empereur français*, Calmann-Levy, Paris.

Gagliardi-Baysse, A. (2008) 'Dynamique de formation et de reproduction des elites centrafricaines,' Unpublished MA dissertation, Université Paris I Panthéon-Sorbonne. Available from: <http://www.fasopo.org/reasopo/jr/memoire_gagliardi.pdf>.

Giddens, Anthony (1981) *A Contemporary Critique of Historical Materialism. Volume I: Power, Property, and the State*, University of California Press, Berkeley, US.

Giddens, Anthony (1985) *A Contemporary Critique of Historical Materialism. Volume II: The Nation-State and Violence*, University of California Press, Berkeley, US.

Kalck, P. (1974) *Histoire de la République centrafricaine*, Berger-Levrault, Paris.

Kinata, C. (2008) 'Barthélémy Boganda et l'eglise catholique en Oubangui Chari', *Cahiers d'études africaines*, no. 191.

Lemarchand, R. (1986) 'Chad: the misadventures of the north–south dialectic', *African Studies Review*, vol. 29, no. 3, September.

Lombard, L. (2012) 'Raiding sovereignty in Central African borderlands', Unpublished PhD dissertation, Duke University. Available from: <http://dukespace.lib.duke.edu/dspace/bitstream/handle/10161/5861/Lombard_duke_0066D_11603.pdf?sequence=1>.

Lombard, L. and E. Berman (2007) 'The Central African Republic and small arms', *Small Arms Survey*, Geneva. Available from: http://www.smallarmssurvey.org/fileadmin/docs/D-Book-series/book-07-CAR/SAS-Central-African-Republic-and-Small-Arms.pdf.

Marchal, R. (1998) 'France and Africa: the emergence of essential reforms', *International Affairs*, vol. 74, no. 2.

Marchal, R. (2006) 'Chad/Darfur: How to merge two crises', *Review of African Political Economy*, vol. 33, no. 106.

Marchal, R. (2008) 'The roots of the Darfur conflict and the Chadian civil war', *Public Culture*, vol. 20, no. 3.

Marchal, R. (2009) 'Aux marges du monde, en Afrique centrale', *Les Etudes du CERI*, n°153–154, 2009. Available from: <http://www.sciencespo.fr/ceri/en/content/aux-marges-du-monde-en-afrique-centrale>.

Marchal, R. (2011) 'Baba Laddé: Robber and robin hoods?' *Africa Confidential*, vol. 52, no. 19, September.

Marchal, R. (2014) 'South Africa and France: A rising versus a declining power in Africa?', *Centre for Conflict Prevention*: Cape Town, South Africa.

Shaw, M. (2001) 'A regressive crystallization of global state power: theorising a response to the 'war against terrorism' *MartinShaw.org*. Available from: <http://martinshaw.org/2009/12/13/a-regressive-crystallization-of-global-state-power-theorising-a-response-to-the-war-against-terrorism-2001/>.

Tubiana, J. (2011) 'Renouncing the Rebels: Local and Regional Dimensions of Chad–Sudan Rapprochement', *Small Arms Survey*, Available from: <http://www.smallarmssurveysudan.org/fileadmin/docs/working-papers/HSBA-WP-25-Local-and-Regional-Dimensions-Chad-Sudan-Rapprochement.pdf>.

9 Pathologies of Peacekeeping and Peacebuilding in CAR

Nathaniel Olin

In the past two decades, the Central African Republic (CAR) has played host to nearly a dozen different peacekeeping and peacebuilding initiatives, including formal UN missions, regional coalitions, and long-term French bilateral military engagement. This contrasts with the much larger international intervention in the neighbouring Democratic Republic of the Congo, for example, which has been primarily carried out within the UN mission (MONUC/MONUSCO),[1] or the interventions in Sudan, in which most international and regional peacekeeping efforts have been integrated attempts.[2] CAR also received substantial humanitarian aid considering its small population, with approximately $227 million in official humanitarian aid in 2012 alone (OECD, 2014). Yet in 2013, the regime was overthrown, and the country descended into widespread sectarian violence, unravelling the very limited progress in peacebuilding and prompting even deeper international intervention to try to stabilize the situation. Despite their myriad forms, multiple international interventions have failed to manage instability or to build peace in CAR. Why is this the case?

While its low profile on the international scene has limited the aid it has received in the past few decades, being off the radar has allowed international actors to adopt a broader variety of approaches to peacekeeping and peacebuilding. CAR has thus served as an 'early adopter' for many peacekeeping concepts that have since been implemented elsewhere—the regional peacekeeping force the Mission interafricaine de surveillance des accords de Bangui (MISAB), deployed in 1997, predated the African Union Mission in Somalia by a full decade, while the country was one of the first to be inscribed on the Peacebuilding Commission Agenda or receive an 'integrated' peacebuilding operation. Peacekeeping operations in CAR have involved a mix of bilateral engagement and regional support, while peacebuilding operations focus on two primary goals: disarmament, demobilization, and reintegration (DDR) of combatants along with reform of the armed forces (FACA), and the creation of an 'inclusive political dialogue' between relevant stakeholders. However, these efforts have failed for several reasons. One is the failure to profit from periods of stability, and the search for cheap solutions leading to quick exits. Even during periods of relative calm, international peacebuilders, and the UN system in particular, made incredibly slow progress in both disarmament and in promoting the inclusive political dialogue. Neither could be achieved without some measure of buy-in from the Central African regime. However, peacebuilding actors did not adjust their objectives in the face of these obstacles, instead pursuing them ineffectually in multiple formats including the in-country peacebuilding mission the Bureau des Nations Unies pour la consolidation de la paix en République Centrafricaine (BONUCA), later the Bureau Intégré de l'Organisation des Nations Unies en Centrafrique (BINUCA), the NY-based Peacebuilding Commission, and through bilateral aid. As a result, peacebuilding efforts came to mirror CAR's own government, existing more in name than in substance, and this problem became self-reinforcing.

A second reason for failure was the tendency of regional partners and the former colonial power France to interfere in Central African politics. Participating in regional peacekeeping missions temporarily improved the image of many of CAR's neighbours in the eyes of the international community, but it also allowed them to extend their influence into CAR, and to play kingmaker when the opportunity presented itself. By supporting

Bozizé's overthrow of the Patassé regime without much backlash, CAR's neighbours sent a clear signal that the international community was not committed to CAR's democratic institutions—a sufficiently credible threat to the regime could win international support, a lesson Seleka exploited years later.

Finally, members of the international community often worked at cross-purposes. The efforts of the United Nations system often did not align with the political agendas of the regional states or of France, who provided the military and logistical support (and thus, the leverage) for most of this period. Regional and subregional organizations struggled with each other for control of interventions, and peacekeepers from different countries even came into direct conflict with one another. All these factors worked to undermine the effectiveness of international interventions.

This chapter will provide an overview of the regional and international peacekeeping and peacebuilding operations deployed to the Central Africa Republic, beginning with the creation of MISAB in 1997. While peace operations in CAR have evolved over the past seventeen years, interference by CAR's international partners, a focus on cheap solutions, and incoherence in the international response, all contributed to the comprehensive failure of international peacekeeping and peacebuilding missions in the country. With the recent collapse of state institutions and deployment of a substantial UN peacekeeping mission, understanding the reasons why past interventions failed will be crucial for avoiding the same tragic mistakes in the future.

Box 9.1: International interventions in the Central African Republic

January 1997: The deployment of the Mission Interafricaine de Surveillance des Accords de Bangui (MISAB).

March 1998: France phases out logistics support. MISAB is replaced with the Mission des Nations Unis en République centrafricaine (United Nations Mission in CAR, or MINURCA).

February 2000: MINURCA is replaced by the Le Bureau des Nations Unies pour la consolidation de la paix en République centrafricaine (United Nations Peacebuilding Support Office in the Central African Republic, or BONUCA).

August 2002: The Community of Sahel–Saharan States (CEN-SAD) deploys 300 soldiers to Bangui.

October 2002: The Economic and Monetary Community of Central African States (CEMAC) deploys the Multinational Force in the Central African Republic (FOMUC).

September 2007: In order to respond to the armed activities in Chad and Darfur, and its humanitarian spillover, the United Nations Mission in the Central African Republic and Chad (MINURCAT) is authorized.

June 2008: CAR is inscribed on the agenda of the UN Peacebuilding Commission.

July 2008: Control of FOMUC is transferred from CEMAC to the Economic Community of Central African States (CEEAC), and the mission is renamed Mission de consolidation de la paix en Centrafrique (MICOPAX).

January 2010: BONUCA is succeeded by an integrated peacebuilding office, the Bureau Intégré de l'Organisation des Nations Unies en Centrafrique or BINUCA.

December 2010: MINURCAT is withdrawn at the request of the government of Chad.

January 2013: The Seleka reaches the outskirts of Bangui; MICOPAX prevents them from taking the capital. The Libreville Accords are signed.

March 2013: The Libreville Accords break down. Seleka overthrows Bozizé without resistance from MICOPAX, and takes power.

July 2013: Violence escalates; MICOPAX reinforces Bangui with French support. The AU authorizes the Mission internationale de soutien à la Centrafrique sous conduite africaine (MISCA), replacing and reinforcing MICOPAX.

> December 2013: After months of looting and spiralling violence, France deploys 1,000 troops to Bangui (Operation Sangaris).
>
> January 2014: In a regional summit in N'Djamena, the Seleka administration is convinced to step down. The UN Security Council authorizes MISCA and a new EU force, EUFOR-RCA.
>
> April 2014: The UN Security Council authorizes the 12,000-strong UN peacekeeping force Mission multidimensionnelle intégrée des Nations Unies pour la stabilisation en Centrafrique (MINUSCA) to replace MISCA and absorb BINUCA in September.

Patassé in peril: from regional to UN peacekeeping

In 1996, the armed forces of CAR (FACA) mutinied on several occasions, due to a combination of unpaid wages and unrest over Patassé's perceived or real ethnic favouritism in military appointments (International Crisis Group, 2007). Multiple interventions by French forces brought the mutineers to the negotiating table, but each incident was more serious than the last, with the third mutiny resulting in hundreds of soldiers occupying parts of the capital, causing French casualties and French reprisals with dozens of civilian casualties. The French government, unwilling to sustain further costs to prop up Patassé's regime, but reluctant to watch it collapse, pushed for an international force to replace its troops in providing security (International Crisis Group, 2007, 10). France convened a summit of its regional allies in Ouagadougou, comprised of Burkina Faso, Gabon, Mali, Senegal, Chad, and Togo, and offered logistical and financial support for a regional peacekeeping operation. The resulting force, MISAB, was mandated to monitor the implementation of the January 1997 Bangui Accords. At its head was General Amadou Toumani Touré, former president of Mali, as the personal representative of the various African heads of state. While France was only an advisor for the Bangui agreements, MISAB was underwritten by French support, and existed largely as a means for French forces to exit without destabilizing the situation in Bangui. MISAB's plan of action for the implementation of the Bangui Accords was ambitious: the formation of a government of national unity, adoption of an amnesty law for participants in the third rebellion, disarmament of militias and civilian populations, determining the status of former Central African heads of state, and various steps of national reconciliation, including a National Reconciliation Conference, 'awareness-raising seminars', creation of an electoral code, and access by political parties to state media.

There was some tension between this ambitious political mandate, and MISAB's operations on the ground, which focused primarily on re-establishing day-to-day order and cracking down on banditry and organized crime in the capital, as well as 'actions aimed at preventing confrontation between the two main forces in question: the loyalists of the Central African Armed Forces and the former rebels' (United Nations Security Council, 1997a). A focus on immediate security was necessary: violence broke out in March and June, resulting in six deaths and twenty wounded within the MISAB force. Once day-to-day order had been restored, the mission focused on disarmament, described as 'Without a doubt, the most delicate phase of the national reconciliation process' (United Nations Security Council, 1997b). The mission also recognized that the need for disarmament went beyond the rebel forces—MISAB requested that the United Nations Development Programme (UNDP) establish a reintegration programme for FACA soldiers wishing to demobilize, to 'make it possible to reduce the cost of operating the armed forces and facilitate their restructuring' (United Nations Security Council 1997c, 3).

In general, MISAB was successful in restoring order to Bangui, and in creating the conditions necessary for progress along the political dimensions of the mandate. The mission's success was important for shaping international peacekeeping policy in Africa going forward, suggesting that regional alliances could provide the long sought-after 'African solutions for African problems'. The French RECAMP[3] initiative, established in 1997 to train African troops for peacekeeping operations, was heavily influenced by MISAB's experience, and based on the principles of UN- or AU-mandated peace operations, African provision of peacekeeping forces and leadership, and provision of hardware, training, and logistical support by external actors. In 2008, RECAMP was expanded into an EU–AU training initiative entitled Amani Africa ('Peace in Africa' in Kiswahili).

While the international community perceived MISAB to be a success, it faced greater difficulty going beyond restoring order to engage in peacebuilding. After a relatively successful voluntary disarmament process, MISAB began oversight of an enforced disarmament programme, accompanying the Central African security forces in conducting searches and seizures in Bangui neighbourhoods. These attempts yielded no results, and the efforts were quickly abandoned (United Nations Security Council, 1998a). Financing and supplying the mission was also a continuous problem. By September 1997, MISAB's reports noted that the political mission might be cut short should UNDP cease funding the International Monitoring Committee. The Committee's staff was reduced at the end of September. In response, MISAB listed the remaining components of the roadmap, and noted that 'it is difficult to see how the mediation effort, and thus the rest of the process, can continue without a mediator' (United Nations Security Council, 1997d). Reports to the UN Security Council noted that 'the material conditions of the troops stands in need of improvement, as they are far inferior to those enjoyed by other similar forces operating in other conflict areas' (United Nations Security Council, 1997e, 3). The trust fund established by the UN for international contribution was substantially under-resourced.

The acute lack of resources for even political engagement left MISAB almost entirely dependent on French logistical support. However, France was unwilling to bankroll the mission any longer than necessary. As early as July 1997, remaining French forces had begun their plans to depart. In order to secure a swift exit, France lobbied for and secured a UN peacekeeping mission to take over MISAB's role. The turnaround was swift: the Security Council authorized the UN Mission for the CAR (MINURCA) on 27 March 1998, with a start date of 15 April, barely three weeks later. By June, MINURCA had deployed 1,200 of its total component of 1,350. Like MISAB, MINURCA was limited to maintaining security in the capital, but had the additional mandate of supporting the legislative elections scheduled for 1998, later extended to the presidential elections of 1999. The mission did not take up any remaining disarmament or demobilization efforts, leaving these to UNDP and the Central African government.

MINURCA's experience mirrored that of MISAB. Where the mission was not able to secure its mandate through force of arms, it was stymied by the lack of a credible national interlocutor. The mission was able to maintain security in Bangui, but was much less successful in making real progress either in the political sphere, or in addressing the government's substantial financial problems. Preparations for elections were contentious at every step, from membership of the national electoral council, to the number of districts and deputies in the National Assembly (United Nations Security Council, 1998b). President Patassé refused to make concessions to the opposition, and MINURCA was unable to exert leverage on the President to enforce his cooperation. Central Africans had just experienced the French government's withdrawal, and with its limited mandate to secure Bangui and push through elections, MINURCA was even less invested in CAR's stability than France had been through MISAB. The regime would not make serious concessions to an unfriendly opposition at the behest of a mission that would surely depart at the first available opportunity.

The intuition proved to be correct. While the mission's mandate was extended to cover presidential elections, the

Secretary-General's report noted that 'The exit strategy for the operation would be firmly linked with the conduct of presidential elections... The Mission would be terminated no later than 60 days after the announcement of the election results' (United Nations Security Council, 1998b, 12). This arbitrary deadline signalled the urgency on the part of the UN to withdraw its mission as quickly as possible, despite the very real possibility of elections destabilizing the tenuous equilibrium CAR had reached. The results of the 1998 legislative elections had already proved contentious. Because the opposition had won the election, Patassé began to bypass the National Assembly and issue orders directly. In response, three of the four opposition deputies Patassé tapped to form a government were forced by their parties to resign. As such, there was every reason to expect that presidential elections would prove contentious.

Beyond elections, the situation in CAR was only superficially stable. The government was still unable to pay the salaries of its civil servants or soldiers, and the FACA was still in dire need of reform. FORSDIR (Force spéciale de défense des institutions républicaines), the Presidential Guard, was implicated in the deaths of multiple civilians after intervening in a trade dispute, encroaching on the mandate of the national police and gendarmerie. Patassé flatly refused to fulfil his earlier commitments to bring the Presidential Guard under control, arguing that FORSDIR was the only branch of the security forces on which he could rely (United Nations Security Council, 1997e). He also held up promulgation of legislation from the National Assembly restructuring the armed forces, referring it to the Constitutional Court which blocked its progress. The Special Representative of the Secretary-General (SRSG) was aware of these warning signs, and wryly noted in his reports that 'the Security Council might therefore wish to consider what measures it can take to persuade the Government of the CAR to fulfil the commitments which formed the basis for the establishment of MINURCA in the first place' (United Nations Security Council, 1997e)'.

Presidential elections were held in September 1999. The opposition pre-emptively denounced the results, declaring that they would not accept any outcome that showed Patassé to be the winner. Nevertheless, observers from MINURCA, the EU, and the International Organization of la Francophonie (IOF) declared the elections to be largely free and fair. Patassé was declared the winner with 52 per cent of the vote. MINURCA reports moved in one breath from discussing how FACA soldiers occupied and threatened to blow up the Finance ministry, along with the Treasurer-General, over unpaid salaries, to outlining the 'transition to post-conflict peacebuilding' (United Nations Security Council, 1998a). Drawdown of MINURCA forces began fifteen days after the presidential elections, and by April 2000, the peacekeeping forces had departed.

BONUCA and FOMUC: peacebuilding during conflict, peacekeeping during war

Upon its departure, MINURCA was replaced by the UN Peacebuilding Support Office in the Central African Republic (BONUCA). While the mission was mandated to 'assist national efforts to strengthen democratic institutions and mechanisms for fostering reconciliation and dialogue', its concrete tasks were primarily the coordination of peacebuilding efforts across the UN system and Bretton Woods institutions, and to 'follow' the situation in the country, in the domains of human rights and security reform. Like MINURCA, BONUCA had little political or financial clout with which to encourage Patassé and the opposition to work together. Unlike MINURCA, however, BONUCA had no military component, and security in Bangui as well as the broader country continued to deteriorate. Armed banditry in the capital increased and the activity of *coupeurs de route*—highwaymen—intensified (United Nations Security Council, 2001). Ironically, security deteriorated despite the government's efforts to reform and reorganize the national military, which proceeded haltingly notwithstanding the international community's failure to adequately fund the demobilization and reintegration programme.

In spite of the continuing serious political tensions and social unrest due to unpaid wages, an attempted coup in May 2001 was 'wholly unexpected' by the UN Secretary-General (United Nations Security Council, 2001). Lacking the support of peacekeepers, Patassé put down the coup with the assistance of Libyan troops and Congolese rebels (from le Mouvement de libération du Congo—MLC),[4] causing substantial loss of life, displacement, and destruction of property (United Nations Security Council, 2001). The Secretary-General dispatched General Touré to reprise his role as special envoy in the aftermath. The attempted coup and subsequent fighting destabilized the situation, rolling back the (incomplete) progress MISAB and MINURCA had made on disarmament and the collection of heavy and light weapons. BONUCA could only call on the international community to assist CAR's agencies in their disarmament efforts—efforts which had proved difficult for regional peacekeepers backed by French logistical support.

BONUCA's mandate and resources were too limited to address the escalating security situation. The UN Secretary-General requested that the UN Security Council strengthen BONUCA's mandate, to more explicitly support the process of national reconciliation, the restructuring of the security forces, training of the national police, and disarmament. However, the fundamental weakness of state institutions remained a problem that BONUCA could not address, and without an armed component, it could not manage crises when they did occur. In October 2001, President Patassé attempted to arrest the FACA chief of staff, General François Bozizé, for alleged complicity in the May 2001 coup. The head of BONUCA, General Lamine Cissé, negotiated an agreement under which Bozizé and his troops would stand down in return for another position and a pardon from Patassé. However, Patassé broke the agreement before it was formalized, attacking Bozizé's positions and forcing him to retreat to Chad. The FACA fragmented as a result, with a number of soldiers joining Bozizé and others deserting outright.

With the crisis now explicitly regional, Patassé reached out to neighbouring states for military assistance. Burkina Faso, Djibouti, Libya, and Sudan deployed some 300 soldiers to Bangui through the Community of Sahel–Saharan States (CEN-SAD). After violent border incidents allegedly involving the Chadian military in August 2002, the Central African Economic and Monetary Community (CEMAC) deployed a small force mandated to ensure the President's safety, monitor the Chadian border, and to participate in FACA's restructuring (United Nations Security Council, 2003). The proposed mission was endorsed by the UN Security Council, but in October, before it could be deployed, Bozizé's forces attacked the capital, only pushed back by Libyan and MLC forces after several days of fighting. The CEMAC mission, known as Force Multinationale en Centrafrique (FOMUC), arrived in December, but at this point Patassé's regional partners had lost confidence in his ability to maintain control without Bozizé. They pushed Patassé into a national dialogue, but the President undercut the process by assaulting Bozizé's positions with MLC support. Finally, regional heads of state as well as the French lost patience with Patassé. While the President was attending a CEN-SAD summit, Bozizé and two columns of Chadian troops took Bangui without a fight. FOMUC was ordered to stand by as the coup occurred, and the CEMAC heads of state formally endorsed the transfer of power at their June 2003 summit. In a telling show of support, French forces arrived the following day to secure the airport. BONUCA could only condemn the unconstitutional transfer of power, and had little choice but to begin working with the new regime.

Thus, while international engagement in CAR from 2000 to 2003 was configured as 'peacebuilding' with a light footprint, both domestic and international actors were able and willing to pursue their political agendas by force throughout. Not only was

BONUCA unable to make substantial progress in promoting a national dialogue, it could not maintain the secure space necessary for political progress, army reform, or disarmament. However, this period also highlighted the double-edged sword of regional peacekeeping. On the one hand, states in CAR's neighbourhood proved more willing to provide the military assistance necessary to maintain order at least in the capital, if not the interior of the country. On the other hand, these states had ulterior motives for intervening in CAR. Stability in CAR mattered only insofar as it prevented spillover into their countries; the reputational benefits of participating in FOMUC were also quite important.

'Peacekeeping' thus provided a win–win proposition for the countries of the region, as they were able to curry favour with the UN, France, and broader international community by contributing (or being perceived to contribute) to regional peace and security, while at the same time, they were able to interfere in the internal affairs of the country, extending their own influence in the region. Such interference set a dangerous precedent: if an outside force could pose a sufficiently credible threat to the regime in power, regional allies were willing to endorse a forceful transfer of power for the sake of expediency and in order to increase their influence in the region.

2003–2008: deterioration of the periphery, expansion of international presence

While the regional peacekeepers of FOMUC (again with French financial support) maintained a measure of order in Bangui, security in the rest of the country deteriorated over the next several years. Rebellions in the west and north-east led to violent reprisals by the ineffective FACA, and French forces intervened directly in the north-east on several occasions. In 2006, French support for the Central African state in retaking the town of Birao rebounded poorly in domestic media when the FACA burned the houses France had helped to liberate from rebels

(International Crisis Group, 2008). Again France began reducing its engagement in the country, and the Bozizé regime began looking for expanded regional support, both in the form of peacekeepers and to expand the FACA's capabilities outside of the capital. FOMUC and the European Union began construction of permanent barracks in each of the six military regions, starting as FOMUC facilities and then transitioning to house FACA battalions. While these operations planned an ambitious increase in CAR's ability to secure its own territory, the scheme was still heavily dependent on bilateral aid. Fully 80 per cent of the budget was left to bilateral donors. In addition, funding for the FOMUC force was uncertain throughout this entire period. This uncertainty limited FOMUC's ability to carry out long-term strategic efforts to create a sustainable security force in CAR, or to address underlying political tensions.

In July 2008, FOMUC was reformed into the Mission for the Consolidation of Peace in the Central African Republic (MICOPAX), under the control of the Economic Community of Central African States (CEEAC) and incorporated soldiers from the DRC and Cameroon, expanding the force's capabilities. In the same year, the escalating crisis on the Chad–Sudan border led to the deployment of an EU force (EUFOR) in Chad and north-eastern CAR, with the understanding that the mission would be replaced by UN peacekeepers within a year. This provided France with a more graceful exit from north-eastern CAR, and was eventually incorporated into MINURCAT.

Peacebuilding and national dialogue stymied

Meanwhile, in Bangui, the UN peacebuilding office BONUCA was focusing primarily on national elections in 2005, and on drafting the new constitution, in order to help establish the democratic credentials of Bozizé's regime. While the elections were by most external reports free and fair, despite Patassé being prevented from running, rebel groups began emerging in 2006 in part to protest the Bozizé presidency and lack of government support. In 2006, Bozizé announced his intention to hold a political dialogue on peace and security, ostensibly including both the political and armed opposition. The dialogue did not begin until 2008. Though participants reached agreement on the demobilization of rebel groups and other issues, substantive political issues remained off the table. The dialogue was organized by the Centre for Humanitarian Dialogue, and BONUCA operated only as bystander. At the same time, international donors organized a separate national forum on security, cutting many of the national dialogue participants (including rebel groups) out of discussions regarding army reform, undermining the credibility and usefulness of both processes (International Crisis Group, 2008).

Also in 2008, before the start of the national dialogue, President Bozizé formally requested that CAR be added to the agenda of the UN Peacebuilding Commission (PBC). A subsidiary body of the UN Security Council established in 2006, the PBC was created specifically to harmonize international efforts to support countries emerging from conflict, particularly to ensure predictable financing for recovery activities in the medium to long term. In principle, the conclusion of the Inclusive National Dialogue made CAR a perfect country case for the PBC, as its low profile on the international stage had led to unpredictable financing and hobbled regional efforts to maintain stability in the country. The PBC accepted the President's proposal in June 2008 and identified three priority areas for its focus in CAR: security sector reform (SSR), including DDR; governance and the rule of law; and the 'development poles' supported by the European Union to rebuild local economies. In all cases, the PBC committed to focusing on the mobilization of resources; it also put a particular focus on coordination where bilateral and multilateral assistance for SSR and DDR was concerned.

Any optimism generated by the events of 2008 was quickly checked in 2009. President Bozizé proved reluctant to implement many of the reforms to which he had committed in the dialogue, focusing instead on ensuring his victory in the 2010 elections (ultimately held in 2011 and marred by allegations of fraud). Meanwhile the disarmament process faltered on multiple levels. Rebel groups demanded living allowances and splintered into new factions while waiting for the programme to commence, and the implementing partners disputed who was in control over particular aspects of the process. SSR remained underfunded by internationals and unsupported by the Central African ministries. The FACA remained effectively a tribal militia, rather than the nationally-representative force envisioned by peacebuilders (International Crisis Group, 2008).

In an effort to reinvigorate the United Nations presence, and with the addition of CAR to the PBC agenda, the UN Secretariat combined BONUCA with other UN presences in the country and re-established it as the Integrated UN Peacebuilding Support Office in CAR (BINUCA) in 2010. The new integrated mission was granted an ambitious mandate to assist with the outcomes of the national dialogue, assist with SSR and DDR processes, support the re-establishment of state authority in the provinces, support efforts to enhance human rights and the rule of law, and coordinate with the PBC. The reconfiguration of BONUCA into BINUCA coincided with a peacekeeping transition next door, as the EU force on the Chad–Sudan border (EUFOR) was reconfigured as the UN mission in the Central African Republic and Chad (MINURCAT), nominally operating in north-eastern CAR and coordinating with BINUCA. Despite BINUCA's nominal increase in stature, however, the mission remained either unable or unwilling to exert effective pressure either on a recalcitrant regime or on the rebel groups involved in the disarmament process. National actors stonewalled the follow-on to the national dialogue, citing the lack of funds from international partners, or the lack of cooperation from the other national parties to the accords (United Nations Security Council, 2009).

The situation mirrored past episodes of international engagement: much like MINURCA's inability to encourage Patassé to implement the Bangui Accords, BINUCA did not have the political clout to pressure Bozizé to uphold his end of the bargain, while FOMUC did not have the military capacity to enforce disarmament or demobilization of the rebel groups. Meanwhile, MINURCAT did little to improve the security situation in north-eastern CAR. The mission was unable to operate over its mandated terrain, and could not even adequately defend its headquarters in Birao, which was attacked by rebels on multiple occasions during its deployment (United Nations Office for the Coordination of Humanitarian Affairs, 2009). The mission had no political role, thanks to its limited mandate from the UN Security Council, and even in this context its operations in CAR were an afterthought, constituting 300 of the 5,200-strong force (International Crisis Group 2008; International Crisis Group 2009). MINURCAT was discontinued in 2010 at the insistence of the Government of Chad, and UN peacekeepers were withdrawn from north-eastern CAR, which remained unstable. With political deadlock and limited military capacity, the security situation only continued to deteriorate.

Ultimately, peacebuilding efforts were unable to advance while the Central African regime remained unwilling to devote serious political capital either to the inclusive national dialogue, or to reform of the security sector, both of which could have undermined Bozizé with respect to his domestic opponents. Although the international community cannot be expected to achieve its objectives in the face of Central African resistance, it made no attempt to adjust its goals despite the lack of progress, or even to report candidly on the Bozizé regime's recalcitrance. As a result, BONUCA/BINUCA stagnated, while PBC efforts saw no results on the ground. The peacebuilding efforts came to mirror CAR's own political institutions: existing more in name than in substance.

Seleka and the limits of international support

In 2012, the increasingly unstable political and security landscape of CAR finally collapsed. Multiple rebel groups in the north-east, citing the government's unmet obligations under various peace accords as well as the failure of the DDR process, began advancing on the capital. As the rebels advanced, elements of Bozizé's former supporters from 2003 defected to the new alliance, while Chadian and Sudanese nationals joined the advance opportunistically.

The following events strikingly mirrored the fall of the previous regime and Bozizé's own rise to power. Chad provided support for Seleka's advance, while the other CEEAC heads of state opted for a containment strategy, deploying MICOPAX between the rebel forces and Bangui in order to prevent the fall of the capital. Wary of his regional allies, Bozizé managed to secure aid from South Africa, in the form of 400 soldiers, which deployed to Bangui without any coordination with MICOPAX (International Crisis Group, 2013). CEEAC forced Bozizé to negotiate with the rebels, commit to legislative elections, and give up any hope of a third presidential term. The resulting Libreville Agreement of January 2013 strengthened MICOPAX with reinforcements from additional countries (including Chad, Gabon, the Republic of Congo, Cameroon, and Equatorial Guinea). However, the agreements quickly collapsed. Bozizé refused to implement the agreement's provisions, publicly suggesting his intention of running for a third term. Meanwhile, the Seleka rank-and-file and certain leaders rejected the agreement reached by the alliance's leadership, in some cases taking their own commanders hostage, and threatened to march on Bangui. Again mirroring the collapse of the Patassé regime a decade prior, MICOPAX tacitly withdrew its support from Bozizé, making no effort to implement the Libreville Agreement. Seleka forces overran the capital three months later, overthrowing Bozizé's regime and killing thirteen South African soldiers but encountering no resistance from MICOPAX.

The rise and fall of Seleka and increasing destabilization

The Seleka leadership and combatants alike proved most interested in looting the state as thoroughly as possible. The new president and political elite misappropriated funds, looted public agencies, and signed multiple questionable agreements with mining and oil companies (International Crisis Group, 2014). Other commanders and combatants organized looting and kidnappings in the capital and throughout the country, and informal taxation and poaching increased.

This level of predation proved unsustainable and unendurable for the general population. Moreover, the primarily Muslim composition of Seleka forces prompted counter-mobilization along sectarian lines, adding a new dimension to an already unstable situation. With matters now well out of hand, MICOPAX forces deployed to Bangui to restore order. However, these forces came into conflict with Seleka troops as well, and were unable to deter the escalation. With MICOPAX forces obviously unable to maintain basic order, and French troops limited by their mandate to secure the airport, the African Union entered the fray in July, announcing the expansion of MICOPAX into the International Support Mission for CAR (MISCA). However, competition between the AU and CEEAC instantly hindered the new mission's operations (International Crisis Group, 2014). The military component was increased, but deployment was slow and there was no corresponding improvement in logistical capacity.

By the end of 2013, mass unrest and the mobilization of popular militias had resulted in spiralling violence, with thousands killed in sectarian clashes. An international response was slow in coming, despite calls from non-governmental organizations; France did not begin pushing for an intervention until August, while the UK balked at a European-funded mission and the US considered a UN peacekeeping mission impractical (Marchal, 2014). The UN Security Council authorized French military intervention in early December in the form of Operation Sangaris, composed of 1,200 soldiers. However, the French operation was hobbled by flawed premises inherited from their recent operations in Mali. Seleka forces proved much more resilient than expected, and Operation Sangaris' focus on Seleka with little attention to Anti-Balaka militias exacerbated these concerns (Marchal, 2014).

Later the same month it authorized the official transfer of MISCA from the CEEAC to the AU, with a mandate to protect civilians and restore order, stabilize the country, create space for humanitarian assistance, support the (now-defunct) DDR process, and reform the (now-gutted) security services. In January 2014, France and CEEAC called the Seleka regime to a CEEAC summit in N'djamena, where they effectively forced the President and Prime Minister to resign, deposing their government. Over the next few months, hundreds of troops from Burundi and Rwanda reinforced the ex-MICOPAX elements and French forces, increasing MISCA's force to nearly 6,000 by March 2014. Despite the repeated increase in peacekeepers, the situation continued to spiral out of control. Moreover, different peacekeeping contingents were accused of taking sides or playing favourites (Marchal, 2013)—Muslim populations accused the French of siding with the anti-Muslim militias, while Chadian soldiers reportedly fired into a crowd of Christians, killing twenty-four and injuring over a hundred civilians (and subsequently withdrawing its peacekeepers). The MICOPAX commander was even quoted as stating that his greatest accomplishment was preventing the Chadian and Congolese contingents of the mission from coming to blows.

In April 2014, the UN Security Council authorized the deployment of a new UN peacekeeping mission, MINUSCA, with a maximum capacity of 12,000 personnel, and deployment planned for September. MISCA units would be incorporated into MINUSCA where possible, while BINUCA—its mandate completely derailed by the spiralling violence—would also be folded into the mission. The EU also formally authorized a new EUFOR mission, deployed in June 2014, reinforcing the existing French forces.

Conclusion

The Central African Republic has been host to a long list of regional and international interventions since the FACA mutinies in 1996, but these missions have proved ineffectual at building peace in CAR, and at worst have actively contributed to the country's destabilization. Although regional forces such as MISAB and FOMUC/MICOPAX were able to establish some order in the capital, attempts to stabilize the provinces were unsuccessful. Regional partners actively orchestrated military challenges to the regime in power and abandoned the head of state, particularly when Central African leaders refused to negotiate with the challengers. Once Patassé had lost his credibility in the region, it was easier for FOMUC to stand by and curry favour with Bozizé. The MICOPAX countries applied a similar logic to Bozizé and Seleka ten years later, albeit with disastrous results.

Bilateral military support, primarily from France, proved similarly capricious. While the French government was willing to assist in establishing order where feasible, it focused on minimizing costs to itself, and was particularly sensitive to public opinion. It played a crucial role in the financial and logistical support of the regional peacekeeping missions, but was not interested in contributing the resources necessary for addressing the underlying challenges. The European Union did finance initial efforts by MICOPAX to expand the capabilities of the FACA in the provinces, but these efforts were quickly undone by more fundamental political challenges.

Peacekeeping operations deployed from outside of the region, such as MINURCA and MINURCAT, were arguably successful within the context of their mandates. However, whatever success these missions achieved on the security front was not matched by political progress or longer-term SSR. MINURCA lacked the political clout to pressure the government, while MINURCAT explicitly lacked a political mandate. Peacebuilding missions such as BONUCA or BINUCA were even less successful. Without a military component, the missions could not offer the carrot of security provision, while their political leverage was minor even when staffed with knowledgeable and capable leadership. Ultimately, these peacebuilding missions were not reactive, maintaining the same unrealistic goals despite the lack of buy-in from local actors.

Whether the latest UN peacekeeping mission MINUSCA will have a positive impact on the situation in CAR remains to be seen. The most recent crisis is much deeper than those of the past seventeen years, and the scale of the international footprint has expanded dramatically as regional and international partners scramble to contain the unfolding violence. The complete breakdown of state institutions, and the troubling track record of regional peacekeeping forces, demands a reappraisal of the international community's peacekeeping strategy in CAR.

Going forward, the international community must be attentive to several factors. First is the tendency of regional partners to actively interfere in CAR for their own ends, particularly Chad but also including the Republic of Congo, DRC, and other members of CEEAC. Regional peacekeeping has also served as an important source of payroll subsidization for African countries such as Burundi, which use peacekeeping deployments both to foot the cost of their over-large military forces, and to serve as theatres for training and building unit cohesion— motives which lead countries to prioritize peacekeeping deployment more than actual conflict resolution. While supporting African peacekeeping missions has both normative and practical attractions for Western countries and the UN system, neighbouring states have incentives to interfere in ways that actively destabilize the situation, or at best that complicate international peacekeeping efforts. Despite MISAB's success, the experiences with FOMUC and MICOPAX mean that the countries of the Central African region cannot credibly take the lead on long-term peacekeeping efforts in the CAR. MINUSCA may be positioned to provide a more impartial presence, if it is able to expand its base of troops beyond MISCA, but should approach any transfer to a regionally-led force with caution.[5]

Moreover, any future peacekeeping presence must resist the impulse to search for quick fixes or low-cost solutions at the expense of durable results. In the past, UN peacekeepers departed quickly after securing elections. This left a fragile political transition in the hands of a region, which proved more interested in manipulating Central African politics to their own ends, and ultimately undermined Patassé and UN peacebuilders alike by supporting Bozizé's rebellion. Neither peacekeeping, nor peacebuilding interventions, can resolve the political, economic, and security crises in CAR without buy-in from Central Africans. Nevertheless, the international community (particularly the UN Security Council and France) must consider these geopolitical factors when constructing interventions or considering withdrawal. While the prospect of a longer-term UN presence will not be easy for the UN Security Council to stomach in an era where the appetite for peacekeeping missions is limited, the alternative has clearly proved much more costly. Without a mandate to back up peacebuilding over the long term, with attention to regional factors, CAR will be on international life support until its next crisis.

Notes

1 For example, the 2013 deployment of a 'Force Intervention Brigade' composed of regional forces from South Africa, Tanzania, and Malawi was carried out under UN auspices as an arm of MONUSCO.

2 For example, the African Union–United Nations Mission in Darfur (UNAMID) was constructed as a 'hybrid' mission, and worked closely with an AU-led mediation team. When regional peacekeepers (mostly Ethiopian) were deployed to the Abyei region after South Sudan's independence and the escalation of border disputes, they were placed under UN mandate as an interim security force (UNISFA).

3 Renforcement des Capacités Africaines de Mantien de la Paix (Reinforcement of African Capacity to Maintain Peace).

4   See Chapter 11, 'CAR's Southern Identity: Congo, CAR, and International Justice' by Tatiana Carayannis for greater detail on the strategic calculations of the MLC.
5   For more on the drawbacks of 'backyard peace operations', see Boulden, J. (2003) *Dealing with Conflict in Africa: The United Nations and Regional Organizations*, Palgrave MacMillan, New York, in particular Chapter 9 (Tatiana Carayannis and Herbert F. Weiss, 'The Democratic Republic of Congo, 1996').

Bibliography

International Crisis Group (2007) *Anatomy of a Phantom State*, Africa Report No. 136, Nairobi–Brussels.

International Crisis Group (2008) *Central African Republic: Untangling the Political Dialogue*, Africa Briefing No. 55, Nairobi–Brussels.

International Crisis Group (2009) *Chad: Powder Keg in the East*. Africa Report No. 149, Nairobi–Brussels.

International Crisis Group (2013) *Central African Republic: Priorities of the Transition*, Africa Report No. 203, Nairobi–Brussels.

International Crisis Group (2014) *The Central African Crisis: From Predation to Stabilisation*, Africa Report No. 219, Nairobi–Brussels.

Marchal, Roland (2013) 'Central African Republic: Back to War Again?' *Global Observatory, International Peace Institute*. Available from: <http://theglobalobservatory.org/component/myblog/central-african-republic-back-to-war-again-/blogger/Roland%20Marchal/>

Marchal, Roland (2014) 'As Violence Persists, International Intervention in CAR falls short', *Global Observatory, International Peace Institute*. Available from: <http://theglobalobservatory.org/component/myblog/as-violence-persists-international-intervention-in-car-falls-short/blogger/Roland%20Marchal/>

Organization for Economic Co-operation and Development (2014) 'Aid disbursements to countries and regions (DAC2a)'. Available from: <http://stats.oecd.org/qwids/>.

United Nations Office for the Coordination of Humanitarian Affairs (2009) 'Spiralling Violence in Central African Republic's North East'. Available from: <http://minurcat.unmissions.org/Portals/MINURCAT/Birao%20under%20fire%20-%20June%2022%20OCHA%20Bangui.pdf>.

United Nations Security Council (1997a) 'First report to the Security Council pursuant to resolution 1125 (1997) concerning the situation in the Central African Republic', S/1997/652.
United Nations Security Council (1997b) 'Second report to the Security Council pursuant to resolution 1125 (1997) concerning the situation in the Central African Republic', S/1997/684.
United Nations Security Council (1997c) 'Third report to the Security Council pursuant to resolution 1125 (1997) concerning the situation in the Central African Republic,' S/1997/716.
United Nations Security Council (1997d) 'Fourth report to the Security Council pursuant to resolution 1125 (1997) concerning the situation in the Central African Republic', S/1997/759.
United Nations Security Council (1997e) 'First report to the Security Council pursuant to resolution 1136 (1997) concerning the situation in the Central African Republic', S/1997/954.
United Nations Security Council (1998a) 'Second report to the Security Council pursuant to resolution 1136 (1997) concerning the situation in the Central African Republic,' S/1998/3.
United Nations Security Council (1998b) 'Third report of the Secretary-General on the United Nations Mission in the Central African Republic', S/1998/1203.
United Nations Security Council (2001) 'Third report of the Secretary-General to the Security Council on the situation in the Central African Republic and on the activities of the United Nations Peace-building Support Office in the Central African Republic (BONUCA)', S/2001/660.
United Nations Security Council (2003) 'The situation in the Central African Republic and activities of the United Nations Peace-building Support Office in the Central African Republic (BONUCA)', S/2003/5.
United Nations Security Council (2009) 'Report of the Secretary-General on the situation in the Central African Republic and on the activities of the United Nations Peacebuilding Support Office in that country', S/2009/309.

10 From Being Forgotten to Being Ignored

International Humanitarian Interventions in the Central African Republic

Enrica Picco

Introduction

A neglected country, a silent crisis, a forgotten population: these are the words often used to describe the humanitarian situation in the Central African Republic (CAR). A country bigger than France, with a little more than four million inhabitants and with a life expectancy of only forty-seven years. Recurrent political crises, with the consequent violence, displacement and outbreaks, have led humanitarian agencies to set up timely operations in the country, especially in the last couple of decades. However, most of the time the interventions revealed themselves to be inadequate in efficiently responding to the needs and this mainly happened for two different reasons. On the one hand, the concurrent regional crises in neighbouring countries such as the Democratic Republic of the Congo (DRC) and Sudan, have contributed to further overshadowing a country that was already known as the 'Cinderella of the French empire' (Brustier, 1962), diverting geo-political interests and consequently the attention of donors and aid agencies. On the other hand, when the aid machine did move ahead and intervene, the humanitarian agencies soon had to face the unsustainability of their interventions, more like a series of small patches to treat a large wound in the absence of a global, structural approach.

This chapter will try to explain the reasons behind the difficulties experienced in assisting the Central African population, starting from the assumption that governance, development, security and humanitarian challenges are strictly intertwined.[1] Crisis after crisis, the long-term support that the Central African state needed to strengthen its capacities was progressively reduced because of the lack of good governance and the political instability, with the development actors claiming they lacked the minimum conditions to intervene. In this scenario, the humanitarian agencies scaled up and took over part of the work, extending emergency interventions to cover structural needs. As was easily foreseeable, this system was unsustainable. Working in CAR became a challenge that only a few international NGOs decided to face and the country got trapped in a category mismatch, not fulfilling the conditions for either emergency aid or development aid. Already neglected for a long time by the central state, then abandoned by the aid actors, Central Africans learned to live with very little expectation that a big change in their precarious living conditions would come from outside.

Being aware of the coexistence of many different factors, the focus will be on the interventions carried out by international NGOs, particularly in the health sector. Along the same lines, the analysis will take as its starting point the first substantial emergency interventions in the country of the late nineties. Finally, a large section will be dedicated to the ongoing humanitarian crisis originating from the first Seleka offensive at the end of 2012, widely considered the most severe to ever affect the country.

Off the humanitarian map

An essential preliminary to any analysis of humanitarian intervention in CAR is an overview of the assistance trends in the country in the last few decades. This will provide the background to understand the ups and downs of the aid system; and to better explain how, year by year, crisis after crisis, assuring long-term assistance in the country has first been considered complex, then simply impossible, with a subsequent impact on the capacity to respond to emergencies.

The entire recent history of CAR has been marked by a dependence on foreign aid. Either coming from bilateral cooperation (France, Germany, Japan, China, USA) or from the Bretton Woods institutions (International Monetary Fund – IMF, World Bank), international financial support was vital for the country. In 1991, foreign aid was estimated to cover 61 per cent of the state budget, a percentage that increased to 76 per cent in 1999. This dependence was made evident for instance in 1992–1993, when the suspension of contributions due to the refusal to carry out presidential elections had heavy social and economic consequences.

France has for years been the first contributor in terms of development aid (Centre français du commerce extérieur – CFCE, 1995). Despite the ambivalent relations during the Bokassa Empire (1965–1979), starting from the 1980s Paris basically took CAR under its wing (International Crisis Group – ICG, 2007). From 1989 to 1992, the French government provided 63.9 per cent of the total bilateral funds, being by far the first partner of CAR by volume of activities compared with the multilateral donors. The French aid was channelled through different systems: financial support (with both direct and indirect funds), technical assistance (to key positions in both the state institutions and the private sector) and military cooperation. On the whole, the different donors subjected their disbursements to conditions that generally heavily impacted on the state's financial self-determination (e.g. in the case of the IMF) (Colgan, 2002).

A typical example of this is the health sector where, between 1986 and 1993, foreign aid covered 70 per cent of the total budget for health care (prevention and treatment) and 30 per cent of the budget for training of health personnel due to poor state resources. In the National Health Development Plan (1994–1998), international aid was supposed to meet 80 per cent of the funding needed; in 1995, it represented more than 90 per cent of the total budget (Ministère de la Santé et de la Population – MSPP, 1999). Although it is not easy to quantify the aid allocation as it intervened at different levels (ministerial budget, specific projects, etc.), in different shapes (funds, building rehabilitation, etc.) and from different actors (NGOs, multilateral institutions and governments), it is general opinion that this external support to the Central African health system was essential for the creation of most of the national programmes to fight against specific diseases (e.g. malaria, HIV, tuberculosis). In fact, the national system showed itself to be so dysfunctional that some programmes still struggled to start up even though they were almost completely funded by foreign aid. This was the case of the Expanded Programme on Immunization (EPI), launched in 1979, that despite international efforts never managed to reach more than half of Central African children.[2]

Besides bilateral and multilateral state cooperation, assistance to the population has for years been provided by just a handful of international NGOs.[3] AFVP (Association Française des Volontaires du Progrès) was one of the first aid organizations in CAR. Since 1964, it has supported rural projects related to the cotton industry as well as health programmes. The Italian NGO COOPI (Cooperazione Internazionale) is another veteran of cooperation in CAR, working in close collaboration with the Catholic Church, the GTZ (German Cooperation Agency) and the local community. Present since 1974, mainly in Ouham-Pendé, its projects promoted rural and urban development specifically in the areas of primary health care, education and micro-credits. In the 1990s, the international presence was consolidated by Handicap International which ran training programmes in Bangui, and Médecins du Monde which supported the national HIV programme.

The picture emerging from this is one of a country where bilateral and multilateral aid, as well as international NGOs had been trying for decades to fulfil the state absence in many development sectors, such as health care, education and rural development. Overall, they managed to establish lasting relations with the local civil society and long-term programmes, especially in the west and north-west of the country. This work was also enhanced by the capillary presence of Christian missions that have worked closely with local communities since the beginning of the last century. Some examples are the Capuccini Fathers, who in Ouham and Ouham-Pendé worked hard to strengthen rural cooperatives in the villages; the Saint Joseph Sisters, who for years have provided assistance to communities in the villages around Markounda in health care (running a dispensary and training health workers), education and agriculture; and finally the Association des Oeuvres Médicales pour la Santé en Centrafrique (ASSOMESCA), an ecumenical association formed in 1989 regrouping Catholic and Protestant churches in CAR.

That was the background to what we can call the first large emergency intervention in the country in 1997. Ironically, the switch in the assistance model in CAR was not provoked by internal needs but by external factors. At that time, thousands of Rwandan refugees were fleeing across the border from Zaire (the current DRC) into Congo-Brazzaville and CAR. The Hutu refugees were in an extremely poor condition, suffering from exhaustion and malnutrition. Many had trudged hundreds of kilometres through the mountains and forests of central Zaire to escape the advance of the mainly Tutsi rebels ('ICRC steps up aid for Rwandan refugees in Congo', 1997).[4]

Despite the lack of a proper coordination system among the humanitarian agencies present in Bangui, the aid actors mobilized resources to provide the Rwandan refugees with shelters and primary health care. At that time, Médecins Sans Frontières (MSF) also set up in CAR and intervened on both sides of the Congo-Brazzaville and Central African border, struggling with difficult access to the refugees who were reachable only by boat, and the poor data collection and alerting system. Due to the persistence of the conflict in DRC, in the following years the influx of refugees was constant. In 1999, there were an estimated 20,000 Congolese in CAR, around 2,000 of them in Bangui in the camp of Port Amont. The aid system scaled up accordingly: at the end of the 1990s, several international NGOs, (e.g. COOPI,

Oxfam Quebec, MSF) increased their presence in Bangui to bring assistance to the refugees.

At that time, the influx of Congolese refugees was not the only concern of President Ange-Félix Patassé (1993–2003). A long-lasting internal discontent in the Forces Armées de la République Centrafricaine (FACA), mainly due to delays in salary payments and ethnic favouritism, fuelled the repeated mutinies of the second half of the nineties.[5] Fighting, looting and disorder deeply affected Bangui and forced people to flee, despite the presence of international troops first sent by the neighbouring countries through the Mission Interafricaine de Surveillance des Accords de Bangui (MISAB), which was then replaced by the Mission des Nations Unies en République Centrafricaine (MINURCA), authorized by the UN Security Council in March 1998. Later on, only one year after the withdrawal of the blue helmets, a renewed political instability culminated with the violent coup attempts in 2001 and 2002 that affected a big part of the country and led to the taking of power by François Bozizé in 2003.[6]

It was at the beginning of the 2000s that the aid agencies started consistently addressing the internal emergency needs of the Central African population. At the same time, a new trend first emerged that would mark the humanitarian intervention in the coming years: a gearing up of the relief system and a simultaneous scaling down of the development aid as a consequence of the conflict.

In October 2002, CAR was devastated by a huge humanitarian crisis, especially in terms of violence against civilians and population displacement. For instance, in the first two weeks of hostilities in Bangui, MSF treated 546 wounded civilians, 50.6 per cent of whom had gunshot wounds. Violence was perpetrated by both parties in the conflict: while Chadian mercenaries regrouped by Bozizé were looting and spreading fear in the north, the Congolese rebel troops of Bemba's Mouvement pour la Libération du Congo (MLC), called up by Patassé, were carrying out mass rapes, especially along the road between Bangui and

Damara (see Carayannis, Chapter 11). Rapes were systematically perpetrated house by house against all women found in the household, whatever their age, allegedly following the orders of the Central African president to punish civilians supporting the coup. In general, in the small villages the people managed to flee into the bush before the arrival of the MLC, but the women living in Bangui (especially in Pk12 and Pk22) were the most affected, with 199 cases of rape registered by MSF in the first week alone.[7]

The second relevant pattern of the events between 2002 and 2003 was massive displacement inside and outside the country. The World Food Programme recorded approximately 210,000 internally displaced civilians in 2003. Although this was a rough estimate due to the difficulties of collecting information, the reality of villages completely empty all around the country confirmed the gravity of the situation. According to the United Nations High Commissioner for Refugees (UNHCR), around 40,000 people crossed the border between CAR and Chad between November 2002 and March 2003.

The few aid agencies present in the country at that time[8] scaled up assistance in the camp settings to provide first relief to Internally Displaced Persons (IDPs) and refugees, but have been unable to respond to the broader humanitarian and long-term needs. Once again, the reason is to be found outside the country. In fact, the 2003 conflict in CAR, although one of the biggest experienced by the country, was exceeded by the other humanitarian crises affecting the region, in terms of the number of people involved, geo-political interest of the international community and subsequent donor attention. In the same years, the crisis of the Great Lakes region and the war in the DRC, together with the conflicts in Chad and Darfur, monopolized the international agenda in Africa and absorbed most of the humanitarian aid. At this time, CAR did not appear on any priority list for humanitarian assistance (Development Initiatives, 2005)[9] despite the alarming and progressively worsening indicators in the country for health, education and development (in the Human Development Indicators [HDI], CAR was ranked 168 out of 175 countries). This trend marked the first half of the 2000s and to a certain extent has remained until today.

A window of opportunity for change

Once the emergency was over, and during the following couple of years of relative stability, the remaining NGOs in CAR struggled to rebuild long-term sustainable aid on the ashes of the progress made in the pre-coup period. At that time, as Olin notes elsewhere in this book (see Chapter 9) the international community in Bangui mainly consisted of three stakeholders: Bureau de l'ONU en Centrafrique (BONUCA), the political bureau left in place by the UN after the departure of the MINURCA; United Nations Development Programme (UNDP), as coordinator of the international aid; and France. While the first two were often trapped in the dichotomy of political (BONUCA) and technical (UNDP) criteria for aid response, the third one was reaffirming its role in the country through substantial support: financial (more than 100 million US dollars between 2003 and 2006), technical (with seventy French technical advisors) and military (to the international troops and the French-only Operation Boali). In addition to the sometimes contradictory conditions and restrictions imposed by the international community, internally, President Bozizé was also responsible for never establishing a system of transparency and good governance able to reassure his external partners (ICG, 2007).

This situation could have continued for years, if not for a few new and coincidental factors that paved the way for a turnaround. Indeed, at the end of 2006, the rebellions against the central power started again. New groups were progressively taking over important towns, controlling entire areas, and threatening the leadership of President Bozizé: L'Armée pour la Restauration de la République et de la Démocratie (APRD) in the north-west and Union des Forces Démocratiques pour le Rassemblement (UFDR) in the east of the country. Extensive violence and human rights abuses were perpetrated by both government forces (FACA and the Presidential Guard), and rebels. Despite its presence since 2000, the BONUCA human rights unit was 'largely passive' and 'did not effectively monitor or report on human rights abuses in the north', as denounced by a Human Rights Watch report in 2007.

Despite a scenario that required immediate intervention, there were a series of constraints that did not allow an effective humanitarian response. A multidisciplinary UN mission carried out in November 2006 identified two main reasons for this lack of response: first, UN agencies continued to 'experience difficulties to gear up their humanitarian response', especially in terms of resources to carry out emergency programmes; and second, 'UN and NGO presence in the most affected areas remains insufficient' because of the scant number of NGOs in the country and the discontinuous physical presence of UN agencies where the needs were greater (Fall, 2006). This was made even more difficult by their security measures, such as the obligation to travel under military escort when accessing those areas.

This acknowledgement of the inadequate humanitarian intervention in the country came together with the intuition that 'addressing humanitarian challenges in CAR must go hand in hand with addressing the root causes of the crisis' and that 'humanitarian assistance must be accompanied by increased recovery and development programs' (Fall, 2006). Meanwhile, CAR was also seen to be going through a protracted protection crisis,[10] with frequent human rights abuses and a non-existent justice system with consequent widespread impunity. The condition of CAR as a fragile state defined by governance, development and security crises was taken into consideration to evaluate the results of the humanitarian intervention and to plan its possible revision.

Most of the recommendations included in the report of this multidisciplinary mission were put in place in the following year. The arrival in the country of a new Humanitarian Coordinator,

Toby Lanzer, was, if not the engine, at least the accelerator of this change. Playing on the idea of 'do no harm', Lanzer launched the more positive idea of 'do more good', where 'impartial and effective humanitarian action can have a positive impact beyond its primary aim of saving lives and relieving suffering, i.e. to create some breathing space for conflict-torn communities and lay the foundations for stability and development (Lanzer, 2008).

A coinciding pull factor to gear up the assistance is also retraceable in the regionalization of the conflict: CAR was becoming a destabilizing country in an already greatly destabilized area. Paradoxically, the conflict in Darfur represented a big chance for CAR and provoked a leverage effect in attracting worldwide interest. A real risk of 'darfurization' (meaning a high fragmentation of violence) was pointed out in the north-east, and especially in the Vakaga prefecture. This area had already for a long time been considered a different country – because of a long-standing state absence, a total lack of infrastructure and an ethnic composition completely different from that of the capital region and the west – and consequently more exposed to degenerate into chronic instability. In 2007, the Darfur crisis led the international community to deploy troops in the CAR/Chad region, first under the European Union (EU) and then under UN control,[11] and to substantially invest in the reform of the FACA to secure the country.

In 2007, the aid system in the country increased significantly and turned into an unprecedented internationalization of the assistance if compared with the previous decade. Between January and July 2007, as a result of consistent UN advocacy to the international community, the number of international NGOs increased from five to twenty-two.[12] Examining the UN system, new coordinators were assigned to most of the agencies (UNICEF, WHO, WFP and UNFPA) and an effective coordination system was put in place through clusters and 'sectorial working groups', as the United Nations Office for the Coordination of Humanitarian Affairs (OCHA) defined the particular approach adopted in CAR where the clusters were merged with existing development sector groups with the aim of 'bridging the often artificial divide between what is humanitarian and what is developmental'. Similarly, the members of the Humanitarian and Development Partnership Team (HDPT) in the field increased from seven to thirty-five organizations (Lanzer, 2008).

Furthermore, the new aid actors in the country could count on more humanitarian funding in 2007 than in 2004, 2005 and 2006 all together: a total of 69 million US dollars, which represents one of the biggest humanitarian investments per capita, even if compared with the aid giants of the region, like DRC and Sudan. In the same year, with the aim of funding the start-up costs and response to emergencies, the Emergency Response Funds mechanism was set up in the country, and in its first year alone funded sixty-six projects for a total of ten million US dollars (Lanzer, 2008). In this new UN-led humanitarian system, the International Committee of the Red Cross (ICRC) also drastically reviewed its engagement in the country, becoming a delegation independent from the one in Cameroon with a budget increasing from almost three million US dollars to almost ten million US dollars, and going from four to twenty international staff and from zero to three bases in the field (Paoua, Kaga Bandoro and Birao).

However, the gearing up of the humanitarian intervention was not a sufficient catalyst for the other essential piece of the pie: development aid. After having abandoned the country during the 2002 to 2003 conflict, in 2008 development donors finally pledged 600 million US dollars over three years to finance the first Poverty Reduction Strategy in the country's history, and engaged in the restructuring of CAR's external debt. A drop in the ocean if we consider the estimated 1.3 billion US dollars needed for Security Sector Reform (SSR), economic recovery, infrastructure, health care and education. On top of this, the impact of these funds in the remote areas of the country most in need was substantially insignificant: in 2007 'less than twenty percent of development aid was spent in projects outside the capital, Bangui' (Jauer, 2009), enhancing the perception of oblivion of those regions.

More generally, during these years, CAR experienced a special and perhaps unrepeatable window of opportunity to make a definitive shift in the future of the country. Unfortunately, this chance was not exploited as much as it could have been, for two reasons. Looking at the external factors, the situation of the country made many people wonder if any development was possible with the persistent insecurity, or if some stability was a preliminary condition for any economic reprisal. As shown by other countries' experience, there was a general agreement within the international community that in CAR security and development should also go hand in hand. However, from an internal perspective, Bozizé was always reluctant to commit to a durable change and his continual resistance annoyed most of the development donors: one example being the SSR that, although funded, never really started because of a clear lack of political will. The choice of delegating any kind of assistance to the international aid, with a consequent and progressive disengagement from the state, did not allow the country to take the opportunity to make some substantial reforms, despite high-level international pressure.

The curve of the assistance in CAR dropped again in the following years, in the worst trend of our age. Not only did the development funds remain scant, concentrated in very few sectors and limited to the capital, but also the humanitarian funds – that often played the important role of temporarily picking up on some long-term need – dropped significantly in 2009. One of the main reasons can be identified in the 'aid category mismatch' that CAR was trapped in, with humanitarian actors eager to quickly disengage after the peak of the crisis and development partners reluctant to invest in a country with limited capacity and will to carry out long-term programmes (Jauer, 2009). The fact of being a fragile state with recurrent humanitarian crises had cut CAR off from access to the assistance most adapted to the country's needs.

The time of disillusion

This is where we were before the crisis originating from the Seleka coup of March 2013. In the years before, CAR seemed to be affected by a long-term crisis that was slowly eroding the country. A 2011 MSF report on the country reported (MSF, 2011) mortality rates above the emergency threshold, especially for children under five and even in areas not affected by conflict (like the south-west); high mortality and morbidity caused by easily treatable and preventable diseases (malaria, HIV, tuberculosis and malnutrition); and a phantom health care system, with a chronic lack of facilities, skilled medical staff, diagnostic and treatment tools, medicines and supplies, and surveillance. Before the recent crisis, around 70 per cent of the Central African population was living in poverty, on less than 1.25 US dollars a day, and more than 30 per cent of households were living with food insecurity. Life expectancy dropped from fifty years in the 1990s to forty-seven in 2007, showing a constant downhill trend (Niewiadowsky, 2014) despite being in a period of relative stability and peace during the first part of the Bozizé era.

Between 2009 and 2012, the number of international NGOs working in the country dropped again. The Consolidated Appeal Processes (CAP) has constantly been underfunded (48.4 per cent in 2010 and 45.9 per cent in 2011) and the funds have been concentrated mainly in unstable areas. For example, the largest single donor to the country, the European Commission's Aid and Civil Protection Department (ECHO), prioritized the conflict zones in the east and north-east, and deprioritized the supposedly 'post-conflict' north-west. In a country so dependent on external technical expertise, the UN agencies stepped back and played a very marginal role, lacking funds and qualified international staff. The key position of Humanitarian Coordinator was left vacant several times. BONUCA's governance structure and lack of management received severe criticism (UN Office of Internal Oversight Services – OIOS, 2009) and was then replaced by a UN Integrated Peacebuilding Support Office in 2010 (BINUCA). A general feeling of resigned hopelessness at the frequent mismanagement and diversion of international funding was quite widespread within Bangui's foreign community, consequently limiting all new initiatives and leading the main international humanitarian and long-term donors to either leave the country or drastically reduce their presence. For instance, looking at the French bilateral cooperation, the estimated number of expatriates was around 1,000 people at the beginning of the 1970s, about 350 in the mid-1990s, 65 in 2000 and only 14 in December 2012; what should have been a natural reduction of external support did not coincide with any empowerment of the local human resources.

Another example is the Global Fund to fight AIDS, Tuberculosis and Malaria (GFATM), the single largest funder of health programmes in the country. Eight separate grant agreements have been signed: four for HIV (CAR had one of the highest rates in Africa, reaching 9 per cent of those aged between fifteen and forty-nine in 1999),[13] two for tuberculosis and two for malaria. Between the first grant disbursements in 2003 and 2011, the fund disbursed 66.2 million US dollars of the 84 million US dollars pledged (The Global Fund, 2013). Furthermore, since 2009, there have been massive, often months-long disruptions and suspensions in disbursements, principally due to concerns about accountability and very low performances achieved by the national programmes, especially in surveillance and supply. The effect has been most dramatically seen in malaria disbursements, which have flatlined since 2008, some years featuring zero disbursements, with major effects on the availability of medicines and therefore on patients.

In the social sector, another significant case is related to education (OIOS, 2009). Despite external donors funding programmes, the public education system has progressively collapsed. Teachers were often poorly trained and badly paid, with months of delay. Furthermore, due to the increasing insecurity in the country, a large percentage of teachers abandoned their place of work. In the last years, most of the primary schools have only been functioning thanks to the 'maître-parents' system, whereby the children's parents are paid directly from the community to cover the role of teacher without any specific training to do so. Only the schools run by religious centres managed to maintain a minimum standard of education. In 2010, UNICEF estimated the Gross Enrolment Ratio (GER) at only 28.6 per cent, meaning only a little more than one out of four children were being enrolled in school.

Fragile state, fragile response: the Seleka/Anti-Balaka crisis

It is not surprising that, starting against such a discouraging backdrop, humanitarian actors were not prepared to face one of the darkest periods in the history of CAR. The Seleka (coalition, in Sango) finds its roots in the far and marginalized north-east of the country, where some local rebel groups joined forces and took advantage of the favourable regional circumstances and support to upset the Bozizé regime. Starting in December 2012, after a first offensive and the subsequent peace agreement signed in Libreville in January 2013, the rebellion launched a second and definitive attack culminating in the coup of 23 March 2013 and the self-proclamation of the Seleka leader, Michel Djotodia, as president of the CAR.

Their rapid takeover of power in March 2013 was followed by weeks of uncontrolled robbery and looting all around the country. All the international NGOs and UN agencies present at that time were also affected and lost significant resources. OCHA reported that in April 2013 six UN offices were looted. Unprepared to face the emergency, humanitarian actors reacted with the immediate evacuation of all national and international staff from the bases in the remote areas of the country: Bouar, Paoua, Kaga Bandoro, Bambari and Ndele bases were closed down, just to mention the UN agencies. Some of them (OCHA, UNICEF, PAM, WHO) remained in Bangui with a reduced team and a higher security level (e.g. bullet-proof jackets); others (UNHCR) withdrew entirely from the country (MSF, 2013a).

Despite the increasing insecurity, at that time remaining in the field was shown to be possible. For instance, MSF bases have also not been spared by the wave of violence. Nevertheless, apart from some temporary evacuations of the international teams, the health facilities supported have never been completely shut down, assuring a constant access to health care for the population.[14] Working in the new environment was also extremely pertinent due to the increased needs. In summer 2013, OCHA stated there were at least 225,000 people displaced all around the country, noting the lack of humanitarian access in the northern and western parts of the country (an increase of 320 per cent before the crisis), and consequently more exposed to various types of diseases (OCHA, 2013). For instance, in the case of malaria, the primary killer in the country, MSF facilities experienced a 33 per cent increase in the number of cases in the first quarter of 2013 compared to the same period of 2012.

The aid agencies' withdrawal from remote areas has not only left thousands of people without assistance, but it has also led to progressively losing the pulse of the country and an understanding of the volatile context. With very few exceptions, the Central African population was left without assistance by the international humanitarian agencies, who generally used the argument of security to justify their lack of response to the crisis: the presence of new and unknown actors in the conflict was taken as justification for not having staff based in remote areas, instead of sending analysts to improve the understanding of the context and security situation as well as experienced international staff to engage with those groups and negotiate humanitarian access.

The evolution of the context of the following months worsened this picture. In August to September 2013, especially in the Ouham region, self-defence groups called Anti-Balaka started to attack the Seleka fighters and to take revenge after months of abuses. At that time, aid agencies present in Bangui had just started to carry out assessments in the field, but the continuous instability, the lack of human and logistical resources and the poorly funded CAP for 2013 (only 35 per cent) did not allow them to set up permanent bases. The fact that most of the international NGOs were still absent from the field had a double consequence: first, there were very few actors able to respond to the direct violence and to the needs of the displaced population; second, the simple fact of being present may have contributed to making the civilians exposed to the conflict feel safer.

Emblematic in this sense is the example of Bossangoa, a town to the north of Bangui: following the Anti-Balaka attacks in September 2013, around 30,000 people were forced to leave their houses and find a temporary refuge in the compound of the Catholic Church, which provided first aid assistance. These people, terrified by the violence they experienced, were left for weeks without decent humanitarian assistance or protection. Action Contre la Faim (ACF) and MSF first assessed the IDP camps in town where people were living without shelter, adequate water supplies and a sufficient number of latrines.[15] It took almost two months, and extensive media coverage of the IDPs' living conditions, for other actors to begin mobilizing their resources, even though Bossangoa is only 300 kilometres from the state capital and connected to it by one of the very few tarmac roads in the country.

The dramatic escalation of the conflict in December 2013, with the Anti-Balaka attack on Bangui and the brutal inter-confessional violence between Christians and Muslims that followed, made everybody finally realize the magnitude of the emergency. As had happened in the past, the regionalization of the conflict played a key role in raising interest in the crisis: this time, the threat was seen coming from the Sahel Jihadist groups, potentially attracted by a conflict taking on a religious dimension and by a land completely out of state control.

This period also marked the beginning of an unprecedented protection crisis: the Central African social fabric was deeply hurt by the extended human rights abuses committed by all the actors and will remain damaged for a long time. Between December 2013 and June 2014, the Muslim community living in

CAR was forced to either leave or die: it is estimated that almost 150,000 Muslims have fled from Bangui and the western regions, mainly by plane or on trucks towards Chad and Cameroon, without the institutions in charge of protecting them being able to put effective contingency mechanisms in place (Kleijer, 2014). Many of them have died along the road; thousands are still prisoners in enclaves, in schools and religious compounds, under the protection of the international forces.

Throughout 2013, MSF took a leading role among the humanitarian stakeholders and progressively expanded its advocacy and lobbying efforts to call for an immediate scale up of humanitarian assistance (MSF, 2013b). In a parallel and complementary way, on the donor side, ECHO significantly strengthened its capacity response in the country and it is common opinion that it was de facto taking over important coordination tasks from the UN. On 11 December, the UN system finally reviewed the classification of the Central African crisis and upgraded it to Level 3, the level of maximum emergency. This procedure was meant to allow the UN agencies to scale up their intervention, through increasing available funds, simplifying procedures and, especially, mobilizing senior experienced international staff from other missions. Unfortunately, this turnaround was late (nine months after the coup) and insufficient to drastically reverse the UN trend – some external factors like the coincidence of other huge humanitarian crises in Syria, the Philippines and South Sudan were also a factor.

This became clear during the emergency in Bangui. In January 2014, OCHA estimated there were more than 500,000 people internally displaced within the city boundary, more than 70 per cent of its total population. Fleeing the violence between ex-Seleka[16] and Anti-Balaka, civilians were leaving their houses and seeking refuge mainly in religious compounds. Among them, around 100,000 people occupied the airport of M'poko, where they felt more protected because of the nearby presence of international troops. Despite the presence of around twenty of the biggest international NGOs and all the UN agencies in the capital, in the first days only a few of them provided a proper response to the displaced in town. Later on, when surveys showed that the population was too scared to return home and a massive humanitarian intervention in the camps was urgently needed, a shameful game of passing the buck of responsibility to intervene started among the different stakeholders on the ground. In public and private meetings, UN agencies complained about the lack of implementing partners (e.g. the measles vaccination of January 2014),[17] while international NGOs were demanding greater support from the UN umbrella, in terms of needs assessment, security analysis and mobilization of funds (e.g. the distribution in the M'poko camp in December 2013).[18]

Underfunding is uniformly mentioned as the principal limitation to launch timely programmes, as also acknowledged by the UN Operational Peer Review carried out in March 2014. Although clearly not the only reason, this is immediately evident looking at the funding status quo today. During the High Level Meeting held in Brussels in January 2014, 254 million US dollars were pledged to respond to the emergency needs in CAR. However, the disbursement of the funds promised has been delayed for months, unlike what happened in other countries like South Sudan where higher commitments (754 million US dollars) corresponded to faster cash outlays. This is having a direct impact on the aid response capacity: the high costs associated with starting up projects for incoming international NGOs cannot be covered by the few available funds, leading a number of actors to look for new activities around the capital (where costs are lower) instead of responding to the needs in isolated rural areas, leaving tens of thousands of vulnerable civilians to fend for themselves without assistance. As a further consequence, salary payments for civil servants – most needed to restart administrative, education and health services all around the country – are constantly delayed and the transitional government of Catherine Samba-Panza, established after Djotodia's (forced) resignation, struggles to extend beyond the borders of Bangui. CAR is passing from being forgotten to being ignored.

Conclusion: a humanitarian accordion

Limiting analysis of the aid response in CAR to the underfunding would, however, be to oversimplify the reality. What are the root causes of this lack of reaction by the humanitarian community to the huge humanitarian crisis of 2013–2014? Previously, the aid system had shown itself to be able to gear up when necessary, but it is evident that something went wrong this time. For instance, the UN agencies, the same ones that led the response and challenged the system in 2007, have been unable to do the same in the last eighteen months. Why has this happened? Certainly, the deprioritization of the country carried out by the UN in the last years has led to the progressive loss of both the donor network and the involvement of experienced, qualified human resources. Reversing this downward spiral trend took months. The process of bringing it up to a standard level is still far from complete and will require strong internal accountability to prevent it happening again. But going one step further, would it then be reasonable to say that the humanitarian system was not prepared for this because of its own limitations in dealing with fragile countries?

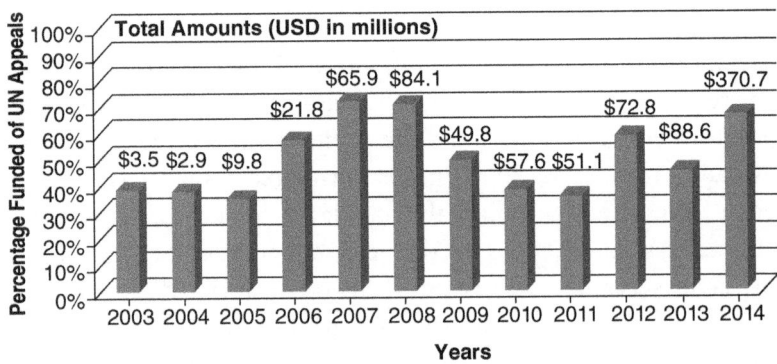

Figure 10.1 Funding UN humanitarian appeals for CAR
Source: http://fts.unocha.org/

As shown in Figure 10.1, historically, humanitarian intervention in CAR has always expanded and contracted like an accordion: a scale-up of the response during the peaks of conflict (external, in the 1990s, and internal, in 2002 to 2003 and 2006 to 2007) and a subsequent return to oblivion when the acute phase was over. On top of this, the baseline of the intervention, marked by the fragility of the state system, became progressively lower over the years. This is what made it very difficult to make the turnaround necessary to respond to the recent humanitarian crisis, which required deploying enormous resources in a short period of time. On the one hand, the immediate emergency response capacity – that the humanitarian system should be able to activate in a very short period of time (e.g. in the case of displaced people) – was not put in action because of the low international attention and understanding of the country dynamics, and consequent scarce forecast and preparedness. On the other hand, the broader aid response needed by the country in all sectors was blocked by the structural and long-term deficiencies of the state.

The windows of opportunity to make a significant change in the intervention have been lost one after another. The last one, in 2007, could have been key to inventing such a mechanism, taking advantage of the relatively stable context and integrating the humanitarian approach with a much needed development perspective to intervene where the structural needs were greater. Looking at the current situation of the country, it seems very unlikely that there will be similar chances anytime soon. After more than one year without any kind of control from the state authorities, the CAR is now a phantom country that needs to be rebuilt from zero. The minimum requirements for effective development aid are now completely lacking, while the needs arising from the widespread humanitarian and protection crisis are increasing day by day. Making the mistake again of responding to the latter, while ignoring the former, could definitely condemn this country.

Notes

1 As this chapter focuses on the humanitarian interventions in the country, it will not provide any in-depth analysis of the political–economic factors backing those interventions (definition of fragile state, regional context, etc.). For this analysis, please refer to the respective chapters of the first section of the book.
2 According to the External Review of the National Immunization Programme in Central African Republic (13 January 2013 from Auguste Ambendet, AFRO Central Inter-country Support Team): 'The main weaknesses are a) the low rate of fully immunized children (31 per cent) identified by the coverage survey, b) frequent shortage of vaccines and finally c) weak vaccine management.'
3 The information included in this session was collected through MSF internal documents review and unstructured key informant interviews.
4 In May 1997, they were crossing the Zaire River into Congo at the rate of some 500 a day, settling in locations like Liranga, Lukulela and Makotipoko to the north of the Congo capital Brazzaville. Some of them continued their journey and arrived in CAR.
5 In April 1996, 400 deserters of the national army attacked Bangui. In December of the same year, the capital saw clashes among different sections.
6 In May 2001, the attempted coup by Kolimba was stopped by Chad and Congolese rebels called up by President Patassé. In October 2002, the attempted coup by Bozizé was stopped by the Libyan intervention.
7 In February 2003, the Féderation International des Droits de l'Homme (FIDH) brought a lawsuit to the International Criminal Court (ICC) for war crimes against Patassé, Bemba and Miskine.
8 At that time, in CAR there were five international NGOs (COOPI, Handicap International, Oxfam Quebec, AELES-lèvres and MSF), the ICRC and some UN agencies (WHO, UNICEF, FAO, UNHCR, WFP, UNDP and UNFPA).
9 The top ten recipients of humanitarian assistance in 2003 were: Iraq, Ethiopia, Afghanistan, Sudan, Angola, Democratic Republic of the Congo, Eritrea, Burundi, Uganda, and Somalia.
10 One of the many definitions of protection was provided by Marguerite Contat Hickel: 'The concept of protection encompasses all activities aimed at obtaining full respect for the rights of the

individual in accordance with the letter and spirit of relevant bodies of law (human rights, humanitarian law and refugee law). Human rights and humanitarian actors shall conduct these activities impartially and not on the basis of race, national, or ethnic origin, language or gender' ('Protection of internally displaced persons affected by armed conflict: Concept and challenges', *IRRC*, September 2001, Vol. 83, N. 84).

11 EUFOR Tchad/RCA was an operational force led by the European Union under the UN Security Council Resolution 1778 of 25 September 2007. MINURCAT (Mission des Nations Unies en RCA et Tchad) took over from EUFOR on 15 March 2009, under the same resolution.

12 The expansion included IRC, Solidarité, ACF, AMI, Triangle, Mercy Corps, Merlin, NRC, Care among others.

13 'Central African Republic' *UNAIDS-AIDS INFO*, available from: <http://www.unaids.org/en/dataanalysis/datatools/aidsinfo/>.

14 According to MSF incident reports, in April 2013, one office and one house were completely looted in Bangui, seven cars stolen (in Bangui, Boguila, Ndele and Batangafo) as well as four offices and houses robbed (in Bangui, Ndele, Batangafo and Boguila) on several occasions.

15 For the water supply, MSF counted only 7.8 litres per person per day, when the minimum standard should be 15–20 litres (Sphere Project). For the latrines, MSF counted one for every 166 users, instead of one for every 20 users (Sphere Project), and no showers were available.

16 Michel Djotodia dissolved the Seleka as a rebel group on 13 September 2013.

17 The measles vaccination of early January 2014 gives us a clear example. With a risk of outbreak, instead of immediately starting a campaign in the IDP camps of the town where some NGOs were ready to intervene, the WHO preferred to use a slower cluster approach to identify the implementing partners.

18 The first food distribution was done by the World Food Programme on 12 December, but its organization in terms of locations and crowd control led to high tensions in the camp. As a consequence, any further distribution was put on standby for security reasons and resumed only three weeks later.

Bibliography

Brégeon, J-N. (1998) *Un rêve d'Afrique: Administrateurs en Oubangui-Chari, la Cendrillon de l'empire*, Denoël, Paris.

Brustier, Louis (1962) *La Cendrillon Africaine*. Editions du Scorpion, Paris.

Centre Français du Commerce Extérieur – CFCE (1995) *République Centrafricaine*, Les éds. du CFCE, Paris.

Colgan, A.L. (2002) 'Hazardous to Health: The World Bank and IMF in Africa', *Africa Action*, Washington, DC, US.

Development Initiatives (2005) 'Global Humanitarian Assistance Update 2004–05', Old Westbrook Farm, Evercreech, Somerset, UK.

Fall, I.D. (2006) 'CAR: A tragedy in making?', *Global Humanitarian Platform*, 4–11 November. Available from: <http://www.globalhumanitarianplatform.org/doc00001965.html>.

Human Rights Watch (2007) 'State of anarchy: rebellion and abuses against civilians', 15 September. Available from: < http://www.hrw.org/reports/2007/09/14/state-anarchy>.

'ICRC steps up aid for Rwandan refugees in Congo' (1997), *AFP*, 16 May.

International Crisis Group – ICG (2007) *Central African Republic: Anatomy of a Phantom State*, Africa Report No. 136, Nairobi–Brussels.

Jauer, K. (2009) 'Stuck in the "recovery gap": the role of humanitarian aid in the Central African Republic', *Overseas Development Institute – Humanitarian Practice Network*, Issue 43, June. Available from: <http://www.odihpn.org/humanitarian-exchange-magazine/issue-43/stuck-in-the-recovery-gap-the-role-of-humanitarian-aid-in-the-central-african-republic>.

Kleijer K. (2014) 'Trucking instead of protecting: how international militaries and aid agencies are failing civilians in CAR' *The Huffington Post*, 7 March.

Lanzer, T. (2008) '"Do More Good" in the Central African Republic', *Overseas Development Institute – Humanitarian Practice Network*, Issue 40, October. Available from: <http://www.odihpn.org/humanitarian-exchange-magazine/issue-40/do-more-good-in-the-central-african-republic>.

Médecins Sans Frontières – MSF (2011) *Central African Republic: A State of Silent Crisis*, MSF, Amsterdam, November.

Médecins Sans Frontières – MSF (2013a) *Central African Republic: Abandoned to its Fate?*, MSF, Amsterdam, 9 July.

Médecins Sans Frontières – MSF (2013b) 'Central African Republic: Open letter to the UN humanitarian system', 12 December. Available from: <http://www.msf.org/article/car-open-letter-un>.

Ministère de la Santé et de la Population – MSPP (1999) *Evaluation du Plan National de Développement Sanitaire 1994–1998*, Bangui.

Niewiadowsky, D. (2014) 'La République Centrafricaine: le naufrage d'un Etat, l'agonie d'une Nation', *Afrilex*, University of Montesquieu, Bordeaux, France.

The Global Fund (2013) 'Central African Republic – Country Index', Available from: <http://portfolio.theglobalfund.org/en/Country/Index/CAF>.

UN Office for the Coordination of Humanitarian Affairs – OCHA (2013) 'Central African Republic: Humanitarian Dashboard' 31 August. Available from: <http://reliefweb.int/sites/reliefweb.int/files/resources/20130831_MYR%20humanitarian_dashboard.pdf>.

UN Office of Internal Oversight Services – OIOS (2009) 'The United Nations Peacebuilding Support Office in the Central African Republic (BONUCA) – Audit Report', 24 December. Available from: <http://usun.state.gov/documents/organization/159875.pdf>.

UN Operational Peer Review (2014) 'Internal Report: Response to the crisis in Central African Republic – Review mission: 24 February–4 March 2014', 23 March (unpublished).

11 CAR's Southern Identity
Congo, CAR, and International Justice

Tatiana Carayannis

In the bureaucratic imaginary of international institutions, the Central African Republic has come to have little to do with Central Africa. It is, instead, more frequently seen as a corollary to the Sahel and to its eastern neighbours, an appendage to Darfur/Sudan and their conflicts, and until recently, in the occasional cross hairs of a meddlesome North African dictator, Muammar Qaddafi, though even that was largely because CAR was on the way to something else – namely, the rest of the African continent. The Central African Republic's giant and troubled neighbour along its southern border, the Democratic Republic of the Congo (DRC), is part of another imaginary, one that is tied to the Great Lakes, which it shares with its own neighbours to the east. The Equator is the invisible frontier that keeps diplomats focused on one or the other, rarely both together. Since CAR straddles both sides, its regional politics are frequently misread.

This is in part because '[B]ureaucracies are formations whose aim is to maximize order, [and] create continuity...'(Davis, 2002). In the UN Secretariat, for example, recent responsibility for CAR and DRC are divided between two Africa regional divisions in the UN Department of Political Affairs. In the UN Department of Peacekeeping, as the situation deteriorated in 2013 and peacekeeping action seemed likely, the brief first resided with the South Sudan team, was later moved to the Great Lakes team, after which it briefly enjoyed its very own CAR team, and, as of this writing, has returned to the Great Lakes team.[1] The politics of knowledge production about the geographies of violence in the region have similarly separated CAR from its southern neighbours. For example, of the three most widely read books on the recent Congo wars that claim a regional approach, CAR merits an index entry in only one.[2]

Understandably, these silos are often workload-driven and sometimes analytically necessary. But they are artificial divides, as CAR is a heavily networked state. It is part of at least two regional blocs at the same time, each with its own geographies of violence. One such geography is rooted among CAR's northern neighbours, linked in particular, to Chad, in the latest crisis; while the other can be found among its southern neighbours. And while Chad today may be more existentially important for CAR, as Smith and Marchal explain elsewhere in the book,[3] this chapter will show that no picture of CAR is complete without an understanding of CAR's historic links and shared national trajectories with its two Congolese neighbours to the south, particularly the DRC.

If today, the Seleka/Anti-Balaka crisis has underscored the importance of Chad and its networks for CAR, the Congo wars of the 1990s drew CAR into their war networks and authority structures. A mere fifteen years ago, it was not the Chadians who Central Africans saw as 'invading foreigners' but the Congolese.

This chapter will look at the relationship between CAR and DRC and in particular, the MLC (Mouvement de libération du Congo) rebellion during the Second Congo War that twice intervened in CAR and which is the basis for the first International Criminal Court (ICC) investigation in CAR. It shows how cross-border contacts can facilitate rebellion or sustain armed actors on one side or the other, and how these rebellions restructure public authority in marginalized areas. Others situate their analysis primarily in remote reaches of the CAR territory—the peripheries of CAR. In the case of the MLC intervention in CAR, the centre of CAR—its capital—becomes the periphery of a neighbouring state's periphery.

CAR is part of the Congo River Basin, a vast network of rivers that spans nearly 800,000 sq km across the centre of the African continent. It shares its longest border with the DRC (1,200 km) and Congo-Brazzaville (400 km) to the south, after Chad (1,100 km) to the north, Sudan (1,000 km) to the east, and Cameroon (700 km) to the west. What would come to be known as the Central African Republic was a territory carved out from between two significant bodies of water. One, the Chari River, flows north from central CAR into Lake Chad. The other is the Ubangui River, which flows south from Bangui into the Congo River as its largest tributary. It is thus not surprising that CAR—first known as Ubangui-Chari, would have these dual regional identities. It sits in between two volatile sub-regions: one that links it to its neighbours to the north of the Equator—Chad, Cameroon, and Sudan and the economic and conflict networks they are part of; and another that links CAR to its two Congolese neighbours and the networks of the Congo wars of the last two decades.

Efforts at regional integration in Central Africa have had a fraught history (Nkama, 2005). In 1959, the four member countries of Afrique Equatoriale Francaise (AEF)—Chad, Congo, Gabon, and Oubangui-Chari—formed the Equatorial Customs Union, which progressively added other countries in the region, and in 1996 became the Communaute Economique et Monetaire d'Afrique Centrale (CEMAC). To date, there are four sub-regional economic blocs in which Central African states are grouped—with each bloc boasting its own grouping of states and objectives. CAR is a member of three out of four of these, an illustration of its split regional identity.

Increasingly, and despite (perhaps partly due to) regional fragmentation, conflicts that are initiated within national borders are fought across entire regions and involve multiple state and non-state actors (Carayannis, 2003). The Central African Republic is no exception. Civilians are caught up in these conflicts as explicit and primary targets of violence, but also as warring parties. Partly as a reaction to this trend, and partly reflecting an evolution in the international peace, security, and justice architecture, efforts to articulate multilateral frameworks and a set of dominant practices to resolve these conflicts have increased over the last two decades. Since the peace process in Northern Ireland, the end of apartheid in South Africa, and in the aftermath of the Rwandan genocide, a new and more diverse generation of conflict management tools and justice institutions has emerged to address these increasingly complex security environments. These include multidimensional peacekeeping operations with complex peacebuilding and peace enforcement mandates, the expansion of a diverse mediation community of practice, the United Nations Peacebuilding Commission, and the establishment of new bodies like the ICC (Carayannis *et al.*, 2014).

Public authority

Another common assumption is that public administration in CAR is weak, has limited legitimacy, and thus is easily overtaken by non-state armed actors and illicit networks. We generally assume that public authority is territorially bound to state frontiers when in fact, as we have seen repeatedly in CAR, authority can be cross border and transnational, or outsourced outright. Moreover, the way in which communities seek to provide justice and security for themselves is often through an amalgam of public authority—by methods that may be outside, but not necessarily disconnected from, the state. It is this hybridity of authority—authority that often is a mix of state and non-state, armed and civilian, benign and predatory and that transcends borders—that makes resolving conflicts, extending state authority, and combating impunity in this region all that more complicated.

There is a growing body of social science literature that explores the emergence of forms of authority in areas where the state is either weak or inexistent—what Lombard and Cakaj refer to as 'autonomous spaces'.[4] This includes the factors shaping the popular legitimacy of justice mechanisms, security providers, taxation and resource governance frameworks. In other words, increasingly, we seek to understand how competing authorities that may be based across national borders and which may consist partly of state and non-state authorities, violent and non-violent actors, contribute to the political order of local communities and to stability (or instability) at local and national levels. As von Benda-Beckmann, Vlassenroot, and others have shown elsewhere, people engage in 'forum shopping' and solicit interventions from the authorities they view as the most powerful, accessible, legitimate, understandable, or effective (von Benda-Beckmann, 1981). At the same time, authorities themselves are 'shopping forums' as they manipulate the processing of disputes to advance their own political and financial interests (ibid.). The shopping that occurs at a regional level is reproduced at very local levels in marginalized areas.

Informal or non-state governance structures are a significant source of the complexity facing researchers and policymakers alike. Various forms of authority across the CAR/DRC border have, at various times, interacted to produce a significant impact both on local populations and on the progression of violence—traditional or customary authorities; rebel administrations; state institutions; and international organizations. Much like Duffield's 'war networks', (2001), this hybridity of public authority implies political projects that go beyond conventional forms of territorial, bureaucratic, or juridical authority (p. 163), since states have increasingly been drawn into 'multi-level and increasingly non-territorial decision-making networks' (p. 11).

A shared history of markets, marginalization, and decline

Bangui was founded in 1889 and lies less than 2 km across the Ubangui River from the Congolese town of Zongo, in DRC's Equateur province. In a pirogue, it takes a mere ten minutes to cross the border. For much of its history, CAR was either a transit zone, or a zone of refuge for mass population displacements—first from the devastating trans-Atlantic slave trade which decimated local populations, and later from conflicts in the region. Forced and voluntary population movements across the Ubangui date back generations and were a coping mechanism for communities under threat in a not very densely populated territory (Cordell, 2002).

The geographic frontiers of CAR and its southern neighbours have largely remained unchanged since a private company under the leadership of King Leopold II of the Belgians, the Association Internationale du Congo, established a private colonial, commercial empire in Central Africa in 1875, and since the French government established a smaller colony in the same region. The boundaries of these colonial empires were largely arbitrary and separated many large precolonial African nations and tribal groups such as the Bakongo who resided in northern Angola, Belgian Congo, and French Congo, as well as in Cabinda; the Lunda, who lived in Angola, Northern Rhodesia (now Zambia), and the Belgian Congo; the Zande, who are found in CAR, South Sudan, and northern Belgian Congo; the Gbandi, Gbaya, and Ngwaka who still reside along both sides of the Ubangui River in CAR, DRC, and Congo-Brazzaville; and the Tutsi and Hutu, who resided mainly in Rwanda and Burundi but also across the frontier in Congo (Weiss and Carayannis, 2004).

A number of trading networks connect markets and communities in Central Africa. These include the illicit trade in diamonds mined in south-eastern CAR and laundered through DRC (see Chapter 6, 'A Multifaceted Business: Diamonds in the Central African Republic' by Ned Dalby), and the much publicized exploitation of 'conflict minerals' in eastern DRC; the not-so-publicized diamond mining and logging in north-western DRC; the exchange of agricultural and manufactured goods between markets in all of CAR's border regions; and networks of arms trafficking. Some of these transborder networks of economic exchange date back to before colonialism, others developed as a result of porous borders and weak state institutions. These regional economic networks often undermine the formal economies, while state authorities reap individual benefits from the revenue-generating capacity of these informal networks. It is not surprising, therefore, to see these commercial networks co-opted by armed actors in conflict situations.

The vast riverine network of navigable waters in Central Africa has meant that rivers and their tributaries have been essential for communication and the primary means of transport for trading communities in the hinterland. That—and the fact that CAR is covered in the same tropical forest found in Congo—means that fishing and logging of tropical timber have dominated local economies and livelihoods.

Before the arrival of the Seleka and the onset of post-2012 violence in CAR, Congolese merchants from the north-western DRC towns of Zongo and Gbadolite were permanent fixtures in Congolese markets along Bangui's small port on the banks of the Ubangui River. There, they supplied Bangui residents with smoked fish, manioc, corn, coffee, sesame, peanuts, and other agricultural products;[5] they then spent their earnings in markets at Pk5 and across Bangui to purchase manufactured goods to sell in local markets back across the river (see Chapter 4, 'Local Dynamics in the Pk5 district of Bangui' by Faouzi Kilembe for more on the Pk5 neighbourhood of Bangui). Markets in Limbongo, Zambi, Nzele and other towns in northern Equateur are typically filled with such goods—clothes, luggage, radios, and a variety of household goods, all imported from Dubai by Muslim traders in Bangui. Early into the Seleka rebellion in 2013, residents of Gbadolite noticed that the price of beef in local markets had declined dramatically and that local markets were suddenly flooded with beef. At closer inspection, local authorities discovered that this sudden influx of beef was the result of local Congolese arms trafficking dealers supplying weapons to the Seleka fighters. At the height of this market, the price was one cow for one machine gun. Unable to stop the flow of weapons and the resulting insecurity through the successful arrest of the traffickers, the mayor of Gbadolite took the drastic measure to ban all beef sales in local markets for several weeks in order to stop the trafficking of weapons. Needless to say, this decision was wildly unpopular among local residents, but it did disrupt the local arms market.

If Bangui is a periphery of the sub-region, then Congo's Equateur province—the poorest and largest province in the DRC, neglected and marginalized by Kinshasa in the post-Mobutu era—has been a periphery of both capitals. Despite its political significance as the home of the DRC's thirty-two-year long dictator and that of many Congolese political and economic elite, Equateur's proximity to Bangui—given that Kinshasa is 1,144 km away as the crow flies[6]—its shared ethnic groups on both sides of the border, and a shared history of political marginalization and rebellion has made the northern part of the Congolese province and its authority structures inter-linked with its Central African neighbour.

CAR and DRC share another attribute that, while more recent in CAR, dates at least to the struggle for independence in Congo—a radicalism of rural populations (Weiss, 1967).[7] During the fight for independence from Belgian occupation in DRC, rural populations proved much more radical in their discourse than the political elites that would lead them. While nationalist leaders sought a replacement of the colonial authorities with indigenous ones, their followers, the masses, were calling for a radical transformation of the state itself. This experience stood in stark contrast to the path of independence followed in French West and Equatorial Africa, where elites were the driving force for independence. In CAR as in DRC today, this 'rural radicalism' has manifested itself in a history of ad hoc self-defence mobilization in rural areas whenever livelihoods and communities are threatened. The Seleka rebellion is one expression of such rural radicalism, as are the Mai Mai auto-defence groups in the

Kivus and the more recent Katakatanga in Congo's mineral-rich Katanga province. The marginalization that underlies the mobilization for violent protest in rural communities similarly explains, at least in part, the rapid expansion of evangelical churches in both CAR and DRC in the last two to three decades as both are responses to alienation and exclusion. As Hollenweger and Anderson explain elsewhere, the social narrative of Pentecostal liturgy is itself revolutionary, as it seeks to empower those who are marginalized to overcome 'the *real* barriers of race, social status, and education' (Hollenweger, 1997).

The Central African Republic gained its independence from France on 13 August 1960, six weeks after Congo's independence and army mutiny that sparked the civil war, and together with another dozen or so newly independent African states. Two young army colonels would take the reins of each country by force—a young Colonel Joseph Mobutu launched his second and relatively bloodless coup on 25 November 1965. A month later, on New Year's Eve 1965, a young Colonel Jean-Bédel Bokassa led a coup in Bangui and seized power from President Dacko. The two new neighbouring leaders grew up alongside each other, and supported and influenced each other's actions. With Mobutu's thirty-two-year rule and Bokassa's shorter-lived reign, both heads of state came to embody the extreme personalization of power. This was the era of great, megalomaniacal Central African leaders, who declared themselves fathers of their nations and launched grand, symbolic architectural projects—they built monuments, stadiums, palaces, and other symbols of national pride in *Kin la belle* and *Bangui la coquette*. In Mobutu's case, in addition to building three palaces (one with imported Chinese labour) in his rural ancestral home in northern Equateur, he also built an airport in the same town with a 4 km runway—for many years the longest runway in all of Africa. This was to enable him to land a Concorde full of guests whom he would host in the palaces. This airport would later come in handy for the Congolese rebels who shored up Patassé's rule.

Bokassa's close personal ties with Mobutu, evident by their frequent meetings in Bangui and in Kinshasa, did not go unnoticed by international actors at the height of the Cold War ('Positions of Zambia Positions of Zambia, Rwanda & C.A.R. VIS-A-VIS MPLA', 1975). Mobutu and Bokassa were both staunchly anti-Angola and opposed Soviet support for the MPLA and other left-leaning regimes in the region and both thus enjoyed strong Western support throughout the Cold War. When President Mobutu dodged a coup in 1975, Bokassa read a public statement that merited a cable to Washington from the US Embassy in Kinshasa:

> The CAR president for life congratulated Mobutu for his successful evasion of the plot against his life and government. Bokassa stated that he, his government, mesan, and all the Central African people rise against the perpetrators of this plot by the forces of imperialism and neocolonialism. Bokassa demanded that the guilty be punished. He condemned coups d'etat in general stating that the forces of imperialism and neocolonialism in Africa must be put down ('Bokassa's Reaction to attempted coup in Zaire', 1975).

No doubt, as the US cable noted, 'Bokassa's message... [was] intended primarily for local consumption and may be considered [a] warning to whoever might be thinking of coup in CAR.'

But the same cable also foreshadowed the growing discontent and nervousness in the West with the potential liability of Bokassa's ostentatious and increasingly erratic behaviour. In 1976, while Bokassa was planning his outrageous coronation, Mobutu was dispatching Dr Bill Close (his long-time personal doctor and father of actor Glenn Close) alongside Centres for Disease Control and Prevention (CDC) staff from Atlanta, to investigate the first case of Ebola that had emerged in the small village of Yambuku in northern Equateur.

> Since Bokassa does not specifically mention USG [United States Government], his speech does not necessarily mean that we will become target of accusations of coup-plotting by Bokassa, however, as reported REFTEL (B) and previous wires, he has still not disspelled [sic] local dissatisfaction over his financial activities and certain of his

ministers. His message does provide a basis for subsequent campaign of charges against USG or others if he wishes find scapegoat ('Bokassa's Reaction to attempted coup in Zaire', 1975).

After Bokassa was overthrown in 1979 by David Dacko with the support of the French and put on trial, Bokassa reportedly said that if he was being accused of eating human flesh then Mobutu was guilty of the same as they ate together frequently. Two years later, with the successful coup by General André Kolingba, Kinshasa's ties with Bangui deepened, as Kolingba was a Yakoma. To signal this ethnic closeness, Mobutu was known to say that Bokassa was his brother but Kolingba was his son. By the 1980s, however, economic decline was beginning to show in both countries, evidenced by the total neglect of agriculture, particularly in then-Zaire, where the Mobutu regime was unable to control productivity in rural areas that declined with each passing year. Unlike the mining sector, which the state could tap with relative ease for revenue even when productivity declined sharply, revenue from agriculture virtually collapsed (Peemans, 1986). Some large-scale agriculture did survive under Mobutu, but it was mostly in the hands of large private capital—former colonial companies, multinational enterprises, and foreign-managed industrial enterprises—and it produced little income for the state coffers. In DRC as in CAR, the rural population was increasingly reduced to subsistence farming or small-scale food production which fed the growing urban population (Peemans, 1986).

CAR and the Congo wars

Bangui played an integral role in the Congo wars of the last two decades. The process of Mobutu's removal began in the Congo as early as January 1990, when President Mobutu, facing growing internal pressures for reform and democratization during a sustained economic crisis, and, facing a significant drop in international support, took steps towards reform. In the meantime, next door in CAR, a fragile democratization process that elected Ange-Félix Patassé president in a UN-led election in 1993, was trying to take root.

In the waning days of Mobutu's rule, while Kabila's Rwandan- and Ugandan-backed putsch was rapidly making its way across Congo, France sought to prop up Mobutu's dying regime through covert military aid to the ailing dictator who spent his last days in Congo on his yacht the *Kamaniola* on the Ubangui River. This covert aid was facilitated by French paratroopers based in CAR and by Patassé. Patassé, however, was preoccupied with his own problems at home, dealing with a series of army mutinies that had erupted throughout 1996–1997 over the non-payment of salaries. As Wohlers notes in Chapter 13, a key event in this evolution was the Chadian deployment of forces to CAR in 1996, at the request of Patassé, to help counter the army mutinies. In this, as in future interventions, Chadian soldiers quickly developed a reputation for undisciplined and abusive behaviour while in CAR.[8] Chadian troops also occupied some Congolese towns across the river in northern Equateur where they acquired the same reputation.

While Kabila's advancing Alliance des Forces Démocratiques pour la Libération du Congo-Zaïre (AFDL, who were mostly Rwandan Tutsi) forces marched towards Kinshasa, they committed 'acts of genocide' against ethnic Hutu refugees who had fled post-genocide Rwanda, and against Congolese civilians in Equateur whom they considered sympathizers. In many cases, AFDL forces pursued fleeing Rwandans into CAR, in a self-authorized right to hot pursuit. This violent episode, confirmed in a UN mapping report on crimes against humanity committed in the DRC since 1993 (Office of the UN High Commissioner for Human Rights—OHCHR, 2010, 114–118), remains part of the psychology of a generation of Congolese and Central Africans. While Mobutu's government fell in May 1997, Patassé hung on to power for another six years, when he was overthrown by a Chadian and French backed coup in 2003.

During the Second Congo War, which broke out on 2 August 1998, the Congo was divided into several rebel-military zones each backed by foreign allies. Control of DRC's Equateur province was divided. Jean-Pierre Bemba's MLC held the northern part of the province, known as Nord- and Sud-Oubangui because of its location along the riverine border with CAR. Bemba's family towns, Gbadolite and Gemena, became the rebel headquarters. Bangui served as the all-important rear supply base for the rebellion. Kabila's Kinshasa government controlled the southern half of the province, including the provincial capital Mbandaka. It is no coincidence that this Maginot line between north and south also largely mirrored the ethnic divisions between the Ngwaka and others in the north (Bemba's ethnic parentage and who are linked with the Gbandi and others in southern CAR and Congo-Brazzaville)[9] and southern Equateur, which is largely ethnically Mongo.

Many ex-FAZ (Zairian army) officers who had been cantoned at the Kitona military base after Mobutu's defeat, or who had gone into exile in CAR and Congo-Brazzaville after the fall of Mobutu, joined Bemba's effort to mount an army with Ugandan training and support. During a nine-month campaign that moved west from Kisangani along two fronts in northern Equateur, Bemba's recruits, with Uganda People's Defence Force (UPDF) battalions and air transport provided by Uganda, ejected Kabila's FAC (Congolese army) and Chadian troops from northern Equateur, and installed the movement's headquarters first in Lisala, and by July 1999, in Gbadolite.

Although the leadership of the movement itself was ethnically diverse, the fact that Bemba was seen locally as a *Mwana Mboke*, or son of the land, who 'liberated' northern Equateur from a foreign (Chadian) occupation, greatly advantaged the movement in that region in the early years of the war. The Chadian troops' brutal treatment of civilians was widely known and feared, whereas the Libyans, who provided financial, air, and at times direct military support both to Bemba and Patassé, did not behave as poorly. It is widely acknowledged, even by critics of the rebellion, that the security situation in Equateur vastly improved under the MLC compared to what it was under Kabila's troops and his Chadian allies.

What makes the MLC stand out from other rebel movements in the DRC wars of the last two decades is its embeddedness in local society and its efforts to govern territories under its control. During the war, as soon as a town or village fell to the MLC, the rebel movement would set up a local administrative structure consisting of an executive branch of the MLC, a territorial council comprised of women's groups, unions, and business, civic and church leaders; and a territorial assembly. In what was in effect a parallel provincial authority, each local administrative structure was given its own budget and the ability to levy taxes, while the MLC provided police and military security. This decentralized administration of local territories, even if still managed from the top by the MLC, permitted a greater inclusiveness of local actors into the administration of northern Equateur. However, given the realities of wartime, these regional and local administrative structures were oriented more towards recruitment and mobilization, than actual administration and local governance.

This support began to erode as the war and negotiations for a unified transition government dragged out. Growing dissatisfaction with the movement's three-fold increase of local taxes and incidents reported by local communities about MLC soldiers stealing produce from villagers' fields in Basankusu and a nurse's bicycle in Bosomodjebo in early 2003, and the allegedly accidental killing of a civilian by two soldiers in Yakoma in July 2003, contributed to the erosion of the population's support. Although the MLC called these incidents isolated, there were enough such isolated incidents being reported throughout rebel-held territory that they were likely part of a pervasive pattern of extortion of civilians by MLC soldiers.

Moreover, the MLC asserted its political authority by intervening twice into Bangui in the Central African Republic to defend the elected (and ethnically related) foreign government of Ange-Félix Patassé against internal rebellions. Indeed, the Patassé regime was the junior partner in this MLC–CAR alliance—an unusual relationship between a rebel movement and a foreign government.

The two MLC military interventions into CAR from October 2002 to March 2003 at Patassé's request tarnished the MLC's image and exposed Bemba to an ICC investigation. Both interventions were efforts to prop up elected president Ange-Félix Patassé against Chadian (and French) backed rebels, François Bozizé among them. Patassé once again outsourced security to an external actor, this time to a neighbouring rebel movement. In December 2002, nearly one thousand MLC fighters joined Libyan troops in Bangui to shore up the Patassé government. Libya's objective was to maintain a friendly government in CAR to allow Tripoli a rear base of operations against Chad's President Déby and his French supporters. For the MLC, preventing a Kinshasa–Bangui alliance was crucial for the rebellion's ability to maintain access in and out of CAR. The MLC sustained heavy losses in the fighting and were widely accused of looting and raping civilians in the suburbs of Bangui.

The events of 2002 and 2003 significantly disrupted the Central African economy and increased food insecurity and civilian displacement in CAR and in DRC. This crisis was exacerbated by Bozizé's army and mercenary supporters who, once in power, exacted retribution against Congolese and Central African civilians, killing and raping many of them and looting their shops and belongings.[10] As Marchal notes, until 2003, nearly half of the foreigners in Bangui were Congolese nationals. Most of them fled CAR.

In February 2003, the French-financed International Federation for Human Rights (FIDH) filed a petition with the ICC accusing both Bemba and Patassé of war crimes. This FIDH petition was widely seen as having been encouraged, if not facilitated, by the French government. When it was clear that the Central African rebels were taking control over large parts of the country, Bemba withdrew his troops. By this time, South Africa had successfully brokered a peace deal among armed groups fighting in the DRC and the MLC leadership was preparing to end the rebellion and assume positions in a new Government of National Unity in Kinshasa. Two years after Patassé was successfully overthrown by François Bozizé and his French supporters in March 2003, CAR's new President Bozizé formally petitioned the ICC to investigate all crimes under its jurisdiction committed on CAR territory after 1 July 2002, the date of entry into force of the Rome Statute—a request he later reconsidered when he realized that he could also be a target.

CAR and the politics of international justice

During the 2003–2006 transition in DRC, Bemba was one of four vice-presidents of the government of national unity. In the first post-war election in 2006, he forced Kabila to a run-off and lost with just under 48 per cent of the national vote. His surprise national showing and his rising popularity among the Congolese electorate allowed him to claim the leadership of the political opposition in Congo.

The ICC's announcement on 22 May 2007 that it was formally investigating allegations of rape in CAR did not mention Jean-Pierre Bemba or the MLC by name, but it was widely assumed that he was the target of the investigation, and this immediately began influencing political calculations in the Congo. The Office of the Prosecutor had initially planned to announce the investigation in March 2007 while Bemba, having just lost the election, was literally under fire by President Kabila's republican guard in Kinshasa, and together with Mission de l'Organisation de Nations Unies en Republique Democratique du Congo (MONUC), was attempting to negotiate his exile. Amidst accusations of 'victor's justice' among Bemba supporters, and alarm in many capitals at the political fallout this would cause in the immediate aftermath of what were the most expensive elections the UN has ever organized, the ICC delayed the announcement. Once it released its statement, the ICC drew widespread criticism both inside and outside the DRC and CAR for the choice and timing of this case. First, it was widely agreed that Bemba was not at the top of the list of worst offenders in either the DRC or CAR and that the MLC's actions did not compare to the levels of mass atrocities found in the Kivus, Ituri, or northern Katanga, for example. In CAR, Central Africans asked themselves why Patassé, Bozizé, Miskine, or any other mercenaries were not also indicted.

Congolese and international human rights advocates publicly expressed concern that the CAR investigation would be spun and exploited by Kabila and his supporters to further marginalize an already weakened opposition since the March 2007 events in Kinshasa, which resulted in Bemba's forced exile. This fear would soon be realized as evidence of the growing repression by the new Kinshasa government and its crackdown against the opposition mounted, as it sought to centralize and consolidate power. Of particular concern was that this would further embolden Kabila and encourage the government's efforts to target individuals from Equateur province, Bemba's province of origin. Equatorian politicians were soon targeted, the provincial governor dismissed, and more recently, the provincial assembly forcibly suspended by the Kinshasa government.

Given the mounting evidence of sexual violence in conflict areas, Moreno-Ocampo, the ICC's first prosecutor (who himself was haunted by accusations of sexual misconduct) (Flint and de Waal, 2009), was under pressure by international advocacy groups to prosecute a case on sexual violence. While the successful prosecution of this case would send the message that rape is, indeed, a war crime, the case was clearly politically motivated. Despite personal assurances by Louis Michel to Bemba that he would not be pursued by the ICC and thus was free to travel in Europe, both the French who had supported the Bozizé coup, and the Americans who had supported Kabila's bid in the 2006 election found it politically expedient to neutralize the popular Congolese opposition leader. Moreno-Ocampo understood this and saw this as high profile, yet low-hanging fruit. He would get one of the big fish and the advocacy community would get its rape case. Bemba thus became a convenient political target.

Bemba's arrest in Brussels while on a family visit was facilitated by the Americans,[11] and based initially solely on testimony provided by the French NGO, FIDH. The ICC charged him with two crimes against humanity (rape and murder) and three war crimes (rape, murder, and pillaging a town or place). Although Bemba was not present in Bangui during either of the two MLC interventions, the Court argued that he was criminally responsible as a military commander, claiming that he had effective authority and control over the MLC rebel troops who allegedly committed these crimes, and that Bemba knew that MLC troops were committing crimes and 'did not take all necessary and reasonable measures within his power to prevent or repress their commission'.[12]

Bemba's arrest immediately and predictably prompted outrage in the DRC, glee among Bozizé's inner circle in Bangui, and accusations throughout Africa that the ICC is a political instrument of Western powers aimed against African leaders. This, and the shortcomings in the way the Court has prosecuted most of its cases thus far, has eroded much of the goodwill initially enjoyed by the ICC among the African human rights community. It has also created such a political backlash in the region against international justice that few in the region believe the ICC will survive.

Leaving aside the fact that the ICC decisions on what cases to investigate and prosecute are steeped in international politics, one of the biggest drawbacks of reliance on the ICC as the sole mechanism of justice in this region is that the Court's temporal jurisdiction means that it cannot address all of the crimes committed in the last two decades, since the end of Cold War competition ushered in a new era of violent political contestation in Africa. Whatever the ICC does in the Central African Republic, its jurisdictional constraints will prevent it from providing a 'full service' justice solution to the Central African people.

Ironically, and in keeping with a running theme in CAR's political life, the ICC's first case in CAR was to prosecute a neighbouring rebel leader rather than the CAR's own predatory leaders and war criminals. By arresting and trying a warlord turned popular leader of the political opposition in one country for crimes he may be responsible for in another country, the ICC served justice neither to Central Africans who seek justice for crimes committed by their own leaders, nor to Congolese who either lost a popular native son or who have their share of grievances against him and wonder why he was not arrested for crimes committed in DRC (Vinck and Pham, 2010; 2014). The ICC's only case in CAR, like most international interventions in CAR, has been about something other than CAR; and like the failures of those interventions, has consequently failed to bring justice either to CAR or DRC.

Conclusion

In the wake of the 2012 crisis, CAR is largely associated with Chad, Sudan, and the Sahel. But as recently as the 1990s, and throughout the Cold War, CAR was very much a part of the vortex of its southern neighbours. This underscores the argument that some of the failures of international intervention in CAR can be attributed to a tendency to treat CAR as a function of other bureaucratic and policy priorities, rather than treating CAR on its own terms.

While the Congolese have played the role of the meddling foreigners over the years as much as the Chadians, Central Africans do not see Congolese as foreign *in the same way* as they do the Chadians. Unlike the Chadians, Congolese are by and large tolerated in CAR, despite their large numbers in Bangui. The idea of a CAR/DRC connection strikes many in the capital and southern part of the country as natural given that they are all 'Bantu' peoples and largely Christian or animist, and given their shared post-colonial history. When asked about their Congolese neighbours, Central Africans in Bangui will often reply, '*ce sont des bandits*'—'they're petty thieves!' They will continue by saying 'they're petty thieves who won't go home. They're argumentative and like their beer and they pretend to come for the day markets but they never leave'. However, they will also quickly add that 'at least the Congolese are not mean and sinister like the Chadians, who, if you anger them, will say nothing and just pull out a knife and kill you on the spot'.[13] Exploring CAR's history with the DRC is a useful reminder of the subjectivity of belonging, and how quickly the terms of autochthony can change.

Also, tracing the CAR's relationship to the Congo wars of the last two decades challenges a dominant assumption that where the state is not present, there is nothing there, hence our perennial need to extend state authority in post-conflict settings. The relationship between peripheries in both countries during the Second Congo War is a useful reminder that the absence of evidence is not evidence of absence. The peripheries of DRC and CAR clearly show that these so-called ungoverned spaces during wartime or peacetime do have authority structures, often hybrid and sometimes transnational. Before we 'rebuild' local governance systems in CAR (or in DRC) we need to understand what these authorities are composed of, how they function, and how they change.

Finally, Central African heads of state have been adept at using security and insecurity in DRC to their advantage. Starting with President Dacko, who already in the early 1960s exploited French fears that CAR would become 'another Congo', these leaders have made use of the DRC conflict arenas for their own ends. Related to this political adeptness is CAR's history of concessionary politics, which has long extended the outsourcing of security to the neighbours, and which now extends to outsourcing the delivery of justice to the ICC when politically expedient.

Notes

1 In 2008, I organized a meeting for the UN Secretariat on the 'Greater' Horn, in which CAR was also featured.
2 Lemarchand, R. (2009) *The Dynamics of Violence in Central Africa*, University of Pennsylvania Press, Philadelphia, US; Reyntjens, F. (2009) *The Great African War: Congo and Regional Geopolitics, 1996–2006*,

Cambridge University Press, Cambridge, UK; only Prunier, G. (2011) *Africa's World War*, Oxford University Press, Oxford, UK, has an index entry for CAR. At over 500 pages, it could afford to.

3 See Chapter 2, 'CAR's History: The Past of a Tense Present' by Stephen Smith and Chapter 8, 'CAR and the Regional (Dis)order' by Roland Marchal.

4 See Chapter 7, 'The Autonomous Zone Conundrum: Armed Conservation and Rebellion in North-Eastern CAR' by Louisa Lombard and Chapter 12 'In Unclaimed Land: The Lord's Resistance Army in CAR' by Ledio Cakaj; and for a more detailed literature review of public authority in these spaces see Hoffmann, K. and T. Kirk (2013) 'Public Authority and the Provision of Public Goods in Conflict-affected and Transitioning Regions', *Justice and Security Research Programme Paper #7*, August, London.

5 Mobutu planted huge rice and palm oil plantations in northern Equateur but these were privately owned by his family and after he was deposed in 1997, were left to fall apart.

6 In the absence of air or commercial river transport, it takes a month to bring produce down to market in Kinshasa on makeshift timber rafts that are like small floating villages as they must be self-sustaining during the long trip. It is not unusual to bring along live provisions in the form of goats and chickens on these rafts.

7 'Rural radicalism' is a term coined by Herbert F. Weiss in his award-winning book on the Congolese independence struggle, *Political Protests in the Congo* (1967).

8 See Chapter 13, 'A Central African Elite Perspective on the Struggles of the Central African Republic' by Laurence Wohlers.

9 The Zande kingdom spans southern CAR, South Sudan, and north-eastern DRC, largely the Congolese province of Haut Uele. However, this is the least populated area of CAR and played little role in the Congo wars.

10 See Chapter 8, 'CAR and the Regional (Dis)order' by Roland Marchal.

11 Interview with former US government official in Washington, 18 November 2011.

12 For further detail, see the 'Case Information Sheet' (2014) *International Criminal Court,* updated 14 November. Available from: <http://www.icc-cpi.int/iccdocs/PIDS/publications/BembaEng.pdf>.

13 Interview, Bangui, June 2012.

Bibliography

'Bokassa's Reaction to attempted coup in Zaire' (1975), *Wikileaks*, 19 June, Bangui. Available from: <http://search.wikileaks.org/plusd/cables/1975BANGUI00843_b.html>.

Carayannis, T. (2003) 'The Complex Wars of the Congo: Towards a New Analytic Approach', *Journal of Asian and African Studies*, vol. 38 no. 2–3, June, 232–255.

Carayannis, T., Bojicic-Dzelilovic, V., Olin, N., Rigterink, A. and Schomerus, M. (2014) 'Practice Without Evidence: interrogating conflict resolution approaches and assumptions', *Justice and Security Research Programme Paper #11*, February, London. Available from: <http://www.lse.ac.uk/internationalDevelopment/research/JSRP/JSRP%20Papers/JSRP-Paper-11.aspx>.

Cordell, D. (2002) 'Des 'réfugiés' dans l'Afrique précoloniale?', *Politique Africaine*, no. 85, pp. 16–28.

Davis, L. (2002) 'Dancing in the Dark: A Manifesto against Professional Organizations,' in Jeffrey Williams, ed. *The Institution of Literature*, SUNY Press, Albany, pp. 153–172.

Duffield, M. (2001) *Global Governance and the New Wars: The Merging of Development and Security*, Zed Books, London.

Flint, J. and de Waal, A. (2009) 'Case Closed: Prosecutor without Borders,' *World Affairs*, April. Available from: <http://www.worldaffairsjournal.org/article/case-closed-prosecutor-without-borders>.

Hollenweger, W. J. (1997) *Pentecostalism: Origins and Developments Worldwide*. Hendrickson Publishers, Peabody; cited in Anderson, A. 'Evangelism and the Growth of Pentecostalism in Africa,' University of Birmingham, Available from: <http://www.artsweb.bham.ac.uk/aanderson/publications/evangelism_and_the_growth_of_pen.htm>.

Nkama, A. (2005) 'Regional Economic Blocs in Central Africa: What Went Right and What Went Wrong?' in Fomin, E. S. D. and Forje, J. eds. *Central Africa: Crises, Reform and Reconstruction*, CODESRIA, Dakar, pp. 17–30.

Office of the UN High Commissioner for Human Rights – OHCHR (2010) *DRC: Mapping Human Rights Violations 1993–2003*, Geneva–New York, pp. 1–566.

Peemans, J-P. (1986) 'Accummulation and Underdevelopment in Zaire: General Aspects in Relation to the Evolution of the Agrarian Crisis,' in Nzongola-Ntalaja, ed., *The Crisis in Zaire: Myths and Realities*, Africa World Press, Trenton, pp. 67–84.

'Positions of Zambia, Rwanda & C.A.R. VIS-A-VIS MPLA' (1975), *Wikileaks*, 28 December, Kinshasa. Available from: <http://search.wikileaks.org/plusd/cables/1975KINSHA11015_b.html>.

Vinck, P. and Pham, P. N. (2010) 'Outreach Evaluation: The International Criminal Court in the Central African Republic', *International Journal of Transitional Justice 2010*, 4 (3): pp. 421–442.

Vinck, P. and Pham, P. N. (2014). 'A La Recherche d'une Paix Durable: Enquête de la Population dans l'Est de la République Démocratique du Congo sur les Perceptions et Attitudes envers la Paix, la Sécurité, et la Justice', *Harvard Humanitarian Initiative – Programme des Nations Unies pour le Développement*, Harvard, pp. 1–75.

von Benda-Beckmann, K. (1981) 'Forum Shopping and Shopping Forums: Dispute Processing in a Minangkabau Village in West Sumatra', *The Journal of Legal Pluralism and Unofficial Law*, 13.19: 117–159.

Weiss, H. (1967) *Political Protests in the Congo*, Princeton University Press, Princeton, US.

Weiss, H. and Carayannis, T. (2004) 'Reconstructing the Congo', *Journal of International Affairs*, Vol. 58, No. 1.

12 In Unclaimed Land
The Lord's Resistance Army in CAR

Ledio Cakaj

In April 2009, Joseph Kony, the leader of the Lord's Resistance Army (LRA), approached the river Mbomou, which forms the eastern border between the Democratic Republic of the Congo (DRC) and the Central African Republic (CAR). Kony and a group of nearly 800 people, including women and children, had just trudged hundreds of kilometres on a hazardous journey from north-eastern DRC, chased along the way by Ugandan aircraft and ground troops. Looking into the vast, sparsely governed south-eastern CAR, Kony led a prayer for safe arrival in what he referred to as 'the land of blessed peace and rest'.

In this country, which was new to the brutality of the long LRA conflict, Kony claimed his people – holies, as he calls them – would live unmolested, free to do as they wanted, in an unclaimed land free for their taking. His fighters proceeded to act as many rebels and other aggressors have before them, preying on the local population with impunity. A range of actors from the Ugandan army to an African Union mission followed the LRA into CAR, often unwittingly behaving as if eastern CAR was indeed unclaimed. Survival for the local population has always been arduous, but the arrival of the LRA has been a particularly depressing chapter. The indigenous people had always struggled for basic services and protection from their own government, which has shown little regard for their problems.

But now they risked becoming collateral damage as foreign armies mandated to hunt Kony's holies occupied their communities.

This chapter examines the activity of LRA groups in CAR and the regional and international response to their presence. While the groups have been mobile, inventive and adaptable, international reaction has been slow, predictable and hampered by regional politics. Geography, location and the absence of local capacities to cope with violent groups are some of the main factors which render the country attractive to the rebels and hinder the counter LRA operations.

The sparsely populated and densely forested areas in the east provide ample shelter and protection from the pursuing Ugandan soldiers, who cannot comb the vast territories LRA groups traverse. Desire to connect with the old backers of the Sudanese Armed Forces (SAF) – in the southernmost bases of southern Darfur – constitutes the reason why the LRA initially entered the country and this so-called bad neighbour issue remains evident in the movements of LRA groups between eastern CAR and southern Darfur. The lack of capable security forces translates to an inability to provide basic protection to civilians or rudimentary support to the ongoing counter LRA military mission.

The study of the LRA in CAR offers more than a description of the violence caused by a gradually declining belligerent group in a so-called unclaimed land. It provides a glimpse into the complicated and often dysfunctional regional geopolitics, while highlighting the inability of weak states and international institutions to cope with versatile border crossing armed groups, of which the LRA is one of many.

Yet, despite all the attention directed at the Ugandan group, in part due to well-coordinated advocacy campaigns in the US and Western Europe, the local population of eastern CAR has seen few tangible benefits while LRA violence has continued, albeit at a decreasing rate. Since the LRA's incursion into CAR, more than 100 million US dollars have been poured into funding military operations and seemingly endless bureaucratic meetings in regional capitals, but only small fractions of such funds and international interest have been invested in helping CAR civilians who have borne the brunt of LRA violence.

The LRA – a background

Part rebel group and part cult with military ethos, the LRA is one of the longest-surviving armed groups in Africa. Founded on the legitimate grievances of northern Uganda's Acholi people, the LRA evolved over nearly three decades into a personal survival vehicle for founder and leader, Joseph Kony. Often described as messianic, Kony is a pragmatic leader who borrows from Acholi rituals and Christian teachings to legitimize and prolong his control.

The LRA of today is in decline. Though the rebels have continued to abduct hundreds across South Sudan, DRC and CAR, Kony's insistence on maintaining predominantly Acholi armed fighters might prove his undoing. LRA groups have not operated near northern Uganda since the end of 2006 lacking thus the opportunity to abduct and indoctrinate new Acholi youth for several years. Yet as weak as the LRA is, it remains exceedingly difficult to wipe out.

The rebel group later to be known as the LRA was formed in 1987 when a small group of former soldiers and civilians, mostly from Acholiland came together in rebellion. Kony's rebellion, as well as two predecessor insurgencies, arose in response to increased violence against civilians committed by the soldiers of the then newly installed and current Ugandan President Yoweri Museveni.[1] The LRA initially enjoyed a limited level of popular support. But that eventually dissipated due to general fatigue with the war's toll on access to basic services, and increased violence against civilians from Ugandan soldiers and LRA fighters who turned to looting and abducting to sustain themselves (Branch, 2010).

The mid-1990s marked a crucial phase in the history of the LRA.[2] The Sudanese government supported Kony financially and militarily in retaliation for President Museveni's backing of the Sudan People's Liberation Army (SPLA). Khartoum's support translated into LRA bases in Sudanese territory protected by the SAF, training of fighters, and a great deal of weaponry and ammunition in return for LRA-led attacks on the SPLA.[3] Given the hardware and territory, Kony resorted to finding the manpower, which meant increased abductions and violence against civilians in both Uganda and South Sudan.

By the mid-2000s, the situation had changed drastically as almost complete cessation of support from Khartoum – which by 2005 had signed a peace agreement with the SPLA – and increased international diplomatic efforts combined with military pressure from the Ugandan army, convinced the LRA leadership to relocate to Garamba Park in north-eastern DRC and eventually commit to peace talks. The peace process, commonly referred to as the Juba Talks because the parties often met in the South Sudanese capital, started in 2006. But by the end of 2008, Kony had repeatedly failed to show up and sign the final negotiated agreement. Ultimately, the Ugandan government launched Operation Lightning Thunder (OLT) on 14 December 2008, bombing LRA bases in Garamba followed by a ground sweep by infantry troops.

The Garamba offensive scattered LRA combatants across DRC, CAR and South Sudan. LRA attacks against civilians increased significantly in 2009 particularly in the immediate aftermath of OLT as the LRA embarked on a retaliatory campaign. Over 1,000 people were killed in the first few weeks following OLT including during the infamous so-called Christmas massacres that took place in the towns of Duru and Faradje in DRC's Haut Uélé region in December 2008 (Human Rights Watch, 2009).

According to the LRA Crisis Tracker, a mapping platform that documents LRA attacks, the LRA killed over 2,898 people and abducted 5,231 between 1 December 2008 and 1 May 2014.[4] However, overall LRA violence diminished significantly in the last two years in part due to significant numbers of fighters deserting or being killed by the Ugandan army. There was a 50 per cent drop in LRA abductions and 75 per cent decrease in LRA killings between 2010 and 2013, according to the US State Department (2014). There have not been mass abductions or promotions into leadership ranks for non-Ugandan fighters, which has further depleted the ranks.[5]

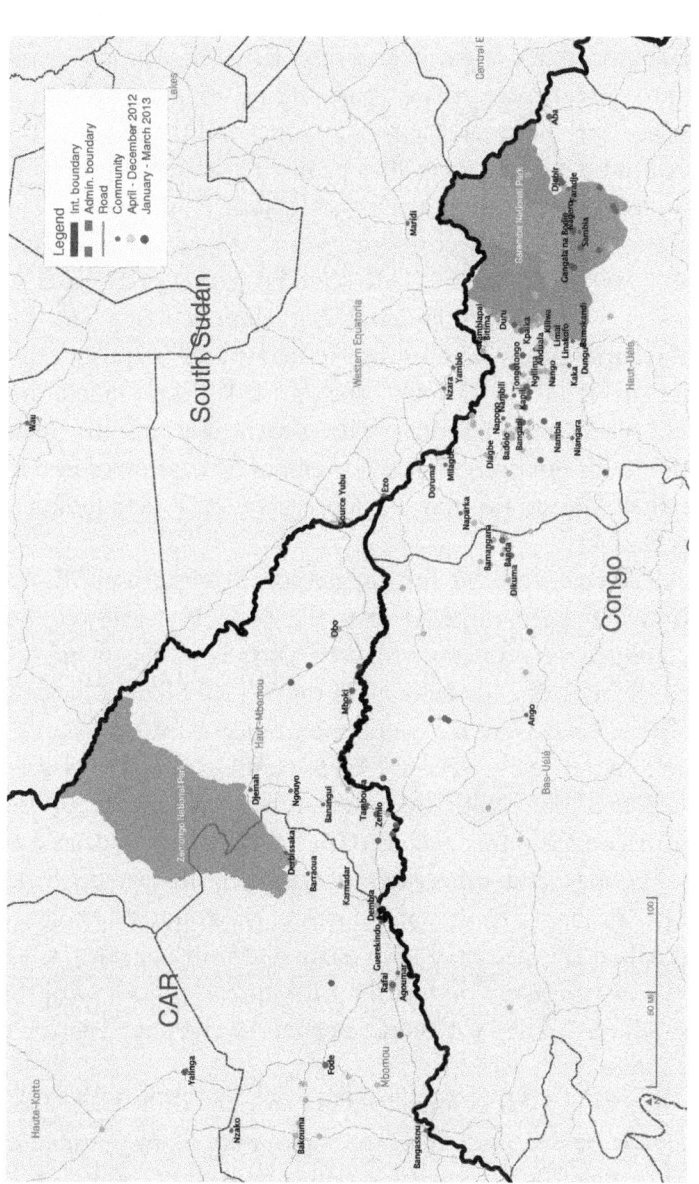

Map 12.1 LRA attacks against civilians, April 2012–March 2013
Source: LRA Crisis Tracker, January–March 2013 Quarterly Security Brief

LRA activity in CAR

Eastern CAR, especially areas adjacent to southern Darfur, is of particular importance to Kony and the LRA. These lands enable forays into Sudanese territory particularly in Kafia Kingi, a disputed territory between the two Sudans, and the bases of the SAF, historic LRA allies, as well as providing escape routes from Ugandan soldiers who operate in CAR and South Sudan. The lack of meaningful CAR security forces and UN peacekeepers has meant that parts of eastern CAR have been preferred areas of operation for LRA top commanders including Kony and his personal security detail. These 'ungoverned spaces' are also fertile operating grounds for various other armed groups, including poachers, rebels and bandits, who often prey on the local population with impunity, but who remain little known, in part because their objectives may be more economic than political (Lombard, 2012).

The LRA was not the first aggressor in eastern CAR. Its population had been targeted over the years by various rebel groups, *'coupeurs de route'* or road bandits, as well as poachers, armed cattle herders and elements of the SPLA.[6] SPLA attacks in south-eastern CAR were fairly common at least until the signing of the Comprehensive Peace Agreement in 2005 between Khartoum and the South Sudanese rebels.[7] Elements of the Central African national army, FACA, have also been accused of unlawful killings and other acts of violence against civilians, particularly in the north-east and north of the country.[8] Violence against civilians in eastern, and in particular north-eastern, CAR predated and will likely outlast the LRA threat at least until the security vacuum is filled with competent and well-trained national security forces.

LRA attacks in CAR commenced in February 2008 as the Juba peace talks were ongoing. The Juba Talks were likely doomed as early as October 2007, soon after Kony ordered the execution of his deputy, Vincent Otti, fearing the latter's defection and potential splits in the LRA.[9] Looking for options after Otti's death, Kony instructed one of his trusted commanders, Okot Odhiambo, to make contact with SAF troops stationed in Kafia Kingi – the southernmost SAF base in Sudan – an area south of southern Darfur and adjacent to CAR's Haut Kotto prefecture with no international presence.

According to former LRA combatants, by the end of 2008 Odhiambo had twice tried and failed to enter SAF-controlled territory due to the harsh weather conditions in areas crisscrossed by many armed groups. Ironically, Odhiambo's security situation was so dire he later warned Kony that eastern CAR was a dangerous region.[10]

Failing to make contact with the SAF and on the way back to Garamba, Odhiambo abducted many in Obo, reportedly on Kony's express orders.[11] Immediately after Otti's death, Kony told his fighters to prepare for war and the decision to abduct *en masse* – something the LRA had refrained from for about two years while in Garamba Park – was likely made in preparation for the inevitable clash. Otti had been the main LRA interlocutor in the Juba Talks and his execution unravelled months of negotiations and effectively amounted to a death sentence for the peace process.[12] The newly-abducted from Obo were trained as fighters, given as wives to LRA commanders and were used as guides and translators when LRA groups moved to CAR.

Odhiambo led the first known LRA attack in CAR on 25 February 2008 in Bassigbiri, 50 km north of the Congolese border in close proximity to the South Sudanese border town of Source Yubu. Over sixty people were abducted and taken to LRA camps in Garamba National Park, forty in Bassigbiri and another twenty from nearby villages. Six people abducted in Bassigbiri were later killed.[13] About a week later, on the night of 5 March, a large LRA group attacked the neighbourhood of AIM (named after the evangelical Africa Inland Mission's church) in Obo. Seventy-three people were abducted. More than one-third of the kidnapped are believed to be dead or still with the LRA, while the others later returned home.[14]

After Ugandan's OLT in December 2008 in Garamba, LRA groups filtered into CAR from DRC and South Sudan, likely arriving in April 2009. Bassigbiri, Aboissi and Selim in the southeastern corner of CAR, were attacked by hungry fighters searching for food and abductees to porter the loot. By the end of 2009 more than 800 LRA members had made it to CAR, with an estimated 300 remaining in DRC.[15] Despite increased international military pressure, LRA fighters, including Kony, reportedly moved frequently between CAR and southern Darfur's Kafia Kingi between 2009 and 2013. Access to Kafia Kingi is a main reason why LRA groups continue to operate in eastern CAR, particularly the large Zemongo reserve, adjacent to Kafia Kingi and southern Darfur.

But LRA groups have always been highly mobile throughout their time in CAR, and LRA attacks have been registered over vast areas predominantly to the east but also in the north. By April 2014 attacks had been registered in and around Obo, Mboki, Zemio, Rafai in the south and Birao in Vakaga prefecture in the north (UN Office for the Coordination of Humanitarian Affairs – OCHA, 2014). According to raw data from the LRA Crisis Tracker, between June 2009 and May 2014, there were 341 reported LRA attacks resulting in 414 civilian fatalities and 1,721 abductions of civilians in CAR. The violence has also caused mass displacement. By the end of March 2014, there were 21,000 internally displaced people due to LRA violence in CAR, in addition to over 3,200 Congolese refugees (OCHA, 2014).

Counter LRA operations – Uganda People's Defence Force

Following Kony's move to CAR in May 2009, the Uganda People's Defence Force (UPDF) established a forward operating base in Obo in early June 2009, having already set up headquarters in Nzara in South Sudan's Western Equatoria State (WES). It is likely the UPDF entered CAR after the two national armies signed a bilateral agreement in early June 2009.[16] President

Museveni discussed with President Bozizé the possibility of LRA movement in CAR and possible ways to counter Kony as early as August 2007 while the Juba Talks were ongoing (US Embassy – Kampala, 2007).

Since 2009, the UPDF has maintained the bulk of its anti-LRA forces in Obo, Derbysaka, Dembia and Djema. But their presence has not consistently led to fewer attacks on the population. In the first quarter of 2014, seventeen out of twenty-one registered LRA attacks took place in Haut Mbomou, while the rest took place in Haut Kotto.[17] That the majority of attacks in CAR in 2014 took place in Haut Mbomou, where most of the Ugandan armed forces are based, shows the enormous difficulties of dealing decisively with the small but highly mobile LRA groups over vast sparsely inhabited lands.

The current number of overall Ugandan soldiers in the LRA theatre of operations is reportedly between 500 to 700 troops.[18] An increase in Ugandan presence operating in Somalia, a large deployment of Ugandan troops in South Sudan in support of President Kiir, and a reliance on soldiers for domestic operations account for the relatively small number of Ugandan soldiers in CAR. Strategy plays an important role too, according to a Ugandan top commander, who argued that large numbers of soldiers would not be helpful since the LRA is composed of small mobile groups.[19]

The local population of Haut Mbomou initially welcomed the deployment of the Ugandan army, effectively the sole force providing any protection against LRA attacks. But a prolonged stay in CAR – the UPDF entered its fifth year in CAR in June 2014 – and a lack of results have caused disappointment and at times outright anger. 'The UPDF is our army now, they decide who stays [in power] in the south-east' said a local NGO worker immediately after a recent incident in Obo that had the UPDF display policing powers. On 14 January 2014, Ugandan soldiers dispersed a group of youth demonstrating against the outgoing prefect of Obo.[20] At least one civilian died and four were injured after the Ugandan soldiers opened fired against the Obo youths who allegedly threatened the soldiers ('Obo, une person tuée et cinq autre blessées', 2014).

In contrast to DRC, CAR officials have not publicly criticized the Ugandan military operations in their country. The Ugandan army faced significant political opposition in DRC, as well as allegations of profiteering and poaching. Congolese officials publicly stated that very few LRA fighters remained in DRC and that the Ugandan army was now after Congolese minerals (Thompson, 2011). The Congolese army commander stationed in Dungu – the epicentre of LRA attacks in Haut Uélé – Lieutenant Colonel Nasibu Babu Nadoo told the British Broadcasting Corporation that, 'Over the last two years we have successfully neutralized Kony', and 'It has become a business for Ugandan officers to enrich themselves by telling the international community that the LRA is a big problem here' (Thompson, 2011).

Despite Ugandan government claims that the UPDF is not operational in DRC, there have been allegations that the Ugandan army has slaughtered elephants in Garamba National Park. On 15 March 2012 at least twenty-three elephants were killed by snipers who were likely on board a helicopter, as park rangers later found no ground tracks surrounding the slain elephants whose tusks had been removed. Rangers suspected a Ugandan army helicopter, photographed two weeks later flying suspiciously low over Garamba, was involved. Ugandan officials, denying any army involvement, admitted the helicopter was part of the UPDF flying to Nzara, South Sudan, as part of the counter LRA operations, even though Ugandan army aircraft have no permission to use DRC's airspace ('Ugandan Army Chopper Cited in Elephant Poaching', 2012).

In CAR, the Ugandan army found a general absence of any national military apparatus and relative indifference from Bangui officials towards the far-flung corner where the Ugandans were initially based.[21] CAR security forces, notably the national army (FACA), have never been a significant factor in the fight against the LRA. By early 2012 FACA only had about 200 troops spread throughout Haut Mbomou and Mbomou prefectures.[22] Poorly trained and under-resourced, FACA troops were unwilling to chase LRA groups or protect civilians. Numerous reports detailed how FACA soldiers displayed a frequent tendency to flee during LRA attacks or to turn up hours after an attack had ended (Cakaj and Lancaster, 2012).

Following the Seleka takeover of March 2013, the FACA was disbanded throughout the country. The Ugandan army became and remains the sole de facto recognizable authority in south-eastern CAR, providing a degree of safety to the local population and local leaders who in turn have little choice but to support the Ugandan presence. Fears of a possible advance by Seleka, who the Ugandan soldiers halted at Rafai, and the arrival of US Special Forces in Obo which helped improve the Ugandan army's conduct, has led to grudging acceptance of the foreign guests.[23]

Some leaders in Obo and Mboki have publicly supported the presence of the UPDF, in large part due to the personal security the Ugandan army provides, but at a local level there has been sizeable discontent. Interviews on the ground in March 2010 and December 2011 indicated that many, both in the south-east and Bangui, regarded the UPDF as engaging in predatory behaviour, particularly towards local women. United Nations and NGO representatives with presence in Haut Mbomou spoke of Ugandan soldiers and 'cases of public drunkenness and disorderly conduct', and of 'a market for prostitution often involving underage girls often as young as twelve'.[24]

An internal United Nations report stated that it is not 'unusual to see girls and women sneak into the UPDF base at night, or find UPDF personnel embroiled in brawls over girls or women'.[25] And as an international aid worker noted most recently, 'there are a number of children in Obo fathered by Ugandan soldiers who have returned home raising the question of how will these children be brought up and treated by the community'.[26]

While the local anger towards the UPDF was linked to soldiers' poor conduct and exploitation of women and girls, government representatives in Bangui were more concerned with theft of resources. In late 2011 officials alleged that UPDF commanders were involved in illicit activities such as illegal logging and looting of mineral resources and the sale of 'everything you can think of, from bicycles brought from Uganda on UPDF vehicles to fuel, AK 47s and bullets'.[27]

July 2010 marked a turning point for the UPDF presence in CAR. President Bozizé asked the UPDF to leave their base in Sam Ouandja and to stay only in Obo and Djema (International Crisis Group, 2010). It is unclear why, but the proximity of Ugandan soldiers to the diamond mines of Sam Ouandja might well have been a concern for Bozizé.[28]

Increasingly, CAR officials began to openly voice their dissatisfaction with the Ugandan army. The Minister of Commerce, herself a resident of Haut Mbomou, said that the UPDF were not welcome in CAR and that they were more interested in looting resources rather than chasing the LRA.[29] The Minister produced a handwritten report from the highest local official in Obo detailing the 'destruction of the Obo forest by UPDF soldiers cutting timber and transporting it in army trucks towards Bambouti and South Sudan'.[30]

According to the Minister, when UPDF commanders were confronted about the timber, they claimed they needed it to fix bridges and roads. While it is true that the roads in CAR are in a poor condition, the Minister stated, it is 'not the job of the UPDF to fix roads. Certainly not the roads of southern Sudan where most of the timber is going'.[31] Allegations of the UPDF's illicit logging are not new. Similar claims were made in Sudan in the past (Schomerus, 2007). Ugandan officials contacted about such claims have categorically denied the army's involvement in theft of natural resources.[32]

With the arrival of Djotodia in March 2013, the relationship between the Ugandans and the new CAR authorities deteriorated. Djotodia publicly asked for the UPDF to leave CAR. Kampala responded by withdrawing an army liaison based in Bangui and officially suspending the counter LRA mission (Kasasira, 2013). But after several meetings between Djotodia and African Union officials, the CAR president agreed to allow the Ugandan army to continue its operations, which resumed officially in October 2013 (Candia, 2013).

President Catherine Samba-Panza has paid little attention so far to the LRA or the Ugandan army presence in CAR given pressing concerns in Bangui and other parts of the country. This might yet change as reports of Ugandan soldiers clashing with Seleka in the north-east continue.[33] Involvement in the Seleka fights and an expressed desire to join the nascent peacekeeping mission could mean that Ugandan soldiers will stay in CAR, regardless of Kony and the LRA (Baguma, 2014).[34]

The African Union Mission to counter the LRA

In July 2010, at the fifteenth AU summit in Kampala, countries in the region agreed to an AU intervention against the LRA, though the UPDF was already carrying out a military offensive in several countries. The summit participants decided that the AU would, 'organise without delay action-oriented consultations with countries affected by the LRA and other interested parties, with a view to facilitating a coordinated regional action against the threat posed by the LRA'.[35]

Ultimately, the African Union merely provided a political umbrella for the ongoing Ugandan military operations. The fragile security situation of participating regional members and a lack of funds hampered the successful deployment of a strong AU mission. The promise of money – akin to the AU mission in Somalia – brought the regional actors together in the first place. In its absence, as Addis was unable to secure donor funding of the Somalia level – regional capitals slowly lost interest. Recent violence and instability in South Sudan and CAR also limited each country's participation. Congolese politics and long-standing animosity towards the Ugandan army curtailed DRC's involvement. Ultimately, the UPDF is the sole member of the AU counter LRA mission largely supported by US contributions.

Bozizé understood the importance of using military operations against Kony and the LRA to attract international attention, as well as to gain political legitimacy and financial support for his regime. He seized the AU summit agreements and organized a regional ministerial meeting on 13 and 14 October 2010 in Bangui under AU auspices. He opened the meeting himself and the sole agenda item was how to tackle the LRA. Security ministers from Uganda, CAR, South Sudan and DRC, AU Commissioner for Peace and Security, Ramtane Lamamra[36] as well as representatives of the United Nations, the European Union, France and the United Sates attended the meeting. The military and security plan recommendations included enhancing the capacity of regional armies, creating a joint centre of operations aimed at increasing information and coordination between the regional armies, a joint brigade composed of soldiers from the regional armies to chase LRA groups, joint border patrols and improved communications in areas with LRA presence (African Union, 2010).

At a second regional ministerial meeting on the LRA[37] held in Addis Ababa from 6–8 June 2011[38] participants agreed that 'an AU authorized mission with international support' should be established, aiming to secure the 'elimination of the LRA leading to the creation of a secure and stable environment in the affected countries'.[39] Other important decisions included supporting the appointment of a Special Envoy of the President of the African Union Commission (AUC) to coordinate the efforts against the LRA, the creation of the Joint Coordination Mechanism to be based in Bangui, the establishment of the Regional Task Force (RTF) operational headquarters in Yambio, South Sudan and sector headquarters in South Sudan, CAR and DRC. The AU was also asked to strive to secure the funds necessary.[40]

On 23 November 2011, the AU appointed former Mozambique diplomat Francisco Madeira as the AU Special Envoy for LRA issues. The African Union Peace and Security Council authorized the African Union Regional Cooperation Initiative (AU-RCI) against the LRA in November 2011 and officially launched in Yambio, South Sudan in March 2012 (Marinkovic and Benner, 2012).

Despite the media fanfare, the AU-RCI was riddled with problems from the start, most of which persist today. The RTF never comprised even close to the targeted 5,000 soldiers. A battalion of 500 SPLA soldiers deployed to Nzara, South Sudan for a few months, but appear to have disintegrated following the alleged coup attempt in South Sudan on 15 December 2013 and infighting in the SPLA.[41] Roughly 500 FACA soldiers were also supposed to deploy in areas of CAR where the LRA was operational but only 300 had arrived by early 2013. Ultimately, most fled following the Seleka advance.[42] A handful of FACA troops in Obo by late 2013 reportedly lived off the local population, with some help from the Ugandan army contingent based in Obo.[43] After much resistance from Kinshasa, the Congolese army dispatched 500 troops to north-eastern DRC but refused to allow Ugandan soldiers pursuing LRA groups to enter Congolese territory ('Congo sends 500 soldiers to join Uganda-led hunt for fugitive warlord Joseph Kony', 2013).

With the exception of the Ugandan troops, who receive financial and logistical support from the United States government unrelated to the AU, and who operate almost independently of the AU-RCI, all other contributing forces remain in dire need of training and basic supplies. The RTF headquarters in Yambio was so badly funded by July 2013 it could only afford to switch on the generators for two hours a day during working hours.[44] By February 2014 the headquarters had little to no communication capacity with its sectors in DRC and CAR.[45]

Some positives from the AU-RCI included the work of outgoing Ambassador Madeira, who in conjunction with the former head of United Nations Regional Office for Central Africa (UNOCA), the UN mission in charge of LRA issues' Special Representative of the Secretary-General (SRSG) Abu Moussa, engaged the governments of the involved countries in maintaining their commitment to dealing with the conflict. For instance, SRSG Moussa and Ambassador Madeira travelled to Bangui in May and June 2013 to ensure that Djotodia allowed the AU-RTF to resume operations in CAR (AU Peace and Security Council, 2013). Despite securing permission from Djotodia in June in the form of a written letter, the Ugandan army continued to be formally on standby at least until October 2013, perhaps confirming the weaknesses of the AU-RCI and the independence of the Ugandan troops from the AU mission.

'The letter does not mean much to me', said a Ugandan army commander, 'does Djotodia control all of his forces in CAR? I don't think so'. The Ugandan commander also added that the African Union needed to clarify its official policies. 'They [AU officials] cannot, on one hand, not recognize Djotodia's rule and yet show us a letter signed by him as the legitimate leader of CAR.'[46]

Even without the political chaos in Bangui, the African Union could have played a more assertive role in pushing for effective collaboration between LRA-affected countries. But ultimately, the AU failed to use its political muscle to keep political leadership focused on the counter LRA operations. Khartoum's participation in the counter LRA operations under the auspices of the AU could have stopped Kony from finding refuge in southern Darfur's Kafia Kingi region. Similarly, decisive AU action could have helped mediate long-standing problems between the Ugandans and the Congolese as well as convincing Kinshasa not to dismiss the LRA as a transient or temporary problem. But the signs from Addis over the years showed that dealing with the LRA was not a high priority. Rather, it was an agenda which appeared to be pushed by Uganda and to a lesser extent other countries, in large part to secure a closer working relationship and financial gain from the United States.

Immediately after the Bangui meeting where the idea of the RTF was introduced, the CAR foreign minister said, 'the international community must not be stingy with the means to help Centrafrica to get rid of the insecurity created by this rebellion' ('Central Africa says "fight LRA like Al Qaeda"', 2010). As a SPLA senior officer told an international diplomat referring to the South Sudanese promised deployment to the RTF, 'we have assigned two battalions to go, now pay us'.[47]

Demands by the member states to be reimbursed by the AU for contributing troops would have created prohibitive costs – over seventy million US dollars – for only a six-month rotation.[48] At least ten million more were envisioned as needed for the office of the Special Envoy and other civilian posts such as political and humanitarian affairs officers. Two AU officials expressed dismay at the way regional governments were 'forcing the AU to beg for funds for their armies while attempting also to control the entire process'.[49]

If there ever was much interest in Addis in the LRA mission, it cooled significantly after the AU was called on to play an increasingly significant role in dealing with events in Bangui by overseeing the evolution of MICOPAX into MISCA. Planners for the new UN backed mission, MINUSCA, seemed content to cede control of a large swathe of south-eastern CAR to the Ugandan army as initial plans of peacekeepers' deployment became available in the fall of 2014.[50]

US involvement in fighting the LRA

To a large extent, the United States' steadfast focus on the counter LRA efforts has compelled the countries in the region to maintain participation. The US has been supportive of the Ugandan efforts to address the LRA since the Juba Talks.[51] Officials in the administration of George W. Bush put pressure on the DRC government to permit Ugandan troops to enter Congolese territory for OLT, and the US army provided planning and logistics support to the tune of 'millions of dollars'.[52] US support to the Ugandan government in the shape of logistics aid and intelligence gathering continued under President Obama who signed a law on 24 May 2010 that significantly increased US commitment to the LRA fight.

'The Lord's Resistance Army Disarmament and Northern Uganda Recovery Act of 2009' requires the US government to develop a multilateral interagency strategy, 'to protect civilians from the Lord's Resistance Army, to apprehend or remove Joseph Kony and his top commanders from the battlefield in the continued absence of a negotiated solution, and to disarm and demobilize the remaining Lord's Resistance Army fighters' (US Congress, 2010).[53]

Until November 2011, the US strategy as required by 'The Lord's Resistance Army Disarmament and Northern Uganda Recovery Act of 2009' was to continue to support the Ugandan army's efforts against the LRA. Between 2009 and 2012 the US State Department allocated $56 million for supplies, equipment and logistics support to African forces engaged in dealing with the LRA, primarily the Ugandan army. In 2012, US Congress authorized the Department of Defense (DoD) to assist African forces, primarily the UPDF, involved in the counter LRA operations. DoD authorized $22.5 million in 2012 and $17.7 million in 2013 (Arieff and Ploch, 2014).

Most of the funds from the US government are used to provide transport and logistical support to the UPDF troops on the ground. Specifically, the US government hires private contractors who manage, through third party contractors, transportation of food and troops from Uganda to Sudan and CAR. US funds are also used to cover fuel for aircraft and vehicles for the UPDF as well as collecting intelligence.[54] The cost of the US involvement, however, is much larger than the sums allocated to the Ugandan army. Such costs include contracts for providing housing, food and medical care for the US Special Forces and a series of classified items believed to be part of Intelligence, Surveillance and Reconnaissance systems.[55]

In an effort to galvanize the operations against the LRA and responding to pressure from US based advocacy groups, President Obama authorized, 'a small number of combat-equipped U.S.

forces to deploy to Central Africa to provide assistance to regional forces that are working toward the removal of Joseph Kony from the battlefield' on 14 October 2011 (The White House, 2011). State Department officials have said that 100 of the US Special Forces deployed on the ground only act as military advisers to the UPDF and the regional forces on the ground and do not engage LRA fighters.[56]

Fewer than thirty of the US Special Forces are based in Obo while the rest are in Nzara, South Sudan and Entebbe, Uganda. By mid-2013, a handful of military advisers were deployed to Dungu, DRC as part of an effort by the US government to coordinate the regional militaries, a large gap that the African Union had been unable to resolve.[57] A large part of the US Special Forces based in Entebbe have carried out training exercises for the UPDF, including air-dropping food supplies for ground forces intended to increase the mobility of UPDF forces hunting LRA groups in CAR (Butagira, 2011).

The US military advisers have been perhaps at their best when working mostly within their own chain of command, independently or semi-independently of the Ugandan army. Such has been the case with their work in encouraging defections by producing and distributing demobilization leaflets and creating so-called safe reporting sites where LRA fighters can surrender without being harmed by the local population.[58] Another benefit of the presence of the US military advisers on the ground has been an improvement in behaviour on the part of the Ugandan army. Anecdotal evidence suggests that Ugandan army behaviour towards the local population in Obo and surrounding areas improved with the arrival of the US Special Forces.[59]

Apart from assisting the Ugandan army with intelligence gathering and logistics, the US government has also provided regional humanitarian assistance as well as funds aimed at promoting the rehabilitation of communities which experienced LRA violence. A recent factsheet published by the US State Department states that between 2010 and 2013 the United States

Agency for International Development (USAID) provided $8.5 million to the United Nations Children's Fund (UNICEF) to support the rehabilitation of formerly abducted youth in CAR and DRC in addition to US government humanitarian funds of $8.25 million given to CAR, DRC and South Sudan since 2010 (US State Department, 2014). These sums, which pale in significance to the more than $100 million spent on the military effort between 2009 and 2014, cannot sufficiently cover the great needs for the reintegration and rehabilitation of former fighters and entire communities and the rebuilding of homes and other infrastructure damaged by the LRA and military operations.[60]

Despite a few significant achievements such as the defection of top commander Caesar Achellam in March 2012 and the unconfirmed demise of Kony's deputy, Okot Odhiambo at the end of 2013, the fight against the LRA is far from over. Three years after the deployment of US Special Forces to Central Africa, Kony remains on the loose and LRA attacks against civilians in CAR and DRC continue, albeit at significantly reduced rates compared to previous years. It is not, however, inconceivable that the US involvement in the counter LRA operations could evolve into a larger Central Africa role, particularly as the LRA threat declines while deadlier conflicts in South Sudan and CAR emerge.[61]

Conclusion

The case of the LRA in CAR highlights a number of failures of previous CAR governments and international institutions over the years. The disconnect between Bangui and the many national semi-autonomous zones, the lack of security sector reform, and the inability of local leaders and international actors to adequately address the influence of neighbouring countries have created a security vacuum that has easily been exploited by the LRA and other unregulated militias. Failure to address these root causes means that the LRA phenomenon in CAR risks being replicated. The kinds of operations that have been mustered to counter the

LRA so far have remained always a kind of Band-Aid for the specific problem of LRA violence, as if the LRA could be dealt with separately from the broader problems of militarization in the region. Such an approach is doomed to failure from the outset.

Notes

1 For more on the context of the LRA's formation see: Branch, A. (2010) 'Exploring the Roots of LRA Violence: Political Crisis and Ethnic Politics in Acholiland', in Tim Allen and Koen Vlassenroot, eds., *The Lord's Resistance Army, Myth and Reality*, Zed Books, London.
2 For an understanding of the LRA's history see: Cakaj, L., Lacaille, G. and Lancaster, P. (2011) 'Diagnostic study of the Lord's Resistance Army', *Transitional Demobilization and Reintegration Program – World Bank*, Washington DC. Available from: <http://www.tdrp.net/PDFs/LRA_DiagnosticStudy_1.pdf>.
3 For a more detailed account of LRA's training in Sudan see: Ledio Cakaj (2011) 'Lords of War', *Jane's Intelligence Review*, September.
4 See LRA Crisis Tracker, http://www.lracrisistracker.com, last accessed 24 May 2014.
5 For a detailed description of numbers and composition of LRA groups by mid-2013 see: Cakaj, L. and Lancaster, P. (2013) 'Loosening Kony's Grip: Effective Defection Strategies for Today's LRA', *The Enough Project*, Washington DC, July.
6 A report published in early 2009, a year after the first LRA attack in CAR, classified the LRA threat against civilians in CAR as last in a series of other factors including rebel groups and bandits. Spittaels, S. and Hilgert, F. (2009) 'Mapping Conflict Motives: Central African Republic', *IPIS*, Antwerp, February.
7 SPLA elements often crossed into south-eastern CAR to loot food as well as force South Sudanese refugees in CAR towns to return to Sudan. See for instance, 'CAR, Report on the Anticipated Sudanese Peace Accord', (2004) *IRIN*, 24 March.
8 'State of Anarchy, Rebellion and Abuses against Civilians in CAR', (2007) *Human Rights Watch*, September.
9 For a discussion of the relationship between Kony and Otti and what transpired in the LRA camps leading to and following Otti's death see Cakaj *et al.* (2011).

10 Interviews with former LRA combatants, Gulu, October 2010, March and June 2011.
11 Interviews with G. O., June 2010, March 2011. Gulu, Uganda.
12 Interview with G. O., March 2011, Gulu. According to this testimony and others, Kony believed that Otti was offered money to kill Kony and destroy the LRA and that Ugandan officials were not serious about the talks.
13 Interview with official, 8 March 2010, Obo.
14 Interview with representative from a non-governmental organization (NGO), 9 March 2010, Obo.
15 Estimates based on interviews with former LRA combatants, Uganda, CAR, DRC, South Sudan, August 2009–July 2013.
16 A US Embassy cable from Bangui states that the then US Ambassador spoke on 6 November 2009 with the CAR deputy foreign minister who stated that the UPDF entered CAR in early June 2009 at the request of CAR to deal with the LRA. http://cablegatesearch.wikileaks.org/cable.php?id=09BANGUI243
17 LRA Crisis Tracker, 'LRA Crisis Tracker Quarter 1 Security Brief', http://reports.lracrisistracker.com/en/q1-2014/
18 Estimate based on interviews with various experts as the Ugandan army does not disclose force strength.
19 Interview with Colonel Mike Kabango, 22 July 2013, Yambio, South Sudan.
20 Phone interview with NGO representative, 5 April 2014.
21 As a political commentator in Bangui stated, 'Obo is more than a 1,000 km away from here and the saying goes "the state's authority ends at kilometre 12 from the capital"'. Interview, Bangui, 3 December 2011.
22 Interview with Colonel Arthure Bengue, Yambio, South Sudan, 19 July 2013.
23 Various interviews with local NGO and religious leaders, Brussels and Washington DC, 2013.
24 Interviews with NGO and UN representatives, Bangui, 6 December 2011.
25 Confidential.
26 Email exchanges with aid worker who travels frequently to south-eastern CAR, July 2014.

In unclaimed land

27 Interviews with various officials in Bangui. No evidence was produced for these claims except a report written on the cutting of timber in Obo. Some of the claims of cases of UPDF soldiers selling Chinese made bicycles in Djema and AK47s and bullets to a Chadian trader in Mboki were brought out by different sources too. A local official told this author in March 2010 that the UPDF base commander in Djema held a public meeting with the people of Djema asking them 'not to buy bullets from UPDF soldiers and report the soldiers immediately'.
28 Despite rumours that the Ugandans moved to Sam Ouandja to get involved in the diamond trade and not to stop the LRA from moving to south darfur, there has been no evidence so far to support such claims. It is possible that UDFR leader Zakaria Damane, who controlled many mines in the area, complained to the then CAR President.
29 Interview with Marlyn Mouliom Roosalem, Minister of Commerce and Industry and Resident of Haut Mbomou, Bangui, 6 December 2011.
30 A local NGO worker also claimed to have seen the report, stating, in addition, that the local officials in Obo were annoyed that the UPDF took the timber 'without even asking them'. Interview with NGO worker. Bangui, 2 December 2011.
31 Ibid.
32 Telephone interviews with Lieutenant Colonel Felix Kulaigye, Ugandan army spokesperson, Kampala, 11 and 13 July 2012.
33 Various sources including the Ugandan army spokesperson Paddy Ankunda reported a UPDF attack on Seleka in Nzako on 30 June 2014, where eleven Seleka fighters were killed. Ankunda also published photos, via his Twitter account, of alleged weapons recovered from Seleka during a UPDF disarmament campaign in the north-east.
34 In a visit to Paris on 13 May 2014, Ugandan Foreign Minister Sam Kutesa stated that 400 Ugandan troops would be part of the peacekeeping force in CAR.
35 'Conclusions de la réunion régionale ministérielle sur l'Armée de Résistance du Seigneur (LRA).' Not public.
36 Ambassador Lamamra headed the Peace and Security Department (PSD) until 2013, of the AU Commission. Similar to the UN Department of Peacekeeping Operations, the PSD provides peace support and other conflict management practices. The PSD and the Political Affairs Department are the main executive bodies of the AUC.

37 The meeting was chaired by Mr Lamamra and was attended by Minister of Defence of Uganda Crispus Walter Kiyonga, Minister of Defence of the DRC Charles Mwando Nsimba, Minister of Defence of the CAR Jean-Francis Bozizé and Minister of Internal Affairs of South Sudan Major General Gier Chuang Aluong. Sudan (and Chad) sent their AUC representatives. See the press release on the second regional ministerial meeting on the Lord's Resistance Army (LRA), Addis Ababa, Ethiopia, 6–8 June 2011.
38 This was the follow up to the first regional ministerial meeting that took place in October 2010 in Bangui, a full eight months later, even though the follow-up mechanism agreed to in Bangui stipulated that the ministers from the regional countries would meet every four months. The second regional ministerial meeting was initially scheduled to take place in Kampala but was moved to Addis instead.
39 'Conclusions on the second regional ministerial meeting on the Lord's Resistance Army (LRA), Addis Ababa, 6–8 June, 2011.' Not public.
40 Ibid.
41 Interview with NGO worker, 15 February 2014, Kampala, Uganda.
42 Interview with Colonel Bengue, AU-RTF headquarters, Yambio, 19 July 2013.
43 Interview with CAR NGO representative, Washington DC, 20 November 2013.
44 Interview with Colonel Bengue, AU RTF headquarters, Yambio, 19 July 2013.
45 Interview with AU official, 15 February 2014, Entebbe, Uganda.
46 Interview with Ugandan army commander who asked not to disclose name, rank or location for fear of repercussions from superiors.
47 Interview with diplomat, Washington DC, 22 August 2011.
48 Interview with AU officials, 22 and 23 July 2011. Addis Ababa, Ethiopia.
49 Various interviews and email correspondence.
50 Unpublished initial deployment plans indicated no role for peacekeepers in the south-east. This might yet change, particularly as some Ugandan officials want to incorporate current UPDF in CAR into MINUSCA.
51 Assistant Secretary of State Jendayi Frazer met with Museveni in September 2007 to discuss, among other things, 'contingencies to dealing with the LRA', according to a diplomatic cable made public by Wikileaks. http://wikileaks.org/cable/2007/09/07KAMPALA1449.html

52 'Armed US advisers to help fight renegade group', (2011) *The New York Times*, 14 October. The article specifies that, 'the administration of President George W. Bush, which authorized the Pentagon to send a team of seventeen counterterrorism advisers to train Ugandan troops and provided millions of dollars' worth of aid, including fuel trucks, satellite phones and night-vision goggles, to the Ugandan Army'.
53 'S 1067 The Lord's Resistance Army Disarmament and Northern Uganda Recovery Act of 2009' http://www.govtrack.us/congress/bill.xpd?bill=s111-1067
54 Interview with US officials, Kampala, 14 March 2011.
55 Interview with researcher, Washington DC, 10 May 2013.
56 Various phone and face to face interviews with State Department officials, Washington DC, 2010–2013.
57 Phone interview with US diplomat, 11 May 2014.
58 See Ledio Cakaj and Phil Lancaster, 'Loosening Kony's Grip: Effective Defection Strategies for Today's LRA', *The Enough Project*, Washington, DC, July 2013.
59 More research is needed to support such a claim based on informal interviews with at least three different foreign researchers visiting Obo and surrounding areas between March 2010 and June 2014.
60 The Obo-Tambura road, for instance, linking south-eastern CAR with South Sudan has been destroyed by years of movement of heavy vehicles used by the Ugandan army. In addition, the civil society of CAR, but also neighbouring countries, have pointed out the immediate needs faced by their communities. See for instance, 'Resolution of the Civil Society Task Force' (2014) *Conciliation Resources*, 29 May, Kinshasa. http://www.c-r.org/sites/default/files/RCSTF_DRC_EN.pdf
61 US officials, both at the State Department and the White House, claimed that there were no plans by early 2014 to turn the counter LRA operation into a larger, more diverse, mission but did not exclude the possibility it could happen in the future 'based on US interests'.

Bibliography

African Union Commission (2010) 'Communique de presse sur la réunion régionale ministérielle sur l'Armée de Résistance du Seigneur

(LRA) tenue a Bangui en République Centrafricain (RCA), les 13 et 14 Octobre 2010', 16 October, Addis Ababa.

Arieff, A. and Ploch, L. (2014) 'The Lord's Resistance Army: The US Response', *Congressional Research Service*, 15 May. Available from: <http://fas.org/sgp/crs/row/R42094.pdf>.

Atkinson, R. (1994) *The Roots of Ethnicity: The origins of the Acholi of Uganda before 1800*, Fountain Publishers, Kampala.

AU Peace and Security Council (2013) 'Report of the Chairperson of the Commission on the Implementation of the African Union-led Regional Cooperation Initiative for the Elimination of the Lord's Resistance Army,' PSC/PR/2.(CCCLXXX), 17 June, Addis Ababa.

Baguma, R. (2014) 'Uganda to Send 400 Peacekeeping Troops to CAR', *The New Vision*, 14 May. Available from: <http://www.newvision.co.ug/news/655500-uganda-to-send-400-peacekeeping-troops-to-car.html>.

Branch, A. (2010) 'Exploring the Roots of LRA Violence: Political Crisis and Ethnic Politics in Achoiland', in Tim Allen and Koen Vlassenroot, eds., *The Lord's Resistance Army, Myth and Reality*, Zed Books, London.

Butagira, T. (2011) 'US commandos venture into Kony's killing fields', *Daily Monitor*, 7 December, Kampala.

Cakaj, L. and Lancaster, P. (2012) 'On the Heels of Kony: The Untold Tragedy Unfolding in the Central African Republic', *The Enough Project*, Washington, DC.

Cakaj, L., Lacaille, G. and Lancaster, P. (2011) 'Diagnostic study of the Lord's Resistance Army', *Transitional Demobilization and Reintegration Program – World Bank*, Washington, DC. Available from: <http://www.tdrp.net/PDFs/LRA_DiagnosticStudy_1.pdf>.

Candia, S. (2013) 'UPDF Launches Fresh Bid to Capture Kony', *The New Vision*, 6 October. Available from: <http://www.newvision.co.ug/news/648048-updf-launches-fresh-bid-to-capture-kony.html>.

'Central Africa says "fight LRA like Al Qaeda"', (2010) *Agence France-Presse*, 14 October. Available from: <http://www.rnw.nl/africa/bulletin/central-africa-says-fight-lra-al-qaeda>.

'Congo sends 500 soldiers to join Uganda-led hunt for fugitive warlord Joseph Kony', (2013) *Associated Press*, 15 February.

Human Rights Watch (2009) 'The Christmas Massacres: LRA attacks on civilians in Northern Congo', Kinshasa–New York, 16 February.

Available from: <http://www.hrw.org/sites/default/files/reports/drc0209webwcover_1.pdf>.

International Crisis Group (2010) *Dangerous Little Stones: Diamonds in the Central African Republic*, Africa Report No. 167, Nairobi–Brussels.

Kasasira, R. (2013) 'UPDF ordered out of CAR, Suspends Hunt for Kony', *Daily Monitor*, 3 April. Available from: <http://www.monitor.co.ug/News/National/UPDF-ordered-out-of-CAR - suspends-hunt-for-Kony/-/688334/1737582/-/ydtcw/-/index.html>.

Lombard, Louisa (2012) 'Raiding and Refuge: The Political Economy of a Central African Buffer Zone'. Working paper prepared for the Conflict Prevention and Peace Forum, New York.

'LRA Crisis Tracker Quarter 1 Security Brief', (2014) *LRA Crisis Tracker*. Available from: <http://reports.lracrisistracker.com/en/q1–2014/>.

Marinkovic, N and Benner, A. (2012) 'African Union Launch Initiative against the LRA but Key Questions Remain', *Enough Project*, 2 April. Available from: <http://www.enoughproject.org/blogs/african-union-launches-initiative-against-lra-key-questions-remain>.

'Obo, une personne tuée et cinq autre blessées' (2014) *Réseau de Journalistes pour le Droit de l'Homme an RCA*, 14 January. Available from: <http://www.rjdh-rca.net/actulites/actualite/obo-une-personne-tuee-et-cinq-autres-blessees.html>.

Schomerus, M. (2007) 'The Lord's Resistance Army in Sudan: A history and overview', *Small Arms Survey*, Geneva.

Spittaels, S. and Hilgert, F. (2009) 'Mapping Conflict Motives: Central African Republic', *IPIS*, Antwerp, Belgium, February.

The White House, Office of the Press Secretary (2011) 'Letter from the President to the Speaker of the House of Representatives and the President Pro Tempore of the Senate regarding the Lord's Resistance Army', 14 October, Washington, DC. Available from: <http://www.whitehouse.gov/the-press-office/2011/10/14/letter-president-speaker-house-representatives-and-president-pro-tempore>.

Thompson, M. (2011) 'Who can stop the LRA?' *BBC News*, 18 February.

'Ugandan Army Chopper Cited in Elephant Poaching', (2012) *The East African*, 16 June. Available from: <http://www.theeastafrican.co.ke/news/UPDF-chopper-cited-in-Congo-elephant-hunt/-/2558/1509340/-/item/0/-/l0l0iz/-/index.html>.

UN Office for the Coordination of Humanitarian Affairs – OCHA (2014) 'LRA Regional Update, CAR, DRC and South Sudan', January–

March. Available from: <http://reliefweb.int/sites/reliefweb.int/files/resources/LRA_Regional_Update_Q1-2014-14Apr2014_final.pdf>.

US Congress (2010) 'The Lord's Resistance Army Disarmament and Northern Uganda Recovery Act of 2009', S. 1067, Enacted 24 May, Washington, DC.

US Embassy – Kampala (2007) 'NORTHERN UGANDA NOTES (AUGUST 25 – SEPTEMBER 7, 2007)' *Wikileaks*. Available from: <http://www.wikileaks.org/plusd/cables/07KAMPALA1435_a.html>.

US State Department (2014) 'US Support to Regional Efforts to Counter the Lord's Resistance Army', 24 March. Available from: <http://www.state.gov/r/pa/prs/ps/2014/03/223844.htm>.

13 A Central African Elite Perspective on the Struggles of the Central African Republic

Laurence D. Wohlers[1]

No attempt to make sense of the political trajectory of the Central African Republic can avoid examining the role that Central African elites have played. The role of elites and their strategic decision-making in moments of transition has long been the object of study by those seeking to understand democratic transitions. CAR is no exception. However, whereas much of social science literature looks solely at elite bargaining, pact formation, or the contextual variables that condition the choices and strategies adopted by elites, this chapter seeks to understand how the Central African elites themselves understand their fifty year history of failed political and economic development.

This chapter is based on extensive interviews with members of the Central African elite, both before and after the Seleka takeover.[2] Those elites are profoundly aware that the country has failed to realize its potential since independence. What went wrong is a question that preoccupies them. Indeed, even among those who have to one degree or another drifted into rent-seeking themselves, a certain wistful idealism remains for what the country might have been.

At the same time, elites' analysis of the root causes of the country's woes differs significantly from that of outside observers. Particularly in recent years, the latter have portrayed CAR as a nation caught in a never-ending cycle of conflict, characterized by deep ethnic and religious divisions. Even more than a failed state, it is seen by the outside world to be a hopeless one. However, that is not the view of Central African elites. While not minimizing the extent of governance failures, they consistently reject the implication of inevitability. Instead, the people who lived through these years and were directly involved emphasize that the country's slow and painful collapse was in large part due to the personal mistakes of its most senior leaders.

Which view is correct? This chapter will suggest that the truth lies somewhere in the middle. The conditions that the country inherited at independence – a population that was uneducated even compared to the low standards of colonial Africa, an underdeveloped economy, and a virtually non-existent political class certainly created ideal conditions for strongman rule and the consequential misgovernment that the country has suffered for so long. Further, the personalization of CAR's troubles is also tied to the nature of power in CAR. The issue is not just that the country inherited the highly-centralized structure of France's Fifth Republic, but that, in the absence of either powerful traditional leaders or a modern private sector, there was no countervailing political force. As a result, Central African heads of state started with very strong legal and constitutional advantages – and then proceeded to add on additional extra-constitutional powers virtually at will. The elites, generally senior civil servants without an independent power base, had little choice but to go along.

At the same time, the choices made by those strongmen were by no means inevitable and were in fact unique to each. In this sense, the elite too are right: CAR's post-independence history more than most is heavily shaped by the idiosyncrasies, and frequently the failings, of its presidents.

Finally, the bulk of this chapter, which focuses on the presidents themselves, demonstrates that governance failure became self-reinforcing. Just as successful governance can lay the foundation for future prosperity and stability, so too in CAR did the policy failures of the first presidents create the political weakness that led to future problems. It is, for example, difficult to imagine that General François Bozizé, a man of little education or political sophistication and who commanded minimal loyalty even among his fellow army officers, could have mounted a successful takeover in a country that had not already been considerably weakened. In short, CAR's history demonstrates that decline is self-reinforcing and cannot be easily reversed.

The elites

Who are these Central African elites? First, they are an extremely small portion of the population. Even by the standards of former colonies, CAR was extraordinarily poorly prepared for independence. The first Bangui *lycée* graduated its first class only in 1956, five years before independence. Thus, the severe shortage of educated cadres has been a persistent problem for both the economy and every Central African government. Even the first president, David Dacko, had only a non-university degree as a public school teacher. Further, the elite interviewed for this chapter were largely educated in a very narrow window, from independence until about 1980, a period of an intensive push to create an educated cadre. By the mid-1980s, that window was closing as the quality of Central African schools deteriorated and opportunities for outside study, especially in Europe, collapsed. Thus, overall educational achievement has actually declined in recent decades instead of expanding.

Second, almost without exception, this generation of elites went into government. That is what they were trained for and expected to do. At independence, a modern business sector simply did not exist and for various reasons the country never succeeded in creating one. Thus, as the conditions of government service deteriorated substantially after the mid-1980s, only a very few entered the private sector. Instead, they either left the country entirely or voluntarily became more political, in particular assisting the rent-seeking policies of successive political leaders, sometimes in return for a share of the spoils for themselves.

Third, Central African elites know each other intimately, having typically attended the same few high schools in CAR before travelling abroad, to France and Belgium in the early years of the post-independence era, later to the Eastern bloc, for their studies. Back in Bangui, they intermarried, worked together in the government, and largely socialized together as well. These intense connections meant that politics in CAR, although certainly influenced by ethnic and ideological affinities, were more often determined by the nature of personal relationships.

An interesting example of this phenomenon is the relationship between President Bozizé and his 2013 transitional prime minister, Nicolas Tiangaye. An articulate and courageous human rights lawyer, Tiangaye made his first reputation defending the former Emperor Jean-Bédel Bokassa at his 1986 trial.[3] When several years later, Bozizé was tried for coup plotting by the Kolingba regime, it was Tiangaye who undertook Bozizé's defence, protected his family, conducted a public campaign to improve Bozizé's detention conditions, and even personally gave money to the then destitute Bozizé. When Bozizé took power years later, the two found themselves together in the secretive, but politically powerful, Central African Masonic Lodge.[4]

Their political break-up, beginning soon after Bozizé's 2003 takeover, was both vicious and personal. Tiangaye's public resistance to Bozizé's efforts to consolidate power infuriated the latter, leading to physical attacks on Tiangaye supporters. When Bozizé's Presidential Guard beat up Tiangaye's son, the outraged Tiangaye showed up in his pyjamas at the presidential palace, publicly daring Bozizé to try to kill him. Later, after the flawed 2011 elections, it was Tiangaye who helped push the political opposition into rejecting the very legitimacy of Bozizé's victory. It was therefore particularly ironic that the Communauté Économique des États de l'Afrique Centrale (CEEAC) leaders chose Tiangaye to be the prime minister of the transitional government they imposed on Bozizé in January 2013.⁵ It was a relationship destined to fail, and it soon did.

Like Bozizé and Tiangaye, many others of the elite have bounced in and out of power over the past four decades. Men such as Jean-Jacques Démafouth, a cousin and current adviser to President Samba-Panza, who boasts on his resume experience as a defence minister, a rebel leader, and the distinction of having been the subject of an arrest warrant under every president since Kolingba. That he survived multiple political intrigues is not an aberration, however, the list of the political elite killed by their opponents in CAR is remarkably short. Despite the fact that political rivalries have been bitter, CAR's political leadership has rarely sought to kill or permanently expel its rivals. Instead, the members of the elite have managed to continuously reinvent themselves and return to the political game.

An elite oral history of CAR's decline

Press reports since the Seleka takeover frequently portray the violence in CAR as the result of long-standing ethnic and religious divides. That is not, however, the perspective of elites. In my conversations with them, they insisted that in the early years, ethnic and religious origin mattered little. A leading Muslim politician married to a Christian told me that his fiancée's parents worried about his political views, not his religion. Even the first Imam of Bangui had a Christian wife. Others noted that the 1990s democracy movement that finally forced Kolingba to hold the free elections, which he ultimately lost, did not have a strong ethnic connotation. In fact, a key leader of that movement, Aristide Sokambi, was from a southern ethnic group closely related to Kolingba's Yakoma. Similarly, many of the key leaders who spear-headed the coup of François Bozizé were not of his ethnic group: for example, Parfait Mbaye and Charles Doubane were both from the south and Karim Meckassoua was Muslim.

Elites do acknowledge that ethnic and religious tensions did become more prominent with later regimes. Tensions of the different ethnic groups of the majority Christian population developed as successive presidents, beginning with André Kolingba, began to surround themselves with their own family and ethnic followers. Even there, however, interviewees point out that the spoils went to a relatively small elite and ethnic groups as a class did not benefit. The development of Christian–Muslim tensions, on the other hand, tended to arise over specific conflicts, such as between the largely Christian consumers and the mostly Chadian shopkeeper community or between the Peuhl cattle herders and the mostly Christian farming communities.

A lack of non-governmental institutions

There was however a darker, flip side to the relative lack of ethnic tensions: interviewees frequently noted the lack of strong, non-governmental institutions – including traditional ethnic ones – that could have provided social stability and a counter-balance to the excesses of an overly strong presidential system. A key reason they cite is the country's colonial and pre-colonial past. A century of devastating attacks by slavers followed by an unusually harsh colonial experience had not just depopulated the country; it had largely destroyed traditional institutions. Apart from several relatively small sultanates that successfully resisted the slavers, there were neither traditional authorities left of any consequence or ethnic-based organizations. This did not mean that political leaders did not favour members of their ethnic group – Kolingba, Patassé and Bozizé all did to varying degrees. However, ethnic groups themselves never developed into powerful political or social forces. One key result is that the country only developed one political party with a substantial following (Patassé's MLPC – Le Mouvement pour la Libération du Peuple Centrafricain). Instead, political parties, of which there are currently over fifty, were simply the private appendages of opportunistic politicians hoping to attract enough attention to win a ministerial post.

A parallel problem that interviewees cited frequently was the failure to develop a successful and independent local merchant class. At independence, virtually all commerce and industry was in the hands of foreigners – French, Portuguese and some Greeks. When they pulled out, especially during the chaos and destruction of the 1990 mutinies, the void was largely filled by Lebanese, Chadians, and West Africans. Central Africans freely admit their lack of commercial experience and ability. A key problem, they say, was that colonial regulations forbade Central Africans from entering commerce, reportedly in order to ensure sufficient availability for farm labour. After independence, the drive to train a new class of civil servants led the government to neglect the creation of a commercial class.[6] The result, lamented one former prime minister, was that the country never had a significant middle class that was not dependent on government jobs and that might have resisted the political mistakes and corruption that gradually accumulated in the government. As one elite said, the country had some excellent senior civil servants but the government lacked *rigueur* (rigour) and *suivi* (follow-up).

A state both predatory and incompetent?

Interviewees agree that every Central African government perceived the private sector as a source of revenue (and patronage), rather than as an instrument of development. This was not, however, a perception limited only to presidential entourages. Indeed, very few of the Central African elite had ever worked in business and as a result senior civil servants tended to assume that companies were hiding their wealth. As a result, rather than nurture businesses, governments would continually push for more tax revenue. This not only slowed business development, it skewed the private sector towards those who were willing to embrace graft as a business model, as the best way to avoid excessive taxation was to pay bribes.[7]

Interviewees recounted examples of predatory political attacks on businesses on the part of political leadership in all of the administrations. In addition, they noted the willingness of successive leaders – Kolingba, Patassé, and Bozizé – to tolerate a degree of rent-seeking within their entourages that undermined their rule and much of the time did not even benefit the leaders personally.

A series of accidental presidents and its consequences

As a result, elites believe, the elite lacked a collective capacity to resist the culture of greed, the mismanagement, and the political incompetence that gradually evolved and eventually became deeply rooted in Central African governance. Further, interviewees noted that, with the exception of Patassé, none of CAR's heads of state had an obvious claim to power either by experience, popular power base or lineage of legitimacy. Instead, they were largely accidental presidents – Dacko because of Boganda's death, Bokassa because he seized the moment of Dacko's weakness, Kolingba because Dacko wanted to leave, and Bozizé because he came along at a moment when the region was ready for anyone to replace Patassé. None was obviously 'presidential' before coming to power – indeed, the better educated in the Central African elite had reason to look down on them.

Poorly prepared for governing, without an inherent claim to legitimacy, with weak institutions to support them, and with chronic revenue shortages, the vulnerability of these heads of state was obvious. Each strove to reduce that vulnerability, though often in unorthodox ways. André Kolingba, for example, found emotional support in the latter years of his regime in an illiterate fisherman from his hometown, whose 'visions' Kolingba found credible. The fisherman became so close to Kolingba that he once insisted on seating him at an official dinner in Paris, despite French protocol objections. Eventually, the fisherman was assassinated, reportedly at the instigation of Kolingba's own family.[8] Bozizé was also well-known for the influence on him of the Benin-based Celestial Church of Christ, of which he served as a deacon. Senior government officials spoke of using the Church's priests as an effective vehicle for passing messages to the President.

Each president also strove to reduce his vulnerability by turning heavily to family and ethnic allies to hold key positions. In the short run, CAR's constitution facilitated this strategy, as it vested extraordinary powers in the head of state. In the long run, however, it inevitably led to greater political isolation of the leadership, heightened corruption, and a steadily shrinking base of support.

The unravelling of the elite's ethos of service and the expanding culture of corruption

It is difficult to define precisely when the civil service lost its ethos of service. Several senior interviewees point to the second half of the Kolingba regime as a key turning point when the growth of corruption grew among the presidential entourage, combined with cuts in real income of government employees, this led to a breakdown in the social contract between the rulers and the senior civil service. The result was a steady expansion of corruption, which then exploded during the latter half of the Patassé regime when the successive governments failed to pay salaries. By the time that François Bozizé was firmly in power, corruption had become so pervasive that it appeared to be the principle *raison d'être* of the government. The most lucrative sources of corruption – principally diamonds or mining contracts – were reserved for Bozizé and his closest associates. Although it is unclear how much money Bozizé diverted, a foreign pilot for a small private airline recounted having repeatedly flown the President, accompanied by large trunks of cash, to neighbouring countries.

Opportunities for rent-seeking, however, were hardly limited to the President's family. Several interviewees noted that Bozizé was generally tolerant of corruption, particularly if he received a cut. For example, the government's chief prosecutor was widely reported to have arrested and deported several foreign businessmen. He then confiscated their investments, splitting the proceeds with one of Bozizé's sons. Other businessmen complained of repeated tax inspections, conducted for the purpose of soliciting pay-offs. Meanwhile, the CAR coordinator for the Global Fund's HIV programme was finally forced to resign after foreign press reporting on the disappearance of large sums.

The rampant corruption at senior levels naturally influenced the comportment of civil servants as well. Elites speak of a general collapse of government discipline, such that increasingly civil servants would not even show up for work. Assignments outside of Bangui were particularly disliked, and civil servants would frequently make only cursory visits to such posts. One result was that district courts were unable to try cases because either the judges or the prosecutors were absent. There were also many mechanisms for civil servants to steal government funds; an inventive one was to fake an illness serious enough to require evacuation to a foreign hospital, and then pocket the money once the government approved the evacuation. Lower-level civil servants could not aspire to such largesse. However, as the international community began to fund basic national health and education operations, those civil servants would increasingly insist that they be paid substantial per diems in order to accept training or travel to carry out their functions.

To the interviewees, this was all a far cry from the image they retained of a disciplined and committed civil service in the early years after independence.[9]

Presidents and their mistakes (as seen by elites)

Because my interlocutors were heavily focused on critiquing their heads of state, this section will take a chronological approach, beginning with David Dacko and ending with François Bozizé. The short presidency of Michel Djotodia is not within its purview.

David Dacko: the father of Central African authoritarianism?

David Dacko has the unfortunate distinction of being, twice, made to be 'France's solution' to a political crisis in CAR: first, after the country's spiritual founder, Barthélemy Boganda died just before independence, and secondly in 1979 when he was brought back to Bangui by the French paratroopers who overthrew Emperor Bokassa. His close association with French *dirigisme* (interventionism) inevitably colours elites' view of Dacko, a president who moreover never demonstrated much political savvy and failed in the end to shake off his aura of illegitimacy. That being said, Dacko won high marks for his personal commitment to development and building up the Central African economy. It was in fact during Dacko's first term in office that the government created the local textile industry, thus making it possible to use the cotton crop domestically. Dacko also put an enormous emphasis on education. Moreover, although corruption was not unknown in Dacko governments, Dacko did not enrich himself.

Dacko's greatest flaw, interviewees say, was his intolerance of political dissent or competition. Unable to manage the complications of political pluralism, Dacko turned to one-party governance. Without charisma or a populist political base, Dacko then repeatedly resorted to strong-arm tactics to try to protect his regimes. The arrest, trial, and expulsion of the popular leader Abel Goumba in the early 1960s was one example. Worse, one interviewee pointed out, it was Dacko who created all of the legal tools of repression that would serve his successors so well.[10] Bokassa did not need to enact any measures himself; he merely applied those developed by Dacko. The measures did not serve Dacko as well, in both of his presidencies, popular pressures eventually built up for change that Dacko could not resist.

Bokassa: the 'Golden Era'

For many in the elite, the Bokassa period passes for something of a golden era. That may be surprising to outsiders who associate

Bokassa largely with his extravagant and costly imperial coronation, the allegations that he ate human flesh, and his famously encyclopaedic tastes in women.[11] However, elites recall his reign nostalgically as a time of infrastructure building, agricultural expansion, and a sense of national direction. Schools were well furnished and staffed, both in the capital and in the provinces. Further, Bokassa is remembered for the perception that he stood up to a French presence that, under Dacko, had been perceived as largely supporting the interests of the French colonial business sector.[12]

Moreover, one interviewee noted, Bokassa's grand projects such as the agricultural expansion programme, Operation Bokassa and the building of the national university gave the country a sense of national purpose and identity. It was under Bokassa, interviewees said, that people first began to think of themselves as Central Africans. Bokassa, another added, understood that the people wanted strong leadership and an ambitious vision of the future.

That being said, elites acknowledge that Bokassa's rule became steadily more capricious and violent. A former senior minister recounted the terror of working for Bokassa, saying that he avoided social contacts for fear of being accused of coup plotting.[13] A younger civil servant told of whisking his wife onto a plane to France after Bokassa's eye turned to her. Moreover, the reality was that many of Bokassa's grandiose projects were poorly planned and implemented. Finally, Bokassa faced the same revenue problems that Dacko did – even before the expenses of his gaudy coronation in 1977, the government was nearly bankrupt.

Nevertheless, the elite remember the Bokassa period as a time when the senior civil service responded to a sense of larger national purpose. Bokassa himself may have enriched himself at the state's expense, but he did not tolerate the same in others. Indeed, the sort of conspicuous consumption by elites that became commonplace under later presidents would have been extremely dangerous under Bokassa. As a result, the civil service itself was still perceived to be relatively disciplined and incorrupt.

In particular, multiple interviewees recounted nostalgically stories of police and gendarmes who were respectful, professional, and did not ask for money.

Kolingba: the inventor of ethnic-based governance

The elite also speak positively of the early years of the Kolingba regime, and particularly the disciplined and effective governance by Kolingba's military committee for national reconstruction. Backed by strong levels of French assistance, this was a period of a strong, active civil service and an expansion of social services. School attendance reached its peak with 75 per cent of school age children. The agricultural sector was relatively prosperous and growing. The government's authority and reach extended to most of the country. Borders were generally secure, roads were safe – though thanks in large part to the sizeable presence of French troops.[14] Although Kolingba ruled with a strong hand and was not interested in multi-party democracy, the regime was not particularly oppressive. Opponents were generally exiled to remote parts of the country where they lived in relative freedom.[15]

That said, interviewees widely condemned Kolingba for turning ethnic favouritism into a highly-organized system that reached deeply not only into the security forces but the rest of government. This had catastrophic long-term consequences for the country. Although both Dacko and Bokassa created ethnic-based personal guards, neither practiced ethnic favouritism on a wide scale. Interviewees agreed that Kolingba's ethnic policy first appeared following an amateurish, failed coup attempt by Ange-Félix Patassé and his close associate, François Bozizé (a future president himself) in 1982. A former minister under Bokassa and a member of the Gbaya, the nation's largest ethnic group, Patassé was arguably the most charismatic politician CAR ever had. Kolingba moved initially to purge Gbaya from the security services following the failed coup.

However, he did not stop there. Interviewees say that Kolingba's closest advisers, largely members of the Yakoma, a small ethnic group from the south, then moved rapidly to assert their control over the entire government. One interviewee noted that by the end of the regime, the heads of thirty of the thirty-one parastatals and 75 per cent of the army were Yakoma. Kolingba also used the parastatals to absorb the hiring of their friends and family after the international financial institutions forced the government to halt induction into the civil service. Since there were few private sector modern enterprises, Kolingba's hollowing out of the parastatals, interviewees say, had serious long-term economic consequences. Production of cotton, coffee, tobacco and palm oil dropped severely by the end of Kolingba's time in office, largely as a result of mismanagement and corruption.[16]

In addition, interviewees criticize the Kolingba regime for the economic *désolidarisation* (separation) of the ruling leadership with the middle class. Unable to finance the burgeoning civil service, the Kolingba governments cut salaries and benefits significantly.[17] A consequence of these policies, and the eventual cause of Kolingba's downfall, was the resulting dissatisfaction in the middle class. This class was certainly small and largely confined to those working in Bangui's formal economy. Yet its political influence would prove decisive in forcing the country's first, and last, truly democratic elections in 1993.

Patassé: the catastrophic result of CAR's one free election
Although Bokassa is the best known, and most controversial, Central African leader outside of the country, in the eyes of the Central African elite, Ange-Félix Patassé is the most dominant political figure of the post-independence era. Patassé's charismatic appeal to the population, his dominance of the country's only political party to develop a grass roots following, the MLPC, and his mercurial and provocative politics destabilized successive regimes, including his own, from 1980 onwards.[18]

Yet, even Patassé's detractors agree that he inherited a very difficult set of political and economic problems after winning the 1993 elections. Politically, his Gbaya ethnic group in particular expected compensation for the years of discrimination under Kolingba. Economically, the 50 per cent devaluation of the Central African franc soon after his inauguration caught Patassé unprepared for what proved to be a disastrous reduction in the standard of living of the country's import-dependent middle class. Moreover, with French budget subsidies at an end and forced to divert substantial revenues to repaying debts to international financial institutions, Patassé faced a serious budgetary crisis from the outset. Indeed, even his critics criticized the international community for the lack of external support to this, the first democratically-elected government in the country's history.

However, interviewees fault Patassé particularly on three points. First, he terribly mismanaged the ethnic problem. His first step – reintegrating back into the military and civil service the non-Yakoma who had been pushed out by the previous regime, was broadly supported by the population. However, the decision required resources that the government did not have. Moreover, Patassé's decision to restore promotions that the former employees would have theoretically received if they had not been fired suddenly expanded the senior ranks of the government with largely untrained newcomers. Finally, far from eschewing ethnic politics, Patassé quickly promoted his own ethnic group into senior positions.

Second, interviewees say that Patassé had a gift for provocation that angered his potential partners, both at home and abroad. Externally, his 1960s-style, anti-Western rhetoric offended the French and scared the financial institutions. As a result, successive Patassé governments had trouble accessing Western financial assistance. IMF assistance, suspended initially in 1989 under Kolingba, would not begin again until 1998 (five years into Patassé's rule).

Interviewees also emphasized that Patassé managed to anger his closest neighbours. His close relationship with DRC rebel leader turned opposition vice-president Jean-Pierre Bemba (who used Bangui as a transit point for clandestine diamond shipments, reportedly with Patassé's assistance) angered President Kabila, who responded by cutting off CAR's critical access to oil refined in Kinshasa. When Patassé then turned to Qaddafi for oil (and military support) he thereby angered Chadian President Déby. By the end of his time in office, Patassé had offended every important regional actor, thereby inadvertently helping to stimulate the external coalition that would overthrow him.

Third, interviewees say that Patassé paid little attention to the details of governance, especially economics. He rarely attended cabinet meetings or travelled around the country. He drank large quantities of wine. He failed to control the excesses of his political party, the MLPC, that many interviewees agreed was more interested in rent-seeking and internal intrigues than in governing.

As his political isolation grew, several interviewees alleged that Patassé's paranoia began to cloud his judgment. Patassé became a regular reader of intelligence files (the infamous *fiches*), in a system that was highly politicized and unprofessionally administered. The result was a growing web of arrests and treason trials that demotivated the army and ultimately destabilized the regime.[19] The army thus largely failed to fight when Bozizé's small force descended from Chad in March 2003. The respected commander of the Presidential Guard, unwilling to risk bloodshed in support of Patassé, simply left town to allow Bozizé's forces an uncontested entry.

Bozizé: The cautious CEO

Interviewees describe Bozizé as polar opposite in personality to Patassé. Where Patassé was impulsive and mercurial, Bozizé was cautious and indecisive; Patassé drank copiously, Bozizé never touched alcohol; Patassé was charismatic and never happier than in front of a crowd, Bozizé was taciturn and spoke poorly. It is unclear if Bozizé really was guilty of the coup plot allegations that forced his flight in 2001. In any case, Bozizé initially thought himself too weak to attempt a takeover.[20] Ultimately, however, he benefited by being available at a moment when both CAR's neighbours and many Central African elites were ready to replace Patassé.

The country that Bozizé ultimately did take over in 2003 was in desperate shape. Interviewees agreed that the country's small modern economy was wrecked. What the mutinies from 1996 to 1998 had not already destroyed, Bozizé's mercenary army, pillaged in their own turn.[21] Nevertheless, the consensus of the political elite is that Bozizé initially received significant support, both externally and internally. Domestically, Central Africans at all levels were exhausted by the instability and chronic conflict of the Patassé years. Interviewees agree that the desire for stability was intense, a desire that Bozizé continued to benefit from up to the 2011 elections. Given those positive trends, interviewees agree that Bozizé had every chance of success if only he had shown moderately good governance. They are therefore nearly unanimous in blaming Bozizé personally for the governing mistakes that eventually destabilized his regime and set the stage for the Seleka takeover in 2013.

His first and most critical mistake, they say, was to increasingly rely on a poorly-educated entourage of family and tribal loyalists. Interviewees say Bozizé's electoral victory in 2005 convinced him that he no longer needed his technocratic supporters. One interviewee formerly close to him said that Bozizé was convinced that the intellectuals had 'betrayed' Bokassa, and thus could not be trusted. Instead, egged on by his entourage, Bozizé after 2005 increasingly focused on how to stay in power indefinitely. To do so, he gradually replaced his ethnically-diverse and technocratic government team with what one commentator ridiculed as 'tribalism from the bottom'. In fact, many interviewees argued that family played a far greater role with Bozizé than with any of his predecessors.

Second, suspicion and cynicism were hallmarks of Bozizé's style of governance. In fact, one interviewee deadpanned that Bozizé never trusted a man he could not buy. For example, interviewees says that one reason that the critical issue of DDR (Disarmament, Demobilization and Reintegration) for rebel groups stalled for years was that Bozizé obstructed the process, apparently hoping that he could buy off the rebel groups' leaders rather than spend the larger sums of DDR funds allocated for the rank and file. Interviewees, however, say that this approach eventually backfired. Bozizé had enough money to buy off individuals here or there but that only increased frustrations in the rank and file, both in the Bangui political opposition and the fighters in the northern-based rebel groups.

Third, interviewees say that Bozizé destroyed what was left of government administration. In the case of the army, this was intentional: it was widely known that, mistrustful of the army's loyalty, he denied it ammunition and opportunities for field exercises and kept it largely deployed in Bangui.[22] The result was that he steadily lost control of the outlying prefectures to politico-military groups, poachers, and bandits. Less intentionally, he ignored growing indiscipline and corruption in the administration, with the result that civil servants outside of Bangui simply abandoned their posts and returned to Bangui. By the end of the Bozizé regime, the government barely existed outside of the capital. As one senior civil servant noted, 'Bozizé made sure we civil servants were paid and so we went along. However, the rest of the population felt abandoned and so eagerly supported the arrival of the Seleka, even though Seleka was a foreign force'.

Eventually, therefore, like Patassé before him, Bozizé simply exhausted the collective goodwill that had brought him to power in 2003. Though interviewees do not fully agree on the extent of the collaboration between the Seleka leadership and Bozizé's political opponents inside the country, it is clear that Seleka's rapid advance to the capital was at a minimum facilitated by the exasperation on all sides with Bozizé.

Dependency: France, Chad, and a dangerous neighbourhood

Although the elite invariably speak of CAR as a country rich in natural resources, the reality is that no government has ever put together a sufficient combination of revenues, infrastructure, technical capacity and governance to exploit effectively those resources, much less provide the population with much needed improvements in services and infrastructure. The result is that Central African governments have always been dependent on outside support.

For the first twenty years of its existence, that essentially boiled down to one country: France. France provided the bulk of budgetary support, French *coopérants* (advisers) played key roles in most ministries, French military provided training and defence support, France trained the civil service, and French businesses controlled much of the economy. Central African elites, most of whom are French-trained, have had a difficult time coming to terms with the end of that era. As one noted nostalgically, 'we still think that the road to power in CAR lies through Paris'.

The winding down of French dominance in CAR stretched over a decade, beginning with reductions in assistance in the 1980s and culminating in the departure of French troops and many French businesses during the successive mutinies of the late 1990s. Given that CAR had by far the smallest army in a region dominated by conflict, the French departure made CAR's security situation precarious. The consequences for Central African elites were tremendous, ushering in a new era of regional politics for which the elites and the country were unprepared, and at a serious political disadvantage. The result was that CAR's presidents, opposition, and rebels all increasingly made their way to neighbouring capitals as the best way to obtain an edge in their quests to achieve or maintain power. Increasingly in the later years, the key regional relationship was Chad. Interviewees agree that, despite their substantial other failings, the ultimate undoing of both Patassé and Bozizé was their failure to successfully manage their relationship with Chadian President Déby.

Conclusion

Outsiders seeking to understand CAR's history of chronic instability frequently conclude that deep-seated social or ethnic conflict is the primary source of the nation's problems. While acknowledging ethnic and religious tensions, those interviewed for this chapter did not dwell on them. Although they speak consistently of mismanagement of ethnic relations by successive heads of state, elites rarely mention ethnic or religious conflict *per se* as being a root cause of the nation's weakness. They have a point. In fact, ethnicity did not appear to play a major role in how any of CAR's leaders rose to power. The sole and partial exception to that is Ange-Félix Patassé, who clearly catered to and was supported by a large majority of his Gbaya tribe in the 1993 elections. In general, however, leaders resorted to ethnicity only later, when they feared for their ability to remain in power.

Instead, the elites I talked to repeatedly returned to the theme that the country's failure was primarily due to the political and management failures of the country's presidents. In one sense, they are not wrong. The country was not lucky in its leaders, and one can imagine that, given CAR's highly-centralized government, a single competent leader would have faced as few obstacles to positive governance as the nation's actual presidents met in carrying out their ultimately destructive policies. The difference between national success and failure may have been as simple as that.

Nevertheless, the ability of weak and unpopular leaders to dominate the body politic for long periods also reflects the country's chronic lack of counter-vailing institutions, either traditional or modern. With the lone exception of the popular democracy movement that forced the 1993 elections, the elite never coalesced around political interest groups or movements that could have acted as a check on the government's mistakes and misdeeds. Again, with the exception of the 1993 elections, political change always came either from the outside or from lone actors who faced little opposition. Indeed, despite the country's reputation for coup d'états, taking power in Bangui was generally a tepid affair, with little violence and opponents melting away rather than putting up a fight.

It was not that the Central African elite lacked honest and courageous individuals. I have known personally a number of individuals whose commitment, despite the odds, to continue to pursue positive change I admire tremendously. However, the elite's inability to establish genuine political interest groups, coupled with the weakness of the middle class generally and the unfortunate choice of France's Fifth Republic as a governance model, set the stage for chronic misrule by authoritarian presidents. A few of the first generation of the elite recognized this failure. Most, however, have learned to reinvent themselves in order to survive with each new leader.

Whether they will be able to continue to do so, however, is an open question. The Seleka takeover and its aftermath has seriously weakened the elite's role in the body politic. The short period of the Djotodia regime was the first in CAR history in which those who effectively held power were not drawn from the post-independence elite. For the first time, the elite were truly outsiders looking in. In turn, the Anti-Balaka forces that eventually rebelled against Seleka, although Christian and mostly from the south, are largely illiterate and drawn heavily from outside the elite. The lawlessness, chronic violence, and economic devastation of the past eighteen months is something for which the elite has had no answer. Yet the post-Seleka transitional president, Catherine Samba-Panza, has staffed her government with many familiar faces from the old elite. However, progress in restoring government effectiveness has been slow and the population is clearly frustrated.

This raises the question about how the population will judge the elite in elections planned for the end of the transition. Although well over a dozen of these familiar elite have already indicated their intention to run for president, they may well face competition from a new generation derived not from the civil service but from the Anti-Balaka groups. It may then be difficult to return to the old, pre-Seleka political order. That will not be good for the elites, but it is not clear what it will mean for the country.

Notes

1 The opinions and characterizations in this book are those of the author, and do not necessarily represent official positions of the United States Government.
2 This chapter developed from discussions with many Central Africans during my tenure as US ambassador to the Central African Republic (2010–2013) and was then buttressed by more formal interviews with a dozen Central Africans, chosen for their knowledge of the country. The result is meant to be neither a scientific survey of Central African opinion nor an in-depth study of CAR's governance failure, but rather an impressionistic look at how local elites view their country's, and their own, failure.
3 Emperor Jean-Bédel Bokassa was arrested by CAR authorities immediately upon his return from exile in France on 24 October 1986 and put on trial on fourteen different charges including: murder, treason, embezzlement, illegal use of property, and cannibalism. In December, he was convicted of thirteen counts (all except cannibalism) and was jailed until 1993, three years before his death in 1996.
4 Central Africa's highly secretive Masonic lodge reportedly is led by Republic of Congo President Sassou Nguesso and includes many of CAR's senior elite. Ironically, Bozizé was a latecomer to the lodge and was therefore a junior member to many of his political opponents, including Tiangaye and 2011 presidential candidate Martin Ziguélé.
5 The January 2014 Libreville conference, convoked by CEEAC president Déby, forced Bozizé to accept a transitional government in which his powers were to be severely curbed and he was to be barred from any effort to change the constitution to run for a third term.
6 See Chapter 3, 'Being Rich, Being Poor: Wealth and Fear in the Central African Republic' by Roland Marchal, for further discussion about the reasons for the paucity of a non-Muslim, Christian commercial class in CAR.
7 See Chapter 5, 'The Elite's Road to Riches in a Poor Country' by Stephen Smith, for more on the workings of this concessionary mode of politics.

8   Several contacts confirmed this account of the fisherman's power over Kolingba, adding that ministers at the time regularly complained of the power that Kolingba's fisherman had over government policy.
9   Yarisse Zoctizoum, in his history of CAR published in 1983, would disagree with this perspective. He argues that at independence, Central African elites became '*munju voko*' (foreign/white blacks) – in other words, just as exploitative and entitled as colonial officials (Zoctizoum, 1983). Kalck, too, cites the fact that early parliamentary discussions were obsessed with such topics as the cost of alcohol and government elite perks. Salaries for elites exploded during the 1960s (Kalck, 1972).
10 Dacko went so far as to ban visits to diplomatic missions or showing movies without government approval. In this obsession with controlling public information, interviewees say, he was particularly influenced by the Communist ideology popular at the time.
11 See Titley (1997) for a detailed discussion of Bokassa's many wives and mistresses, who were customarily referred to by their nationalities.
12 See O'Toole (1986). In 1960, total French aid approximately equalled total exports.
13 Several participants speculated that the fear of authority Bokassa inspired continued long after his reign, contributing to a general reluctance of civil servants to challenge abuses of authority.
14 A senior military commander recounted that as a young lieutenant in the 1980s he had led patrols along the Sudanese border to stop poaching. The armed forces at that time, he said, largely fulfilled its security mandate, though he noted that French training and logistical support was vital. In contrast, during the Bozizé era, the army had largely given up patrolling both its borders and large sections of the interior.
15 Aristide Sokambi, a leader of the 1990s democracy movement, recalled how, during his forced exile to a remote village, he organized the villagers to build a tennis court and had friendly relations with the local gendarmes. When he was released, the villagers gave him a farewell party.
16 For example, CAR preceded Ivory Coast in growing high-quality Robusta coffee. Kolingba, however, reportedly allowed family members to import lower-quality coffee from Zaire and mix it with the Central African coffee. The result was that buyers began turning away from Central African coffee.

17 Under pressure from the international financial institutions, it instituted a semi-voluntary reduction in force (le Départ Volontaire Assisté), which pressured many civil servants to leave government service in return for a one-time severance payment.
18 Interviewees agree that Patassé's political manoeuvres particularly destabilized Dacko's second term in office leading to its early demise and the subsequent coup d'état by Kolingba.
19 Although Patassé's Minister of Defence, Jean-Jacques Démafouth, and his Army chief of staff, François Bozizé, were implacable enemies; each was in turn accused of treason. Démafouth went to trial and was ultimately acquitted; Bozizé refused arrest and fled into exile.
20 A contact well-placed in the Patassé government noted that, even after fleeing, Bozizé was ready to cut a deal with Patassé in order to avoid more years of exile. Bozizé had good reasons to do so: his standing within the army was not high (only thirty-five soldiers had joined his flight north to Chad), and well-informed interviewees agree that Chadian President Déby was unimpressed by Bozizé and initially offered no support. A senior minister at the time speculated that even an ambassadorship at that moment might have neutralized him.
21 Indeed, Bozizé's fighters destroyed the economically important cotton mill located, ironically, in Bozizé's home town of Bossangoa. It took most of Bozizé's ten years in power to replace it.
22 One source reported that even in the middle of heated combat with the Seleka in December 2013, Bozizé refused to distribute heavy weapons to the regular army, trusting only his ethnic-based Presidential Guard to remain loyal.

Bibliography

Kalck, Pierre (1972) *Central African Republic: A Failure in Decolonization*. Praeger, New York.

O'Toole, T. (1986) *The Central African Republic, the Continent's Hidden Heart*, Westview Press: Boulder, US.

Titley, B. (1997) *The Dark Age: The Political Odyssey of Emperor Bokassa*, Liverpool Press: Liverpool, UK.

Zoctizoum, Y. (1983) *Histoire de la Centrafrique: violence du développement, domination et inégalités*, L'Harmattan: Paris.

14 A Concluding Note on the Failure and Future of Peacebuilding in CAR

Tatiana Carayannis and Louisa Lombard

The chapters assembled in this volume offer a range of arguments about how the Central African Republic ended up in the predicament it is currently in, precisely to underscore that there is no one factor that explains the increase in violence at the end of 2012. Rather, they point to a convergence of very complex dynamics – internal and external – that developed over many decades.

The at-times staggering length of the country's list of challenges notwithstanding, there was nothing *necessary* about the trajectory taken by the Central African Republic in late 2012. The comparative wisdom of hindsight might make it seem like CAR was on an inevitable course toward 'failure' or 'fragility' from the start, but that would be an ahistorical argument. The various problems and challenges Central Africans have faced do not add up to the country's current condition – there were roads not taken, as well as a number of instances of bad luck. Who knows how things would have been different had Barthélemy Boganda not taken that fateful flight in March 1959. The structural and political difficulties would not have disappeared, but the personalities and strategies may have been quite different indeed. Counterfactuals can be interesting as thought experiments. But it strikes us that the most important reason to reject the arguments that would portray CAR as having been on an inevitable path toward disaster is that they let all of us who have been involved in the country off the hook too easily.

Peacebuilding efforts in the country have been a marked failure. Mistakes have been made, and opportunities have slid away. In this conclusion, we review some of the dynamics of these failures. Our interest is not to point fingers but to facilitate learning from mistakes. We also discuss the social faultlines that have taken on such great importance over the course of the 2013–2015 'crisis,' particularly the role of religion in questions of belonging and predation. Our interest in doing so is to begin pointing to the conditions under which existing cracks in social relations can become chasms (if only temporarily), with devastating consequences. While we are aware how difficult it will be to bring about changes in the reigning Central African and diplomatic political cultures and structures, the extent of the violence seems to have spurred a new intensity of reflection on the part of both international interveners and Central Africans and a recognition that things *should* be done differently. Evidence so far suggests that old patterns are going to be difficult to change, but perhaps the recognition that they should is at least the first step in a long process toward a more peaceful and prosperous future.

The 2013–2015 'Crisis': A brief history

The Seleka takeover of Bangui in March 2013 that ousted President François Bozizé brought to power Michel Djotodia, a leader in the rebel alliance and First Deputy Prime Minister for National Defence.[1] By late March 2013, the Central African Armed Forces (FACA) had disintegrated. Seleka commanders, never organized into a particularly unified hierarchy, ruled towns and cities as their fiefdoms. The failure of some among them to speak Sango fed the perception among people living in these places that their lives, lands, and livelihoods were being despoiled by rapacious foreigners. In fact, Seleka drew on a motley assortment of men – a number of them were itinerant men-in-arms recruited in the Chad/Darfur borderlands; others were from northeastern CAR rebel groups that had mobilized over the past decade; and still others joined amid the rush on the capital in the hopes that by doing so they might gain a government job or at least access to a disarmament, demobilization, and reintegration (DDR) programme.

During these months of ad hoc Seleka rule and widespread criminality, a violent response began building, drawing initially on vigilante or auto-defence groups of varying levels of organization that have long been widespread in the country. These fighters became known as anti-Balaka. The various groups and loosely-organized bands using this moniker had diverse origins but some of the most brutal (and best-equipped) were Bozizé supporters and from Pentecostal church movements. As the vengeance impulse seems so often to do, the anti-Balaka reprisal attacks quickly exceeded their ostensible targets – the Seleka enemy became the Seleka/Muslim-foreign enemy, with membership in either of these categories sufficient grounds for persecution.

On 5 December 2013, the same day the UN Security Council passed resolution 2127 authorizing an African Union peacekeeping force in CAR, MISCA, to be supported by French troops (the Sangaris mission), anti-Balaka groups launched a spectacular night-time attack on the capital. More than 600 civilians were killed in Bangui and more than 214,000 fled from their homes. Widespread violence continued in the following months, claiming the lives of two French soldiers, and leaving entire villages torched across the country. A mass exodus of Muslims out of the country followed, with many seeking refuge in neighbouring countries or in predominantly-Muslim north-eastern CAR.

The fact that the grievances and animosities were expressed in a religious idiom provided a convenient shorthand narrative to the outside world of what the conflict was about – it was Christians against Muslims. This simplification has been misleading, in that it reduces to a question of differing ideologies or identities what are, in fact, a wide range of tensions and identity-related concerns, all of which have a degree of fluidity or situational definition. To understand how religion came to be such a flashpoint, it is worth parsing how religion became newly politicized over the last decade in CAR.[2]

CAR's population is majority Christian (about 50 per cent Protestant and 35 per cent Catholic), with a substantial Muslim minority (about 15 per cent). People who today say that Central Africans of different religions have always gotten along can point to the very few incidents of religious violence or religious intolerance over the last century and the many marriages across religious lines (as described in Kilembe, Chapter 4). However, Muslim-led slave raiding was prevalent within a few generations of those alive today, ending only once the twentieth century was well under way. At that time, the area now known as CAR was subject to two competing processes of centralization: one trans-Saharan and Muslim; and the other French-led, Christian, and directed toward the Atlantic. The French 'won,' and thus everything that is related to the state in CAR is coded Christian-French (the colonial language, Sango, falls into this heritage). Muslims are coded as foreigners, seen as inherently suspicious though also useful for their commercial prowess and networks. This partly explains why in early 2013, the Seleka – then mostly but not exclusively Muslim – were perceived as a group of dubious nationals, not fully Central African but instead 'hinterlanders' who raided the capital seeking a slice of the public cake, angry that former President Bozizé failed to fulfil the promises made in earlier peace accords and in the Libreville Agreement of January 2013.

Concerns about 'Muslim-foreigners' had also been inculcated by Bozizé over his decade in power. At the same time as he relied on Chadian support and even Chadian soldiers for his security, (and people of Chadian heritage benefited from total impunity for the various crimes they were accused of committing), he gave speeches in which he vilified the Muslim-foreigners who were, according to him, ruining the country. Bozizé used religion, and especially membership in his evangelical Christian congregation, as a criterion determining political access and positions. A Muslim awakening was also beginning during this time, with a new Wahhabi presence in the capital. The politicization of religion further mapped onto the dynamics described in Chapter 3 (Marchal), whereby Muslims, as commercial actors frequently involved in long-distance networks of trade and connection, are often wealthier than their Christian neighbours, another source of stress amid the uncertainty, anomie, and economic decline of the past few decades in CAR. So while the violence was expressed using a religious idiom, it had less to do with doctrinal differences or hatred, and more to do with the uncertainty, mistrust, and manipulation whose unfortunate long roots in CAR are bearing fruit. As Debos (2014) writes, 'The polarization of identity is more often a consequence of than a cause for war.'

By early 2014, nearly a quarter of CAR's total population of 4.5 million was displaced, and more than half of it in need of emergency humanitarian assistance. In fact, according to Médecins Sans Frontières (MSF), there were more deaths from the absence of health services than from violence (Centrafrique, 2014). Confronted with an unprecedented level of violence and mass displacement, international actors finally authorized and deployed the extensive international peacekeeping forces that at least some analysts had long argued would be necessary to bring back some order to the country.[3] In April 2014, after twelve months of increasing violence, the Security Council, by resolution 2149, transformed the pre-existing African Union mission (MISCA) into the United Nations Multidimensional Integrated Stabilization Mission in the Central African Republic (MINUSCA), supported by French (Sangaris) and European Union (EUFOR) forces. In what was a long and difficult internal UN handover process, the former UN peacebuilding mission, BINUCA, was subsumed within the new UN peacekeeping mission. The transition from regional to international stewardship was not unexpected. The AU International Support Mission had no unified command structure, and suffered both from rivalries among troop contributors and varying commitments to meet the goals of its mandate. After the AU's failures in Mali, few in the Security Council or in the UN Secretariat wanted to be seen as 'piling on' to the AU's failures, despite growing public pressure throughout 2013 for a more robust international intervention. This explains why MINUSCA was authorized in April 2014 – a year into MISCA's deployment, but with a five-month 'preparation' period for the transition of authority from MISCA to MINUSCA in September 2014.

By early 2015, CAR was host to three peacekeeping missions – one each from the UN, the EU, and a Security-Council authorized deployment by France,[4] and to nearly 12,000 international troops,[5] an enormous military presence as compared to the national army's strength of a mere 8,000 soldiers in 2012. CAR also saw an exponential growth in the number of humanitarian actors in this period, with 49 international NGOs (UN OCHA, 2014) starting programmes in CAR, including 11 new NGOs in the health sector alone. UN international staff in the country almost tripled from 49 in December 2014 to 139 in January 2015, and then again to 385 by March 2015 (Inter-Agency Standing Committee, 2014). Two new positions for Senior Humanitarian Coordinators were created, and cluster coordinators were upgraded to full-time positions. While this greatly increased the international presence in areas most affected by the conflict outside the capital, international staff remained concentrated in Bangui and some of the larger towns.

While an increased peacekeeper presence may reflect a greater importance of CAR on the international agenda, a position that many with ties to the country had long advocated for, the deployment occurred only after many of the worst atrocities had already occurred. Moreover, the mode of operating of these international actors re-inscribes some of the old patterns of ineffectiveness. The future, though not as grim as it might have looked at the height of the fighting, remains darkly clouded.

The failures of peacebuilding in CAR

The cascading magnitude of violence beginning late 2012 seemed to catch everyone by surprise – the Bozizé regime, the French, and the UN peacebuilding mission in the country. The label applied to it captured this sense that it was a period out of the normal: a *crisis*. A hashtag made it official: this was the #CARcrisis. While effective in galvanizing humanitarian aid, the label does not help us understand how CAR got into this predicament, or how politics in the country work. A crisis would imply that at other times, people in the country lived under normally peaceful conditions. However, the war that began in late 2012 was not an aberration or break with a past of normalcy. Rather, it is only the latest instantiation of weak statehood (that is, limited institutionalization of capacity, and a large role played by outside actors called in by the CAR state in the concessionary model described in Chapter 5) that has existed since independence. Since the string of army mutinies that began in 1996, crisis has been quasi-permanent. The permanent disorder in CAR is most evident at the subnational (local) and regional levels where the boundary between peace and wartime has been increasingly blurred.

Time and again, the international response – by France, or by African countries or by the UN (all more or less remote-controlled by France)[6] – has been spavined by a fundamental but, from a policy point of view, conveniently expedient misconception of the crisis of the day in CAR. The latter is understood as a 'critical' situation, i.e. one that is qualitatively different compared to the presumed normalcy of whatever preceded it, and which could easily be restored. The assumption that, following the deployment of international troops and the partial restoration of state authority (usually just) in Bangui, the situation will get 'back to normal,' misses the fact that for the Central African people there has never been such a thing as 'normalcy.' Life before the onset of violence in 2013 was one of permanent insecurity, internal displacement, and absent state services. In this forgotten country, state institutions have been dysfunctional at best, and non-existent at worse, for nearly two decades. Civilians live in a chronic crisis marked by periods of low intensity violence that are punctuated by periodic spikes in fighting.[7]

One of the reasons the quasi-permanence of the crisis has, at times, been easy to forget relates to the temporality and trajectory of international responses mustered to deal with CAR's conflicts. As the country has gone through various elements of the peacebuilding toolkit – peace talks, national dialogues, elections, and so forth – these episodes, despite their political emptiness, provide the narrative that is supposed to describe the state of the country. As each hurdle passes, a transition is imagined to have occurred, for instance, from a state of conflict to one of 'post-conflict,' even if there exists pressing evidence (such as the emergence of new rebel groups) to the contrary (Lombard, 2012a). This is understandable; no donor wants to fund *yet another* peace process just at the moment when they thought it would be possible to move onto elections and then wash their hands of this benighted place. But it is also arguably a major cause of the difficulty of emerging from the quasi-permanent crisis: the tools in the box never quite fit the problem, and even this limited number of tools only diminishes, because once it has been used it gets put aside, unless a major upheaval starts the cycle again. This begs for a bespoke peacebuilding approach rather than a one size fits all, and a good deal of contextual knowledge to tailor the approach.

International actors, who may have some sense of this history of perpetual crisis in CAR, nevertheless ignore it when it comes time to design peacebuilding programmes. Thus for instance, the UN default is to work to 'restore' the CAR national army, without any accounting for the fact that the army has been a source of predation and insecurity for decades. The fairly constant level of conflict potential since the mid-1990s would have been better met with a sustained *political* commitment (that is, a real reckoning as regards impunity and the distribution of political and economic power in the country) rather than repetitive military–humanitarian interventionism. Only a year into the massive response to the 2013 violence, talk of 'normalization' and the restoration of 'social cohesion' was premature in a way long-term CAR observers found painfully familiar. External actors continue to prioritize quick-fix solutions, an overly military approach to stabilization, and the promotion of elections at all costs over the broader structural needs of re-defining state/society responsibilities. With each cycle of rebellion, once the fighting subsided and displacement figures dropped, international actors ran for the exits.

As a result, though CAR has seen many peacebuilding initiatives, these have occurred in name only. Much like the Central African state, these initiatives have been a kind of public theatre that provides rents, yet without ever delving into the kinds of substantive political or institutional reforms that would be necessary to definitively put violent politics in the past (Lombard 2011 and Picco, Chapter 10). While it is common (and often warranted) to castigate Central African public officials for their lack of political will or for their obstructionism, multilateral actors also bear some of the burden of responsibility. Two examples will illustrate some of the shortcomings of the peacebuilding toolkit in CAR – one that targets the level of elites and another a more popular level.

The first is political dialogue. The Central African Republic has had three major political dialogues since 1998. This long history of mediation initiatives in the country is matched in length by an equally long history of failure in implementing their recommendations (see, for example, Lombard 2012b). While plans for a new national dialogue, the 'Bangui Forum,' are under way in 2015, nearly all of the recommendations from the Inclusive Political Dialogue (PDI) of December 2008, an earlier initiative supported and funded by BONUCA (the UN Peacebuilding Support Office in CAR), and other international partners, remain valid, yet were never implemented.[8] The Bangui Forum is also regrettably though aptly named, as it once again emphasizes elite bargaining among Bangui-based elites.[9] That earlier dialogue brought together six elite (and largely Bangui-based) constituencies: the presidential majority in the national assembly, rebel movements, opposition parties, non-aligned parties, the civil service, and civil society. Yet, soon after the process concluded, electoral politics took over and reforms were postponed. The election only further polarized Central African society, as President Bozizé's immediate family ended up with 11 of the 105 seats in the national assembly (his extended family and other close associates brought the tally up into the 20s). To most international and regional actors, Bozizé seemed like the least bad option at the time, and everyone involved was eager to move on to other matters. Thus, the notion of truly inclusive governance was all but forgotten.

Political dialogue shows the failures of peacebuilding at an elite level, and specifically, the ease with which elites agree on the platitudes of good governance and the difficulty of making those platitudes a reality. Disarmament, demobilization, and reintegration (DDR) programmes, of which CAR has seen several, show how the peacebuilding toolkit has repeatedly failed CAR at a more popular level.

UN planners conceived of DDR as a way to help former combatants rejoin their communities as productive, unarmed workers.[10] But DDR proceeds from the faulty assumption that in order to bring about security, the post-peace agreement state has only to *regain* its monopoly on violence. This assumption is flawed because in most places where DDR is proposed, the state generally never held such a monopoly in the first place. This is the case in much of CAR.[11] Nor will the state have any such monopoly in the foreseeable future. The self-defence-groups-cum-rebels in CAR are sources of predation, but they are also many communities' best hope of protection.

However, on the ground, DDR has taken on a different meaning, partially divorced from the content implied by the terms that make up its acronym: namely, the promise of patrimonial largesse as a way of tiding over dispossessed youth. In theory, a pay-off to members of armed groups might be a useful way to placate them. In practice, the long run-up to DDR was accompanied by a spike in recruitment, conferred a special status without an expiration date to one segment of the population, and only fueled armed group members' unrealistic expectations. When these were not met, the cycle of grievance continued. Moreover, in the process, valuable space, energy, and resources for a more realistic and just organization of security provision and economic opportunities – the necessary conditions for armed groups to disband – were all commandeered by the DDR undertaking, which in its two major CAR iterations to date (the Programme de Réinsertion et appui aux communautés, PRAC, from 2004–2007; and the Steering Committee-led efforts from 2009–2011) was spectacularly unsuccessful.

Despite the patent unsuitability of DDR for the CAR context, the response has primarily been to say that with proper technical procedures, it will work. Thus, the failures of the PRAC were attributed in part to the corruption of the National DDR Commission that ran it with funding from international donors. The subsequent effort (a 'second generation' approach to DDR) was instead led by a Steering Committee composed of members of the government, rebel groups, and the international community. This committee was to take the key political decisions that would move the process forward. Instead, they met in Bangui and stalled. The Steering Committee chair, the UN Special Representative of the Secretary-General (UNSRSG) in CAR presided, effectively mute, over the stalling. Six-hour Steering Committee meetings (all of which started at least an hour late) would result in a slight tweaking of minutae, such as a document's wording ('youth' or 'young people'?), and silence on sensitive political issues. Key steering committee members would frequently cancel at the last minute, forcing the re-scheduling of the meeting, usually not until some date several weeks hence given the limited availability of all involved. The Steering Committee had been envisioned as part of a division of labor: it would make the political decisions necessary to move the process forward, while UNDP would prepare and carry out the technical side of things. With the Steering Committee's stalling, the resources spent on technical preparations were for naught.

The military observers sent by the Communauté Economique de l'Afrique Centrale (CEAC) could have completed their mandate within six months of deployment, but they, too, stood waiting for more than a year while the Steering Committee avoided making the political decisions that would allow the technicians to do their jobs. By early 2011, more than fifty Steering Committee meetings into the process and yet with all the key political issues remaining to be resolved, the United Nations Development Programme's (UNDP) DDR funding (a total of US $27 million, from several sources) had more or less run out before any activities on behalf of ex-combatants had taken place.[12] In short, not only was DDR as conceived ill-suited to the CAR context, there were no mechanisms for accountability as the process became a farce.

Meanwhile, on their DDR-funded junkets to the hinterland locations of the armed group members, the Bangui-based leaders of these armed groups made promises about the pay-out that awaited fighters through DDR, and the ranks of the groups ballooned – all after the signing of peace agreements. At the time of active hostilities with the government, estimates placed the size of the APRD at about 1,000 and the UFDR at some 600. The numbers rose during the Libreville peace conference (the UFDR, for instance, then listed its ranks at 1,240 fighters), and again during the process of developing the lists of DDR participants. The 'Bozizé model' looms large in armed group members' minds: like the fighters who helped Bozizé seize power, they were encouraged to join armed groups with the promise of material rewards. Fighters would discuss amongst themselves how much cash they will receive – 800,000 CFA? One million? Two million?

By the time initial lists were prepared for DDR, the APRD contained some 6,000 fighters. Field commanders kept recruiting, calling on people who had lost a relative to APRD fighting to join to claim the rewards of the fallen. Promises about DDR fostered expectations on the part of the people who joined up, but these expectations have led nowhere. Central African leaders used the DDR process to actively prevent the objectives that theoretically should have been at the heart of DDR, namely greater transparency of governance and opportunities for marginalized youth.

This lamentable experience was the second major internationally-funded DDR programme in CAR in seven years. The earlier programme, the PRAC, was if anything less successful (Clemont et al., 2007). And yet DDR remains a key element of post-conflict 'common sense.' While certain international actors wish to move away from DDR (the World Bank, for instance, has tried to shift toward programmes for youth in vulnerable regions, rather than use armed group membership as a criterion for participation), it has become an expectation on the part of many Central Africans, and vague or not-so-vague promises about DDR frequently enter into peace negotiations, including the Nairobi negotiations of early 2015. Finding ways to avoid incentivizing the rebellion mentality – on both an elite and a popular level – might not be easy, but is absolutely critical. The extent of the violence and suffering from 2012 to 2015 seems at least to have encouraged a new interest in reflection and making a new way forward. The challenge will be to structure it in productive ways; toward that end, DDR as we know it is a step in the wrong direction.

A humanitarian accordion

At the same time as the relentless focus on a sequential peacebuilding toolkit has made it difficult to appreciate the perpetual quasi-crisis in CAR, it has also taken up agenda space that could have been used to profit from periods of relative stability by prioritizing development goals like modest, sustainable growth for the education and health sectors. Instead, an emergency/humanitarian mode of aid (distributions, taking over for stressed state services, etc.) has predominated. Consider the case of MSF's programmes in CAR. Most began as emergency projects in support of the country's health structures, justified as a result of the acute level of conflict at the mode of deployment/ programme conception. They have transmogrified into a progressive replacement of the Ministry of Health in the areas where they work. For instance, in the northern town of Batangafo, MSF has almost completely substituted for the state not only in life-saving activities but also in the long-term and routine programmes for which the Ministry of Health receives funding from entities like UNICEF and the Global Fund to Fight AIDS, Tuberculosis, and Malaria. If MSF were to depart, the number of health workers in the sub-prefecture would drop to ten from 171, and there would be not a single physician.

Humanitarian initiatives are supposed to be temporary measures, a kind of Band-aid, that allow the wound underneath to heal. But in this case, the Band-aid covers a wound that rather than heal, only suppurates. Without going so far as to say that the Band-aid in this analogy is causing the wound not to heal, it seems apposite to suggest that a different treatment is needed. The tendency has been for an uptick in humanitarian aid around moments of 'crisis,' funding levels that decline once the atrocities are less obvious, not to be replaced by development aid, until the cycle begins again. This is precisely the bridge to development for post-conflict states that the United Nations Peacebuilding Commission (PBC) was established in 2005 to fill within the UN peacebuilding architecture. In 2014, the humanitarian budget for CAR was nearly US $400 million, three to four times the budget allocated for development.

This is another example of the 'humanitarian accordion' (see Picco, Chapter 10), where international actors rush in to replace a weak social service sector rather than build capacity, and then slowly retreat until the next crisis. This leaves the country weaker than it had been prior to the intervention and requires an even larger humanitarian presence the next time around. The Bekou Fund, launched in July 2014 by the European Union, was an attempt to bridge the humanitarian-to-development process, but its lofty plans have yet to become a reality.

The Gordian knots of peacebuilding and politics in CAR

It would be unfair to blame international actors for this state of affairs, however. Rather, they are locked in an uncomfortable embrace with CAR's leaders: both depend on each other's participation in ways that make it difficult to enforce any genuine progress in terms of political accountability. So while there have been some useful projects focusing on employment and economic reconstruction, the key, underlying systemic questions such as the history of concessionary politics, have never been tackled. This is because they require, at least partially, difficult processes of political contestation that are a Pandora's Box no one wants to open. Ironically, the time frame of the most ambitious and necessary projects launched in the country aimed at structural reform have often conflicted with the political priorities set up by the same donors (for instance, security sector reform, which conflicted with promised amnesty/DDR provisions), who, in the process, end up sabotaging the very programmes they themselves have set up.

One of the key dilemmas in terms of international engagement with CAR leaders is what to do when these leaders contradict the spirit of inclusive, anti-corruption policies that they are supposed to be enacting. So far the international response has tended to be to privately rant or scoff at the ineptitude of the government, and publicly mostly look the other way, with the assumption being that whoever is in power is the least bad option, or put there by France and the region. This reasoning seems to be undergirded by the hope that it will be possible to pull back and leave Central Africans to endure their (sorry) fate. Thus, though there have been a number of incidences of apparent corruption scandals under President Catherine Samba-Panza (for instance, the Angola affair in early 2014),[13] the French-led response has been the equivalent of a shrug: elites are all corrupt anyway, so what difference would it make if we tried to switch one for another? The CAR state is currently run through two separate budgets. One is funded entirely by foreign aid and managed by international advisers and experts with the explicit goal of making sure no foreign money is embezzled or otherwise improperly used. The other consists of money made by the government, mostly from sale of public companies or resources to private actors (who then rehabilitate the service/facility and rent back to the government at a higher price); other kinds of concessions; or from bilateral aid (Angola has been an eager donor). This budget is managed by the presidency with no international (or domestic) oversight. (At the strong suggestion of the French, the IMF does not delve into this obvious problem.) Central Africans, when they learn of particularly egregious misuses of funds, are incensed. But what leverage do they have when even international financial institutions look the other way?

In short, there are a variety of vicious cycles, or Gordian knots, involved in the relationship between CAR elites and international actors. The latter want quick solutions and to be able to pull out quickly; the former want to maintain power and privilege in a context of 'paradoxical scarcity' (Smith, Chapter 1). So while international actors might be able to retreat in the short term, they end up having to return, and in greater numbers, once the problems return worse than before. Ideally, then, the debate should not be about whether the international system has patience for a long engagement in CAR. Unless there is a total international exit (and regardless of the merits of such an approach, this seems an unlikely outcome given the human suffering that would result at least in the short term, and the international structures meant to respond to it), the engagement will be long, one way or another. The question should rather be how to make that long engagement a sustained, coherent one, such that it would be possible to avoid the cycle of mistakes that has characterized the last twenty years of responses to CAR's conflicts.

Regional and 'local' complications

The Angolan government donations bring up another issue, namely the involvement of regional powers in CAR politics.[14] Some of these regional elites have private interests that run at cross purposes to those of international donor organizations or western diplomats. For instance, Angolan President José Eduardo dos Santos's daughter has pursued a friendship and business relationship with President Samba-Panza, presumably to get in on the new state-run diamond company (Diamonds' best friend, 2015). This is but the latest in a long history of interference by regional actors and French domination, whose goals and interests do not always translate a sustainable peace in CAR. There is a historical tendency for CAR's leaders to look to Paris, N'Djamena, or Brazzaville for protection and guidance rather than trying to build any kind of social contract with the Central African population. President Patassé's call for military support from Jean-Pierre Bemba and his MLC rebels from the Democratic Republic of the Congo (DRC) in 2002 and Bozizé's employment of Chadian mercenaries (many of whom eventually joined Seleka and overthrew him) are but two examples of how even security is a concession to be outsourced. On the political front, the continued reliance on an assortment of dishonest brokers, for example, President of Congo-Brazzaville Sassou Nguesso, who strive to extract diplomatic mileage out of their involvement in CAR rather than truly assist its leaders in a peacebuilding process is another challenge. As Chief International Mediator, Sassou Nguesso has oriented his efforts toward France to curry favour for a constitutional mandate extension for a third term.

The biggest losers in this litany of failures are the people of CAR. However, it would be wrong not to include them in the story of the country's decline. Too often, there is a fable that 'the people' are good, and the elites bad. Without judging, it is possible to notice that in the context of anomie and uncertainty that marks CAR today, it is immensely difficult for Central Africans to act in favour of the common good beyond certain circumscribed social groupings. Moreover, widespread practices of popular punishment (Lombard and Batianga-Kinzi, 2015), and the rapidity of the descent into mass violence should at the very least necessitate some deep reflection on the part of Central Africans about the place they accord physical violence in the repertoire of effective political action. Regime change – or elections – do little to nurture effective civic and commercial engagement of the many. Trust is not so much something that will need to be 'rebuilt' as it is something in need of building, afresh, for the first time.

The future of peacebuilding in CAR

Combined, MINUSCA and the 800,000 Euro/day French Sangaris mission in CAR represent the largest interventions in the country's history.[15] And yet at the same time as there has been this unprecedented involvement, there remains an eagerness to pass through elections so that these international actors can pull out. It is perhaps useful to remind, yet again, that there are no quick fixes for a defective system, and that while short-term solutions may have blunted outbreaks of violence, they have done nothing to address structural problems. Quite the opposite, as Smith (Chapter 5) reminds us: 'CAR's ruling elite has transacted the country's sovereignty wholesale and no longer piecemeal, and is now asking to be generously funded to take it back. It's been an all-out triumph of concessionary politics. A country which has descended into chaos by dint of outsourcing its state attributes in the first place is digging itself deeper into a hole with the altruistic help of the outside world.'

As much as anything, then, the current crisis is a failure of imagination: among international actors, among CAR political elites, among Central Africans more broadly. Lackluster attempts to create an ideal-type state have yielded only a state that does even less for its people then before. What other possibilities might there be for developing political compacts between rulers and ruled, whether those rulers are from the national or international ruling elites? There has been very little energy placed on processes of imagination like these. Terms like 'reconciliation' get used ad nauseum, yet without anyone ever taking the time to define in specifics what reconciliation might consist of. It gets left to religious authorities, who, though good at drawing international support and fronting a face of a united CAR, have little control over the kinds of mistrust and spiritual insecurity that prevent Central Africans from working together to build wealth (see Marchal Chapter 2).[16] Should the reconciliation be between Seleka and anti-Balaka? Between Christians and Muslims? Between Bangui and the peripheral areas? Between the elites and the population? And what about the difficult question of citizenship, so central as elections approach: with many voter rolls destroyed in the violence of 2013–14, how will citizenship be determined? Similar problems have lurked within the other main donor priority, namely the restoration of 'social cohesion.' Once taken as the stock in trade of anthropology, decades ago anthropologists discarded the concept of social cohesion because it actively obscures political power dynamics. In this donor-funded iteration, what would social cohesion look like? Who does it involve? These kinds of questions have mostly been either reduced to their material components – a refurbished market area, a new school – or relegated to the beaux mots of religious leaders rather than considered on an existential or historical-political level. Who, at the end of the day, belongs in CAR? Who counts? These kinds of discussions have been sorely lacking.

There is a long history of trying to make sense of CAR's problems through narratives developed elsewhere, for other contexts – rebellion, genocide, humanitarian crisis, ungoverned spaces, 'Darfur spillover'… These externally-driven models and narratives have hindered the development of workable solutions to CAR's myriad problems. This book is intended as one small step taken with the hope of facilitating greater attention to the ways that CAR's particular history and political economy leave this place and its people with any number of challenges that, though certain among them might be shared with other contexts, have become a uniquely troubling constellation in the case of CAR.

Notes

1 For a discussion of the failures of the political negotiations between Seleka's arrival on the scene in December 2012 and the coup in March 2013, see Tumutegyereize, K. and N. Tillon (2013) 'Central African Republic: Peace Talks Without the Talks.' *African Arguments*. March 15.
2 For a discussion of the war in CAR and the role of the media, see Ceriana Mayneri, A. (2014). 'La Centrafrique, de la rébellion Séléka aux groupes anti-balaka (2012–2014): Usages de la violence, schème persécutif et traitement médiatique du conflit.' *Politique Africaine*, Vol. 2, pp. 179–193.
3 See for instance the discussion of missteps on recognizing the security challenges described in Marchal, R. (2014) 'CAR: As Violence Persists, International Intervention Falls Short.' IPI Global Observatory, 5 February.
4 The Security Council authorized French forces to use 'all necessary means' to provide operational support to MINUSCA. United Nations Security Council (2014) Resolution 2149, 10 April, paragraph 47.
5 Before the EUFOR withdrawal on 15 March 2015, there were: 9,421 MINUSCA, 2,000 Sangaris and 750 EUFOR.
6 The EU is critical of some French choices but eventually foots the bill. There is no political interest strong enough in Brussels to start a critical conversation with Paris on CAR.
7 MSF, for example, has repeatedly reported on the alarming conditions of the health system, even during periods of non-crisis. For example see: Médecins Sans Frontières – MSF (2011) Central African Republic: A State of Silent Crisis, MSF, Amsterdam, November; and Médecins Sans Frontières – MSF (2013) Central African Republic: Abandoned to its Fate? MSF, Amsterdam, 9 July.

8 For more information on the 2008 process, please see: United Nations Peacebuilding Commission (2008) 'Background Paper on Inclusive Political Dialogue' October 8; or International Crisis Group (2010) Central African Republic: Keeping the Dialogue Alive, Africa Briefing No. 69, Nairobi/Brussels.
9 Though there were initially some plans to make grassroots consultations a key part of the dialogue process, they were rushed in the interests of pushing the process forward as quickly as possible. A report was written, but a framework for real grassroots participation was not included.
10 DDR became part of the post-Cold War 'post-conflict reconstruction orthodoxy'; for a critical, yet ultimately supportive, analysis of DDR, see Schulhofer-Wohl, J. and N. Sambanis (2010) 'Disarmament, Demobilization, and Reintegration Programs: An Assessment,' *The Folke Bernadotte Academy*, Stockholm. And Muggah, R. (2005) 'No Magic Bullet: A Critical Perspective on Disarmament, Demobilization and Reintegration in Post-Conflict Contexts', *The Round Table*, Vol. 94, No. 379, pp. 239–252.
11 The Central African Armed Forces count only about 1,500 decently-trained soldiers among their ranks. International state-builders who look to these forces – more often predatory than protective – to secure the country's territory and people tend to downplay or ignore how long term, not to say unlikely, such an outcome is.
12 Some of these funds had been used for the creation of state-of-the-art databases and other monitoring tools intended to promote transparency and accountability. In the end, the Steering Committee decided not to use them, preferring their own personalized methods.
13 The Angolan government gave US $10 million to the CAR government in April 2014. Some of this was given in cash in Luanda and exchanged to CFA in Cameroon at an extortionate rate (some US $810,000 was lost in the transaction); another instalment, believed to be more than US $5 million, reached Bangui and then disappeared. See 'Allies Lose Faith.' (2014). *Africa Confidential.* Vol. 55, No. 17, 29 August.
14 Although the perception that CAR is a puppet to the wills of foreigners is common both within and outside CAR, this idea prevents a necessary 'crucial interrogation on the nature of its elites

and the multiple connections built over time (often through the former colonial power) with their regional counterparts' (Marchal, Chapter 9).

15 MINUSCA's yearly budget of US $628,724,000 vastly exceeds any of the previous peacekeeping or political missions deployed; See the current and early 5th committee reports for the specific comparison; United Nations General Assembly (2014) 'Financing of the United Nations Multidimensional Integrated Stabilization Mission in the Central African Republic', Report of the 5th Committee, A/69/684, 24 December.

16 As Marchal writes, 'No regional narrative has been defined to provide a sense of living together, despite differing on religion. It is so because this issue relies not specifically on religious differences as such but on positions of power and wealth accumulation, on the control of the invisible world, which is a crucial issue in all societies of the region and on rivalries between regional players' (Chapter 8).

Bibliography

'Allies Lose Faith.' (2014). *Africa Confidential.* Vol. 55, No. 17, 29 August.

'Centrafrique : "Il y a plus de morts par défaut de soins que par violence selon MSF"' (2014) *Le Monde Afrique,* 26 February.

Clémont, C. *et al.* (2007) 'Rapport Final – RCA: Le DDR sans GPS', Mission indépendente d'évaluation du Programme de Réinsertion des ex-combattants et Appui aux Communautés, *Programme Multi-Pays de Démobilisation et Réintegration,* December.

Debos, M. (2014) '"Hate" and "Security Vacuum": How Not to Ask the Right Questions about a Confusing Crisis' *Cultural Anthropology – Fieldsights,* 11 June.

'Diamonds' best friend' (2015) *Africa Confidential,* Vol. 56, No. 6, 20 March.

Inter-Agency Standing Committee (2014), 'Operational peer review: Response to the crisis in the Central African Republic', 23 March. IASC, Geneva.

Lombard, L. (2012a). 'Rébellion et les limites de la consolidation de la paix en Centrafrique.' Politique Africaine.

Lombard, L. (2012b). Inclusive Political Dialogue: Central African Republic. In Stan, Lavinia, and Nadya Nadelsky, eds. *The Encyclopedia of Transitional Justice*. Cambridge University Press, Cambridge.

Lombard, L. (2011). 'Election Briefing: Central African Republic.' The Monkey Cage. Joshua Tucker, moderator.

UN OCHA (2014), 'CAR: Operational presence' *United Nations Office for the Coordination of Humanitarian Affairs*, 6 June, Bangui.

About the contributors

Ledio Cakaj is an independent researcher focusing on armed groups, demobilization and reintegration of former combatants, and security sector reform. He has worked for more than a decade in the Balkans and East and Central Africa. Cakaj spent seven years working almost exclusively on the Lord's Resistance Army for organizations including the World Bank, the Enough Project, Small Arms Survey and Resolve. He has carried out extensive field research in Uganda, the Democratic Republic of Congo, South Sudan and Central African Republic. Cakaj has written a series of reports and articles on the LRA for publications such as the Washington Post, Jane's Intelligence Review, Africa Report and The Journal of East African Studies.

Ned Dalby is East and Central Africa Projects Manager at Conciliation Resources, a peacebuilding organisation, where he works with civil society groups to prevent violence through analysis, advocacy and community-based programmes. Previously as an Analyst at International Crisis Group, a conflict resolution think-tank, he conducted field research in West and Central Africa, including the Central African Republic. Seeking to understand the drivers of conflict there, he investigated the political, economic, social and cultural life of the country. Ned holds master's degrees from the School of Oriental and African Studies in London and Warwick University and a bachelor's in Classics from the University of Oxford.

Faouzi Kilembe Faouzi Kilembe is a national of the Central African Republic and an expert on local development and civil society. Since March 2012, he has worked as a Technical Assistant for the Programme Pôles de Développement in CAR, funded by the European Union.

Roland Marchal is a senior research fellow at CNRS, based at the CERI/Sciences Po Paris. He has published extensively on conflicts in the Central African Republic, Greater Horn of Africa (From Chad to Somalia) and the policy of international actors on the continent including France. Besides his personal research, he has been the Editor of the French academic Quarterly *Politique Africaine* from 2002 to 2006 and a consultant for European States, the European Union, the United Nations and the World Bank.

Nathaniel Olin is a doctoral student in political science at the University of Wisconsin-Madison, studying civil conflict and insurgency in francophone Africa. Before coming to Madison, Nathaniel worked as the Africa Program Associate at the Conflict Prevention and Peace Forum, a program of the Social Science Research Council, where he organized high-level consultations and commissioned research providing senior UN policymakers with access to external analysis on conflict or conflict-risk situations throughout the African continent. He also worked briefly in the UN advocacy office of the International Crisis Group. Nathaniel received his B.A. in International Relations in 2009 from Stanford University, and was born and raised in Philadelphia.

Enrica Picco is a lawyer, specialized in International Law with post-graduate education in Peace and Democracy Building and

Peacekeeping Management. She has been involved in humanitarian work with Médecins Sans Frontières since 2006, with experience in DRC, Sudan, Haiti and CAR among others, in positions progressively evolving from Field Coordinator to Humanitarian Affairs Officer. Since January 2013, she is based in Barcelona as Humanitarian Affairs Advisor for MSF, with the Central African Republic as her main research focus.

Stephen W. Smith is a Professor of the Practice at Duke University where he teaches African Studies since 2007. Until 2013, he also lectured as an adjunct at Johns Hopkins School of Advanced International Studies (SAIS) in Washington, DC. He holds a PhD in semiotics from Berlin's Free University and graduated in anthropology at the Sorbonne in Paris. The deputy editor of the foreign desk at Le Monde for five years and, previously, the Africa editor at Libération for twelve years, he had worked as a roving correspondent in West and Central Africa for Reuters and Radio France International (RFI). He is the (co-) author of sixteen books, of country reports (Nigeria, CAR) for the International Crisis Group, and a consultant for the UN and other international bodies. He contributes to the London Review of Books and also works for the film industry as a historical consultant and script writer.

Laurence D. Wohlers was the US Ambassador to the Central African Republic from 2010 until the embassy was evacuated in December, 2012. He then led the US government response to the crisis in CAR until his retirement in October, 2013. In April, 2014, he returned to CAR temporarily as the Deputy SRSG for MINUSCA to help start up that new peacekeeping operation. During a 36 year career in the State Department, Ambassador Wohlers served numerous assignments in Africa, Japan and Europe. Significant assignments abroad included Minister Counselor for Political Affairs at the US Mission to the European Union and Minister Counselor for Public Affairs at the US Embassy in Moscow. In Washington, he was Executive Assistant to the

Under Secretary of State for Public Affairs and Public Diplomacy and Senior Advisor for International Programs at the Smithsonian Institution. Ambassador Wohlers served previously in the Central African Republic from 1985 to 1987 as the Director of the Centre Martin Luther King. He received an M.S. from the National War College and a B.A from Washington University in St. Louis.

Index

Abidjan, 67
ACCB, 91
Achellam, Caesar, 286
ACOBECA, 91
Action Contre La Faim, 235
African nations, pre-colonial, 249
African Union, *see* AU
AFVP, 222
Ahmed, Bashir, 185
aid: 220–1, 225, 230, 232, 238, 285; agencies remote areas withdrawal, 234; CAR 'category mismatch', 23; emergency/humanitarian mode, 332
Al-Bahir, Omar, 183
Al-Sanusi, Muhammad, 19
Amani Africa, EU-AU training initiative, 200
Anderson, Allan, 252
Angola, CAR involvement, 187; 2014 'Affair', 334–5
antelopes, radio collars, 155
Anti-Balaka, 7–8, 45, 59, 87, 190, 234, 236; anti-Muslim, 189; attacks of, 235; French support, 9;

militias, 213; non-elite, 315; Pk5 attacks, 97
anti-poaching, militias, 152, 156–7
APFC, 152
APRD (Army for the Restoration of the Republic and Democracy) 38–9, 226, 330
Areva, French parastatal, 108–10
arms traffickers, Congolese, 250
Ashforth, Adam, 12, 55
Association Internationale du Congo, 249
ASSOMESCA, 223
AU (African Union), 8–9, 187, 189, 267, 279, 283, 285; -CEEAC competition, 212; Commissioner for Peace and Security, 280; International Support Mission, 323; Mali failures, 324; Mission in Somalia, 195; -RCI, 281–2
autochthony, 168–9
'autonomous spaces/zones', 143, 248
Awakening Churches, hostility to Islam, 63; individuation promoting, 62

Bangui, 3, 22, 225; Accords, 199, 210; aesthetic improvements, 5; Congolese in, 258; elites, *see* elites; first Muslim families, 80; 'Forum', 32; foundation of, 77, 248; market neighbourhood, *see* Pk5; postcolonial, 18; 2001 violence, 34; 2003 plundering, 37; University of, 4
Bayart, Jean-François, 14
Bemba, Jean-Pierre, 36, 178, 224, 256, 258–60, 309, 335
Bierschenk, Thomas, 143
BINUCA, 195, 209, 213, 231, 323; power lack, 210
Birao, 206
Biya, Paul, 180, 186
Boganda, Barthélemy, 24, 81, 302, 319; death of, 170, 305
Bokassa, Jean-Bédel, President/Emperor, 4, 31, 35, 58, 67–9, 81, 123, 132, 172–3, 178, 252, 298, 302, 308, 311; coup of, 25; Empire, 221; era, 151; French dumping of, 28, 305; French indulgence of, 26; Islam conversion, 27; nostalgia for, 306; overthrow of, 254
Boko Haram, 186, 189; Cameroon spillover, 167
Bonezoui, Alain Fred Pépin, 112
Bongo, Omar, 36, 180, 184; Freemasonry of, 171
BONUCA, 195, 206, 207, 208, 226, 327; criticism of, 231; effectiveness lack, 203–4; human rights unit, 227
Bouar, French military base, 4, 29, 34
Bozizé, François, 1, 5, 8, 29, 35–7, 58, 69, 88, 92, 96, 105–7, 109, 113, 133–6, 158, 176, 180, 184–5, 204–5, 207–8, 210, 214, 216, 224, 226, 230, 233, 260–1, 275, 278, 280, 297, 299–300, 302, 304, 307, 310, 312–13, 320–1, 325; -CEMAC relations, 183; Chadian mercenaries, 181; 335; corruption, 303; diamonds control, 124, 132; evangelical Christian support, 322; 'family politics', 38; fleeing of, 43; French support, 259; *la Bozizé*, decade, 6; 'least bad option', 6, 328; 'model', 330; privatized national budget, 116; overthrow of, 42, 110, 196; South African support, 41, 186, 211; successful coup of, 89, 98; -Tiangaye personal history, 298; 'tribalism from the bottom', 311
Brazzaville, 22, 149, 170; Agreement 2014, 187
Burundi, 215
Bush, George W., 283

Cakaj, Ledio, 247
Cameroon, 186, 207
Cappucini Fathers, 223
Carayannis, Tatiana, 178
cash crops, price/economy collapse, 56, 58
Catholic Church, 59, 171, 222
CEEAC (Economic Community of Central African States), 113, 207, 211, 213, 330; AU competition, 212; leaders, 298
Celestial Church of Christ, 303
CEMAC (Central African Economic and Monetary Union), 36–7, 183, 184, 186, 205, 246
CEMIDO, 110
CEMIFI, 110
CEN-SAD, 205
Central African Armed Forces, 5, 9
Central African Empire, creation of, 27

Central African Republic (CAR), 172; aid, 23, 220–1, 225, 230, 232, 234, 238, 285; alluvial diamonds, 126, 135; Angolan involvement, 187; budgets, 68, 115, 234; cash-crop production, 26; Chadian role, 89, 113, 181–2, 211, 224, 255; Christian coded nationalism, 147; commercial links, 123; Congo border, 251; Congolese refugees, 224; customs service, 102, 110; de-population, 3; December 2012 war, 2; donor funds wasted, 14; DRC wars relation, 263; eastern, 267, 272–3; elites, *see below*; Emergency Response Funds mechanism, 229; endemic state violence, 57; external misconceptions, 325; foreign aid dependence, 221; forest management, 106 'forest production zone', 104; French centralized model, 315; French military bases, 34, 174–5; hybrid authority, 247–8; IDP scale, 323; Independence of, 4, 24, 252, 297; inheritance issue, 54; international interventions, 11, 173, 262, 335; land borders, 130; Libyan role, 173, 205, 234, 256, 310; life expectancy, 114, 231; long-term investment lack, 66; military concessions, 113; natural resource wealth, 312; neighbouring states, services delivery, 166; 1993 election, 1, 31, 255, 308, 314; hunting, see below; North East, *see below*; personalized troubles, 296; pre-colonial, 18; Presidential extraordinary power, 303; refugees influx, 223; regional politics impact, 167, 215, 228, 244–5; regional states system, 167; rentier state, 12, 105; self-defence groups, 7; social relations mistrust, 131; South African role, 6, 113, 258; south eastern, 283; state expertise lack, 2, 65; state diamond dependence, 129; state privatization, 12; trafficking hub, 88; trans-border networks, 249; 'true' populations, 8; Ugandan military in, *see below*, UPDF; untrained Presidents, 302

Centre for Humanitarian Dialogue, 208

centre-periphery relations, 17–18

Chad, 2, 4–6, 23, 35, 40, 66, 89, 215, 313; CAR trading class, 170; demobilizations, 5; Libya role, 17; mercenaries from, 89, 113, 224; Seleka support, 211; soldiers brutal reputation, 256; Southern, 188; 2006 rebellion, 182

China National Petroleum Corporation, 106

Chirac, Jacques, 33, 180, 183

Christians, -Muslim tensions/ violence, 235, 300; *see also,* Evangelical

Cissé, Lamine, 204

citizenship, CAR question of, 337

civil servants, 296; ethos loss, 304; parasitic caste, 25; revenue access, 70

Close, Bill, 253

Côte d'Ivoire, 63

COAC, 96

COCORA, 96

Cold War: Bokassa Western support, 253; end of consequences, 175

Colombe mines, 132
colonialism, 2, 169; French low-cost, 12, 65; microbial shock, 19; poll tax, 170; traditional institutions destruction, 300
commerce, government tax weakening, 301
Community of Sahel and Saharan States, 35
Compagnie des Sultanats du Haut-Oubangui, 21
concessionary companies, 68; colonial subcontracted, 103; French Equatorial Africa, 64; militias, 59; model of, 65
'concessionary politics', 102, 110–11, 115, 124, 132, 336; cycles of, 104
conflict dynamics, transnational, 2
Congo Free State, 20–2
Congo-Brazzaville, 189; crises cycles, 178
Congo-Ocean railroad, construction of, 79, 170
conservation, wildlife: armed, 151–3, 157, 160; EU financed, 152; hunting regulation, 143–4; surveillance, 155
Consolidated Appeal Processes, 231
Convention of Patriots for Justice and Peace (CPJP), 137–8, 182, 184
COOPI, 222
cotton, price collapse impact, 179
Counter Reform movement, anti-sorcery movement, 60
counterfeit medications, trade in, 84
coupeurs de route, 57, 156, 203, 272
Customs service, private-public venture, 111–12

Dabaab refugee camp, Kenya, 114
Dacko, David, 24, 28, 68, 173, 252, 254, 263, 297, 302, 304, 306; 'France's solution', 25, 29, 305
Dalby, Ned, 12
Damane, Zakaria, 39, 41, 136–7, 158
Dar al-Kuti, Islamic frontier state, 19
Darfur, 84, 182, 228; caravans from, 18; conflict effects, 180–1; crises of, 167; southern, 40, 268; 'spillover, 13; Sultanate, 169
DDR (Disarmament, Demobilization and Reintegration) programmes, 148, 321; issue of, 311; mistaken assumptions of, 328–31; PRAC failures, 329, 331; Steering Committee corruption, 329–30
De Gaulle, Charles, 26
De Sardan, Olivier, 143
Déby Itno, Idriss, 5–6, 8, 36–7, 41–2, 89, 107, 173, 175–6, 180, 184–8, 258, 310, 313; CAR kingmaker perception, 183; French support, 181
Démafouth, Jean-Jacques, 35, 182, 299
Debos, Marielle, 323
desertification, 151
diamonds: artisinal mining, 12, 126, 131; CAR zones, 124; global price fall impact, 129; illegal trading, 130–1, 249; industrial mining taxes, 133; miners spiritual beliefs, 128; north east CAR rebels link, 135–7; production chain hierarchy, 127–8; smuggling, 123, 138
Dieng, Adama, 44

Djimwei, Laurent, 39
Djotodia, Michel, 7–8, 39, 41, 43, 45, 88, 97, 116, 134, 142, 158, 233, 237, 278–9, 282, 304, 315, 320
Dolisie, Albert, 77
Dos Santos, José Eduardo, 335
Doubane, Charles, 299
DRC (Democratic Republic of Congo), 2, 61, 167, 207, 215, 245; international intervention, 194; 'rural radicalism', 251;1990s wars, 178, 245; 2006 election, 259; Ugandan military presence, 276; 'conflict minerals, 249
Dubai, CAR imports from, 250
Duffield, Mark, 248

Ebola, first case of, 253
ECHO, 231, 236
ECOFAC, 152
Ed Din Adam, Nur, 186
education: decline, 297; Gross Enrolment Ratio, 233; Muslims low level, 93
Elf, 106
elite(s) CAR, 13, 31, 71, 117, 313; Bangui-based, 133, 328; concessionary politics, 103; Francophile, 171; individual ethics, 315; inevitable failure rejection, 296; nomenclature, 115; personal relationships, 291; political, 56; political sidelined, 6; reinventions, 299; regional connections, 168; responsibility denial, 58; role of, 295
entrepreneurs: military, 142; political, 134, 138; political-military, 7, 151
Equateur province, DRC, 251, 255–7; Kabila targeted, 260

Equatorial Customs Union, 246
Equatorial Guinea, 69
escapism, 72
Essongo, Noel Léonard, 188
EU (European Union), 44, 175, 207, 214, 228; Bekou Fund, 333; conservation archives, 154; 'development poles', 208; EUFOR, 41, 209, 213, 323; state fetishisation, 152
evangelical churches: anti-Islam, 63, 86; Awakening Churches, 62; Celestial Church of Christ, 303; fast expansion of, 252
Expanded Programme on Immunization, 222
Extractive Industry Transparency Initiative, 133
Extraversion, 14
Exxon Mobil, 106

FACA (Central African Armed Forces), 32, 35, 38, 40, 272, 276, 281; as tribal militia, 209; 2013 disintegration, 320; mutinies 1990s, 32, 198, 311, 313, 325
Fadlallah, Rabih, 19
'Fashoda incident', 20
FDPC, 39
FIDH, 258, 261
Floch-Prigent, Loïc Le, 106
Foccart, Jacques, 26
Fodio, Usman Dan, 80
FOMUC, 205–7; MICOPAX, 214; military capacity lack, 210
forced labour, colonial, 3, 23, 79
forced migration, 169
'foreigner': business people, 71; category of, 66; Chadians as, 67; invasion fear, 70
FORSDIR, Patassé Presidential Guard, 202

France, 1, 187, 324, 333; African gendarme role retreat, 30; -African summit 1990, 31; aid, 221, 226, 232; Barkhane Operation, 187; CAR elites dominated, 313; CAR interference, 195; centralized model, 296; colonial underinvestment, 145; engagement reduction, 207; -Great Britain colonial disputes, 20; Mobutu support, 255; Operation Barracuda, 28; Operation Boali, 37; Operation Sangaris, 44–5, 71, 212–13, 323, 336; postcolonial-African network, 26; RECAMP initiative, 200; underfunded interventions, 214
Freemasonry, 171, 180, 184; Central African Masonic Lodge, 298; regional forum, 171
French Equatorial Africa (AEF), 145–6, 170, 246; French Congo, 20, 23; population displacements, 79; -UN disparate agendas, 196
French Foreign Trade Bank, 27
French National Assembly, 24
French Somaliland, 19
French West Africa, 24
FROLINAT, 176
Fula movement, 80

Gabon, 19, 36, 171
Garang, John, 177
Gbanda ethnic group, 18
Gbaya, ethnic group, 18, 189, 307–8, 314
Geschiere, Peter, 62
Giscard d'Estaing, Valéry, 26–8
Global Fund to fight AIDS, TB and Malaria (GFATM), 232, 332; HIV programme CAR coordinator, 304
Goumba, Abel, 24, 31, 37–8, 305
governance, outsourced, 115
government documents sale, 93
Grynber, Jack J., 107
GTZ (German Cooperation Association), 222

Habré, Hissène, 172–4, 176
Handicap International, 222
Hardin, Rebecca, 103
head tax, colonial, 22
health: foreign aid, 221; services lack, 323
herders: Mbororo, 156; militarization of, 176
Hissene, Adoukaye, 137
HIV: CAR, 232; mining sites, 128
Hollande, Francois, 41, 185
Hollenwegger, W.J., 252
hostage camps, colonial, 23
Human Rights Watch, 227
'humanitarian accordion', 332
humanitarian aid, 194, 234, 285; agencies, 220; CAR non-priority, 225; system limits, 238
Humanitarian Development Partnership Team, 113, 229
hunting, 149–50; 'industrialized 'elephant, 151; regulation, 149; safari industry, 153
Hutu refugees, 223, 255
hybrid authority, 263

Ianarelli, Armand, 111–12
ICC (International Criminal Court), 14, 245, 247, 258–60, 263; selectivity of, 261–2
Idongo 'model village', 154
IMF (International Monetary Fund), 116, 309, 334
immigrant origins, 79

Inclusive Political Dialogue 2008, 327
informers, private-public customs, 112
insecurity, 54, 72; economic, 71; sources, 14; 'spiritual', 11–12, 55, 73
Insurrection, 1928, 23
Inter-African Mission to Monitor the Bangui Accord, 33
internally displaced people, 9, 225, 234–5,; January 2014, 236; LRA violence, 274; scale of, 39
international actors, quick-fix failures, 327, 334
International Monitoring Committee, 200
International Socialist Organisation, 185
IOF (International Organization of la Francophonie), 203
IRC (International Red Cross), 229
Islam: conversion to, 129; issue of, 168
ivory, 21, 65; hunting of, 150
Izamo, Jean, 25–6

'Janjaweed', 156–7
jealousy, social, 55
Jihadist groups, Sahel, 235
Juba Talks, 270, 272–3, 275, 283
Justin, Hassan, 39

Kabara, Hassan, 81
Kabila, Joseph, 36; 256, 260, 309; Chadian allies, 257; DRC putsch, 255
Karl, Terry L., 103
Kiir, President, 275
Kilembe, Faouzi, 12
Kimberly Process, 133–4
King Leopold II, 20, 249; public outcry, 22

Kitchener, Horatio, 20
Kivus, 252
Kolelas, Bernard, 180
Kolingba, André, 29–31, 35, 58, 66, 88, 171, 174, 178, 254, 298–300, 302, 309; ethnic favouritism, 307; Yakoma favouritism, 308
Kongo-wara, 'war of', 23
Kony, Joseph, 113, 267–75, 280, 284–5; Southern Darfur refuge, 282
Kougou, Adoum Yakoub, 176
Koumtamadji, Martin, aka Abdoulaye Miskine, 33
Kribi, Cameroon, 106
Kwa na Kwa party, 38, 148–9

Laboureur, Jean, 153
Laboureur, Matthieu, 153–4
Laddé, Baba, 182
Lakoué, Maradas, 39, 182
Lala, Idi, 173
Lamamra, Ramtane, 280
Lanzer, Toby, 228
Lauvergeon, Anne, 108
Layama, Imam Kobine, 97–8
leasing, French colonial, 3
Lebanese business community, 67–8
legal system, pay-offs, 72
Libreville Agreement 2013, 186, 211, 233, 322
Libya, 28, 179, 181; CAR involvement, 173, 205, 310; National Oil Company, 106; Patassé support, 204
Lissouba, Pascal, 180
logging: illicit, 278; industry, 104; tax on, 105
Logone Republic, idea of, 174
Lombard, Louisa, 247
Londres, Albert, 147

Lord's Resistance Army (LRA), 9, 57, 160, 177; AU against, 279, 281; decline, 269; Eastern CAR arrival, 267–8, 272, 275, 278; Haut Uélé massacres, 270; LRA Crisis Tracker, 270, 274; Obos seized, 273; Ugandan troops against, 280; USA counter efforts, 283–4, 286

M'poko, airport, 236
Machiavelli, 57
Madeira, Fancisco, 280–2
Mai-Mai auto-defence groups, 251
malaria, 232
Mali, French intervention, 44
Malloum, Félix, 172
Mamadou M'Baïki market, Pk5, 76, 82
Mamang-Kanga, Jean-Baptiste, 155
Mandja, ethnic group, 18
Mantion, Jean-Claude, 31; coup foiling, 29; dismissal of, 175; dominance of, 30
Marchal, Roland 8, 12, 15, 143, 245, 258
Massi, Charles, 138; killing of, 184
Mbaikoua, Alphonse, 29, 174
Mbaye, Parfait, 299
MCLN, 173
Médecins du Monde, 222
Médecins Sans Frontières (MSF), 114, 223, 231, 235, 323; advocacy role, 236; state replacement, 332; violence afflicted, 234
Mecca, pilgrims to, 79
Meckassoua, Karim, 299
Michel, Louis, 260
MICOPAX, 42, 188, 207, 211, 212
migrations, history of, 72
Military Committee for National Recovery, 29

militias, concessionary companies, 59
mining, immigrant attraction, 80
MINURCA, 34, 201, 209–10, 224; Chadian troops, 96; departure of, 226; drawdown of, 203; failure of, 202; political mandate lack, 214
MINUSCA, 1, 45, 213, 215, 323–4, 336
MISAB, 34, 195, 201, 214, 224; Chadian contingent, 90, 96; creation of, 196, 198; French logistical support, 200; French underwritten, 199; success perception, 201
MISCA, 44, 188–9, 212–13, 216, 283, 321, 323–4
Miskine communities, 39, 78, 260
Mitterand, François, 31, 60
MLC (Movement for the Liberation of Congo), 36, 178, 205, 224, 245, 256–61
MLPC, 27, 29, 300; grass roots support, 308; rent-seeking, 310
Mobutu, Joseph, 178, 252–4; demise of, 5; French support, 255
MONUC, 194, 259
Moreno-Ocampo, 260
Moussa, Abu, 281–2
Movement for the Social Evolution of Black Africa, 24
Muslims: business sector, 64, 98, 250; CAR fleeing, 236; -Christian relations, 81, 86, 90; community devastation, 235; dehumanized, 43; diamond buying offices, 129; flight of, 45; foreigner categorised, 66, 147, 322; France anti-accusations, 213; identity, 60; mass exodus, 321; massacre of, 99; new Wahhabi influence, 323; Ngawi market culture, 84;

persecution of, 8; Pk5 market, 78, 80; place of, 13; Rwandan and Burundian support, 9; state discrimination, 91–4
Musuveni, Yoweri, 269, 275

Nadoo, Nasibyu Babu, 276
Nahor, Mahmouth, 182
Nairobi negotiations 2015, 331
Namsio, Obed, 108
Ndele town, 144–6
Ndjamena, 8, 172–3
Ndoutingaï, Sylvain, 108–9, 133, 183
Nganga, 61
Ngaragba prison massacre, 28
Ngoupandé, Jean-Paul, 28, 32
NGOs: few, 227; health sector, 220; international, 324; lack, 300
Niamey, Niger, 6, 142
Nigerians, Pk5 market, 85
nomenklatura, CAR, 41, 102
'normalcy', non-existence of, 325
North East CAR: autonomous zone, 149, 151–2, 159; colonial non-investment, 145; French interventions, 206; humanitarian interventions, 285; rebel groups, 320; violent raiding history, 159

Obama, Barack, 283–4
Obo, US Special Forces in, 277
OCHA, 234
Odhiambo, Okot, 273, 286
oil, 106, 127, 172, 184; Doséo basin, 107
Olin, Nathaniel, 226
Operation Barracuda, 28
Operation Boali, 37
Operation Bokassa, 306
Operation Closing Gate, 133
Otti, Vincent, execution of, 272–3

Oubangui-Chari colony, 18–20, 24; colonial scandals, 22; ivory hunting, 149; safari hunting, 150; under-invested, 21
Ougadougou summit 1997, 198
Ouham-Pende prefecture, 9
Oursel, Luc, 108

'paradoxical scarcity', 102–3, 334
parastatals: companies, 69; Kolingba hollowing, 308
Paris, 1931 colonial exhibition, 20
Patassé, Ange-Félix, 4–5, 27, 29, 31, 34–9, 58, 89, 92, 105–7, 132, 172, 175–6, 178–9, 196, 198, 201–3, 205, 207, 209, 211, 214, 216, 224, 252, 255, 257, 259–60, 300, 302–3, 307–8, 312–14, 335; coup attempt against 2001, 204; companies of, 69; ethnic politics, 309; French-Chadian coup against, 255; Libyan support, 177, 256, 310; MLC support, 258; overthrow, 180; personal militia, 33; Togo exile, 30
patronage, 69
PBC (UN Peacebuilding Commission), 208–10, 247, 332
PDRN, 152–3
peace processes, conflict management tools, 247
peacebuilding, 134; failures, 320; nominal initiatives, 327
peacekeeping, 8, 116, 168; chronology, 196–8; concepts early adopting, 194; failures of, 209–10, 214; forces, 6; missions, 1, 9, 324; regional ulterior motives, 206; under-resourced, 200
Pentecostal Churches, influence, 55, 100, 321

Index ■ 355

People's Republic of China, Dacko recognition of, 25
'periphery of peripheries', CAR, 167
Petronas, 106
Peulh, 189
Picco, Enrica, 13–14
Pk5, Bangui market zone, 76; anti-Muslim militias, 96; Chadians, 182; heterogenity, 80–1; illegal activities, 88; melting pot, 78; Muslim-Christian relations, 77, 87, 95; Muslim presence, 79, 97; nightlife, 86; specialized zones, 82–5
political dialogue, implementation failure, 327
politicians, 'big man' persona, 132; power personalization, 252
Pompidou, Georges, 26
Poverty Reduction Strategy, CAR, 229
PRAC, failures of, 329, 331
private sector, foreign, 56
production, concessionary mode, 56
PTIAL, China oil company, 107
pygmies, 18

Qaddafi, Muamar, 27–8, 35–6, 81, 172, 175

Ramadan, Caliph Yaya, 157–8
rape, 225; sexual violence in conflict zones, 260
reciprocity, crisis of, 62
refugees, 9; Congolese, 245
regional states, CAR interference, 195
religion: 'hatred rhetoric', 8; politicized, 322; role of, 320
Revolution Justice, rebel group, 9

'rival resource regimes', 154
'river people', Oubangui river, 18
Rosicrucian societies, 171
Rousseau, Jean-Jacques, 57
RSM Production Corporation, 107
rubber, 22, 65; 'boom', 21

Sabone, Abakar, 39, 41, 158
Saint Joseph Sisters, 223
Saleh, Ibni Oumar Mahamat, 185
Sam Ouandja town, 137, 278; diamond wealth, 136
Samba-Panza, Catherine, 8, 45, 116, 187, 237, 279, 299; Chad hostility, 188; corruption scandals, 334–5; old elites with, 315
Sangba Ecosystem Protection Zone, 154
Sango, CAR *lingua franca*, 30, 33, 39, 66, 80, 129, 144, 147, 153, 171, 320, 322
Sanusi, Sultan, 144–6, 152
Sara-Kaba ethnic group, 32
Sarkozy, Nicholas, 41, 109, 183
Sassou Nguesso, Denis, 36, 178, 180, 184, 186–8, 335
Savorgnan de Brazza, Pierre, 22
Schmitt, Carl, 115
Scott, James C., 160
Seleka coalition, 1, 6, 9, 42–3, 70, 87, 96, 103, 124, 134, 137, 158, 183–4, 196, 213–14, 236, 250, 311, 315, 320; ad hoc rule, 321; Chad support, 9, 211; coup, 98–9; crisis, 72–3; diamond business link, 137; 'disbanded', 7; foreign recruits/identity, 142, 182–3; Islamic dimension, 186, 212; Muslim attitudes, 97; offensive's humanitarian crisis, 220; rebellion, 251; secession discourse, 188; state looting,

211; takeover, 277, 295; 2013 power seizure, 116
sexual violence, conflict zones, 260; rape, 225
'shopping forums', 248
slavery, 145; slave-raiding, 3, 18, 169, 322; trade, 19, 57, 168; traditional institution destruction, 300; trans-Atlantic trade, 249
Smith, Stephen W., 12, 245, 336
SODIF, 111
Sokambi, Aristide, 299
Somalia, Uganda presence, 275
sorcery: accusation targets, 56, 61–2; court cases, 59; Penal Code, 59; prevalence, 60; wealth link, 63
South Africa, 6; Bozizé military advisors, 113
South Sudan, 2; SPLA, 269, 272, 281; Ugandan troops, 275; Western Equatorial State, 274
sovereignty, relational, 14; 'rent', 17, 103
SSR, underfunded, 209
state, the CAR; absence of experience, 143; building process, 167; *experience* of, 154; fetishizing of, 152; flawed 'dysfunctional' argument, 166; long-term perspectives lack, 115; monopoly of violence misconception, 328; 'phantom', 17; rent-seeking, 303; wealth legitimized, 63
Steering Committee DDR, corrupt, 329–30
structural adjustment, 4
Sudan, 2, 66; Armed Forces, 177, 268; Comprehensive Peace Agreement 2005, 272; crisis, 89; LRA support, 269, 273; SPLM, 177

Sultans, 19th century trade links, 3, 144; 19th century, 3

Trans-Saharan networks, 3
taxe de pacage, 155–6
terrorism, colonial, 23–4
textile industry, 305
Tiangaye, Nicolas, 43, 116, 298–9
timber, 127
Tongo-Tongo, 57
trade, foreigner dominated, 301
Transitional National Council, 45

Ubangui-Chari, 246
UFDR, 40, 42, 135–8, 143, 148, 157–9, 182, 226, 330
Uganda: Acholi people, 269; CAR presence, 277, 283; DRC presence, 276; *see also* UPDF
unemployment, Muslim, 94; urban youth, 42
'ungoverned spaces', 272
United Nations (UN), 1, 187, 189; CAR election 1993, 255; Department of Peacekeeping, 244; Department of Political Affairs, 244; Development Programme (UNDP), 199–201, 226, 330; High Commissioner for Refugees (UNHCR), 233; Office for the Coordination of Humanitarian Affairs (OCHA), 113, 228, 233; Operational Peer Review, 237; Peacebuilding Commission, 208–10, 247, 332; Peacebuilding Support Office in the Central African Republic, 34; Regional Office for Central Africa (UNOCA), 281; Security Council, 9, 44, 216, 321; UNICEF, 233, 286, 332; see also, MINURCA, MINUSCA, MONUC, MONUSCO

Union of Democratic Forces for Unity, 39
United States of Latin Africa, 170
UPDF (Ugandan Defence Force), 113, 160, 256, 267, 274; army of, 267; CAR logging, 278; counter LRA mission, 280; military, 113; Operation Lightning Thunder, 270, 274; USA support, 281, 282, 284–5
UraMin, 108, 109
uranium, 127; Bakouma, 108
USA (United States of America): counter LRA, 283; Déby support, 181; LRA fight, 284; military, 113; Special Forces, 277, 285; troops, 9; USAID, 286

Vakava province, 'Darfurianization', 40
'verge of genocide' rhetoric, 8
von Benda-Beckmann, Keebet, 248

Waddai Sultanate, 169; slave-trading, 19
'war networks', 248
water and electricity, 112
wildlife: guards, 142; official policy, 149
witch doctors, 63
witchcraft accusations, epidemic, 55–6
Wohlers, Laurence D., 13, 255
World Bank, 110, 147, 331; adjudicating branch, 107
World Food Programme, 225

Yakoma ethnic group, 30, 35, 80
Younnous, Oumar, 137

Zaghawa, 181
'Zaribas system', 144
Ziguélé, 38
Zindenko, Joseph, 142, 159
Zuma, Jacob, 183